CIMA

TUDY TEXT

OPERATIONAL

PAPER F1

FINANCIAL OPERATIONS

Our text is designed to help you study **effectively** and **efficiently**.

In this edition we:

- **Highlight** the **most important elements** in the syllabus and the **key skills** you will need

- **Signpost** how each chapter links to the syllabus and the learning outcomes

- **Provide** lots of **exam alerts** explaining how what you're learning may be tested

- **Include examples** and **questions** to help you apply what you've learnt

- **Emphasise key points** in **section summaries**

- **Test your knowledge** of what you've studied in **quick quizzes**

- **Examine your understanding** in our **exam question bank**

- **Reference all the important topics** in the **full index**

FOR EXAMS IN NOVEMBER 2011 AND MAY 2012

LEARNING MEDIA

First edition 2009
Third edition June 2011

ISBN 9780 7517 9478 6
(Previous ISBN 9780 7517 8460 2)

e-ISBN 9780 7517 9608 7

British Library Cataloguing-in-Publication Data
A catalogue record for this book
is available from the British Library

Published by

BPP Learning Media Ltd
BPP House, Aldine Place
London W12 8AA

www.bpp.com/learningmedia

Printed in the United Kingdom

Your learning materials, published by BPP
Learning Media Ltd, are printed on paper sourced
from sustainable, managed forests.

We are grateful to the Chartered Institute of
Management Accountants for permission to
reproduce past examination questions. The
suggested solutions in the exam answer bank have
been prepared by BPP Learning Media Ltd.

Contents

How our Study Text can help you pass

Streamlined studying	• We show you the best ways to study efficiently
	• Our Text has been designed to ensure you can easily and quickly navigate through it
	• The different features in our Text emphasise important knowledge and techniques
Exam expertise	• **Studying F1** on page vii introduces the key themes of the syllabus and summarises how to pass
	• We highlight throughout our Text how topics may be tested and what you'll have to do in the exam
	• We help you see the complete picture of the syllabus, so that you can answer questions that range across the whole syllabus
	• Our Text covers the syllabus content – no more, no less
Regular review	• We frequently summarise the key knowledge you need
	• We test what you've learnt by providing questions and quizzes throughout our Text

Our other products

BPP Learning Media also offers these products for the F1 exam:

Practice and Revision Kit	Providing lots more question practice and helpful guidance on how to pass the exam
Passcards	Summarising what you should know in visual, easy to remember, form
Success CDs	Covering the vital elements of the F1 syllabus in less than 90 minutes and also containing exam hints to help you fine tune your strategy
i-Pass	Providing computer-based testing in a variety of formats, ideal for self-assessment
Interactive Passcards	Allowing you to learn actively with a clear visual format summarising what you must know

You can purchase these products by visiting http://www.bpp.com/mybpp

CIMA Distance Learning

BPP's distance learning packages provide flexibility and convenience, allowing you to study effectively, at a pace that suits you, where and when you choose. There are four great distance learning packages available.

Online classroom	Bringing the classroom experience to you via the web and offering you great flexibility, with the quality for which BPP classroom courses are renowned
Basics Plus	Combining the paper-based and e-learning approaches of our Basics and Basics Online distance learning packages
Basics	Consisting of high quality BPP Learning Media study materials and access to BPP Professional Education subject experts
Basics Online	Including the best online learning and practice

You can find out more about these packages by visiting http://www.bpp.com/courses/examination-courses/accounting--finance/cima-2011/ways-to-study.aspx

Features in our Study Text

 Section Introductions explain how the section fits into the chapter

 Key Terms are the core vocabulary you need to learn

KEY TERM

 Key Points are points that you have to know, ideas or calculations that will be the foundations of your answers

KEY POINT

 Exam Alerts show you how subjects are likely to be tested

 Exam Skills are the key skills you will need to demonstrate in the exam, linked to question requirements

 Formulae To Learn are formulae you must remember in the exam

LEARN

 Exam Formulae are formulae you will be given in the exam

EXAM

 Examples show how theory is put into practice

 Questions give you the practice you need to test your understanding of what you've learnt

 Case Studies link what you've learnt with the real-world business environment

CASE STUDY

 Links show how the syllabus overlaps with other parts of the qualification, including Knowledge Brought Forward that you need to remember from previous exams

 Website References link to material that will enhance your understanding of what you're studying

 Further Reading will give you a wider perspective on the subjects you're covering

 Section Summaries allow you to review each section

Streamlined studying

What you should do	In order to
Read the Chapter and Section Introductions	See why topics need to be studied and map your way through the chapter
Go quickly through the explanations	Gain the depth of knowledge and understanding that you'll need
Highlight the Key Points, Key Terms and Formulae To Learn	Make sure you know the basics that you can't do without in the exam
Focus on the Exam Skills and Exam Alerts	Know how you'll be tested and what you'll have to do
Work through the Examples and Case Studies	See how what you've learnt applies in practice
Prepare Answers to the Questions	See if you can apply what you've learnt in practice
Revisit the Section Summaries in the Chapter Roundup	Remind you of, and reinforce, what you've learnt
Answer the Quick Quiz	Find out if there are any gaps in your knowledge
Answer the Question(s) in the Exam Question Bank	Practise what you've learnt in depth

Should I take notes?

Brief notes may help you remember what you're learning. You should use the notes format that's most helpful to you (lists, diagrams, mindmaps).

Further help

BPP Learning Media's *Learning to Learn Accountancy* provides lots more helpful guidance on studying. It is designed to be used both at the outset of your CIMA studies and throughout the process of learning accountancy. It can help you **focus your studies on the subject and exam**, enabling you to **acquire knowledge, practise and revise efficiently and effectively**.

Syllabus and learning outcomes

Paper F1 Financial Operations

The syllabus comprises:

Topic and Study Weighting

A	Principles of Business Taxation	25%
B	Regulation and Ethics of Financial Reporting	15%
C	Financial Accounting and Reporting	60%

Learning Outcomes				
Lead		**Component**		**Syllabus content**
A	**Principles of business taxation (25%)**			
1	Explain the types of tax that can apply to incorporated businesses, their principles and potential administrative requirements.	(a)	Identify the principal types of taxation likely to be of relevance to an incorporated business in a particular country;	(i) Concepts of direct versus indirect taxes, taxable person and competent jurisdiction.
		(b)	Describe the features of the principal types of taxation likely to be of relevance to an incorporated business in a particular country;	(ii) Types of taxation, including direct tax on the company's trading profits and capital gains, indirect taxes collected by the company, employee taxation and withholding taxes on international payments, and their features (e.g. in terms of who ultimately bears the tax cost, withholding responsibilities, principles of calculating the tax base).
		(c)	Explain key administrative requirements and the possible enquiry and investigation powers of taxing authorities associated with the principal types of taxation likely to be of relevance to an incorporated business;	(iii) Sources of tax rules (e.g. domestic primary legislation and court rulings, practice of the relevant taxing authority, supranational bodies, such as the EU in the case of value added/sales tax, and international tax treaties).
		(d)	Explain the difference in principle between tax avoidance and tax evasion;	(iv) Indirect taxes collected by the company:
		(e)	Illustrate numerically the principles of different types of tax based on provided information.	– in the context of indirect taxes, the distinction between unit taxes (e.g. excise duties based on physical measures) and ad valorem taxes (e.g. sales tax based on value);

          –   the mechanism of value added/sales taxes, in which businesses are liable for tax on their outputs less credits for tax paid on their inputs, including the concepts of exemption and variation in tax rates depending on the type of output and disallowance of input credits for exempt outputs.

(v)   Employee taxation:

          –   the employee as a separate taxable person subject to a personal income tax regime;

          –   use of employer reporting and withholding to ensure compliance and assist tax collection.

(vi)   The need for record-keeping and record retention that may be additional to that required for financial accounting purposes.

(vii)   The need for deadlines for reporting (filing returns) and tax payments.

(viii)   Types of powers of tax authorities to ensure compliance with tax rules:

          –   power to review and query filed returns;

          –   power to request special reports or returns;

          –   power to examine records (generally extending back some years);

          –   powers of entry and search;

          –   exchange of information with tax authorities in other jurisdictions.

(ix)   The distinction between tax avoidance and tax evasion, and how these vary among jurisdictions (including the difference between the use of statutory general anti-avoidance provisions and case law based regimes).

2	Explain fundamental concepts in international taxation of incorporated businesses.	(a)	Identify situations in which foreign tax obligations (reporting and liability) could arise and methods for relieving foreign tax;	(i)	International taxation:
		(b)	Explain sources of tax rules and the importance of jurisdiction.		– the concept of corporate residence and the variation in rules for its determination across jurisdictions (e.g. place of incorporation versus place of management);
					– types of payments on which withholding tax may be required (especially interest, dividends, royalties and capital gains accruing to non-residents);
					– means of establishing a taxable presence in another country (local company and branch);
					– the effect of double tax treaties (based on the OECD Model Convention) on the above (e.g. reduction of withholding tax rates, provisions for defining a permanent establishment).
3	Prepare corporate income tax calculations.	(a)	Prepare corporate income tax calculations based on a given simple set of rules.	(i)	Direct taxes on company profits and gains:
					– the principle of non-deductibility of dividends and systems of taxation defined according to the treatment of dividends in the hands of the shareholder (e.g. classical, partial imputation and imputation);
					– the distinction between accounting and taxable profits in absolute terms (e.g. disallowable expenditure on revenue account, such as entertaining, and on capital account, such as formation and acquisition costs) and in terms of timing (e.g. deduction on a paid basis);

4					– the concept of tax depreciation replacing book depreciation in the tax computation and its calculation based on the pooling of assets by their classes, including balancing adjustments on the disposal of assets;
					– the nature of rules recharacterising interest payments as dividends (e.g. where interest is based on profitability);
					– potential for variation in rules for calculating the tax base dependent on the nature or source of the income (scheduler systems);
					– the need for rules dealing with the relief of losses;
					– principles of relief for foreign taxes by exemption, deduction and credit.
					– the concept of tax consolidation (e.g. for relief of losses and deferral of capital gains on asset transfers within a group).
4	Apply the accounting rules for current and deferred taxation.	(a)	Apply the accounting rules for current and deferred taxation, including calculation of deferred tax based on a given set of rules.	(i)	Accounting treatment of taxation and disclosure requirements under IAS 12.
B	**Regulation and ethics of financial reporting (15%)**				
1	Explain the need for and methods of regulating accounting and financial reporting.	(a)	Explain the need for regulation of published accounts and the concept that regulatory regimes vary from country to country;	(i)	The need for regulation of accounts.
				(ii)	Elements in a regulatory framework for published accounts (e.g. company law, local GAAP, review of accounts by public bodies).
		(b)	Explain potential elements that might be expected in a national regulatory framework for published accounts;	(iii)	GAAP based on prescriptive versus principles-based standards.
				(iv)	The role and structure of the IASB and IOSCO.

		(c)	Describe the role and structure of the International Accounting Standards Board (IASB) and the International Organisation of Securities Commissions (IOSCO);	(v)	The IASB's Framework for the Presentation and Preparation of Financial Statements.
		(d)	Explain the meaning of given features or parts of the IASB's Framework for the Presentation and Preparation of Financial Statements;	(vi)	The process leading to the promulgation of a standard practice.
				(vii)	Ways in which IFRSs are used: adoption as local GAAP, model for local GAAP, persuasive influence in formulating local GAAP.
		(e)	Describe the process leading to the promulgation of an IFRS;	(viii)	The powers and duties of the external auditors, the audit report and its qualification for accounting statements not in accordance with best practice.
		(f)	Describe ways in which IFRSs can interact with local regulatory frameworks;		
		(g)	Explain in general terms, the role of the external auditor, the elements of the audit report and types of qualification of that report.		
2	Apply the provisions of the CIMA Code of Ethics for Professional Accountants.	(a)	Explain the importance of the exercise of ethical principles in reporting and assessing information;	(i)	Ethical requirements of the professional accountant in reporting and assessing information (the fundamental principles).
		(b)	Describe the sources of ethical codes for those involved in the reporting or taxation affairs of an organisation, including the external auditors;	(ii)	Sources of ethical codes (IFAC, professional bodies, employing organisations, social/religious/personal sources).
		(c)	Apply the provisions of the CIMA Code of Ethics for Professional Accountants of particular relevance to the information reporting, assurance and tax-related activities of the accountant.	(iii)	Provisions of the CIMA Code of Ethics for Professional Accountants of particular relevance to information reporting, assurance and tax-related activities (especially section 220 and Part C).

C	Financial accounting and reporting (60%)					
1	Prepare the full financial statements of a single company and the consolidated statements of financial position and comprehensive income for a group (in relatively straightforward circumstances)	(a)	Prepare a complete set of financial statements, in a form suitable for publication for a single company;	(i)	Preparation of the financial statements of a single company, as specified in IAS 1 (revised), including the statement of changes in equity.
		(b)	Apply the conditions required for an undertaking to be a subsidiary or an associate of another company;	(ii)	Preparation of the statement of cash flows (IAS 7).
		(c)	Prepare the consolidated statement of financial position (balance sheet) and statement of comprehensive income for a group of companies in a form suitable for publication for a group of companies comprising directly held interests in one or more fully-controlled subsidiaries and associates (such interests having been acquired at the beginning of an accounting period);	(iii)	Preparation of the consolidated statement of financial position (balance sheet) and statement of comprehensive income where: interests are directly held by the acquirer (parent) company; any subsidiary is fully controlled; and all interests were acquired at the beginning of an accounting period. (IFRS 3 and IAS 27, to the extent that their provisions are relevant to the specified learning outcomes).
		(d)	Apply the concepts of fair value at the point of acquisition, identifiability of assets and liabilities, and recognition of goodwill.		
2	Apply international standards dealing with a range of matters and items.	(a)	Apply the accounting rules contained in IFRSs and IASs dealing with reporting performance, non-current assets, including their impairment, inventories, disclosure of related parties to a business, construction contracts (and related financing costs), post-balance sheet events, provisions, contingencies, and leases (lessee only);	(i)	Reporting performance, prior period items, discontinuing operations, and segment reporting (IAS 8 and IFRS 5 and 8). Recognition of revenue (IAS 18) Measurement of profit or loss (IAS 1 (revised))
				(ii)	Property, Plant and Equipment (IAS 16): the calculation of depreciation and the effect of revaluations, changes to economic useful life, repairs, improvements and disposals.

(b) Explain the accounting rules contained in IFRSs and IASs governing share capital transactions.

(iii) Research and development costs (IAS 38): criteria for capitalisation.

(iv) Intangible Assets (IAS 38) and goodwill: recognition, valuation, amortisation.

(v) Impairment of Assets (IAS 36) and Non-Current Assets Held for Sale (IFRS 5) and their effects on the above.

(vi) Inventories (IAS 2).

(vii) The disclosure of related parties to a business (IAS 24).

(viii) Construction contracts and related financing costs (IAS 11 and 23): determination of cost, net realisable value, the inclusion of overheads and the measurement of profit on uncompleted contracts.

(ix) Post-balance sheet events (IAS 10).

(x) Provisions and contingencies (IAS 37).

(xi) Leases (IAS 17) – distinguishing operating from finance leases and the concept of substance over form (from the Framework); accounting for leases in the books of the lessee.

(xii) Issue and redemption of shares, including treatment of share issue and redemption costs (IAS 32 and 39), the share premium account, the accounting for maintenance of capital arising from the purchase by a company of its own shares.

Old and new syllabuses

The syllabus for the F1 *Financial Operations* paper is similar to the syllabus for the old syllabus paper P7 *Financial Accounting and Tax Principles*. The main difference is that the section on managing short term finance which was included in P7 under the old syllabus has moved to P1 *Performance Operations* in the new syllabus.

The other three main areas are roughly the same for both the old and new syllabus exams. There have been changes in study weightings and some new topics introduced.

The following topics have been added into the syllabus, with references to the chapter in which they are covered:

- Ethics (2)

- Group accounting (13-16)

- Tax depreciation based on the pooling of assets by their classes (18)

Studying F1

1   What's F1 about

F1 consists of three fairly distinct areas covering:

- Regulation and ethics
- Financial accounting standards and accounts preparation
- Taxation

1.1 Regulation and ethics

In F1 you are expected to know about the regulation of accounts; why regulation is necessary and the processes of establishing and enforcing the rules that accountants are expected to apply when they prepare company accounts. As accountants, you will have to deal with external auditors; this syllabus also therefore requires you to understand the role of external auditors and interpret external audit reports. Finally, you are expected to know the CIMA *Code of ethics for professional accountants* and be able to apply this to a given scenario. Regulation and ethics are covered in Chapters 1 to 3 of this Study Text.

1.2 Financial accounting standards and accounts preparation

The financial accounting part of the syllabus consists of two main areas. The first area is concerned with the preparation of accounts for a single company and is dealt with in Chapters 4 to 12. It is assumed that you know the basic elements of accounts preparation from previous studies. F1 requires more detailed knowledge of the contents of the main financial statements (statement of comprehensive income, statement of financial position and statement of cash flows) and also how accounting standards impact upon the main statements and the notes to the accounts.

The second area you will need to know is how to prepare accounts for a simple group. Chapters 14 and 15 look at how to prepare accounts for a parent plus subsidiary company and then Chapter 16 applies the same principles for an associate.

1.3 Taxation

As F1 is designed to be an international paper you don't need specific knowledge of any individual country's tax regime. Instead the paper focuses on the elements that are common to most of the major tax regimes. F1 aims to give you knowledge of different kinds of taxation, how tax is administered, the role of the taxation authorities and what is regarded as tax avoidance and evasion. As this is an international paper, you also have to be aware of the international tax dimension and how foreign tax obligations can arise. Taxation is covered in Chapters 17 to 19 of this Study Text.

2 What's required

2.1 Knowledge

As the majority of marks are available for questions worth 5 marks or less, the examiner has a lot of opportunity to test your knowledge of the detail of the syllabus, in particular key definitions, the features of tax regimes and the accounting regulatory process. You will also not only have to answer short questions on the requirements of accounting standards, but in addition use your knowledge of the standards to prepare extracts from accounts that comply with those standards.

2.2 Calculations

Calculation questions will be of two types:

- Short calculations for five marks or less, including taxation calculations and calculations that are required by accounting standards

- Longer calculations for which you will have to prepare proformas. The majority of marks in Section C of F1 will be available for these. The proformas you will need to know are those for the main financial accounting statements

2.3 What the examiner means

The table below has been prepared by CIMA to help you interpret the syllabus and learning outcomes and the meaning of exam questions.

You will see that there are 5 levels of Learning objective, ranging from Knowledge to Evaluation, reflecting the level of skill you will be expected to demonstrate. CIMA Certificate subjects were constrained to levels 1 to 3, but in CIMA's Professional qualification the entire hierarchy will be used.

At the start of each chapter in your study text is a topic list relating the coverage in the chapter to the level of skill you may be called on to demonstrate in the exam.

Learning objectives	Verbs used	Definition
1 Knowledge		
What are you expected to know	• List	• Make a list of
	• State	• Express, fully or clearly, the details of/facts of
	• Define	• Give the exact meaning of
2 Comprehension		
What you are expected to understand	• Describe	• Communicate the key features of
	• Distinguish	• Highlight the differences between
	• Explain	• Make clear or intelligible/state the meaning of
	• Identify	• Recognise, establish or select after consideration
	• Illustrate	• Use an example to describe or explain something

3 Application

How you are expected to apply your knowledge	• Apply	• Put to practical use
	• Calculate/compute	• Ascertain or reckon mathematically
	• Demonstrate	• Prove with certainty or to exhibit by practical means
	• Prepare	• Make or get ready for use
	• Reconcile	• Make or prove consistent/compatible
	• Solve	• Find an answer to
	• Tabulate	• Arrange in a table

4 Analysis

How you are expected to analyse the detail of what you have learned	• Analyse	• Examine in detail the structure of
	• Categorise	• Place into a defined class or division
	• Compare and contrast	• Show the similarities and/or differences between
	• Construct	• Build up or compile
	• Discuss	• Examine in detail by argument
	• Interpret	• Translate into intelligible or familiar terms
	• Prioritise	• Place in order of priority or sequence for action
	• Produce	• Create or bring into existence

5 Evaluation

How you are expected to use your learning to evaluate, make decisions or recommendations	• Advise	• Counsel, inform or notify
	• Evaluate	• Appraise or assess the value of
	• Recommend	• Propose a course of action

3 How to pass

3.1 Study the whole syllabus

All of the marks available to you will be for compulsory questions. This gives the examiner plenty of opportunity to test all major areas of the syllabus on **every** paper, but sadly doesn't give you much opportunity to avoid questions you don't like. In particular you must spend some time on the rules and regulatory background issues as these may be covered in 5 mark, as well as shorter 2 mark, questions.

3.2 Lots of question practice

Our Text gives you lots of opportunity to practise by providing questions within chapters, quick quiz questions and questions in the exam question bank at the end. In addition the BPP Learning Media Practice and Revision Kit provides lots more question practice. It's particularly important to practise:

- Banks of objective test questions so that you get used to doing a number together

- More complicated shorter calculations. We highlight within the Text calculations that can cause problems and it's worth doing as many of these as possible

- Longer calculations and proformas. You will need to do these to answer the Section C question well.

3.3 Develop time management skills

Time management is often a problem, with some candidates not leaving themselves enough time to do the shorter calculations. Particularly therefore towards the end of your course, you need to practise all types of question, only allowing yourself the time you will be given in the exam.

3.4 Develop business awareness

Although this is not a higher level paper, candidates with good business awareness can score well in a number of areas.

- Reading articles in CIMA's *Financial Management* magazine and the business press will help you understand the practical rationale for accounting standards and make it easier for you to apply accounting requirements correctly

- Looking through the accounts of major companies will familiarise you with the contents of accounts and help you comment on key figures and changes from year-to-year

4 Brought forward knowledge

Paper F1 builds on the knowledge learned in the certificate level paper C2: *Fundamentals of Financial Accounting*. You should make sure that you are familiar with basic financial accounting terminology and techniques. If it is a long time since you studied basic financial accounting, it may be worth revising the fundamentals before you begin paper F1.

5 Links with other Operational level exams

Regulation and ethics are part of the **global business environment** which is covered in E1 *Enterprise Operations*.

Your financial accounting studies in this paper will be useful when studying working capital and investment appraisal in P1 *Performance Operations*.

The exam paper

Format of the paper

		Number of marks
Section A:	A variety of compulsory objective test questions, 2 – 4 marks each	20
Section B:	6 compulsory questions, 5 marks each	30
Section C:	2 compulsory questions, 25 marks each	50
		100

Time allowed: 3 hours, plus 20 minutes reading time

May 2011 exam paper

Section A

1   Tax rate structures, employee tax, tax residence, VAT, tax avoidance and tax evasion, IAS 8 and retrospective adjustments, IFRS 8 and reportable segments, calculation of goodwill, calculation of investment in associate, intra-group trading and PUP.

Section B

2   (a)   Corporate income tax and deferred tax
     (b)   Capital gains tax
     (c)   Underlying tax and double tax relief
     (d)   Principles based versus rules based standards
     (e)   IASB's *Framework*
     (f)   Ethics

Section C

3   Preparation of a statement of comprehensive income and a statement of changes in equity for a single entity, including discontinued operations and a warranty provision.

4   Preparation of a statement of cash flows for a single entity, calculation of amounts to be included in the financial statements relating to a finance lease.

November 2010 exam paper

Section A

1   Interaction of corporate and personal tax, employee tax, formal incidence of VAT, administration of tax, calculating VAT, audit opinions, treasury shares, IASB's *Framework*, related parties, IFRS 8.

Section B

2   (a)   Relieving trading losses (company income tax)
     (b)   Withholding tax, including calculation of double tax relief
     (c)   *Framework*: qualitative characteristics
     (d)   Group accounts: calculation of goodwill and IFRS 3
     (e)   Group accounts: classification of investments
     (f)   Provisions, events after the reporting period

Section C

3   Financial statements preparation for a single entity, including an income tax computation and deferred tax.

4   Preparation of a statement of cash flows for a single company, ethical considerations.

May 2010 exam paper

Section A

1   Ideal tax principles, tax rate structures, deferred tax, IASB's *Framework,* qualitative characteristics, revenue recognition, development expenditure, finance leases, discontinued operations, cash flows.

Section B

2   (a)   Tax evasion and tax avoidance
     (b)   Indirect taxes
     (c)   International tax
     (d)   External audit and audit reports
     (e)   Construction contracts
     (f)   Discontinued operations, restructuring provisions, CIMA's Code of ethics

Section C

3   Financial statements preparation for a single entity, including a share issue, operating lease and revaluation of property, plant and equipment.

4   Preparation of consolidated statement of financial position and consolidated statement of comprehensive income, calculation of income tax and deferred tax for the group.

Specimen exam paper

Section A

1   Tax avoidance and evasion, calculating income tax, VAT, systems of taxing corporate income, IASB's *Framework,* CIMA Code of ethics, external audit, IFRS 3, inventories, related parties.

Section B

2   (a)   Tax residence
     (b)   VAT explanation and calculation
     (c)   Principles vs. rules based accounting standards
     (d)   Discontinued operations
     (e)   Accounting treatment of leases
     (f)   Accounting treatment of preference shares

Section C

3   Financial statements preparation for a single entity, including deferred tax calculation.

4   Preparation of consolidated statement of financial position, including the treatment of an associate in group accounts.

REGULATION AND ETHICS OF FINANCIAL REPORTING

Part A

THE REGULATORY FRAMEWORK

Accounting is regulated by local statute (such as company law), by Stock Exchange requirements and by accounting standards.

In this chapter we first examine the role of the International Accounting Standards Board (IASB), the development of International Financial Reporting

Standards and some criticism of the IASB. We then spend some time on the IASB's *Framework*. This is a key document, providing the conceptual framework within which International Financial Reporting Standards are formulated.

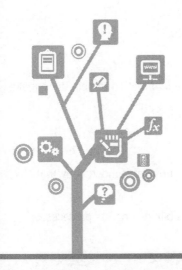

topic list	learning outcomes	syllabus references	ability required
1 The International Accounting Standards Board (IASB)	B1(c)	B1(iv)	comprehension
2 Setting of International Financial Reporting Standards	B1(e)	B1(vi)	comprehension
3 Progress towards global harmonisation	B1(f)	B1(vii)	comprehension
4 Conceptual framework and GAAP	B1(a)	B1(i), (iii)	comprehension
5 The IASB *Framework*	B1(b), (d)	B1(ii), (v)	comprehension
6 Qualitative characteristics of financial statements	B1(b), (d)	B1(ii), (v)	comprehension
7 The elements of financial statements	B1(b), (d)	B1(ii), (v)	comprehension

1   The International Accounting Standards Board (IASB)

Introduction

In this section we cover the role and structure of the IASB.

1.1 Impact of globalisation

The current reality is that the world's capital markets operate more and more freely across borders. The impacts of rapid globalisation are epitomised by the words of Paul Volker, Chairman of the IASC Foundation Trustees in November 2002, in a speech to the World Congress of Accountants.

'Developments over the past year and more have strongly reinforced the logic of achieving and implementing high-quality international accounting standards. In an age when capital flows freely across borders, it simply makes sense to account for economic transactions, whether they occur in the Americas, Asia, or Europe, in the same manner. Providing improved transparency and comparability will certainly help ensure that capital is allocated efficiently. Not so incidentally, generally accepted international standards will reduce the cost of compliance with multiple national standards.'

As the modern business imperative moves towards the globalisation of operations and activities, there is an underlying commercial logic that also requires a truly global capital market. Harmonised financial reporting standards are intended to provide:

- A platform for wider investment choice
- A more efficient capital market
- Lower cost of capital
- Enhanced business development

Globally, users of financial statements need transparent and comparative information to help them make economic decisions.

1.2 Formation of the IASB

The International Accounting Standards Board (IASB) is an independent, privately funded body that develops and issues International Financial Reporting Standards (IFRSs).

From April 2001 the IASB assumed accounting standard setting responsibilities from its predecessor body, the International Accounting Standards Committee (IASC).

KEY POINT

The IASB adopted the 41 International Accounting Standards (IASs) issued by its predecessor body, the IASC. All new standards issued by the IASB are now called International Financial Reporting Standards (IFRSs). The term 'IFRSs' is commonly used to refer to all international standards in issue, which currently comprises 41 IASs and 9 IFRSs.

The 15 members of the IASB come from nine countries and have a variety of backgrounds with a mix of auditors, preparers of financial statements, users of financial statements and an academic.

The IASB operates under the oversight of the **IFRS Foundation**.

1.3 The IFRS Foundation

The IFRS Foundation was known as the IASC Foundation until its name was changed in 2010. In March 2001 the IASC Foundation was formed as a not-for-profit corporation incorporated in the USA.

The formal objectives of the IFRS Foundation are to:

(a)   develop a single set of high quality, understandable, enforceable and globally accepted international financial reporting standards (IFRSs) through its standard setting body, the IASB

(b)   promote the use and rigorous application of those standards

(c)   take account of the financial reporting needs of emerging economies and small and medium-sized entities

(d)   bring about convergence of national accounting standards and IFRSs to high quality solutions.

The IFRS Foundation is currently made up of 18 Trustees, who essentially monitor and fund the IASB, the IFRS Advisory Council and the IFRS Interpretations Committee. The Trustees are appointed from a variety of geographic and functional backgrounds.

The structure of the IFRS Foundation and related bodies is shown below.

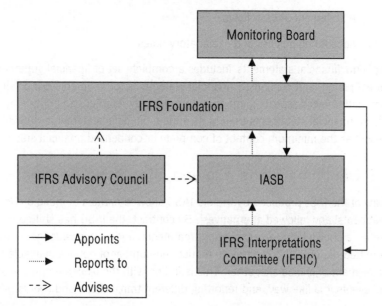

IFRS Advisory Council. The IFRS Advisory Council (formerly called the Standards Advisory Council or SAC) is essentially a forum used by the IASB to consult with the outside world. It consults with national standard setters, academics, user groups and a host of other interested parties to advise the IASB on a range of issues, from the IASB's work programme for developing new IFRSs, to giving practical advice on the implementation of particular standards.

The IFRS Advisory Council meets the IASB at least three times a year and puts forward the views of its members on current standard setting projects.

IFRS Interpretations Committee (IFRIC). The IFRS Interpretations Committee (formerly called the International Financial Reporting Interpretations Committee*) was set up in March 2002 and provides guidance on specific practical issues in the interpretation of IFRSs. The IFRIC is discussed in more detail in the next section.

*Note: despite the name change, the IFRS Interpretations Committee is still known by the acronym IFRIC.

1.4 Scope and authority of IFRSs

IFRSs set out recognition, measurement, presentation and disclosure requirements dealing with transactions and events that are important in general purpose financial statements. IFRSs are based on the IASB *Framework*, which:

•   Addresses the concepts underlying the information presented in general purpose financial statements

•   Facilitates the consistent and logical formulation of IFRSs

•   Provides a basis for the use of judgement in resolving accounting issues.

IFRSs are designed to apply to the general purpose financial statements and other financial reporting of all profit-oriented entities. General purpose financial statements are directed towards the common information needs of a wide range of users, for example, shareholders, suppliers, employees and the public at large. The objective of financial statements is to provide information about the financial position, performance and cash flows of an entity that is useful to those users in making economic decisions.

A complete set of financial statements includes:

- A statement of financial position

- A statement of comprehensive income

- A statement of all changes in equity, showing only owner changes in equity (Non-owner changes are in the statement of comprehensive income)

- A statement of cash flows

- Accounting policies and explanatory notes

The term 'financial statements' includes a complete set of financial statements prepared for an interim or annual period, and condensed financial statements for an interim period. In the interest of timeliness and cost, and to avoid repeating information previously reported, an entity may provide less information in its interim financial statements than in its annual financial statements. IAS 34 *Interim financial reporting* prescribes the minimum content of complete or condensed financial statements for an interim period.

1.5 Benchmark and allowed alternative treatment

Many of the IASs produced by the old IASC allowed entities to make a choice between 'benchmark treatments' and 'allowed alternatives'. By contrast, the IASB has shifted the emphasis away from allowing entities a choice between accounting treatments, and is reconsidering all those IASs where choices are permitted. Its objective is either to reduce the number of options available to choose from, or to eliminate the element of choice altogether. This is in line with the IASB's emphasis on reporting like transactions and events in a like way, and reporting different transactions and events differently.

Any limitation of scope of an IFRS will be made clear in the standard.

Section summary

The IASB replaced the IASC in 2001. It is responsible for setting International Financial Reporting Standards (IFRSs).

2 Setting of International Financial Reporting Standards

Introduction

This section looks at the process of developing an IFRS and the impact this has on different countries.

2.1 IFRS due process

IFRSs are developed through an international due process that involves accountants, financial analysts and other users of financial statements, the business community, stock exchanges, regulatory and legal authorities, academics and other interested individuals and organisations from around the world. The IASB consults the IFRS Advisory Council in public meetings on major projects, agenda decisions and work priorities, and discusses technical matters in meetings that are open to public observation.

The overall agenda of the IASB will initially be set by discussion with the IFRS Advisory Council. The process for developing an individual standard would involve the following steps.

During the early stages of a project, the IASB may establish an **Advisory Committee** to give advice on issues arising in the project. Consultation with the Advisory Committee and the IFRS Advisory Council occurs throughout the project.

 The IASB may develop and publish Discussion Papers for public comment.

 Following the receipt and review of comments, the IASB develops and publishes an Exposure Draft for public comment.

 Following the receipt and review of comments, the IASB issues a final International Financial Reporting Standard.

2.1.1 Interpretation of IFRSs

The IFRIC assists the IASB by improving existing IFRSs. It was established in March 2002 by the then IASC Foundation (now the IFRS Foundation) to replace the Standards Interpretations Committee (SIC). Where before SIC Interpretations were issued, now IFRIC Interpretations are issued.

The IFRIC has two main responsibilities:

- Review, on a timely basis, newly identified financial reporting issues not specifically addressed in IFRSs

- Clarify issues where unsatisfactory or conflicting interpretations have developed, or seem likely to develop in the absence of authoritative guidance, with a view to reaching a consensus on the appropriate treatment.

The IFRIC also helps the IASB move towards international harmonisation by working with its equivalent national-level bodies (such as the Urgent Issues Task Force, or UITF, in the UK).

The IFRIC, like the IASB itself, adopts a principles based approach. Its intention is to provide guidance that is in line with the rest of the IFRSs. It therefore bases itself, like each of the individual Standards, first and foremost on the IASB *Framework*. It will then look at any relevant IFRSs for principles applying the *Framework* to that particular area.

It is absolutely essential to the work of the IFRIC that its interpretations are in line with IASB *Framework* principles, rather than any other accounting principles.

The IFRIC then in turn informs the IASB of any inadequacies that it finds in the *Framework* or in existing IFRSs. If it believes that they should be modified or that a new Standard should be developed, the IFRIC informs the IASB so that it can consider whether or not to do so. This helps to ensure that the *Framework* and existing IFRSs are kept up to date for the actual financial reporting issues that the IFRIC has found with them.

The IFRIC develops its interpretations through a due process of consultation and debate which includes making Draft Interpretations available for public comment. The IFRIC Interpretations that it makes publically available are the consensus views that it has reached as a result of this process.

2.1.2 Comment periods

The IASB issues each Exposure Draft and Discussion Paper for public comment, with a normal comment period of 120 days. In certain circumstances, the IASB may expose proposals for a much shorter period. However, such limited periods would be used only in extreme circumstances. Draft IFRIC Interpretations are exposed for a 60-day comment period.

2.2 Co-ordination with national standard setters

Close co-ordination between the IASB due process and due process of national standard setters is important to the success of the IASB's mandate.

The IASB is exploring ways in which to integrate its due process more closely with national due process. Such integration may grow as the relationship between IASB and national standard setters evolves. In particular, the IASB is exploring the following procedure for projects that have international implications.

(a)   IASB and national standard setters would co-ordinate their work plans so that when the IASB starts a project, national standard setters would also add it to their own work plans so that they can play a full part in developing international consensus. Similarly, where national standard setters start projects, the IASB would consider whether it needs to develop a new Standard or review its existing Standards. Over a reasonable period, the IASB and national standard setters should aim to review all standards where significant differences currently exist, giving priority to the areas where the differences are greatest.

(b)   National standards setters would not be required to vote for IASB's preferred solution in their national standards, since each country remains free to adopt IASB standards with amendments or to adopt other standards. However, the existence of an international consensus is clearly one factor that members of national standard setters would consider when they decide how to vote on national standards.

(c)   The IASB would continue to publish its own Exposure Drafts and other documents for public comment.

(d)   National standard setters would publish their own exposure document at approximately the same time as IASB Exposure Drafts and would seek specific comments on any significant divergences between the two exposure documents. In some instances, national standard setters may include in their exposure documents specific comments on issues of particular relevance to their country or include more detailed guidance than is included in the corresponding IASB document.

(e)   National standard setters would follow their own full due process, which they would ideally choose to integrate with the IASB's due process. This integration would avoid unnecessary delays in completing standards and would also minimise the likelihood of unnecessary differences between the standards that result.

2.2.1 IASB liaison members

Seven of the full-time members of the IASB have formal liaison responsibilities with national standard setters in order to promote the convergence of national accounting standards and IFRSs. The IASB envisages a partnership between the IASB and these national standard setters as they work together to achieve convergence of accounting standards world-wide.

In addition all IASB members have contact responsibility with national standards setters not having liaison members and many countries are also represented on the IFRS Advisory Council.

2.3 Other international influences

2.3.1 European Commission (EC)

The EC regulations form one part of a broader programme for the harmonisation of company law in member states. The commission is uniquely the only organisation to produce international standards of accounting practice which are legally enforceable, in the form of directives which must be included in the national legislation of member states.

However, the EC has also acknowledged the role of the IASB in harmonising world-wide accounting rules.

Prior to the EC adoption of IFRSs in 2005 the IASB undertook an improvements project, dealing with revisions to IFRSs, for example in the area of materiality, presentation, leases, related parties and earnings per share. This has been matched in, for example, the UK, by a convergence project, bringing UK accounting standards into line with IFRSs where these are better.

2.3.2 International Organisation of Securities Commissions (IOSCO)

IOSCO is the representative of the world's securities markets regulators. IOSCO has been active in encouraging and promoting the improvement and quality of IFRSs over the last ten years. This commitment was evidenced by the agreement between IASC and IOSCO to work on a programme of 'core standards' which could be used by publicly listed entities when offering securities in foreign jurisdictions.

The 'core standards' project resulted in fifteen new or revised standards and was completed in 1999 with the issue of IAS 39 *Financial instruments: recognition and measurement.* IOSCO spent a year reviewing the results of the project and released a report in May 2000 which recommended to all its members that they allow multinational issuers to use IFRSs, as supplemented by reconciliation, disclosure and interpretation where necessary, to address outstanding substantive issues at a national or regional level.

IASB staff and IOSCO continue to work together to resolve outstanding issues and to identify areas where new IASB standards are needed.

2.3.3 Financial Accounting Standards Board (FASB)

The US standard setter, the FASB and the IASB have been undertaking a project of harmonisation between US accounting standards and IFRSs.

In September 2002, both parties acknowledged their commitment to the process of developing accounting standards that can be used for domestic and international purposes. Both the FASB and the IASB have worked together to make amendments to current accounting standards in the short term, and to work together on a long term basis to ensure new standards issued are compatible.

The IASB is currently involved in a joint project with the FASB to develop a common conceptual framework. This would provide a sound foundation for developing future accounting standards. The aim is that future standards should be principles based and internationally converged. This represents a movement away from the rules based approach which has characterised US accounting standards. The new framework will build upon the existing IASB and FASB frameworks and take into account subsequent developments.

The FASB is a important influence on the current and future work of the IASB.

2.4 Current IFRSs

The current list is as follows.

International Accounting Standards/International Financial Reporting Standards		Date of issue
IAS 1 (revised)*	Presentation of financial statements	Sept 2007
IAS 2*	Inventories	Dec 2003
IAS 7*	Statement of cash flows	Dec 1992
IAS 8*	Accounting policies, changes in accounting estimates and errors	Dec 2003
IAS 10*	Events after the reporting period	Dec 2003
IAS 11*	Construction contracts	Dec 1993
IAS 12*	Income taxes	Nov 2000
IAS 16*	Property, plant and equipment	Dec 2003
IAS 17*	Leases	Dec 2003
IAS 18*	Revenue	Dec 1993

International Accounting Standards/International Financial Reporting Standards		Date of issue
IAS 19	Employee benefits	Nov 2000
IAS 20	Accounting for government grants and disclosure of government assistance	Jan 1995
IAS 21	The effects of changes in foreign exchange rates	Dec 2003
IAS 23 (revised)*	Borrowing costs	Jan 2008
IAS 24*	Related party disclosures	Dec 2003
IAS 26	Accounting and reporting by retirement benefit plans	Jan 1995
IAS 27 (revised)*	Consolidated and separate financial statements	Jan 2008
IAS 28*	Investments in associates	Dec 2003
IAS 29	Financial reporting in hyperinflationary economies	Jan 1995
IAS 30	Disclosures in the financial statements of banks and similar financial institutions	Jan 1995
IAS 31	Interests in joint ventures	Dec 2003
IAS 32*	Financial instruments: presentation	Dec 2003
IAS 33	Earnings per share	Dec 2003
IAS 34	Interim financial reporting	Feb 1998
IAS 36*	Impairment of assets	June 1998
IAS 37*	Provisions, contingent liabilities and contingent assets	Sept 1998
IAS 38*	Intangible assets	Sept 1998
IAS 39*	Financial instruments: recognition and measurement	Dec 2003
IAS 40	Investment property	Dec 2003
IAS 41	Agriculture	Feb 2001
IFRS 1	First time adoption of International Financial Reporting Standards	Nov 2008
IFRS 2	Share-based payment	Feb 2004
IFRS 3 (revised)*	Business combinations	Jan 2008
IFRS 4	Insurance contracts	Mar 2004
IFRS 5*	Non-current assets held for sale and discontinued operations	Mar 2004
IFRS 6	Exploration for and evaluation of mineral resources	Dec 2004
IFRS 7	Financial instruments: disclosure	Aug 2005
IFRS 8*	Operating segments	Nov 2006
IFRS 9	Financial instruments	Nov 2009
IFRS 10	Consolidated financial statements	May 2011
IFRS 11	Joint arrangements	May 2011
IFRS 12	Disclosure of interests in other entities	May 2011

*Examinable at F1

KEY POINT

Various exposure drafts and discussion papers are currently at different stages within the IFRS process, but these are not of concern to you at this stage of your studies.

2.5 Scope and application of IFRSs

2.5.1 Scope

Any limitation of the applicability of a specific IFRS is made clear within that standard. IFRSs are **not intended to be applied to immaterial items, nor are they retrospective**. Each individual IFRS lays out its scope at the beginning of the standard.

2.5.2 Application

Within each individual country **local regulations** govern, to a greater or lesser degree, the issue of financial statements. These local regulations include accounting standards issued by the national regulatory bodies and/or professional accountancy bodies in the country concerned.

The IASB **concentrated on essentials** when producing IFRSs. This means that the IASB tried not to make IFRSs too complex, because otherwise they would be impossible to apply on a worldwide basis.

Section summary

IFRSs are set in a similar manner to the previous setting of IASs in accordance with the IASB's due process.

3 Progress towards global harmonisation

Introduction

This section first looks at the arguments for and against having accounting standards, then moves on to consider the global effect of IFRSs and the progress towards global harmonisation of accounting standards.

3.1 Accounting standards and choice

It is sometimes argued that companies should be given a choice in matters of financial reporting on the grounds that accounting standards are detrimental to the quality of such reporting. There are arguments on both sides.

In favour of accounting standards (both national and international), the following points can be made.

- They **reduce or eliminate confusing variations** in the methods used to prepare accounts.

- They provide a **focal point for debate** and discussions about accounting practice.

- They oblige companies to **disclose the accounting policies** used in the preparation of accounts.

- They are a less rigid alternative to enforcing conformity by means of **legislation**.

- They have obliged companies to **disclose more accounting information** than they would otherwise have done if accounting standards did not exist.

Many companies are reluctant to disclose information which is not required by national legislation. However, the following arguments may be put forward **against standardisation** and **in favour of choice**.

LEARNING MEDIA

- A set of rules which give backing to one method of preparing accounts might be **inappropriate in some circumstances**. For example, IAS 16 on depreciation is inappropriate for investment properties (properties not occupied by the entity but held solely for investment), which are covered by IAS 40 on investment property.

- Standards may be subject to **lobbying or government pressure** (in the case of national standards). For example, in the USA, the accounting standard FAS 19 on the accounts of oil and gas companies led to a powerful lobby of oil companies, which persuaded the SEC (Securities and Exchange Commission) to step in. FAS 19 was then suspended.

- Unlike IFRSs, many national standards are not based on a **conceptual framework of accounting**.

- There may be a **trend towards rigidity**, and away from flexibility in applying the rules.

3.2 Criticisms of the IASB

Any international body, whatever its purpose or activity, faces enormous political difficulties in attempting to gain **international consensus** and the IASB is no exception to this. How can the IASB reconcile the financial reporting situation between economies as diverse as third-world developing countries and sophisticated first-world industrial powers?

Developing countries are suspicious of the IASB, believing it to be dominated by the **USA.** This arises because acceptance by the USA listing authority, the Securities and Exchange Commission (SEC), of IFRS is seen as the priority. For all practical purposes it is the American market which must be persuaded to accept IFRSs, and a lot of progress has now been made in this direction.

Developing countries have been catered for to some extent by the development of IAS 41 on **agriculture**, which is generally of much more relevance to such countries.

There are also tensions between the **UK/US model** of financial reporting and the **European model**. The UK/US model is based around investor reporting, whereas the European model is mainly concerned with tax rules, so shareholder reporting has a much lower priority.

The break-up of the former USSR and the move in many **Eastern European countries** to free-market economies has also created difficulties. It is likely that these countries will have to 'catch up' to international standards as their economies stabilise.

3.3 Global effect of IFRSs and the IASB

As far as Europe is concerned, the consolidated financial statements of many of Europe's top multinationals are already prepared in conformity with national requirements, European Commission (EC) directives and IFRSs. These developments have been given added impetus by the internationalisation of capital markets. IFRSs have been implemented in the European Union since 2005 for the consolidated financial statements of public listed companies.

In Japan, the influence of the IASB had, until recently, been negligible. This was mainly because of links in Japan between tax rules and financial reporting. The Japanese Ministry of Finance set up a working committee to consider whether to bring national requirements into line with IFRSs. The Tokyo Stock Exchange has announced that it will accept financial statements from foreign issuers that conform with home country standards, which would include IFRS.

The Japanese standpoint was widely seen as an attempt to attract foreign issuers, in particular companies from Hong Kong and Singapore. As these countries base their accounting on international standards, this action is therefore implicit acknowledgement by the Japanese Ministry of Finance of IFRS requirements. In December 2009 the Japanese FSA announced that Japanese listed companies would be allowed to use IFRS from 31 March 2010.

In the USA, the Securities and Exchange Commission (SEC) agreed in 1993 to allow foreign issuers (of shares, etc) to follow IFRS treatments on certain issues, including statements of cash flows under IAS 7.

The overall effect is that, where an IFRS treatment differs from US GAAP, these treatments will now be acceptable.

In certain countries, the application of IFRSs is mandatory for all domestic listed companies. The following provides an example of some of the countries, but the schedule is not exhaustive: Barbados, Cyprus, Georgia, Jamaica, Jordan, Kenya, Kuwait, Malawi, Mauritius, Nepal, Peru, Serbia and Trinidad and Tobago.

Countries that implemented IFRSs for the 2005 European ruling in respect of the consolidated financial statements of public listed companies include Austria, Belgium, Czech Republic, Denmark, Estonia, Finland, France, Germany, Greece, Hungary, Iceland, Ireland, Italy, Liechtenstein, Lithuania, Luxembourg, Netherlands, Norway, Poland, Portugal, Slovenia, Slovak Republic, Spain, Sweden and the United Kingdom.

Many non-European counties also require their listed companies to adopt IFRSs. These include Australia, Bahamas, Bahrain, Chile, Costa Rica, Egypt, Hong Kong, Kenya, Kuwait, Mauritius, New Zealand, and South Africa.

There are some countries where the implementation of IFRSs is not mandatory but discretionary. These include Aruba, Bermuda, Bolivia, Cayman Islands, Dominica, El Salvador, Gibraltar, Laos, Lesotho, Swaziland, Switzerland, Turkey, Uganda and Zimbabwe.

However, there are several countries where the use of IFRSs is not currently permitted. The following are some of the countries, but the list is not exhaustive: Bangladesh, Cuba, Indonesia, Iran, Senegal, Taiwan, Thailand, Tunisia and Vietnam.

3.4 Harmonisation in Europe

The objective of the European Commission (EC) is to build a fully integrated, globally competitive market. A key element of this is the harmonisation of company law across the member states. In line with this the EC aims to establish a level playing field for financial reporting, supported by an effective enforcement regime. The commission is uniquely the only organisation whose accounting standards are legally enforceable, in the form of directives which must be included in the national legislation of member states. However, the directives have been criticised as they might become constraints on the application of world-wide standards, and might bring accounting standardisation and harmonisation into the political arena.

The EC adopted a regulation under which from 2005 consolidated financial statements of listed companies were required to comply with IFRS. The implications of this measure are far reaching. However, member states currently have the discretion to extend the implementation of IFRS to include non-listed companies. In the UK, for example, small companies report under UK accounting standards, with many taking advantage of the reduced disclosure requirements of the FRSSE (Financial Reporting Standard for Smaller Entities). The IASB has recently issued the IFRS for SMEs (Small and Medium-sized entities) and this is an important step toward the introduction of IFRS for all companies.

Many commentators believe that in the light of the EC's commitment to IFRS it is only a matter of time before national standard setting bodies like the Accounting Standards Board (ASB) in the UK are, in effect, replaced by the IASB, with national standards falling into disuse. However, the IASB will continue to need input and expertise from valued national standard setters like the ASB.

3.5 Harmonisation in the USA

Convergence between IFRSs and US accounting standards (US GAAP) is one of the bigger issues in the global implementation of IFRSs. At present, all US entities must file accounts prepared under US GAAP. However, in 2002 the IASB and its US equivalent, the FASB (Financial Accounting Standards Board) did agree to harmonise their work plans, and to work towards reducing the differences between IFRSs and US GAAP. This is known as the IASB Convergence Project and IFRS 5 *Non-Current Assets Held for Sale and Discontinued Operations* was the first standard to be issued as a result of this agreement.

In 2008 the US Securities and Exchange Commission (SEC) issued a 'roadmap' for the use of IFRSs, proposing the eventual mandatory use of IFRSs for all US public companies. At present, only overseas issuers of securities are allowed to file accounts under IFRSs (without having to provide a reconciliation to US GAAP). The proposals were revised in 2010 and now set out six headings on which progress needs to be made. These headings include:

- Further improvements to IFRS

- Changes to the accountability and funding arrangements for the IFRS Foundation, to demonstrate beyond doubt its independence

- Investor understanding and education regarding IFRS.

If these proposals are adopted and assuming that the SEC judges that sufficient progress has been made under the six headings, then the use of IFRS would become **compulsory** for all US entities, starting in approximately 2015 or 2016.

An essential part of harmonising US GAAP and IFRS is to create a common conceptual framework. An agreement on the underpinning concepts is seen as vital to international convergence. The IASB and the FASB are currently working on a project to develop a **common conceptual framework**.

3.6 Harmonisation in the UK

In the UK a detailed comparison has been carried out between international and UK accounting standards which has been documented in what is called The Convergence Handbook.

The following statement is taken from The Convergence Handbook.

'The ASB is working with the IASB and other national standard setters in order to seek improvements in IFRS and convergence of national and international standards. The ASB is one of several national standard setters that have a formal liaison relationship with the IASB. This relationship involves regular meetings and other consultations as well as several joint standard setting projects, including the ASB's joint project with the IASB on reporting financial performance.

The ASB intends to align UK accounting standards with IFRS whenever practicable. It proposes to do this, in the main, by a phased replacement of existing UK standards with new UK standards based on the equivalent IFRS.'

This is from an article by Sir David Tweedie, Chairman of the IASB.

'The UK is part of an increasingly global economy, and its prosperity depends upon inward and outward capital flows to facilitate investment and promote economic growth. Adopting international standards will remove a hurdle in the way of developments that offer the prospects of benefits for the UK investor and for UK business as a whole.'

3.7 Approaches to implementation of IFRSs

There are generally three ways a country choosing to adopt international standards can go about it.

(a) **Adoption as local accounting standards**. Some countries choose to adopt IFRSs with little or no amendments for their particular countries.

(b) **Model for local accounting standards**. Other countries adopt IFRSs, but adapt them to suit local needs. This is the case in Australia.

(c) **Persuasive influence in formulating local accounting standards**. Some countries already had accounting standards which pre-dated IFRSs. Many of these countries have been working for may years to narrow the gap between their local standards and IFRSs. This is the case in the UK.

International harmonisation

Learning outcome B1(a)

In accounting terms what do you think are:

(a)   The advantages to international harmonisation?

(b)   The barriers to international harmonisation?

Section summary

In its attempt to formulate standards which are accepted internationally, the IASB has met opposition over various issues from companies, interest groups and countries.

Some progress has been made towards global harmonisation of accounting standards, with many countries, including EU member states, requiring mandatory use of IFRSs for listed entities.

Convergence between IFRS and US GAAP is one of the bigger issues in the global implementation of IFRS. The SEC has produced a 'roadmap' for the implementation of IFRS.

4   Conceptual framework and GAAP

Introduction

In this section we introduce the idea of a conceptual framework.

4.1 The search for a conceptual framework

KEY TERM

A CONCEPTUAL FRAMEWORK in the field we are concerned with, is a statement of generally accepted theoretical principles which form the frame of reference for financial reporting.

These theoretical principles provide the basis for the development of new accounting standards and the evaluation of those already in existence. The financial reporting process is concerned with providing information that is useful in the business and economic decision-making process. Therefore a conceptual framework will form the **theoretical basis** for determining which events should be accounted for, how they should be measured and how they should be communicated to the user. Although it is theoretical in nature, a conceptual framework for financial reporting has highly practical final aims.

The **danger of not having a conceptual framework** is demonstrated in the way some countries' standards have developed over recent years; standards tend to be produced in a haphazard and fire-fighting approach. Where an agreed framework exists, the standard-setting body act as an architect or designer, rather than a fire-fighter, building accounting rules on the foundation of sound, agreed basic principles.

The lack of a conceptual framework also means that fundamental principles are tackled **more than once** in different standards, thereby producing **contradictions and inconsistencies** in basic concepts, such as those of prudence and matching. This leads to ambiguity and it affects the true and fair concept of financial reporting.

Another problem with the lack of a conceptual framework has become apparent in the USA. The large number of **highly detailed standards** produced by the Financial Accounting Standards Board (FASB) has created a financial reporting environment governed by specific rules rather than general principles. This would be avoided if a cohesive set of principles were in place.

A conceptual framework can also bolster standard setters **against political pressure** from various 'lobby groups' and interested parties. Such pressure would only prevail if it was acceptable under the conceptual framework.

4.2 Advantages and disadvantages of a conceptual framework

4.2.1 Advantages

(a) The situation is avoided whereby standards are developed on a patchwork basis, where a particular accounting problem is recognised as having emerged, and resources are then channelled into **standardising accounting practice** in that area, without regard to whether that particular issue was necessarily the most important issue remaining at that time without standardisation.

(b) As stated above, the development of certain standards (particularly national standards) have been subject to considerable **political interference** from interested parties. Where there is a conflict of interest between user groups on which policies to choose, policies deriving from a conceptual framework will be **less open to criticism** that the standard-setter buckled to external pressure.

(c) Some standards may concentrate on the **statement of comprehensive income** whereas some may concentrate on the **valuation of net assets** (statement of financial position).

4.2.2 Disadvantages

(a) Financial statements are intended for a **variety of users**, and it is not certain that a single conceptual framework can be devised which will suit all users.

(b) Given the diversity of user requirements, there may be a need for a variety of accounting standards, each produced for a **different purpose** (and with different concepts as a basis).

(c) It is not clear that a conceptual framework makes the task of **preparing and then implementing** standards any easier than without a framework.

Before we look at the IASB's attempt to produce a conceptual framework, we need to consider another term of importance to this debate: generally accepted accounting practice; or GAAP.

4.3 Generally Accepted Accounting Practice (GAAP)

KEY TERM

GAAP signifies all the rules, from whatever source, which govern accounting.

In individual countries this is seen primarily as a **combination** of:

- National company law
- National accounting standards
- Local stock exchange requirements

Although those sources are the basis for the GAAP of individual countries, the concept also includes the effects of **non-mandatory sources** such as IFRS or statutory requirements in other countries.

In many countries, like the UK, GAAP does not have any statutory or regulatory authority or definition, unlike other countries, such as the USA. The term is mentioned rarely in legislation, and only then in fairly limited terms.

There are different views of GAAP in different countries. The IASB convergence programme seeks to reduce these differences.

4.3.1 Rules based versus principles based GAAP   5/11

GAAP can be based on legislation and accounting standards that are either:

(a) rules based, or
(b) principles based.

The USA operates a **rules based** system, where standards are very detailed, attempting to cover all eventualities. Accounts which do not comply in all details are presumed to be misleading. This has the advantage of clear requirements which can be generally understood and it removes any element of judgement. Other advantages of a prescriptive system are that it can be taught and learnt more easily, therefore it should ensure that similar items are treated in a similar way and it should be more obvious if a entity does not follow GAAP.

The IASB *Framework* is a **principles based** system which does not specify all the details but seeks to obtain adherence to the 'spirit' of the regulations. This does leave room for some element of professional judgement, but it also makes it harder for entities to avoid applying a standard as the terms of reference are broader.

Other advantages of having a principles based system include the following.

(a)   Standards based on principles **don't go out of date** in the same way as those based on rules. For example if a prescriptive standard includes a list of common items that would qualify for specific treatment, the list may go out of date as economies progress and develop.

(b)   It is more difficult for a company to **manipulate information** to avoid applying a standard based on principles than it is for a prescriptive standard.

(c)   Standards based on principles are **less likely to contradict each other** than those based on rules as they are all based on the same basic principles.

(d)   Standards based on rules require that many detailed standards covering all possible situations have to be produced. This can result in **complexity in financial reporting** as there are a considerable number of standards to be followed. Having standards based on principles avoids this.

4.3.2 GAAP and a conceptual framework

A conceptual framework for financial reporting can be defined as an attempt to codify existing GAAP in order to reappraise current accounting standards and to produce new standards.

Section summary

A conceptual framework provides the basis for the formulation of accounting standards.

5 The IASB *Framework*

Introduction

This section explains the *Framework* developed by the IASB.

5.1 A conceptual framework   5/10, 11/10

In July 1989 the old IASC produced a document, *Framework for the preparation and presentation of financial statements* ('*Framework*'). The *Framework* is, in effect, the **conceptual framework** upon which all IASs and IFRSs are based and hence which determines how financial statements are prepared and the information they contain.

The *Framework* consists of several sections or chapters, following on after a preface and introduction. These **chapters** are as follows.

- The objective of financial statements
- Underlying assumptions
- Qualitative characteristics of financial statements

- The elements of financial statements
- Recognition of the elements of financial statements
- Measurement of the elements of financial statements
- Concepts of capital and capital maintenance

5.2 Preface

The preface to the *Framework* points out the fundamental reason why financial statements are produced worldwide, ie to **satisfy the requirements of external users**, but that practice varies due to the individual pressures in each country.

These pressures may be social, political, economic or legal, but they result in variations in practice from country to country, including the form of statements, the definition of their component parts (assets, liabilities etc), the criteria for recognition of items and both the scope and disclosure of financial statements.

5.3 Introduction

The introduction to the *Framework* lays out the purpose, status and scope of the document. It then looks at different users of financial statements and their information needs. (Note that the *Framework* refers to the IASC. In practice this now means the IASB.)

5.3.1 Purpose and status

The introduction gives a list of the purposes of the *Framework*.

(a)   Assist the Board of the IASC in the **development of future IFRSs** and in its review of existing IFRSs.

(b)   Assist the Board of the IASC in **promoting harmonisation** of regulations, accounting standards and procedures relating to the presentation of financial statements by providing a basis for reducing the number of alternative accounting treatments permitted by IFRS.

(c)   Assist **national standard-setting bodies** in developing national standards.

(d)   Assist **preparers of financial statements** in applying IFRSs and in dealing with topics that have yet to form the subject of an IFRS.

(e)   Assist **auditors** in forming an opinion as to whether financial statements conform with IFRS.

(f)   Assist **users of financial statements** in interpreting the information contained in financial statements prepared in conformity with IFRS.

(g)   Provide those who are interested in the work of IASC with **information** about its approach to the formulation of IFRS.

The *Framework* is not an IFRS and so does not overrule any individual IFRS. In the (rare) cases of conflict between an IFRS and the *Framework*, the **IFRS will prevail**. These cases will diminish over time as the *Framework* will be used as a guide in the production of future IFRS. The *Framework* itself will be revised occasionally depending on the experience of the IASB in using it.

5.3.2 Scope   11/10

The *Framework* deals with:

(a)   The **objective** of financial statements.

(b)   The **qualitative characteristics** that determine the usefulness of information in financial statements.

(c)   The **definition, recognition and measurement** of the elements from which financial statements are constructed.

(d)   Concepts of **capital and capital maintenance**.

The *Framework* is concerned with **'general purpose' financial statements** (ie a normal set of annual statements), but it can be applied to other types of accounts. A complete set of financial statements includes:

(a)   A statement of financial position
(b)   A statement of comprehensive income
(c)   A statement of changes in financial position (eg a statement of cash flows)
(d)   Notes, other statements and explanatory material

Supplementary information may be included, but some items are not included, namely commentaries and reports by the directors, the chairman, management etc.

All types of financial reporting entities are included (commercial, industrial, business; public or private sector).

KEY TERM

A REPORTING ENTITY is an entity for which there are users who rely on the financial statements as their major source of financial information about the entity.   *(Framework)*

5.3.3 Users and their information needs

The *Framework* identifies the users of accounting information as investors, employees, lenders, suppliers and other trade creditors, customers, government and their agencies and the public.

Question 1.2	Information needs

Learning outcome B1(a)

What do you think are the information needs of the users of financial information listed above?

Financial statements cannot meet all these users' needs, but financial statements which meet the **needs of investors** (providers of risk capital) will meet most of the needs of other users.

The *Framework* emphasises that the preparation and presentation of financial statements is primarily the **responsibility of an entity's management**. Management also has an interest in the information appearing in financial statements.

5.4 The objective of financial statements   5/11

The *Framework* states that:

> 'The objective of financial statements is to provide information about the **financial position, performance** and **changes in financial position** of an entity that is useful to a wide range of users in making economic decisions.'   *(Framework)*

Such financial statements will meet the needs of most users. The information is, however, **restricted**.

(a)   It is based on **past events** not expected future events.
(b)   It does not necessarily contain **non-financial information**.

The statements also show the results of **management's stewardship**.

5.4.1 Financial position, performance and changes in financial position

Information about **financial position** is mainly provided in the statement of financial position. Financial position information is affected by the following and information about each one can aid the user.

(a) **Economic resources controlled**: to predict the ability to generate cash

(b) **Financial structure**: to predict borrowing needs, the distribution of future profits/cash and likely success in raising new finance

(c) **Liquidity and solvency**: to predict whether financial commitments will be met as they fall due (liquidity relates to short-term commitments, solvency is longer-term)

KEY TERMS

LIQUIDITY The availability of sufficient funds to meet deposit withdrawals and other short-term financial commitments as they fall due.

SOLVENCY. The availability of cash over the longer term to meet financial commitments as they fall due.

(Framework)

In all these areas, the capacity to adapt to changes in the environment in which the entity operates is very important.

Information about **financial performance** is primarily found in the statement of comprehensive income. Financial performance information, particularly profitability, is used to assess potential changes in the economic resources the entity is likely to control in the future. Information about performance variability is therefore important.

Information about **changes in financial position** is found in the statement of cash flows. Changes in financial position information is used to assess the entity's investing, financing and operating activities. It shows the entity's ability to produce cash and the needs which utilise those cash flows.

All parts of the financial statements are **interrelated**, reflecting different aspects of the same transactions or events. Each statement provides different information; none can provide all the information required by users.

5.5 Underlying assumptions   5/11

5.5.1 Accruals basis

KEY TERM

ACCRUALS BASIS. The effects of transactions and other events are recognised when they occur (and not as cash or its equivalent is received or paid) and they are recorded in the accounting records and reported in the financial statements of the periods to which they relate.

(Framework)

Entities should prepare their financial statements on the basis that transactions are recorded in them not as the cash is paid or received, but as the revenues or expenses are **earned or incurred** in the accounting period to which they relate.

According to the accruals assumption, in computing profit, revenue earned must be **matched against** the expenditure incurred in earning it. This is also known as the **matching convention**.

5.5.2 Going concern

KEY TERM

GOING CONCERN. The entity is assumed to be a going concern, that is, as continuing in operation for the foreseeable future. It is assumed that the entity has neither the intention nor the need to liquidate or curtail materially the scale of its operations.

(Framework)

This concept assumes that, when preparing a normal set of accounts, the business will **continue to operate** in approximately the same manner for the foreseeable future (at least the next 12 months). In particular, the entity will not go into liquidation or scale down its operations in a material way. The main significance of the going concern concept is that if the entity is not considered to be a going concern, the assets of entity should be included in the accounts at their **'break-up' value** (the amount they would sell for if they were sold off piecemeal and the business were broken up).

If the going concern assumption is not followed, that fact must be disclosed, together with the following information.

(a)   The basis on which the financial statements have been prepared.
(b)   The reasons why the entity is not considered to be a going concern.

Section summary

The *Framework* was produced by the old IASC and adopted by the IASB. It provides the conceptual framework within which IFRSs are formulated. The **accruals basis** and **going concern** are underlying assumptions of the *Framework*.

6 Qualitative characteristics of financial statements   11/10

Introduction

The *Framework* states that qualitative characteristics are the attributes that make the information provided in financial statements useful to users. The four principal qualitative characteristics are **understandability, relevance, reliability and comparability**. This section discusses each of these characteristics in turn.

6.1 Understandability   5/11

Users must be able to understand financial statements. They are assumed to have some business, economic and accounting knowledge and to be able to apply themselves to study the information properly. **Complex matters should not be left out** of financial statements simply due to their difficulty if the information is relevant.

6.2 Relevance   5/11

Only relevant information can be useful. Information should be released on a timely basis to be relevant to users.

KEY TERM

RELEVANCE. Information has the quality of relevance when it influences the economic decisions of users by helping them evaluate past, present or future events or confirming, or correcting, their past evaluations.   *(Framework)*

The predictive and confirmatory roles of information are interrelated. Information on financial position and performance is often used to predict future position and performance and other things of interest to the user, eg likely dividend, wage rises. The **manner of showing information** will enhance the ability to make predictions, eg by highlighting unusual items.

The relevance of information is affected by its **nature and materiality**.

KEY TERM

MATERIALITY. Information is material if its omission or misstatement could influence the economic decisions of users taken on the basis of the financial statements.   *(Framework)*

Information may be judged relevant simply because of its nature (eg remuneration of management). In other cases, both the nature and materiality of the information are important. Materiality is not a primary qualitative characteristic itself (like reliability or relevance), because it is merely a threshold or cut-off point.

An error which is too trivial to affect anyone's understanding of the accounts is referred to as **immaterial**. In preparing accounts it is important to assess what is material and what is not, so that time and money are not wasted in the pursuit of excessive detail.

Determining whether or not an item is material is a very **subjective exercise**. There is no absolute measure of materiality. It is common to apply a convenient rule of thumb (for example material items are those with a value greater than 5% of net profits). However some items disclosed in the accounts are regarded as particularly sensitive and even a very small misstatement of such an item is taken as a material error. An example, in the accounts of a limited liability company, is the amount of remuneration (salaries and other rewards) paid to directors of the company.

The assessment of an item as material or immaterial may **affect its treatment in the accounts**. For example, the income statement of a business shows the expenses incurred grouped under suitable captions (administrative expenses, distribution expenses etc); but in the case of very small expenses it may be appropriate to lump them together as 'sundry expenses', because a more detailed breakdown is inappropriate for such immaterial amounts.

In assessing whether or not an item is material, it is not only the value of the item which needs to be considered. The **context** is also important:

(a)   If a statement of financial position shows non-current assets of $2 million and inventories of $30,000, an error of $20,000 in the depreciation calculations might not be regarded as material. However, an error of $20,000 in the inventory valuation would be material. In other words, the total of which the error forms part must be considered.

(b)   If a business has a bank loan of $50,000 and a $55,000 balance on bank deposit account, it will be a material misstatement if these two amounts are displayed on the statement of financial position as 'cash at bank $5,000'. In other words, incorrect presentation may amount to material misstatement even if there is no monetary error.

6.3 Reliability   5/10, 5/11

Information must also be reliable to be useful. The user must be able to depend on it being a **faithful representation**.

RELIABILITY. Information has the quality of reliability when it is free from material error and bias and can be depended upon by users to represent faithfully that which it either purports to represent or could reasonably be expected to represent.   *(Framework)*

6.3.1 Faithful representation

Information must represent faithfully the transactions it purports to represent in order to be reliable. There is a risk that this may not be the case, not due to bias, but due to **inherent difficulties in identifying the transactions** or finding an **appropriate method of measurement or presentation**. Where measurement of the financial effects of an item is so uncertain, entities should not recognise such an item, eg internally generated goodwill.

6.3.2 Substance over form

Faithful representation of a transaction is only possible if it is accounted for according to its **substance and economic reality**, not with its legal form.

SUBSTANCE OVER FORM. The principle that transactions and other events are accounted for and presented in accordance with their substance and economic reality and not merely their legal form.   *(Framework)*

For instance, one party may sell an asset to another party and the sales documentation may record that legal ownership has been transferred. However, if agreements exist whereby the party selling the asset continues to enjoy the future economic benefits arising from the asset, then in substance no sale has taken place.

6.3.3 Neutrality

Information must be **free from bias** to be reliable. Neutrality is lost if the financial statements are prepared so as to influence the user to make a judgement or decision in order to achieve a predetermined outcome.

6.3.4 Prudence

KEY TERM

PRUDENCE is the inclusion of a degree of caution in the exercise of the judgements needed in making the estimates required under conditions of uncertainty, such that assets or income are not overstated and liabilities or expenses are not understated

Prudence must be exercised when preparing financial statements because of the uncertainty surrounding many transactions. It is not permitted, however, to create secret or hidden reserves using prudence as a justification.

There are three important issues to bear in mind.

(a)   Where **alternative procedures or valuations** are possible, the one selected should be the one which gives the most cautious result.

(b)   Where a **loss is foreseen**, it should be anticipated and taken into account immediately. Even when the exact amount of the loss is not known, an estimate of the loss should be made, based on the best information available. If a business purchases inventory for $1,200 but, because of a sudden slump in the market, only $900 is likely to be realised when the inventory is sold, the prudence concept dictates that the inventory is valued at $900. It is not enough to wait until the inventory is sold, and then recognise the $300 loss; it must be recognised as soon as it is foreseen.

(c)   Profits should only be recognised when **realised** in the form of cash or another asset with a reasonably certain cash value.

6.3.5 Completeness

Financial information must be complete, within the **restrictions of materiality and cost**, to be reliable. Omission may cause information to be misleading.

6.4 Comparability   5/11

Users must be able to compare an entity's financial statements:

(a)   **Through time** to identify trends.

(b)   **With the financial statements** of other entities to evaluate their relative financial position, performance and changes in financial position.

The consistency of treatment is therefore important across like items over time, within the entity and across all entities.

The **disclosure of accounting policies** is particularly important here. Users must be able to distinguish between different accounting policies in order to be able to make a valid comparison of similar items in the accounts of different entities.

Comparability is **not the same as uniformity**. Entities should change accounting policies if they become inappropriate.

Corresponding information for **preceding periods** should be shown to enable comparison over time.

Exam alert

Make sure you know these qualitative characteristics. They are highly likely to be examined in Section A or Section B of your exam.

6.5 Constraints on relevant and reliable information

6.5.1 Timeliness

Information may become irrelevant if there is a delay in reporting it. There is a **balance between timeliness and the provision of reliable information**. Information may be reported on a timely basis when not all aspects of the transaction are known, thus compromising reliability.

If every detail of a transaction is known, it may be too late to publish the information because it has become irrelevant. The overriding consideration is how best to satisfy the economic decision-making needs of the users.

6.5.2 Balance between benefits and cost

This is a pervasive constraint, not a qualitative characteristic. When information is provided, its benefits must exceed the costs of obtaining and presenting it. This is a **subjective area** and there are other difficulties: others than the intended users may gain a benefit; also the cost may be paid by someone other than the users. It is therefore difficult to apply a cost-benefit analysis, but preparers and users should be aware of the constraint.

6.5.3 Balance between qualitative characteristics

A **trade off between qualitative characteristics** is often necessary, the aim being to achieve an appropriate balance to meet the objective of financial statements. It is a matter for professional judgement as to the relative importance of these characteristics in each case.

6.6 True and fair view/fair presentation

The *Framework* does not attempt to define these concepts of true and fair view or fair presentation directly. It does state, however, that the application of the **principal 'qualitative' characteristics** and of **appropriate accounting standards** will usually result in financial statements which show a true and fair view or fair presentation of the information given in them.

Section summary

The four principal qualitative characteristics that make the information provided in financial statements useful to users are **understandability, relevance, reliability and comparability.**

7 The elements of financial statements

Introduction

In this section we look at the elements of financial statements and their recognition and measurement according to the *Framework*.

7.1 The elements of financial statements

Transactions and other events are grouped together in broad **classes** and in this way their financial effects are shown in the financial statements. These broad classes are the elements of financial statements. The *Framework* lays out these elements as follows.

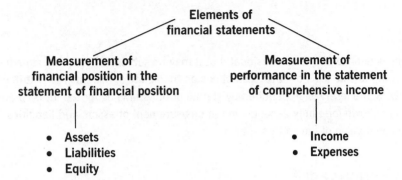

A process of **sub-classification** then takes place for presentation in the financial statements, eg assets are classified by their nature or function in the business to show information in the best way for users to take economic decisions.

7.2 Financial position

We need to define the three terms listed under this heading above.

KEY TERMS

ASSET. A resource controlled by an entity as a result of past events and from which future economic benefits are expected to flow to the entity.

LIABILITY. A present obligation of the entity arising from past events, the settlement of which is expected to result in an outflow from the entity of resources embodying economic benefits.

EQUITY. The residual interest in the assets of the entity after deducting all its liabilities.

These definitions are important, but they do not cover the **criteria for recognition** of any of these items, which are discussed later in this chapter. This means that the definitions may include items which would not actually be recognised in the statement of financial position because they fail to satisfy recognition criteria particularly, as we will see below, the **probable flow of any economic benefit** to or from the business.

Whether an item satisfies any of the definitions above will depend on the **substance and economic reality** of the transaction, not merely its legal form.

Exam alert

These definitions should be learnt. You may be asked to define these terms in your exam.

Question 1.3	Assets and liabilities

Learning outcome B1(b)

Consider the following situations. In each case, do we have an asset or liability within the definitions given by the *Framework*? Explain your answer.

(a)   Pat Co has purchased a patent for $20,000. The patent gives the company sole use of a particular manufacturing process which will save $3,000 a year for the next five years.

(b)   Baldwin Co paid Don Brennan $10,000 to set up a car repair shop, on condition that priority treatment is given to cars from the company's fleet.

(c)   Deals on Wheels Co provides a warranty with every car sold.

7.2.1 Equity

Equity is defined above as a **residual**, but it may be sub-classified in the statement of financial position. This will indicate legal or other restrictions on the ability of the entity to distribute or otherwise apply its equity. Some reserves are required by statute or other law, eg for the future protection of creditors. The amount shown for equity depends on the **measurement of assets and liabilities**. It has nothing to do with the market value of the entity's shares.

7.3 Performance

Profit is used as a **measure of performance**, or as a basis for other measures (eg earnings per share). It depends directly on the measurement of income and expenses, which in turn depend (in part) on the concepts of capital and capital maintenance adopted.

The elements of income and expense are therefore defined.

KEY TERMS

INCOME. Increases in economic benefits during the accounting period in the form of inflows or enhancements of assets or decreases of liabilities that result in increases in equity, other than those relating to contributions from equity participants.

EXPENSES. Decreases in economic benefits during the accounting period in the form of outflows or depletions of assets or incurrences of liabilities that result in decreases in equity, other than those relating to distributions to equity participants.   *(Framework)*

7.3.1 Capital maintenance adjustments

A **revaluation** gives rise to an increase or decrease in equity.

KEY TERM

REVALUATION. Restatement of assets and liabilities.   *(Framework)*

These increases and decreases meet the definitions of income and expenses. They are **not included** in the statement of comprehensive income under certain concepts of capital maintenance, however, but rather in equity.

7.4 Recognition of the elements of financial statements

Items which meet the definition of assets or liabilities may still not be recognised in financial statements because they must also meet certain **recognition criteria**.

KEY TERM

RECOGNITION. The process of incorporating in the statement of financial position or statement of comprehensive income an item that meets the definition of an element and satisfies the following criteria for recognition:

(a)   It is probable that any future economic benefit associated with the item will flow to or from the entity.

(b)   The item has a cost or value that can be measured with reliability.   *(Framework)*

Regard must be given to **materiality**.

7.4.1 Probability of future economic benefits

Probability here means the **degree of uncertainty** that the future economic benefits associated with an item will flow to or from the entity. This must be judged on the basis of the **characteristics of the entity's environment** and the **evidence available** when the financial statements are prepared.

7.4.2 Reliability of measurement

The cost or value of an item, in many cases, **must be estimated**. The *Framework* states, however, that the use of reasonable estimates is an essential part of the preparation of financial statements and does not undermine their reliability. Where no reasonable estimate can be made, the item should not be recognised, although its existence should be disclosed in the notes, or other explanatory material.

Items may still qualify for recognition **at a later date** due to changes in circumstances or subsequent events.

7.4.3 Recognition of items

We can summarise the recognition criteria for assets, liabilities, income and expenses, based on the definition of recognition given above.

Item	Recognised in	When
Asset	The statement of financial position	It is probable that the future economic benefits will flow to the entity and the asset has a cost or value that can be measured reliably.
Liability	The statement of financial position	It is probable that an outflow of resources embodying economic benefits will result from the settlement of a present obligation and the amount at which the settlement will take place can be measured reliably.
Income	The statement of comprehensive income	An increase in future economic benefits related to an increase in an asset or a decrease of a liability has arisen that can be measured reliably.
Expenses	The statement of comprehensive income	A decrease in future economic benefits related to a decrease in an asset or an increase of a liability has arisen that can be measured reliably.

7.5 Measurement of the elements of financial statements

Measurement is defined as follows.

KEY TERM

MEASUREMENT. The process of determining the monetary amounts at which the elements of the financial statements are to be recognised and carried in the statement of financial position and the statement of comprehensive income.   *(Framework)*

This involves the selection of a particular **basis of measurement**. A number of these are used to different degrees and in varying combinations in financial statements. They are:

- **Historical cost**. The amount that was originally paid to acquire an asset.

- **Current cost**. The amount which would be needed at current prices to obtain an equivalent asset.

- **Realisable value**. The net amount expected to be received from selling an asset, or paid to settle a liability.

- **Present value**. The discounted present value of future cash flows that are expected to be received or paid in respect of an asset or liability.

7.6 Concepts of capital and capital maintenance

Most entities use a **financial concept of capital** when preparing their financial statements (see below). The concept of capital selected should be appropriate to the needs of the users of an entity's financial statements.

7.6.1 Concepts of capital maintenance and the determination of profit

First of all, we need to define the different concepts of capital.

KEY TERM

Under a **financial concept of capital**, such as invested money or invested purchasing power, CAPITAL is the net assets or equity of the entity. The financial concept of capital is adopted by most entities.

Under a **physical concept of capital**, such as operating capability, CAPITAL is the productive capacity of the entity based on, for example, units of output per day. *(Framework)*

The definition of profit is also important.

KEY TERM

PROFIT. The residual amount that remains after expenses (including capital maintenance adjustments, where appropriate) have been deducted from income. Any amount over and above that required to maintain the capital at the beginning of the period is profit. *(Framework)*

The main difference between the two concepts of capital maintenance is the treatment of the **effects of changes in the prices of assets and liabilities** of the entity. In general terms, an entity has maintained its capital if it has as much capital at the end of the period as it had at the beginning of the period. Any amount over and above that required to maintain the capital at the beginning of the period is profit.

(a) **Financial capital maintenance**: profit is the increase in nominal money capital over the period.

(b) **Physical capital maintenance**: profit is the increase in the physical productive capacity over the period.

Section summary

The *Framework* groups items into the elements of financial statements. These are assets, liabilities, equity, income and expenses.

Chapter Roundup

✓   The IASB replaced the IASC in 2001. It is responsible for setting International Financial Reporting Standards (IFRSs).

✓   IFRSs are set in a similar manner to the previous setting of IASs in accordance with the IASB's due process.

✓   In its attempt to formulate standards which are accepted internationally, the IASB has met opposition over various issues from companies, interest groups and countries.

✓   Some progress has been made towards global harmonisation of accounting standards, with many countries, including EU member states, requiring mandatory use of IFRSs for listed entities.

✓   Convergence between IFRS and US GAAP is one of the bigger issues in the global implementation of IFRS. The SEC has produced a 'roadmap' for the implementation of IFRS.

✓   A conceptual framework provides the basis for the formulation of accounting standards.

✓   The *Framework* was produced by the old IASC and adopted by the IASB. It provides the conceptual framework within which IFRSs are formulated. The accruals basis and going concern are underlying assumptions of the *Framework*.

✓   The four principal qualitative characteristics that make the information provided in financial statements useful to users are **understandability, relevance, reliability and comparability.**

✓   The *Framework* groups items into the elements of financial statements. These are assets, liabilities, equity, income and expenses.

Quick Quiz

1   How does the *Framework* help promote the harmonisation of accounting standards?

2   What are the four qualitative characteristics of financial statements identified in the *Framework*?

3   Two of the four qualitative characteristics could come into conflict with each other. Which two are these and in what way could they conflict?

4   According to the *Framework* what is the objective of financial statements?

5   Which of the following arguments is not in favour of accounting standards?

    A   They reduce variations in methods used to produce accounts
    B   They oblige companies to disclose their accounting policies
    C   They are a less rigid alternative to legislation
    D   They may tend towards rigidity in applying the rules

Answers to Quick Quiz

1 A conceptual framework provides a basis for reducing the number of alternative accounting treatments permitted by IFRSs, thereby helping to promote harmonisation of accounting standards, procedures and regulations.

2 Understandability, relevance, reliability and comparability.

3 Relevance and reliability. Conflict could arise in terms of timeliness: information must be timely to be relevant, however, if it is reported too soon, then all aspects of a transaction might not be known, so reliability may be compromised.

4 The objective of financial statements is to provide information about the **financial position**, **performance** and **changes in financial position** of an entity that is useful to a wide range of users in making economic decisions.

5 D The other arguments are all in favour of accounting standards.

Answers to Questions

1.1 International harmonisation

(a) Advantages of global harmonisation

The advantages of harmonisation will be based on the benefits to users and preparers of accounts, as follows.

(i) Investors, both individual and corporate, would like to be able to compare the financial results of different companies internationally as well as nationally in making investment decisions.

(ii) Multinational companies would benefit from harmonisation for many reasons including the following.

(1) Better access would be gained to foreign investor funds.

(2) Management control would be improved, because harmonisation would aid internal communication of financial information.

(3) Appraisal of foreign entities for take-overs and mergers would be more straightforward.

(4) It would be easier to comply with the reporting requirements of overseas stock exchanges.

(5) Preparation of group accounts would be easier.

(6) A reduction in audit costs might be achieved.

(7) Transfer of accounting staff across national borders would be easier.

(iii) Governments of developing countries would save time and money if they could adopt international standards and, if these were used internally, governments of developing countries could attempt to control the activities of foreign multinational companies in their own country. These companies could not 'hide' behind foreign accounting practices which are difficult to understand.

(iv) Tax authorities. It will be easier to calculate the tax liability of investors, including multinationals who receive income from overseas sources.

(v) Regional economic groups usually promote trade within a specific geographical region. This would be aided by common accounting practices within the region.

      (vi)   Large international accounting firms would benefit as accounting and auditing would be much easier if similar accounting practices existed throughout the world.

(b)   Barriers to harmonisation

      (i)   Different purposes of financial reporting. In some countries the purpose is solely for tax assessment, while in others it is for investor decision-making.

      (ii)   Different legal systems. These prevent the development of certain accounting practices and restrict the options available.

      (iii)   Different user groups. Countries have different ideas about who the relevant user groups are and their respective importance. In the USA investor and creditor groups are given prominence, while in Europe employees enjoy a higher profile.

      (iv)   Needs of developing countries. Developing countries are obviously behind in the standard setting process and they need to develop the basic standards and principles already in place in most developed countries.

      (v)   Nationalism is demonstrated in an unwillingness to accept another country's standard.

      (vi)   Cultural differences result in objectives for accounting systems differing from country to country.

      (vii)   Unique circumstances. Some countries may be experiencing unusual circumstances which affect all aspects of everyday life and impinge on the ability of companies to produce proper reports, for example hyperinflation, civil war, currency restriction and so on.

      (viii)   The lack of strong accountancy bodies. Many countries do not have strong independent accountancy or business bodies which would press for better standards and greater harmonisation.

1.2 Information needs

(a)   **Investors** are the providers of equity capital

      (i)   Information is required to help make a decision about buying or selling shares, taking up a rights issue and voting.

      (ii)   Investors must have information about the level of dividend, past, present and future and any changes in share price.

      (iii)   Investors will also need to know whether the management has been running the company efficiently.

      (iv)   Investors will want to know about the liquidity position of the company, the company's future prospects, and how the company's shares compare with those of its competitors.

(b)   **Employees** need information about the security of employment and future prospects for jobs in the company, and to help with collective pay bargaining.

(c)   **Lenders** need information to help them decide whether to lend to a company. They will also need to check that the value of any security remains adequate, that the interest repayments are secure.

(d)   **Suppliers** need to know whether the company will be a good customer and pay its debts.

(e)   **Customers** need to know whether the company can continue producing and supplying goods.

(f)   **Government's** interest in a company may be one of creditor or customer, as well as being specifically concerned with compliance with tax and company law, ability to pay tax and the general contribution of the company to the economy.

(g)   The **public** at large would wish to have information for all the reasons mentioned above, but it could be suggested that it would be impossible to provide general purpose accounting information which was specifically designed for the needs of the public.

1.3 Assets and liabilities

(a)　This is an asset, albeit an intangible one. There is a past event, control and future economic benefit (through cost savings).

(b)　This cannot be classified as an asset. Baldwin Co has no control over the car repair shop and it is difficult to argue that there are 'future economic benefits'.

(c)　This is a liability; the business has taken on an obligation. It would be recognised when the warranty is issued rather than when a claim is made.

Now try these questions from the Exam Question Bank			

Number	Level	Marks	Time
Q6	Examination	5	9 mins
Q7	Examination	5	9 mins
Q8	Examination	5	9 mins

EXTERNAL AUDIT

Here we look at the role of the external auditor. If you work for an organisation which is audited (internally or externally), try to talk to the auditors about the audit. Because it is the audit of an organisation you know well, you should gain some insight into the role of the auditor.

The external auditors are employed to check the good **stewardship** of the directors of the company and the truth and fairness of the financial statements. To enable them to do this they have certain **rights and duties**.

When the audit is completed and the auditors are satisfied with the information and explanations provided, an **audit report** is issued. The audit report is the instrument by which the auditors express an **opinion** on the truth and fairness of the financial statements. In Section 4 we look at the standard audit report and its **modification** when the auditors are not completely satisfied with the results of the audit.

Although we refer to ISAs, you are **not** required to learn them for the exam.

topic list	learning outcomes	syllabus references	ability required
1 External audit	B1(g)	B1(viii)	comprehension
2 Accepting audit appointments	B2(c)	B2(iii)	application
3 Duties and rights of auditors	B1(g)	B1(viii)	comprehension
4 The audit report	B1(g)	B1(viii)	comprehension

1   External audit

Introduction

If you work in an organisation you may have come across the auditors and even been asked questions by them. In this section we look at what an audit is and why it is necessary.

1.1 Why is an audit needed?

In the modern commercial environment, businesses which are operated as companies with limited liability need to produce accounts to indicate how successfully they are performing. However the owners of a business require something more than accounts because the managers responsible for preparing them may, either unintentionally or by deliberate manipulation, produce accounts which are misleading. An independent examination of the accounts is needed so that the owners of the business can assess how well management have discharged their *stewardship*.

1.2 Objective of an audit   5/10

KEY TERM

The objective of an AUDIT of financial statements is to enable the auditor to express an opinion whether the financial statements are prepared, in all material respects, in accordance with an identified financial reporting framework.

The phrases used to express the auditor's opinion are 'give a true and fair view' or 'present fairly, in all material respects', which are equivalent terms. A similar objective applies to the audit of financial or other information prepared in accordance with appropriate criteria.

We will look at some of the terms used here later on.

First of all, though, we need to look at what an audit is really about. International Standard on Auditing (ISA) 200 *Overall objectives of the independent auditor and the conduct of an audit in accordance with international standards on auditing* summarises what audits are all about.

ISA 200

The auditor shall comply with all ISAs relevant to the audit.   *(Paragraph 18)*

The standard also comments on the auditor's general approach to audit work.

ISA 200

The auditor shall plan and perform an audit with professional scepticism, recognising that circumstances may exist that cause the financial statements to be materially misstated.   *(Paragraph 15)*

So, for example, the auditor would not simply accept what managers say during the audit of an entity, but would look for supporting evidence.

1.3 Scope of an audit

We talk of the *scope* of an audit here in the sense of the range of audit procedures which are required to achieve the objective of the audit.

> **ISA 200**
>
> To achieve the overall objectives of the auditor, the auditor shall use the objectives stated in relevant ISAs in planning and performing the audit.   *(Paragraph 21)*

1.4 Limitations of an audit

An audit performed under ISAs should provide **'reasonable assurance'** that the financial statements, taken as a whole, are free from material misstatement (we will look at the definition of 'material' later). Reasonable assurance is concerned with the way evidence is built up throughout the audit, which provides the basis of the auditor's opinion. It therefore reflects the whole audit process.

The definition of the audit given above is comprehensive about what an audit is. The standard also makes it clear that the audit is *not*:

(a)   A **guarantee** of the **future viability** of the entity

(b)   An **assurance** of **management's effectiveness** and efficiency

The standard points out that there are inherent (ie existing and permanent characteristic or attribute) limitations in an audit which affect the auditor's ability to discover material misstatements. These inherent limitations arise from the following factors.

(a)   The nature of financial reporting

(b)   The nature of audit procedures

(c)   The need for the audit to be conducted within a reasonable period of time and at a reasonable cost

The auditor's **judgement** is also an issue here. Throughout every stage of the audit, the auditor's judgement is brought to bear. In particular, the auditor's judgement has a great impact on:

(a)   Materiality and audit risk

(b)   The nature, timing and extent of audit procedures

(c)   Evaluating whether sufficient, appropriate audit evidence has been obtained

(d)   The evaluation of management's judgements in applying the entity's applicable financial reporting framework

(e)   The drawing of conclusions based on the audit evidence obtained

1.5 Responsibility for the financial statements

Responsibility for the preparation and presentation of the financial statements rests firmly with the management of the entity. An audit of the financial statements does not relieve management of this responsibility. Many members of the public fail to realise this.

1.6 The expectations gap

There are some common misconceptions in relation to the role of the auditors, even among 'financially aware' people, including the following examples.

(a)   Many people think that the **auditor's report** is to the **directors** of a company, rather than the members.

(b)   Some think that a **qualified audit report** is **more favourable** than an unmodified audit report, whereas the converse is true.

(c)   There is a perception that it is the auditor's duty to detect fraud, when in fact the detection of fraud is the **responsibility** of the **directors**.

These findings highlight the 'expectations gap' between what auditors do and what people in general think that they do. Add the fact that many 'financially aware' people do not look at the report and accounts of a company they are considering investing in, and you have some sobering facts for the auditors to contemplate!

Public concern at large company failures has highlighted problems with the expectations gap. This has formed part of a general debate on corporate governance (ie how companies are governed) in many countries. Corporate governance developments have aimed to make the role of the auditor clearer and to regulate the relationship between the auditors and the management of the entity being audited.

In most countries, audits are required under national statute in the case of a large number of undertakings, including limited liability companies. Other organisations and entities requiring a statutory audit may include charities, investment businesses, trade unions and so on.

Non-statutory audits are performed by independent auditors because the owners, proprietors, members, trustees, professional and governing bodies or other interested parties want them, rather than because the law requires them.

Auditors may also give an **audit opinion** on **statements** other than **annual accounts**, including:

- Summaries of sales in support of a statement of royalties
- Statements of expenditure in support of applications for government grants
- The circulation figures of a newspaper or magazine

In all such audits the auditors must take into account any regulations contained in the internal rules or constitution of the undertaking. Examples of the regulations which the auditors would need to refer to in such assignments would include:

- The rules of clubs, societies and charities
- Partnership agreements

1.7 Auditor independence

The most important characteristics of the external auditor, and one which must never be compromised, is that he is **independent** of the organisation and its directors. For this reason, audit firms will rotate partners so that the same partner is not continually signing off the audit report for a client. This is intended to prevent the development of familiarity as a result of which the auditor's independence may be called into question.

Section summary

- An audit is essentially an independent review. External auditors are regulated by statute and by professional bodies.

- The key stages of an audit are to:
    - Carry out procedures to obtain **sufficient appropriate audit evidence**
    - **Evaluate** the **presentation** of accounts
    - Issue a report containing a **clear expression** of **opinion**

- Audits at best give **reasonable assurance** that the accounts are free from **material misstatement**.

- The **expectations gap** is the difference between the work auditors actually carry out and the work non-auditors think they carry out.

2 Accepting audit appointments

Introduction

This section covers the procedures that the auditors must undertake to ensure that their appointment is valid and that they are clear to act.

2.1 Client acceptance

Before a new audit client is accepted, the auditors must ensure that there are **no threats to compliance with the fundamental principles** of the CIMA Code. For example, if the client is known to be involved in money laundering, this could be a threat to integrity or professional behaviour. We will look at the fundamental principles in more detail in Chapter 3.

The significance of any threats to the Code should be evaluated and if necessary the auditors should **apply safeguards** to eliminate them or reduce them to an acceptable level. If this is not possible, the auditors should decline to enter into a relationship with the client.

Appointment decisions should be **periodically reviewed** for recurring audit clients.

2.2 Engagement acceptance

The significance of any threats to the CIMA Code should be evaluated for each specific audit engagement. If necessary, the auditors should apply safeguards to eliminate them or reduce them to an acceptable level. The Code lists the following examples of safeguards that could be applied.

- Acquiring an appropriate understanding of the nature of the client's business, the complexity of its operations, the specific requirements of the engagement and the purpose, nature and scope of the work to be performed

- Acquiring knowledge of relevant industries or subject matters

- Possessing or obtaining experience with relevant regulatory or reporting requirements

- Assigning sufficient staff with the necessary competencies

- Using experts where necessary, bearing in mind their reputation and expertise

- Agreeing on a realistic time frame for the performance of the engagement

- Complying with quality control policies and procedures designed to provide reasonable assurance that specific engagements are accepted only when they can be performed competently.

The auditors must only agree to accept engagements that they are **competent** to perform. A self-interest threat to professional competence and due care is created if the auditors do not posses the required skills for the engagement or are unable to acquire these through further training.

2.3 Changes in a professional appointment

Companies will change their auditors for various reasons such as the audit fee being perceived as too high or that the company's business has expanded beyond the capabilities of the audit firm. There are certain provisions which the CIMA Code requires a new auditor to follow before accepting such an engagement.

In particular, the new auditors should **communicate** with the existing auditors to establish the facts and circumstances behind the proposed change. Based on this information, the new auditors can decide whether or not it is appropriate to accept the engagement. For example, if it was discovered that the existing audit firm has not been reappointed because of a serious disagreement with the client, the new auditors may decide not to accept the appointment. The incoming auditor must have **permission** from the audit client before communicating with the existing auditors.

Confidentiality rules require that existing auditors can only communicate with the new auditors when the audit client has given permission. All information should be provided honestly and unambiguously.

2.4 Non-audit engagements

The rules for acceptance of non-audit engagements, for example assurance or tax engagements, are the same as those for auditors.

Section summary

Before accepting a new client or engagement, the auditors must ensure the correct acceptance procedures have been carried out.

3 Duties and rights of auditors

Introduction

In this section we look at the duties and rights of the auditor. The duties and rights vary according to national law, we focus here on the UK.

3.1 Duties

The auditors should be required to report on every statement of financial position and statement of comprehensive income laid before the company in general meeting.

The auditors are required to consider the following.

Compliance with legislation	Whether the accounts have been prepared in accordance with the relevant legislation.
Truth and fairness of accounts	Whether the statement of financial position shows a true and fair view of the company's affairs at the end of the period and the statement of comprehensive income (and a statement of cash flows) show a true and fair view of the results for the period.
Adequate records and returns	Whether adequate accounting records have been kept and proper returns adequate for the audit received from branches not visited by the auditor.
Agreement of accounts to records	Whether the accounts are in agreement with the accounting records.
Consistency of other information	Whether the other information presented with the accounts is consistent with the accounts.

3.2 Rights

The auditors must have certain rights to enable them to carry out their duties effectively.

The principal rights auditors should have, excepting those dealing with resignation or removal, are set out in the table below.

Access to records	A right of access at all times to the books, accounts and vouchers of the company.
Information and explanations	A right to require from the company's officers such information and explanations as the auditors think necessary for the performance of their duties as auditors.
Attendance at/notices of general meetings	A right to attend any general meetings of the company and to receive all notices of, and communications relating to such meetings which any member of the company is entitled to receive.

Right to speak at general meetings	A right to be heard at general meetings which they attend on any part of the business that concerns them as auditors.
Rights in relation to written resolutions	A right to receive a copy of any written resolution proposed.
Right to require laying of accounts	A right to give notice in writing requiring that a general meeting be held for the purpose of laying the accounts and reports before the company.

Rights to information

It is an offence for a company's officer knowingly or recklessly to make a statement in any form to an auditor which:

(a)   Purports to convey any information or explanation required by the auditor

(b)   Is materially misleading, false or deceptive

If auditors have not received all the information and explanations they deem necessary, they should state this fact in their report.

Section summary

Auditor's duties generally include the duties to report explicitly on the **reasonableness** of the accounts audited and their **compliance** with legislation. They should also report on whether adequate accounting records have been kept.

Auditor's rights should include the rights of **access to records** and to receive **information** and **explanations**, also rights relating to **attendance** and **speaking** at **general meetings**.

4   The audit report

Introduction

This section looks at the audit report. This is the way that the auditors will report to the shareholders of a company with their findings from the audit. We will look at the structure of the report and the different opinions that the auditor may give.

4.1 Preparing the report

ISA 700 *Forming an opinion and reporting on financial statements* deals with the auditor's responsibility to form an opinion on the financial statements and provides guidance on the form and content of the auditor's report. The auditor's report is the report issued as a result of an audit performed by an independent auditor of the financial statements of an entity.

ISA 700

The auditor shall form an opinion on whether the financial statements are prepared, in all material respects, in accordance with the applicable financial reporting framework.   *(Paragraph 10)*

The applicable financial reporting framework could be either IASs or relevant national standards or practices. Auditors may also have to consider whether the financial statements comply with statutory requirements.

ISA 700

The auditor's report shall be in writing   *(Paragraph 20)*

4.2 Basic elements of the auditor's report

A measure of uniformity in the form and content of the auditor's report is desirable because it helps to promote the reader's understanding and to identify unusual circumstances when they occur. The auditor's report includes the following basic elements, usually in the following layout.

Example: Typical audit report

INDEPENDENT AUDITOR'S REPORT

(APPROPRIATE ADDRESSEE)

Report on the Financial Statements

We have audited the accompanying financial statements of ABC Company, which comprise the statement of financial position as at December 31, 20X1, and the statement of comprehensive income, statement of changes in equity and statement of cash flows for the year then ended, and a summary of significant accounting policies and other explanatory information.

Management's Responsibility for the Financial Statements

Management is responsible for the preparation and fair presentation of these financial statements in accordance with International Financial Reporting Standards, and for such internal control as management determines is necessary to enable the preparation and fair presentation of financial statements that are free from material misstatement, whether due to fraud or error.

Auditor's Responsibility

Our responsibility is to express an opinion on these financial statements based on our audit. We conducted our audit in accordance with International Standards on Auditing. Those standards require that we comply with ethical requirements and plan and perform the audit to obtain reasonable assurance about whether the financial statements are free from material misstatement.

An audit involves performing procedures to obtain audit evidence about the amounts and disclosures in the financial statements. The procedures selected depend on the auditor's judgment, including the assessment of the risks of material misstatement of the financial statements, whether due to fraud or error. In making those risk assessments, the auditor considers internal control relevant to the entity's preparation and fair presentation of the financial statements in order to design audit procedures that are appropriate in the circumstances, but not for the purpose of expressing an opinion on the effectiveness of the entity's internal control. An audit also includes evaluating the appropriateness of accounting policies used and the reasonableness of accounting estimates made by management, as well as evaluating the overall presentation of the financial statements.

We believe that the audit evidence we have obtained is sufficient and appropriate to provide a basis for our audit opinion.

Opinion

In our opinion, the financial statements present fairly, in all material respects, (or *give a true and fair view of*) the financial position of ABC Company as at December 31, 20X1, and (*of*) its financial performance and its cash flows for the year then ended in accordance with International Financial Reporting Standards.

[Auditor's signature]

[Date of the auditor's report]

[Auditor's address]

4.2.1 Title

ISA 700

The auditor's report shall have a title that clearly indicates that it is the report of an independent auditor.

(Paragraph 21)

The term 'independent auditor' distinguishes the auditor's report from reports issued by others, such as by officers of the entity.

4.2.2 Addressee

ISA 700

The auditor's report shall be addressed as required by the circumstances of the engagement.

(Paragraph 22)

The report is ordinarily addressed either to the **shareholders** or **those charged with governance** of the entity whose financial statements are being audited.

4.2.3 Introductory paragraph

ISA 700

The introductory paragraph in the auditor's report shall:

(a)   Identify the entity whose financial statements have been audited;

(b)   State that the financial statements have been audited;

(c)   Identify the title of each statement that comprises the financial statements;

(d)   Refer to the summary of significant accounting policies and other explanatory information; and

(e)   Specify the date or period covered by each financial statement comprising the financial statements.

(Paragraph 23)

4.2.4 Management's responsibility for the financial statements

This section of the auditor's report covers the responsibilities of those in charge of preparing the financial statements. This is often the management of an organisation.

The auditor's report must explain that management are responsible for preparing the financial statements in accordance with an applicable financial reporting framework. It must also describe how management are responsible for internal controls which enable the preparation of financial statements which are free from fraud or error.

4.2.5 Auditor's responsibility

ISA 700

The auditor's report shall state that the responsibility of the auditor is to express an opinion on the financial statements based on the audit.

(Para 29)

The auditor must state that the audit was conducted in accordance with International Standards on Auditing. This section must also contain a description of an audit.

4.2.6 Opinion paragraph

ISA 700

When expressing an unmodified opinion on financial statements ..., the auditor's opinion shall ... use one of the following phrases, which are regarded as being equivalent:

(a)   The financial statements present fairly, in all material respects, ... in accordance with [the applicable financial reporting framework]; or

(b)   The financial statements give a true and fair view of ... in accordance with [the applicable financial reporting framework].

(Paragraph 35)

The terms used to express the auditor's opinion are 'give a true and fair view' or 'present fairly, in all material respects', and are **equivalent**. Both terms indicate, amongst other things, that the auditor considers only those matters that are **material** to the financial statements.

The **applicable financial reporting framework** is determined by IASs, rules issued by professional bodies, and the development of general practice within a country, with an appropriate consideration of fairness and with due regard to local legislation. To advise the reader of the context in which 'fairness' is expressed, the auditor's opinion indicates the framework upon which the financial statements are based.

In addition to an opinion of the true and fair view (or fair presentation, in all material respects), the auditor's report may need to include an opinion as to whether the financial statements comply with other requirements specified by **relevant statutes or law**. These other reporting responsibilities must be addressed in a separate section of the auditor's report.

4.2.7 Signature of the auditor

ISA 700

The auditor's report shall be signed.

(Paragraph 40)

The firm as a whole usually assumes responsibility for the audit, but in some countries an individual partner may be required to take responsibility and sign in his or her own name.

4.2.8 Date of the auditor's report

ISA 700

The auditor's report shall be dated no earlier than the date on which the auditor has obtained sufficient appropriate audit evidence on which to base the auditor's opinion on the financial statements.

(Paragraph 41)

4.2.9 Auditor's address

ISA 700

The auditor's report shall name the location in the jurisdiction where the auditor practices.*(Paragraph 42)*

4.3 Unmodified audit opinion

ISA 700

The auditor shall express an *unmodified opinion* when the auditor concludes that the financial statements are prepared, in all material respects, in accordance with the applicable financial reporting framework.

(Paragraph 16)

This section has introduced you to the standard unmodified audit opinion. The next paragraphs look at how the audit report is affected when problems of varying severity arise in the audit.

Question 2.1	Unmodified audit opinion

Learning outcome B1(g)

The following is an unmodified audit report, which has been signed by the auditors of Kiln, a limited liability company.

INDEPENDENT AUDITOR'S REPORT

TO THE SHAREHOLDERS OF KILN COMPANY

Report on the Financial Statements

We have audited the accompanying financial statements of Kiln Company, which comprise the statement of financial position as at December 31, 20X3, and the statement of comprehensive income, statement of changes in equity and statement of cash flows for the year then ended, and a summary of significant accounting policies and other explanatory information.

Management's Responsibility for the Financial Statements

Management is responsible for the preparation and fair presentation of these financial statements in accordance with International Financial Reporting Standards, and for such internal control as management determines is necessary to enable the preparation and fair presentation of financial statements that are free from material misstatement, whether due to fraud or error.

Auditor's Responsibility

Our responsibility is to express an opinion on these financial statements based on our audit. We conducted our audit in accordance with International Standards on Auditing. Those standards require that we comply with ethical requirements and plan and perform the audit to obtain reasonable assurance about whether the financial statements are free from material misstatement.

An audit involves performing procedures to obtain audit evidence about the amounts and disclosures in the financial statements. The procedures selected depend on the auditor's judgment, including the assessment of the risks of material misstatement of the financial statements, whether due to fraud or error. In making those risk assessments, the auditor considers internal control relevant to the entity's preparation and fair presentation of the financial statements in order to design audit procedures that are appropriate in the circumstances, but not for the purpose of expressing an opinion on the effectiveness of the entity's internal control. An audit also includes evaluating the appropriateness of accounting policies used and the reasonableness of accounting estimates made by management, as well as evaluating the overall presentation of the financial statements.

We believe that the audit evidence we have obtained is sufficient and appropriate to provide a basis for our audit opinion.

Opinion

In our opinion, the financial statements present fairly, in all material respects, (or *give a true and fair view of*) the financial position of Kiln Company as at December 31, 20X3, and (*of*) its financial performance and its cash flows for the year then ended in accordance with International Financial Reporting Standards.

[Auditor's signature]

[Date of the auditor's report]

[Auditor's address]

Required

Explain the purpose and meaning of the following phrases taken from the above extracts of an audit report with an unmodified audit opinion.

(a)   '... which comprise the statement of financial position ..., and the statement of comprehensive income, ... and statement of cash flows ... .'
(b)   '... in accordance with International Standards on Auditing.'
(c)   'In our opinion ...'

4.4 Modified opinions   5/10, 11/10

A modified opinion is required when:

- The auditor concludes that the financial statements as a whole are not free from material misstatements or

- The auditor cannot obtain sufficient appropriate audit evidence to conclude that the financial statements as a whole are free from material misstatement

ISA 705 *Modifications to the opinion in the independent auditor's report* sets out the different types of modified opinions that can result. It identifies three possible types of modifications:

- A **qualified** opinion
- An **adverse** opinion
- A **disclaimer** of opinion

Terminology surrounding audit reports has recently been amended. In your exam and in real-life examples you might see the following terminology used.

New terminology	Equivalent terminology you may see in your exam
Unmodified opinion	Unqualified opinion
Modified opinion	Qualified opinion
Qualified opinion	'Except for' qualified opinion

4.4.1 Types of modifications

The type of modification issued depends on the following:

- The **nature of the matter** giving rise to the modifications (ie whether the financial statements **are materially misstated** or whether they **may be misstated** when the auditor cannot obtain sufficient appropriate audit evidence)

- The auditor's judgement about the **pervasiveness** of the effects/possible effects of the matter on the financial statements

At this point we should look again at the concept of **materiality** which is covered in the IASB's *Framework*.

KEY TERM

A matter is MATERIAL 'if its omission or misstatement could influence the economic decisions of users taken on the basis of the financial statements'.

(Framework)

The concept of materiality is very important to auditors as they do not report on anything which is not material. However, they do have to decide whether something is material or not. They may use guidelines such as treating anything which exceeds 5% of profit or 1% of revenue as material.

Exam skills

Exam questions will make it clear whether or not an item is material. If this is based on amounts, then immaterial amounts will be far less than 5% of profit and material amounts will be far in excess of 10% of profit.

KEY TERM

PERVASIVENESS is a term used to describe the effects or possible effects on the financial statements of misstatements or undetected misstatements (due to an inability to obtain sufficient appropriate audit evidence). There are three types of pervasive effect:

- Those that are not confined to specific elements, accounts or items in the financial statements

- Those that are confined to specific elements, accounts or items in the financial statements and represent or could represent a substantial proportion of the financial statements

- Those that relate to disclosures which are fundamental to users' understanding of the financial statements

4.4.2 Qualified opinions

A qualified opinion must be expressed in the auditor's report in the following two situations:

(1) The auditor concludes that misstatements are material, but not pervasive, to the financial statements.

Material misstatements could arise in respect of:

- The appropriateness of selected accounting policies

- The application of selected accounting policies

- The appropriateness or adequacy of disclosures in the financial statements

Terminology surrounding audit reports has recently been amended. In your exam and in real-life examples you might see this type of modified opinion being referred to as an **'except for' qualified opinion due to a disagreement with management.**

(2) The auditor cannot obtain sufficient appropriate audit evidence on which to base the opinion but concludes that the possible effects of undetected misstatements, if any, could be material but not pervasive.

The auditor's inability to obtain sufficient appropriate audit evidence is also referred to as a limitation on the scope of the audit and could arise from:

- Circumstances beyond the entity's control (eg accounting records destroyed)

- Circumstances relating to the nature or timing of the auditor's work (eg the timing of the auditor's appointment prevents the observation of the physical inventory count)

- Limitations imposed by management (eg management prevents the auditor from requesting external confirmation of specific account balances)

Terminology surrounding audit reports has recently been amended. In your exam and in real-life examples you might see this type of modified opinion being referred to as an **'except for' qualified opinion due to a limitation on scope.**

4.4.3 Adverse opinions

An adverse opinion is expressed when the auditor, having obtained sufficient appropriate audit evidence, concludes that misstatements are both **material and pervasive** to the financial statements.

4.4.4 Disclaimers of opinion

An opinion must be disclaimed when the auditor **cannot obtain sufficient appropriate audit evidence** on which to base the opinion and concludes that the **possible effects** on the financial statements of undetected misstatements, if any, **could be both material and pervasive**.

The opinion must also be disclaimed in situations involving **multiple uncertainties** when the auditor concludes that, despite having obtained sufficient appropriate audit evidence for the individual uncertainties, it is not possible to form an opinion on the financial statements due to the **potential interaction of the uncertainties and their possible cumulative effect** on the financial statements.

Exam alert

You need to be aware of the three different types of modified opinion, however questions in your exam are likely to focus on 'qualified' opinions, where the auditor concludes that misstatements are material, but not pervasive, to the financial statements. Remember that in your exam, this kind of modified opinion may be referred to as an 'except for' qualified opinion due to a disagreement with management.

4.4.5 Effect on the auditor's report

Exam alert

We will focus here on 'qualified' and 'adverse' opinions, as CIMA has stated that the effect of a 'disclaimer of opinion' on the audit report is outside the F1 syllabus.

When the auditor has had to modify the auditor's report, the report must include a paragraph before the opinion paragraph which provides a description of the matter giving rise to the modification. This paragraph will be entitled 'Basis for qualified opinion' or 'Basis for adverse opinion' depending on the type of modification.

The section of the auditor's report containing the opinion will be headed either 'Qualified opinion' or 'Adverse opinion', again depending on the type of modification.

When the auditor expresses a qualified or adverse opinion, the section of the report on the auditor's responsibilities must be amended to state that the auditor believes that the audit evidence obtained is sufficient and appropriate to provide a basis for the auditor's modified audit opinion.

We will now look at some examples of extracts from modified auditor's reports for each of these situations.

Example 1: Qualified opinion due to material misstatement of inventories

---

Basis for qualified opinion

The company's inventories are carried in the statement of financial position at xxx. Management has not stated inventories at the lower of cost and net realisable value but has stated them solely at cost, which constitutes a departure from International Financial Reporting Standards. The company's records indicate that had management stated the inventories at the lower of cost and net realisable value, an amount of xxx would have been required to write the inventories down to their net realisable value. Accordingly, cost of sales would have been increased by xxx, and income tax, net income and shareholders' equity would have been reduced by xxx, xxx and xxx, respectively.

Qualified Opinion

In our opinion, except for the effects of the matter described in the Basis for Qualified Opinion paragraph, the financial statements present fairly, in all material respects, (or *give a true and fair view of*) the financial position of ABC Company as at December 31, 20X1, and (*of*) its financial performance and its cash flows for the year then ended in accordance with International Financial Reporting Standards.

Example 2: Adverse opinion due to material misstatement because of non-consolidation of a subsidiary

---

Basis for adverse opinion

As explained in Note X, the company has not consolidated the financial statements of subsidiary XYZ Company it acquired during 20X1 because it has not yet been able to ascertain the fair values of certain of the subsidiary's material assets and liabilities at the acquisition date. This investment is therefore accounted for on a cost basis. Under International Financial Reporting Standards, the subsidiary should have been consolidated because it is controlled by the company. Had XYZ been consolidated, many elements in the accompanying financial statements would have been materially affected. The effects on the consolidated financial statements of the failure to consolidate have not been determined.

Adverse Opinion

In our opinion, because of the significance of the matter discussed in the Basis for Adverse Opinion paragraph, the consolidated financial statements do not present fairly (or *do not give a true and fair view of*) the financial position of ABC Company and its subsidiaries as at December 31, 20X1, and (*of*) their financial performance and their cash flows for the year then ended in accordance with International Financial Reporting Standards.

Exam alert

You do not have to memorise the wording of audit reports for your exam. A question on audit reports in your exam is likely to ask you to explain what the different types or report are or to decide what kind of report should be issued in a particular circumstance.

4.4.6 Communication with those charged with governance

ISA 705 states that when the auditor expects to express a modified opinion, the auditor must **communicate with those charged with governance** of the entity (usually the directors) the circumstances leading to the expected modification, and the proposed wording of the modification in the auditor's report.

This allows the auditor to give **notice** to those charged with governance of the intended modification and the reasons for it, to **seek agreement or confirm disagreement** with those charged with governance with respect to the modification, and to give those charged with governance an **opportunity to provide further information and explanations** in respect of the matter giving rise to the expected modification.

At this point, those charged with governance may provide additional information and explanations or may decide to change the accounting for an issue raised by the auditors. The auditors may then conclude that a modified opinion is no longer needed.

Question 2.2	Audit problems

Learning outcome B1(g)

During the course of your audit of the non-current assets of Eastern Engineering, a listed company, at 31 March 20X4 the following problem has arisen.

The company incurred development expenditure of $25,000 spent on a viable new product which will go into production next year and which is expected to last for ten years. The expenditure has been debited in full to the statement of comprehensive income. The profit before tax is $100,000.

Required

(a)   List the general forms of modified opinion available to auditors in drafting their report and state the circumstances in which each is appropriate.

(b)   State whether you feel that a modified audit opinion would be necessary for the circumstances outlined above, giving reasons.

(c)   On the assumption that you decide that a modified audit opinion is necessary with respect to the treatment of the development expenditure, draft the section of the report describing the matter (the whole report is not required).

(d)   Outline the auditor's general responsibility with regard to a statement in the directors' or management report concerning the valuation of land and buildings.

4.5 Emphasis of matter paragraphs in the auditor's report

ISA 706 *Emphasis of matter paragraphs and other matter paragraphs in the independent auditor's report* provides guidance to auditors on the inclusion of paragraphs in the auditor's report that either draw users' attention to a matter that is of such importance that it is fundamental to their understanding or that is relevant to their understanding of the audit, the auditor's responsibilities or the auditor's report.

4.5.1 Emphasis of matter paragraphs

KEY TERM

An EMPHASIS OF MATTER is a paragraph included in the auditor's report that refers to a matter appropriately presented or disclosed in the financial statements, that in the auditor's judgment, is of such importance that it is fundamental to users' understanding of the financial statements.

Emphasis of matter paragraphs are used to draw readers' attention to a matter **already presented or disclosed** in the financial statements that the auditor feels is **fundamental** to their understanding, provided that the auditor has obtained sufficient appropriate audit evidence that the matter is **not materially misstated**.

When an emphasis of matter paragraph is included in the auditor's report, it comes **immediately after the opinion paragraph** and is entitled 'Emphasis of matter' (or appropriate). The paragraph must contain a **clear reference** to the matter being emphasised and to where relevant disclosures that fully describe it can be found in the financial statements. The paragraph must state that **the auditor's opinion is not modified** in respect of the matter emphasised.

The following are examples of situations in which the auditor might include an emphasis of matter paragraph in the auditor's report:

(a)   An uncertainty relating to the future outcome of **exceptional litigation or regulatory action**

(b)   **Early application of a new accounting standard** that has a **pervasive effect** on the financial statements

(c)   A **major catastrophe** that has had, or continues to have, **a significant effect** on the entity's financial position

ISA 706 contains an example auditor's report that contains an emphasis of matter paragraph, relevant extracts of which are shown below.

Emphasis of Matter

We draw attention to Note X to the financial statements which describes the uncertainty related to the outcome of the lawsuit filed against the company by XYZ Company. Our opinion is not qualified in respect of this matter.

4.6 The audit report as a means of communication

Unmodified audit reports may not appear to give a great deal of information. The report says a lot, however, by implication.

The real problem here is that, unfortunately, most users do not know what an unmodified audit report tells them. This issue is also confused by the fact that most users do not understand the responsibilities of either the auditors or the directors in relation to the financial statements.

Different countries have tackled this problem in different ways. The role of auditors has been included in the debate on corporate governance in many Western countries, leading to further rules which are nevertheless voluntary, not mandatory.

Section summary

- ISA 700 *Forming an opinion and reporting on financial statements* gives guidance on the form and content of audit reports.

- A **modified opinion** is required when:

    - The auditor concludes that the financial statements as a whole are not free from material misstatements or

    - The auditor cannot obtain sufficient appropriate audit evidence to conclude that the financial statements as a whole are free from material misstatement

- There are three types of **modified opinion**: a **qualified opinion**, an **adverse opinion** and a **disclaimer of opinion**.

- A **qualified opinion** or a **disclaimer of opinion** may arise if the auditor cannot obtain sufficient appropriate audit evidence.

- A **qualified opinion** or an **adverse opinion** may arise if the auditor concludes that the financial statements are not free from material misstatement.

- **Emphasis of matter paragraphs** can be included in the auditor's report under certain circumstances. Their use does not modify the auditor's opinion on the financial statements.

Chapter Roundup

- ✓ An audit is essentially an independent review. External auditors are regulated by statute and professional bodies.

- ✓ The key stages of an audit are to:
  - Carry out procedures to obtain **sufficient appropriate audit evidence**
  - **Evaluate** the **presentation** of accounts
  - Issue a report containing a **clear expression** of **opinion**

- ✓ Audits at best give **reasonable assurance** that the accounts are free from **material misstatement**.

- ✓ The **expectations gap** is the difference between the work auditors actually carry out and the work non-auditors think they carry out.

- ✓ Before accepting a new client or engagement, the auditors must ensure the correct acceptance procedures have been carried out.

- ✓ Auditors' **duties** generally include the duties to report explicitly on the **reasonableness** of the accounts audited and their **compliance** with legislation. They should also report on whether adequate accounting records have been kept.

- ✓ Auditors' rights should include the rights of **access** to **records** and to receive **information** and **explanations**, also rights relating to **attendance** and **speaking** at **general meetings**.

- ✓ ISA 700 *Forming an opinion and reporting on financial statements* gives guidance on the form and content of audit reports.

- ✓ A **modified opinion** is required when:
  - The auditor concludes that the financial statements as a whole are not free from material misstatements or
  - The auditor cannot obtain sufficient appropriate audit evidence to conclude that the financial statements as a whole are free from material misstatement

- ✓ There are three types of **modified opinion**: a **qualified opinion**, an **adverse opinion** and a **disclaimer of opinion**.

- ✓ A **qualified opinion** or a **disclaimer of opinion** may arise if the auditor cannot obtain sufficient appropriate audit evidence.

- ✓ A **qualified opinion** or an **adverse opinion** may arise if the auditor concludes that the financial statements are not free from material misstatement.

- ✓ **Emphasis of matter paragraphs** can be included in the auditor's report under certain circumstances. Their use does not modify the auditor's opinion on the financial statements.

Quick Quiz

1   An audit is the work required to enable the .... to express an .... as to whether the ....
    .... are prepared, in all material respects, in accordance with an identified ....
    ....

2   What is the expectations gap?

3   The main reason why an audit is considered to be necessary is that it gives the financial statements
    credibility

    True ☐

    False ☐

4   Which of the following is not a statutory right of the auditor?

    A   Access to records
    B   Right to speak at general meetings
    C   Right to amend records
    D   Right to receive a copy of any written resolution proposed

5   What are the basic elements of the auditors' report?

6   When will a modified opinion be issued?

Answers to Quick Quiz

1   Auditor, opinion, financial statements, financial reporting framework

2   The **expectations gap** is the difference between the work auditors actually carry out and the work non-
    auditors think they carry out.

3   True

4   C

5   • The report should be addressed to its recipients and have a title indicating it is the report of an
      independent auditor

    • Introductory paragraph including identification of the financial statements audited

    • Separate sections should deal with the responsibilities of management and the responsibility of the
      auditors

    • Opinion paragraph

    • Signature of the auditors

    • Date of the auditor's report

    • Auditor's address

6   A modified opinion is required when:

    • The auditor concludes that the financial statements as a whole are not free from material
      misstatements or

    • The auditor cannot obtain sufficient appropriate audit evidence to conclude that the financial
      statements as a whole are free from material misstatement

Answers to Questions

2.1 Unmodified audit opinion

(a) '... which comprise the statement of financial position ..., and the statement of comprehensive income, ... and statement of cash flows ... .'

Purpose

The purpose of this phrase is to make it clear to the reader of an audit report the part of a company's annual report upon which the auditors are reporting their opinion.

Meaning

An annual report may include documents such as a five year summary and other voluntary information. However, only the statement of comprehensive income, statement of financial position and associated notes are required to be audited in true and fair terms. IAS 7 also requires a statement of cash flows for the financial statements to show a true and fair view. Page references (for instance, 8 to 20) may be used instead to cover the statement of comprehensive income, statement of financial position, notes to the accounts and statement of cash flows. The directors' report, or any equivalent, although examined and reported on by exception if it contains inconsistencies, is not included in these references.

(b) '...in accordance with International Standards on Auditing ....'

Purpose

This phrase is included in order to confirm to the reader that best practice, as laid down in ISAs, has been adopted by the auditors in both carrying out their audit and in drafting their audit opinion. This means that the reader can be assured that the audit has been properly conducted, and that should he or she wish to discover what such standards are, or what certain key phrases mean, he or she can have recourse to ISAs to explain such matters.

Meaning

ISAs are those standards prepared by the International Auditing and Assurance Standards Board (although local/national standards may be mentioned instead).

These prescribe the principles and practices to be followed by auditors in planning, designing and carrying out various aspects of their audit work, the content of audit reports, both modified and unmodified and so on. Members of professional accountancy bodies are expected to follow all of these standards.

(c) 'In our opinion ...'

Purpose

Auditors are required to report on every statement of financial position, statement of comprehensive income and statement of cash flows laid before shareholders. In reporting, they are required to state their *opinion* on those accounts. Thus, the purpose of this phrase is to comply with the requirement to report an opinion.

Meaning

An audit report is an expression of opinion by suitably qualified auditors as to whether the financial statements give a true and fair view, and have been properly prepared in accordance with any relevant local legislation. *It is not a certificate*; rather it is a statement of whether or not, in the professional judgement of the auditors, the financial statements give a true and fair view.

2.2 Audit problems

(a) ISA 705 *Modifications to the opinion in the independent auditor's report* suggests that the auditors may need to modify their audit opinion where they believe the financial statements to be materially misstated.

There are three types of modified opinion:

* Qualified opinion
* Adverse opinion
* Disclaimer of opinion

The following table summarises the different types of modified opinion that can arise.

Nature of circumstances	Material but not pervasive	Material and pervasive
Financial statements are materially misstated	QUALIFIED OPINION	ADVERSE OPINION
Auditor unable to obtain sufficient appropriate audit evidence	QUALIFIED OPINION	DISCLAIMER OF OPINION

(b) Whether a modification of the audit opinion would be required in relation to the circumstances described in the question would depend on whether or not the auditors considered them to be material. An item is likely to be considered as material in the context of a company's financial statements if its omission, misstatement or non-disclosure would prevent a proper understanding of those statements on the part of a potential user. Whilst for some audit purposes materiality will be considered in absolute terms, more often than not it will be considered as a relative term.

Development costs debited to the statement of comprehensive income

The situation here is one of misstatement, since best accounting practice, as laid down by IAS 38, requires that development costs should be taken to the statement of comprehensive income over the useful life of the product to which they relate.

This departure from IAS 38 does not seem to be justifiable and would be material to the reported pre-tax profits for the year, representing as it does 22.5% of that figure.

Whilst this understatement of profit would be material to the financial statements, it is not likely to be seen as pervasive and therefore a **qualified** opinion would be appropriate.

(c) *Basis for Qualified Opinion*

As explained in note ... development costs in respect of a potential new product have been deducted in full against profit instead of being spread over the life of the relevant product as required by IAS 38; the effect of so doing has been to decrease profits before tax for the year by $22,500.

Qualified Opinion

In our opinion, except for the effects of the matter described in the Basis for Qualified Opinion paragraph, the financial statements present fairly, in all material respects, (or "give a true and fair view of") the financial position of Eastern Engineering as at 31 March 20X4, and of its financial performance and its cash flows for the year then ended in accordance with International Financial Reporting Standards.

(d) The auditor's general responsibility with regard to the statement in the directors' report concerning the valuation of land and buildings is to satisfy themselves that this is consistent with the treatment and disclosure of this item in the audited financial statements. If the auditors are not satisfied on the question of consistency then they may have to consider qualifying the opinion in their audit report.

Now try these questions from the Exam Question Bank

Number	Level	Marks	Time
Q9	Examination	5	9 mins
Q10	Examination	5	9 mins

ETHICS

This chapter covers ethical codes, in particular the CIMA *Code of Ethics for Professional Accountants*. It begins by discussing the development of ethical codes in general, before spending time on the CIMA Code.

The ethical matters covered in this chapter are very important. As a CIMA student, you are expected to know and apply the Code in your everyday work.

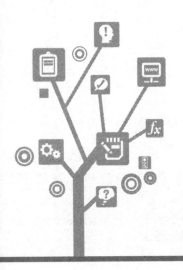

3

topic list	learning outcomes	syllabus references	ability required
1 The need for an ethical code	B2(b)	B2(ii)	comprehension
2 Sources of ethical codes	B2(b)	B2(ii)	comprehension
3 Rules or principles based guidance?	B2(b)	B2(ii)	comprehension
4 Fundamental principles	B2(a)	B2(i)	comprehension
5 Problems facing accountants in public practice	B2(c)	B2(iii)	application
6 Problems facing accountants in business	B2(c)	B2(iii)	application

1 The need for an ethical code

Introduction

In this section we discuss the reasons why ethical codes are considered necessary.

KEY TERM

ETHICS is a set of moral principles to guide behaviour.

A professional accountant has a responsibility to act in the public interest, not just to satisfy the needs of a particular client or employer. Different **stakeholders**, for example investors, governments and employees, **rely on accountants** and their expertise. If the information produced by professional accountants cannot be relied upon, financial markets will not operate effectively.

Professional accountants must be qualified but also have an additional obligation to act ethically by following an ethical code. This ethical requirement may be above that required by laws or regulations in some jurisdictions. An ethical code helps **maintain the reputation** of the accounting profession.

Ethics and ethical codes are **constantly evolving** to adapt with changes in business and society. Cases such as Enron and WorldCom in the USA resulted in the perceived integrity of accountants becoming increasingly important. The CIMA Code was most recently revised in October 2010.

Question 3.1	Ethical issues

Learning outcome B2(b)

Briefly explain the main ethical issues that arise in the following situations.

(a)   Dealing with a repressive authoritarian government abroad

(b)   An aggressive advertising campaign

(c)   Employee redundancies

(d)   Payments or gifts to officials who have the power to help or hinder the payees' operations

Section summary

A need for an ethical code has developed due to various stakeholders relying on accountants and their reputation. An ethical code must evolve to adapt with changing circumstances.

2 Sources of ethical codes

Introduction

This section covers the variety of sources behind the development of ethical codes.

2.1 Early sources of rules

In prehistoric tribes, there were no laws, no court and no police. Rules would have developed through need. The tribe would have a collective idea of what was right or wrong for the good of the group and would have punished a group member who stepped out of line, for example by taking food from others.

Further sources of rules developed as **society** grew and eventually the first laws were laid down to control the larger populations. **Religion** played a major role in developing the rules for the individual, and many of these rules are still in place today.

Business law is relatively new, and has only developed over the last couple of hundred years with industrialisation and the needs that grew from it. **Professional and corporate codes of conduct** are an even more recent development.

Social attitudes have helped shape ethical codes differently in different countries. For example in some cultures (such as Japan) gifts are regarded as an essential part of civilised negotiation, even in circumstances where to Western eyes they might appear ethically dubious. Globalisation has resulted in a move towards standardisation of ethical codes for accountants across the world.

2.2 IFAC

IFAC (the International Federation of Accountants, of which CIMA is a member) is an international body representing all the major accountancy bodies across the world. Its mission is to develop the high standards in professional accountants and enhance the quality of services they provide. To enable this, the IFAC ethics committee published the *Code of Ethics for Professional Accountants*.

The IFAC Code sets out the five fundamental principles of professional ethics and it provides a conceptual framework for applying those principles. Members must apply this conceptual framework to identify threats to compliance with the five fundamental principles, evaluate their significance and apply appropriate safeguards to eliminate or reduce them so that compliance with the fundamental principles is not compromised.

For further information visit www.ifac.org.

2.3 Professional bodies

Professional bodies have their own ethical codes. All CIMA members (and registered students) are required to follow the CIMA *Code of Ethics for Professional Accountants* which is based on the IFAC Code. The CIMA Code has sections which apply to both accountants in business and accountants in public practice.

Although CIMA and IFAC have produced detailed ethical guidance for professional accountants, countries may have their own additional ethical guidance. For example, in the UK, the Auditing Practices Board of the Financial Reporting Council has issued five ethical standards and an ethical standard specific to small entities, which provide an additional source of guidance for UK auditors.

2.4 Employing organisations

Businesses also have ethical values, based on the **norms** and **standards** of **behaviour** that their leaders believe will best help them express their identity and achieve their objectives. Some of these ethical values may be **explicit**, for example, expressed in a mission statement or in employee training programmes. Others may be **unwritten rules and customs** that form part of the organisations' culture.

Business life is a fruitful source of **ethical dilemmas** because its whole purpose is material gain, the making of profit. Success in business requires a constant search for potential advantage over others and business people are under pressure to do whatever yields such advantage.

CASE STUDY

Organisation systems and targets do have ethical implications. The *Harvard Business Review* reported that the US retailer, Sears Roebuck was deluged with complaints that customers of its car service centre were being charged for unnecessary work. Apparently this was because mechanics had been given targets of the number of car spare parts they should sell.

In recent times, trust in business has fallen and increasingly more evidence is required to demonstrate it. In recent years, the UK has seen a procession of corporate disasters including Barings Bank, Northern Rock and HBOS. The US has seen scandals concerning Worldcom, Enron, AIG and Lehman Brothers. Europe did not escape and has seen its share of problems with Parmalat and in India, massive corporate fraud was discovered at Satyam computers. All these scandals have severely knocked public confidence and trust in major corporations.

In an attempt to counter this lack of trust, many corporations have developed **ethical strategies** and **policies** to provide **guidance** and **training** for their employees. Increasing numbers of corporations are developing ethical codes for their employees which must be followed during the course of their employment. The strategy is set by the leadership and this will feed into all areas of the business and become part of the culture of the organisation.

Question 3.2	Employee behaviour

Learning outcome B2(b)

How can an organisation influence employee behaviour towards ethical issues?

An ethical strategy is not always visible to outsiders, and many companies now produce **Corporate Responsibility Policies (CRPs)** and **Corporate Responsibility Reports (CRRs)** for their stakeholders to demonstrate their commitment and to manage their relationships in the wider community.

Section summary

Sources of ethical codes include law, religion, social attitudes, IFAC, professional bodies and employing organisations.

3 Rules or principles based guidance?

Introduction

In this section we look at the advantages and disadvantages of principles based guidance.

The CIMA Code is in the form of a principles-based framework. It contains some rules but in the main it is flexible guidance. It can be seen as being a framework of principles rather than a set of rules. There are a number of advantages of a framework of principles over a system of ethical rules.

3.1 Advantages of principles based guidance

(a) A framework of guidance places the onus on the professional to **consider actively** relevant issues in a given situation, rather than just agreeing action with a checklist of forbidden items. It also requires the professional to **demonstrate** that a responsible conclusion has been reached about ethical issues.

(b) The framework prevents professionals interpreting legalistic requirements narrowly to get around the ethical requirements. There is an extent to which rules engender deception, whereas principles encourage compliance.

(c) A framework allows for variations that are found in every individual situation. Each situation is likely to be different.

(d)   A framework can accommodate a rapidly changing environment, such as the one in which auditors are.

(e)   A framework can contain prohibitions where these are necessary when principles are not enough.

(f)   A code prescribes minimum standards of behaviour that are expected.

(g)   Codes can include examples to illustrate how the principles are applied.

3.2 Disadvantages of principles based guidance

(a)   As ethical codes cannot include all circumstances and dilemmas, accountants need a very good understanding of the underlying principles.

(b)   International codes such as the IFAC Code cannot fully capture regional variations in beliefs and practice.

(c)   The illustrative examples can be interpreted mistakenly as rules to follow in all similar circumstances.

(d)   Principles based codes can be difficult to enforce legally, unless the breach of the code is blatant. Most are therefore voluntary and perhaps therefore less effective.

Section summary

The CIMA Code is a principles based framework. There are advantages and disadvantages of a principles based framework over a system of rules.

4   Fundamental principles

Introduction

This section explains the fundamental principles in the CIMA Code, threats to those principles and the safeguards which can be applied to counteract those threats.

4.1 CIMA fundamental principles of professional ethics   5/10, 11/10, 5/11

CIMA's ethical guidelines are available at **www.cimaglobal.com. Ensure you read them, especially Section 320 and Part B of the 2010 Code as these are specifically referred to in your syllabus. (Note that the syllabus refers to Section 220 and Part C of the Code, however, the recent revision of the Code has reordered the sections so they are now Section 320 and Part B respectively).**

CIMA's *Code of ethics for professional accountants* was last revised in October 2010 and is based on IFAC's *Code of ethics for professional accountants*. It sets out the five fundamental principles of professional ethics and provides a conceptual framework for applying those principles.

CIMA members must not only **know** the fundamental principles, but also **apply** them in their everyday work. There are **serious consequences for failing to follow them**, quite apart from the unacceptability of failure. Whenever a complaint is made against a member, failure to follow the contents of the fundamental principles will be taken into account when a decision is made as to whether a *prima facie* case exists of professional misconduct. The code reflects the standards CIMA expects from both its **members** and **students**.

The five fundamental principles are summarised in the table below.

Fundamental principles	
Integrity	A professional accountant should be straightforward and honest in all professional and business relationships.
Objectivity	A professional accountant should not allow bias, conflict of interest or undue influence of others to override professional or business judgements.
Professional competence and due care	A professional accountant has a continuing duty to maintain professional knowledge and skill at the level required to ensure that a client or employer receives competent professional service based on current developments in practice, legislation and techniques. A professional accountant should act diligently and in accordance with applicable technical and professional standards when providing professional services.
Confidentiality	A professional accountant should respect the confidentiality of information acquired as a result of professional and business relationships and should not disclose any such information to third parties without proper and specific authority unless there is a legal or professional right or duty to disclose. Confidential information acquired as a result of professional and business relationships should not be used for the personal advantage of the professional accountant or third parties.
Professional behaviour	A professional accountant should comply with relevant laws and regulations and should avoid any action that discredits the profession.

Exam alert

You may be asked to list, explain or apply the ethical principles in an exam question so make sure you know them.

4.1.1 Integrity

Integrity is the important principle of honesty and requires accountants to be straightforward in all professional and business relationships. Particular care must be taken when reporting figures and statements. Omitting key information, obscuring the facts or making calculations and decisions without due care could result in false or misleading information being produced and integrity being breached.

Integrity goes further than the work an accountant produces. It also requires the accountant to act in a professional, consistent manner. The accountant must treat everyone the same rather than being friendly to some colleagues but cold to others. It also means that they should not back down over their personal or professional values just to avoid a difficult situation.

4.1.2 Objectivity

Objectivity is a combination of impartiality, intellectual honesty and a freedom from conflicts of interest. Accountants should act fairly and not allow prejudice or bias or the influence of others to affect their judgements. It contrasts with subjectivity which means an individual takes matters into consideration which are important to them, eg friendship and loyalty.

Objectivity is the core value that an accountant brings to their organisation. It is often difficult to separate one's personal interest from a decision, but as accountants it is expected.

Circumstances which may leave accountants in particular risk of breaching this principle include accepting excessive hospitality or forming illicit relationships which could cause embarrassment and the risk of blackmail. Where a threat to objectivity exists, it can be reduced or eliminated by withdrawal, terminating the relationship, involving others in the process and discussing the problem with seniors.

4.1.3 Professional competence and due care

Professional competence and due care means accountants should refrain from performing any services that they cannot perform with reasonable care, knowledge, competence, diligence and a full awareness of the important issues. There is a duty to remain technically up-to-date and apply appropriate technical and professional standards when providing professional services.

Where others perform work on the accountant's behalf, the accountant must ensure that such staff also have adequate experience, qualification and are supervised. Limitations and problems found should be disclosed to those to whom the accountant is reporting. Fact and opinion should be clearly identified to avoid misunderstandings.

4.1.4 Confidentiality

Accountants have a duty to safeguard the security of information in their possession unless there is a legal or professional right or duty to disclose. Also this means not using information obtained in the course of work for personal advantage or for the benefit of others.

Breaches of confidentiality often occur when information is inadvertently disclosed to friends and family and where the accountant has recently changed employers. Care must be taken to keep confidential all information found in the course of performing a professional duty and where a new job is commenced, prior experience may be used in the new role, but not prior information.

CIMA's Code lists circumstances where confidential information may be disclosed. Examples include:

- Disclosure is permitted by law and is authorised by the client or employer

- Disclosure is required by law, such as providing evidence in legal proceedings or assisting public authorities when legal infringements have occurred

- Disclosure is permitted by a professional duty or right, such as complying with technical or ethical requirements, protecting the professional interests of an accountant in a legal action, to respond to a professional body in an investigation or to comply with a quality review.

4.1.5 Professional behaviour

Professional behaviour means, in essence, not doing anything that might bring discredit to the profession and to comply with all relevant laws and regulations. This is defined by the profession as '*actions which a reasonable and informed third party, having knowledge of all relevant information, would conclude negatively affects the good reputation of the profession.*'

Section summary

The five fundamental principles are integrity, objectivity, professional competence and due care, confidentiality and professional behaviour. Compliance with these principles could be threatened by a wide range of circumstances. The professional accountant should apply safeguards to counteract these threats.

5 Problems facing accountants in public practice

Introduction

This section covers the type of threat that a professional accountant in practice might face and the action that should be taken if such a threat arises. We will first look at some general safeguards and then discuss how to apply these to specific threats and situations.

5.1 Threats to compliance with the fundamental principles for accountants in practice

Accountants in practice carry out a variety of work for their clients. They could be asked to perform an **audit of financial statements** which is a statutory requirement for companies of a certain size in most countries. Accountants in practice also carry out **assurance engagements** where they express a conclusion on a subject matter for one party about another. For example, one company buying another company may seek assurance on the forecasts of the company being purchased. Unlike an audit of financial statements, an assurance engagement is not a statutory requirement. Additionally, accountants in public practice perform **non-assurance engagements** during which clients are provided with specialist services such as tax or IT systems advice.

Compliance with the fundamental principles could be threatened by a wide range of circumstances for accountants in practice. The nature and significance of the threats may differ depending on whether they arise in relation to the provision of services to a financial statement audit client, an assurance client or a non-assurance client.

Threat	Examples
Self-interest	Having a financial interest in a client
Self-review	Auditing financial statements prepared by the firm
Advocacy	Advocating the client's case in a lawsuit
Familiarity	Audit team member having family member employed by the client
Intimidation	Threats of replacement due to disagreement

There are two general categories of safeguard identified in the CIMA guidance. These are:

- Safeguards created by the profession, legislation or regulation
- Safeguards in the work environment

5.1.1 Examples of safeguards created by the profession, legislation or regulation

- Educational training and experience requirements for entry into the profession

- Continuing professional development requirements

- Corporate governance regulations

- Professional standards

- Professional or regulatory monitoring and disciplinary procedures

- External review by a legally empowered third party of the reports, returns, communication or information produced by a professional accountant

5.1.2 Examples of safeguards in the work environment

Work environment safeguards comprise firm-wide safeguards and engagement specific safeguards.

Firm-wide safeguards could include the following.

- Leadership of the firm that stresses the importance of compliance with the fundamental principles and acting in the public interest

- Policies and procedures to implement and monitor quality control of engagements

- Documented policies regarding the identification of threats to compliance with the fundamental principles, the evaluation of the significance of these threats and the identification and the application of safeguards to eliminate or reduce the threats, other than those that are clearly insignificant, to an acceptable level

- Documented internal policies and procedures requiring compliance with the fundamental principles

- Policies and procedures that will enable the identification of interests or relationships between the firm or members of engagement teams and clients

- Policies and procedures to monitor and, if necessary, manage the reliance on revenue received from a single client

- Using different partners and engagement teams with separate reporting lines for the provision of non-assurance services to an assurance client

- Policies and procedures to prohibit individuals who are not members of an engagement team from inappropriately influencing the outcome of the engagement

- Timely communication of a firm's policies and procedures, including any changes to them, to all partners and professional staff, and appropriate training and education on such policies and procedures

- Designating a member of senior management to be responsible for overseeing the adequate functioning of the firm's quality control system

- Advising partners and professional staff of those assurance clients and related entities from which they must be independent

- A disciplinary mechanism to promote compliance with policies and procedures

- Published policies and procedures to encourage and empower staff to communicate to senior levels within the firm any issue relating to compliance with the fundamental principles that concerns them

Engagement specific safeguards could include the following.

- Involving an additional professional accountant to review the work done or otherwise advise as necessary

- Consulting an independent third party, such as a committee of independent directors, a professional regulatory body or another professional accountant

- Discussing ethical issues with those charged with governance of the client

- Disclosing to those charged with governance of the client the nature of services provided and extent of fees charged

- Involving another firm to perform or reperform part of the engagement

- Rotating senior assurance team personnel

Exam skills

Remember in this exam, it is important that you can apply the spirit of the guidance to a given situation rather than just learning and regurgitating the guidance.

5.2 Self-interest threat

The CIMA *Code of Ethics for Professional Accountants* highlights a great number of areas in which a self-interest threat to the fundamental principles might arise.

5.3 Self-review threat

The key area in which there is likely to be a self-review threat is where an assurance firm provides services other than assurance services to an assurance client (providing multiple services).

5.3.1 Preparing accounting records and financial statements

There is clearly a significant risk of a self-review threat if a firm **prepares accounting records and financial statements** and then **audits** them. On the other hand auditors routinely assist management with the preparation of financial statements and give advice about accounting treatments and journal entries.

Therefore, audit firms must analyse the risks arising and put safeguards in place to ensure that the risk is at an acceptable level. Safeguards include:

- **Using staff members other than assurance team members** to carry out work

- **Obtaining client approval for any proposed journals entries** or other changes affecting the financial statements

The rules are more stringent when the client is listed. Firms should not prepare accounts or financial statements for listed entities, unless an emergency situation arises.

For any client, audit firms are also not allowed to:

- Determine or change journal entries without client approval
- Authorise or approve transactions
- Prepare source documents

5.4 Advocacy threat

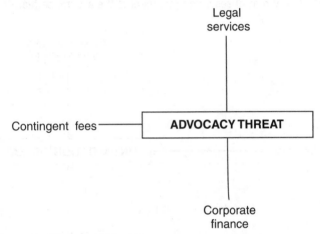

An advocacy threat arises in certain situations where the assurance firm is in a position of **taking the client's part** in a dispute or somehow **acting as their advocate.** The most obvious instances of this would be when a firm offered legal services to a client and, say, defended them in a legal case or provided evidence on their behalf as an expert witness. An advocacy threat might also arise if the firm carried out corporate finance work for the client, for example, if the audit firm was involved in advice on debt reconstruction and negotiated with the bank on the client's behalf.

As with the other threats above, the firm has to appraise the risk and apply safeguards as necessary. Relevant safeguards might be using **different departments** in the firm to carry out the work and making disclosures to the audit committee. Remember, the ultimate option is always to withdraw from an engagement if the risk to independence is too high.

5.5 Familiarity threat

A familiarity threat is where independence is jeopardised by the audit firm and its staff becoming over familiar with the client and its staff. There is a substantial risk of loss of professional scepticism in such circumstances.

We have already discussed some examples of when this risk arises, because very often a familiarity threat arises in conjunction with a self-interest threat.

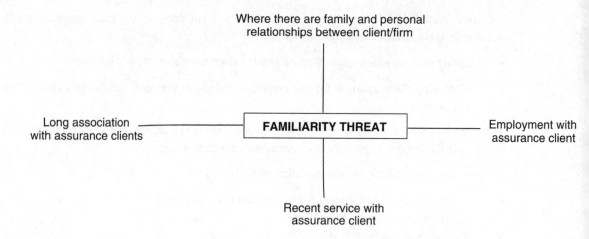

5.6 Intimidation threat

An intimidation threat arises when members of the assurance team have reason to be intimidated by client staff.

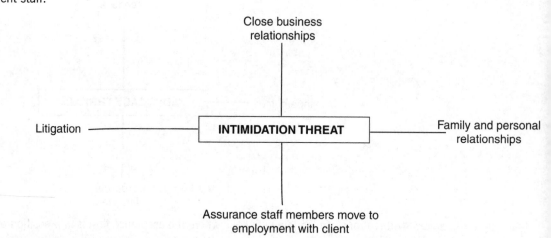

These are also examples of self-interest threats, largely because intimidation may only arise significantly when the assurance firm has something to lose.

5.6.1 Actual and threatened litigation

The most obvious example of an intimidation threat is when the client threatens to sue, or indeed sues, the assurance firm for work that has been done previously. The firm is then faced with the **risk of losing the client, bad publicity** and the **possibility that they will be found to have been negligent,** which will lead to further problems. This could lead for example to the firm being under pressure to produce an unqualified audit report when they have been qualified in the past.

Generally, assurance firms should seek to avoid such situations arising. If they do arise, factors to consider are:

- The materiality of the litigation
- The nature of the assurance engagement
- Whether the litigation relates to a prior assurance engagement

The following safeguards could be considered:

- Disclosing to the audit committee the nature and extent of the litigation
- Removing specific affected individuals from the engagement team
- Involving an additional professional accountant on the team to review work

However, if the litigation is at all serious, it may be necessary to **resign from the engagement**, as the threat to independence is so great.

5.7 Conflicts of interest

Audit firms should take reasonable steps to identify circumstances that could pose a conflict of interest. This is because a conflict of interest could result in the ethical code being breached (for example, if it results in a self-interest threat arising).

A conflict between members' and clients' interests might arise if members compete directly with a client, or have a joint venture or similar with a company that is in competition with the client.

Alternatively, there may be a conflict between the interests of different clients. Assurance firms can have clients who are in competition with each other. However, the firm should ensure that it is **not the subject of a dispute** between the clients. It must also manage its work so that the interests of one client do not adversely affect the other client.

5.7.1 Managing conflicts between clients' interests

When considering whether to accept a client or when there is a change in a client's circumstances, assurance firms should take reasonable steps to ascertain whether there is a **conflict of interest** or if there is likely to be one in the future.

Disclosure is the most important safeguard in connection with conflicts between clients' interests. Safeguards would usually include:

- **Notifying the client** of the interest/activities that may **cause a conflict of interest** and obtaining their consent to act in the circumstances, or

- **Notifying all known relevant parties** that the professional accountant in public practice is **acting for two or more parties** in respect of a matter where their respective interests are in conflict, and obtaining their consent so to act, or

- Notifying the client that the professional accountant in public practice **does not act exclusively for any one client** in the provision of proposed services, and obtaining their consent so to act

Other safeguards

- Using separate engagement teams
- Procedures to prevent access to information (such as special passwords)
- Clear guidelines for the respective teams on issues of security and confidentiality
- The use of confidentiality agreements signed by the partners and staff
- Regular review of the safeguards by an independent senior individual

If a conflict of interest poses a threat to one or more fundamental principles and cannot be eliminated or reduced to an acceptable level through the application of safeguards, the engagement should not be accepted or the accountant should resign from one or more of the conflicting engagements.

Section summary

Accountants in practice may face threats to the fundamental principles in the form of **self-review, self-interest, advocacy, familiarity and intimidation threats**. Appropriate **safeguards** must be put in place to eliminate or reduce such threats to acceptable levels.

6 Problems facing accountants in business   11/10

Introduction

This section covers the type of threat that a professional accountant in business might face and the action that should be taken if such a threat arises.

6.1 The professional accountant in business

Section 320 of the 2010 CIMA Code (previously Section 220 of the 2007 Code as referred to in the F1 syllabus) deals with the preparation and reporting of information. It specifies that a professional accountant in business should maintain information for which they are responsible so that it describes the true nature of transactions, assets and liabilities, is timely, accurate and complete.

6.2 Conflicts between professional and employment obligations

Ethical guidance stresses that a professional accountant should normally support the legitimate and ethical obligations established by the employer. However the professional accountant may be pressurised to act in ways that threaten compliance with the fundamental principles. These include:

*   Acting contrary to law, regulation, technical or professional standards
*   Aiding unethical or illegal earnings management strategies
*   Misleading auditors or regulators
*   Issuing or being associated with a report that misrepresents the facts

If these problems are faced, the accountant should either obtain advice from inside the employer, an independent professional advisor, CIMA, lawyers, or use the formal procedures within the organisation.

6.3 Preparation and reporting of information

As well as complying with financial reporting standards, the professional accountant in business should aim to prepare information that describes clearly the nature of the business transactions, classifies and records information in a timely and proper manner, and represents the facts accurately. If the accountant faces pressures to produce misleading information, superiors should be consulted, such as an audit committee. The accountant should not be associated with misleading information, and may need to seek legal advice or report to the appropriate authorities.

6.4 Acting with sufficient expertise

Guidance stresses that the professional accountant should only undertake tasks for which he or she has sufficient specific training or experience. Certain pressures may threaten the ability of the professional accountant to perform duties with appropriate competence and due care:

*   Lack of information
*   Insufficient training, experience or education
*   Lack of time
*   Inadequate resources

Whether this is a significant threat will depend on the other people the accountant is working with, the seniority of the accountant and the level of supervision and review of work. If the problem is serious, the accountant should take steps to remedy the situation including obtaining training, ensuring time is available and consulting with others where appropriate. Refusal to perform duties is the last resort.

6.5 Financial interests

Ethical guidance highlights financial interests as a self-interest threat to objectivity and confidentiality. In particular the temptation to manipulate price-sensitive information in order to gain financially is stressed. Financial interests may include shares, profit-related bonuses or share options.

This threat can be countered by the individual consulting with superiors and disclosing all relevant information. Having a remuneration committee composed of independent non-executive directors determining the remuneration packages of executive directors can help resolve the problems at senior levels.

6.6 Inducements

Ethical guidance highlights the possibility that accountants may be offered inducements to influence actions or decisions, encourage illegal behaviour or obtain confidential information.

The guidance points out that threats to compliance may appear to arise not only from the accountant making or accepting the inducement, but from the offer having being made in the first place. The guidance recommends that directors or senior managers be informed, and disclosure may be made to third parties. The accountant should also disclose to senior management whether any close relatives work for competitors or suppliers.

Section summary

The accountant in business may face a variety of difficulties including conflicts between professional and employment obligations, pressure to prepare misleading information, a lack of sufficient expertise, financial interests or inducements.

Chapter Roundup

✓   A need for an ethical code has developed due to various stakeholders relying on accountants and their reputation. An ethical code must evolve to adapt with changing circumstances.

✓   Sources of ethical codes include law, religion, social attitudes, IFAC, professional bodies and employing organisations.

✓   The CIMA Code is a principles based framework. There are advantages and disadvantages of a principles based framework over a system of rules.

✓   The five fundamental principles are integrity, objectivity, professional competence and due care, confidentiality and professional behaviour. Compliance with these principles could be threatened by a wide range of circumstances. The professional accountant should apply safeguards to counteract these threats.

✓   Accountants in practice may face threats to the fundamental principles in the form of **self-review, self-interest, advocacy, familiarity and intimidation threats**. Appropriate **safeguards** must be put in place to eliminate or reduce such threats to acceptable levels.

✓   The accountant in business may face a variety of difficulties including conflicts between professional and employment obligations, pressure to prepare misleading information, a lack of sufficient expertise, financial interests or inducements.

Quick Quiz

1   Which of the following is not an advantage of a principles-based ethical code?

     A   It prevents narrow, legalistic interpretations
     B   It can accommodate a rapidly-changing environment
     C   The illustrative examples provided can be followed in all similar situations
     D   It prescribes minimum expected standards of behaviour

2   Fill in the blank.

     .... means that a professional accountant should be straightforward and honest in all business and professional relationships.

3   Give three examples of a familiarity threat.

4   Which of the following is not a legitimate reason to disclose confidential information?

     A   Disclosure is permitted by law
     B   To protect the professional interests of an accountant in a legal investigation
     C   To assist a family member
     D   To provide information to a bank where disclosure is authorised by your employer

Answers to Quick Quiz

1   C   Although the examples may be good guides for conduct in many instances, circumstances will vary, so they should not be seen as totally prescriptive.

2   Integrity

3   •   Making a business decision that will affect a close family member
     •   Long association with a business contact
     •   Acceptance of a gift

4   C   Care should be taken not to disclose confidential information to family members.

Answers to Questions

3.1 Ethical issues

(a)   Dealing with unpleasantly authoritarian governments can be supported on the grounds that it **contributes to economic growth and prosperity** and all the benefits they bring to society in both countries concerned. It can also be opposed as it is **contributing to the continuation of the regime,** and is **fundamentally repugnant**.

(b)   Honesty in advertising is an important problem. Many products are promoted exclusively on image. Deliberately creating the impression that purchasing a particular product will enhance the happiness, success and sex-appeal of the buyer can be attacked as **dishonest.** It can be defended on the grounds that the supplier is actually **selling a fantasy or dream** rather than a physical article.

(c)   Dealings with employees are coloured by the **opposing views of corporate responsibility and individual rights**. The idea of a job as property to be defended has now disappeared from labour relations in many countries, but corporate decisions that lead to redundancies are still deplored. This is because of the obvious **impact of sudden unemployment on aspirations and living standards**, even when the employment market is buoyant. Nevertheless businesses have to consider the cost of employing labour as well as its productive capacity.

(d)   The main problems with payments or gifts to officials are making the distinction between those that should never be made, and those that can be made in certain cultural circumstances.

   (i)   **Extortion**. Foreign officials have been known to threaten companies with the complete closure of their local operations unless suitable payments are made.

   (ii)   **Bribery**. This is payments for services to which a company is not legally entitled. There are some fine distinctions to be drawn; for example, some managers regard political contributions as bribery.

   (iii) **Grease money**. Multinational companies are sometimes unable to obtain services to which they are legally entitled because of deliberate stalling by local officials. Cash payments to the right people may then be enough to oil the machinery of bureaucracy.

   (iv)   **Gifts**. In some cultures (such as Japan) gifts are regarded as an essential part of civilised negotiation, even in circumstances where to Western eyes they might appear ethically dubious. Managers operating in such a culture may feel at liberty to adopt the local customs.

3.2 Employee behaviour

Here are some suggestions.

- Recruitment and selection policies and procedures
- Induction and training
- Objectives and reward schemes
- Ethical codes
- Threat of ethical audit

Now try this question from the Exam Question Bank	Number	Level	Marks	Time
	Q11	Examination	5	9 mins

SINGLE COMPANY FINANCIAL ACCOUNTS

Part B

74

PRESENTATION OF PUBLISHED FINANCIAL STATEMENTS

This chapter covers preparation of the accounts for limited companies. It lays out the IAS 1 (revised) *Presentation of financial statements* format for the statement of financial position, statement of comprehensive income, statement of changes in equity and the disclosures required in the notes to the accounts. The best way to gain familiarity with these formats and disclosures is by doing practice questions.

You will cover the financial statements of group companies in Part C of this Study Text.

topic list	learning outcomes	syllabus references	ability required
1 IAS 1 (revised) *Presentation of financial statements*	C1(a)	C1(i),(iii)	application
2 Statement of financial position	C1(a)	C1(i)	application
3 The current/non-current distinction	C1(a)	C1(i)	application
4 Statement of comprehensive income	C1(a)	C1(i)	application
5 Statement of changes in equity	C1(a)	C1(i)	application
6 Notes to the financial statements	C1(a)	C1(i)	application
7 Approach to answering exam questions	C1(a)	C1(i)	application

1   IAS 1 (revised) *Presentation of financial statements*

Introduction

In this section we look at the requirements for financial statements given in IAS 1 (revised) *Presentation of financial statements*. This standard gives substantial guidance on the form and content of published financial statements and details the statement of financial position, the statement of comprehensive income and the statement of changes in equity (the statement of cash flows is covered by IAS 7). It was revised in September 2007.

You should already be familiar with the preparation of financial statements for sole traders, the basic elements of company financial statements and with the use of double-entry accounting from your studies at CIMA Certificate Level 'Fundamentals of Financial Accounting' or your previous studies if you were exempt from CIMA Certificate. F1 builds on this knowledge, so if you are unsure, it may be helpful to revise these areas first.

1.1 Purpose of financial statements

The purpose of financial statements is to provide users with information about the financial position, financial performance and cash flows of an entity. They show the results of management's stewardship. Per IAS 1, financial statements provide information about an entity's:

(a)   assets
(b)   liabilities
(c)   equity
(d)   income and expenses, including gains and losses
(e)   other changes in equity
(f)   cash flows.

1.2 Responsibility for the financial statements

Responsibility for the preparation and presentation of an entity's financial statements rests with the **board of directors** (or equivalent).

1.3 Components of financial statements

A complete set of financial statements includes the following:

- Statement of financial position

- Statement of comprehensive income (either as a single statement or as two separate statements: the income statement and the statement of other comprehensive income)

- Statement of changes in equity

- Statement of cash flows

- Notes, including a summary of significant accounting policies and other explanatory information.

In addition, IAS 1 encourages, but does not require, a **financial review** by management (which is *not* part of the financial statements), explaining the main features of the entity's performance and position. The report may include a review of the following:

(a)   **Factors/influences determining performance**: changes in the environment in which the entity operates and the entity's policy for investment, including its dividend policy

(b)   The entity's **sources of funding**, the policy on gearing and its risk management policies

(c)   **Strengths and resources** of the entity whose value is not reflected in the statement of financial position under IFRSs

1.4 Fair presentation

Financial statements should **present fairly** the financial position, financial performance and cash flows of an entity. This requires:

- Representing transactions in accordance with the recognition criteria for assets, liabilities, income, expenses and equity set out in the *Framework.*

- Compliance with applicable IFRSs and a statement of compliance.

- Selection, application and disclosure of accounting policies in accordance with IAS 8.

- Presentation of information in a way that provides relevant, reliable, comparable and understandable information.

- Presentation of additional disclosures when the disclosures required by IFRSs are insufficient to give a full understanding of an event or transaction.

In the rare circumstances where management decides that compliance with a standard would not present a true and fair picture, they can **depart** from the requirements of the standard in order to achieve fair presentation. They should disclose:

- That the financial statements are a fair presentation of the entity's position, performance and cash flows

- That the entity has complied with all other relevant IFRSs

- Details of the departure from an IFRS, why it was necessary and the financial impact of the departure

1.5 Going concern

IAS 1 states that an entity should prepare its financial statements on a **going concern basis** unless management either intends to liquidate the entity or to cease trading. The going concern basis assumes that the business will **continue to trade** for the foreseeable future.

1.6 Accruals basis

IAS 1 requires entities to prepare their financial statements, except for the cash flow statement, on the **accruals basis of accounting**. The accruals basis of accounting recognises income when it is earned and expenses when they are incurred, whether or not any cash has been received or paid.

1.7 Other matters covered by IAS 1

IAS 1 also includes the following requirements for financial statements.

(a) Financial statements should be presented at least **annually** and should be produced **within six months of the end of the reporting period.**

(b) The presentation and classification of items in the financial statements should be **consistent** from year to year. Changes in presentation and classification are permitted if required by another IFRS or if the change would result in more appropriate presentation or classification.

(c) **Material** items should be presented separately in the financial statements. Immaterial items can be **aggregated** with similar items.

(d) Assets and liabilities, and income and expenses should **not be offset** except when it is required or permitted by another IFRS.

(e) **Comparative information** should be disclosed for the previous period for all numerical information, unless another IFRS permits or requires otherwise. Comparative information should be reclassified when the presentation or classification of items in the financial statements is amended.

Section summary

Financial statements should **present fairly** the financial position, financial performance and cash flows of an entity.

IAS 1 covers the **form and content** of financial statements. The main components are:

* Statement of financial position
* Statement of comprehensive income
* Statement of changes in equity
* Statement of cash flows
* Notes to the financial statements

2 Statement of financial position

Introduction

First of all we will look at the **suggested format** of the statement of financial position (given in an appendix to IAS 1) and then at further disclosures required.

2.1 Statement of financial position example

XYZ LIMITED
STATEMENT OF FINANCIAL POSITION AT 31 DECEMBER 20X9

	$'000	$'000
Assets		
Non-current assets		
Property, plant and equipment	X	
Other intangible assets	X	
Available-for-sale financial assets	X	
		X
Current assets		
Inventories	X	
Trade receivables	X	
Other current assets	X	
Cash and cash equivalents	X	
		X
Total assets		X
Equity and liabilities	$'000	$'000
Share capital	X	
Retained earnings	X	
Other components of equity	X	
Total equity		X
Non-current liabilities		
Long-term borrowings	X	
Deferred tax	X	
Long-term provisions	X	
Total non-current liabilities		X
Current liabilities		
Trade and other payables	X	
Short-term borrowings	X	
Current portion of long-term borrowings	X	
Current tax payable	X	
Short-term provisions	X	
Total current liabilities		X
Total liabilities		X
Total equity and liabilities		X

As a minimum, IAS 1 requires the following items to be shown in the statement of financial position:

(a)   Property, plant and equipment
(b)   Investment property
(c)   Intangible assets
(d)   Financial assets (excluding amounts shown under (e), (h) and (i))
(e)   Investments in associates
(f)   Biological assets
(g)   Inventories
(h)   Trade and other receivables
(i)   Cash and cash equivalents
(j)   Assets classified as held for sale under IFRS 5
(k)   Trade and other payables
(l)   Provisions
(m)   Financial liabilities (other than (j) and (k))
(n)   Current tax liabilities and assets
(o)   Deferred tax liabilities and assets
(p)   Liabilities included in disposal groups under IFRS 5
(q)   Non-controlling interests (group accounts only)
(r)   Issued capital and reserves

The example shown above is for illustration only (although we will follow the format in this Study Text). IAS 1 does not prescribe the **order or format** in which the items listed should be presented. It simply states that they **must be presented separately** because they are so different in nature or function from each other.

IAS 1 also requires that any **other line items, headings or sub-totals** should be shown in the statement of financial position when it is necessary for an understanding of the entity's financial position.

Management must decide whether to present additional items separately. Their decision should consider the following factors:

(a)   **Nature and liquidity of assets and their materiality**. So monetary/non-monetary assets and current/non-current assets will be presented separately.

(b)   **Function within the entity.** Inventories, receivables and cash and cash equivalents are therefore shown separately.

(c)   **Amounts, nature and timing of liabilities**. Interest-bearing and non-interest-bearing liabilities and provisions will be shown separately, classified as current or non-current as appropriate.

IAS 1 also requires separate presentation where **different measurement bases** (eg cost or valuation) are used for assets and liabilities which differ in nature or function.

2.2 Information presented either in the statement of financial position or by note

Further **sub-classification** of the line items listed above should be disclosed either in the statement of financial position or in the notes. The sub-classification details will in part depend on the requirements of IFRSs. The size, nature and function of the amounts involved will also be important.

Disclosures will vary from item to item and IAS 1 gives the following examples.

(a)   **Property, plant and equipment** are classified by class as described in IAS 16, *Property, plant and equipment*

(b)   **Receivables** are analysed between amounts receivable from trade customers, other members of the group, receivables from related parties, prepayments and other amounts

(c) **Inventories** are sub-classified, in accordance with IAS 2 *Inventories,* into classifications such as merchandise, production supplies, materials, work in progress and finished goods

(d) **Provisions** are analysed showing separately provisions for employee benefit costs and any other items classified in a manner appropriate to the entity's operations

(e) **Equity capital and reserves** are analysed showing separately the various classes of paid in capital, share premium and reserves

IAS 1 lists some **specific disclosures** which must be made, either in the statement of financial position or in the related notes.

(a) **Share capital disclosures** (for each class of share capital)

    (i) Number of shares authorised

    (ii) Number of shares issued and fully paid, and issued but not fully paid

    (iii) Par value per share, or that the shares have no par value

    (iv) Reconciliation of the number of shares outstanding at the beginning and at the end of the year

    (v) Rights, preferences and restrictions attaching to that class including restrictions on the distribution of dividends and the repayment of capital

    (vi) Shares in the entity held by the entity itself or by related group companies

    (vii) Shares reserved for issuance under options and sales contracts, including the terms and amounts

(b) Description of the nature and purpose of **each reserve** within owners' equity

Section summary

IAS 1 suggests a format for the statement of financial position and specifies various items which must be shown in the statement.

3 The current/non-current distinction

Introduction

In this section we look at the requirements of IAS 1 to distinguish between current and non-current assets and liabilities in the statement of financial position.

3.1 The current/non-current distinction

An entity should present **current** and **non-current** assets and liabilities as separate classifications in the statement of financial position, except where a presentation based on liquidity provides more relevant and reliable information. If a presentation based on liquidity is used, all assets and liabilities must be presented broadly **in order of liquidity.**

In either case, the entity should disclose any portion of an asset or liability which is expected to be recovered or settled **after more than twelve months.** For example, for an amount receivable which is due in instalments over 18 months, the portion due after more than twelve months must be disclosed.

3.2 Current assets

KEY TERM

An asset should be classified as a CURRENT ASSET when it:

- is expected to be realised in, or is held for sale or consumption in, the normal course of the entity's operating cycle; or

- is held primarily for trading purposes; or

- is expected to be realised within twelve months of the end of the reporting period; or

- is cash or a cash equivalent asset which is not restricted in its use.

All other assets should be classified as non-current assets.   *(IAS 1)*

3.3 Current liabilities

KEY TERM

A liability should be classified as a CURRENT LIABILITY when it:

- Is expected to be settled in the normal course of the entity's operating cycle; or

- Is held primarily for the purpose of trading; or

- Is due to be settled within twelve months after the reporting period; or

- The entity does not have an unconditional right to defer settlement of the liability for at least twelve months after the reporting period.

All other liabilities should be classified as non-current liabilities.   *(IAS 1)*

Section summary

An entity should present **current** and **non-current** assets and liabilities as separate classifications in the statement of financial position.

---

4   Statement of comprehensive income

Introduction

Income and expenses are presented in the statement of comprehensive income. This section looks at the requirements of IAS 1 for this statement.

4.1 Statement of comprehensive income – format

IAS 1 allows income and expense items to be presented either:

(a)   in a single **statement of comprehensive income**; or

(b)   in two statements: an **income statement** plus a separate **statement of other comprehensive income**.

The suggested format for these statements follows.

XYZ LIMITED
STATEMENT OF COMPREHENSIVE INCOME FOR THE YEAR ENDED
31 DECEMBER 20X9

	20X9 $'000
Revenue	X
Cost of sales	X
Gross profit	X
Other income	X
Distribution costs	X
Administrative expenses	X
Other expenses	X
Finance costs	X
Profit before tax	X
Income tax expense	X
Profit for the year from continuing operations	X
Loss for the year from discontinued operations	X
Profit for the year	X
Other comprehensive income:	
Available-for-sale financial assets	X
Gains on property revaluation	X
Income tax relating to components of other comprehensive income	X
Other comprehensive income for the year, net of tax	X
Total comprehensive income for the year	X

Companies are given the option of presenting this information in two statements as follows:

XYZ LIMITED
INCOME STATEMENT FOR THE YEAR ENDED 31 DECEMBER 20X9

	20X9 $'000
Revenue	X
Cost of sales	X
Gross profit	X
Other income	X
Distribution costs	X
Administrative expenses	X
Other expenses	X
Finance costs	X
Profit before tax	X
Income tax expense	X
Profit for the year from continuing operations	X
Loss for the year from discontinued operations	X
Profit for the year	X

XYZ LIMITED STATEMENT OF OTHER COMPREHENSIVE INCOME
FOR THE YEAR ENDED 31 DECEMBER 20X9

	20X9 $'000
Profit for the year	X
Other comprehensive income:	
Available-for-sale financial assets	X
Gains on property revaluation	X
Income tax relating to components of other comprehensive income	X
Other comprehensive income for the year, net of tax	X
Total comprehensive income for the year	X

Exam skills

In this Study Text, we have used the term **'income statement'** to refer to the section from revenue to profit for the year, whether or not that section is presented as part of a single statement of comprehensive income or as a separate statement. In exam questions, you should make sure that you always call your statement the same name as the statement the examiner asks for in the question.

As a minimum, IAS 1 requires the following items to be disclosed in the statement of comprehensive income:

(a)   Revenue
(b)   Finance costs
(c)   Share of profits and losses of associates and joint ventures accounted for using the equity method*
(d)   Pre-tax gain or loss attributable to discontinued operations
(e)   Tax expense
(f)   Profit or loss
(g)   Each component of other comprehensive income classified by nature
(h)   Share of the other comprehensive income of associates and joint ventures*
(i)   Total comprehensive income.

* These items relate to group accounts.

IAS 1 also requires that any **other line items, headings or sub-totals** should be shown in the statement of comprehensive income when it is necessary for an understanding of the entity's financial position or if another IFRS requires it.

Management must decide whether to present additional items separately. They should consider factors including materiality and the nature and function of the items of income and expense when making this decision.

4.2 Information presented either in the income statement or by note

IAS 1 requires separate disclosure of the nature and amount of items of income and expense if they are material. This disclosure should be in the income statement or in the notes. Examples of items which may require separate disclosure are:

- Write downs of inventories or property, plant and equipment
- Disposals of property, plant and equipment
- Disposals of investments
- Discontinued operations
- Litigation settlements

4.3 Analysis of expenses

IAS 1 requires an analysis of expenses to be given either in the income statement or by note, using a classification based on *either* the **nature of the expenses** or their **function**.

4.3.1 Nature of expenses method

In this method, expenses are aggregated in the income statement **according to their nature** (eg purchase of materials, depreciation, wages and salaries, transport costs). This is by far the easiest method, especially for smaller entities. An example of this classification follows.

	20X9 $'000
Revenue	X
Other operating income	X
Changes in inventories of finished goods and work in progress	(X)
Work performed by the entity and capitalised	X
Raw material and consumables used	(X)
Employee benefits expense	(X)
Depreciation and amortisation expense	(X)
Impairment of property, plant and equipment	(X)
Other expenses	(X)
Finance costs	(X)
Profit before tax	X
Income tax expense	(X)
Profit for the year	X

4.3.2 Function of expenses method

You are likely to be more familiar with this method. Expenses are classified according to their function as part of cost of sales, distribution or administrative activities. This method often gives **more relevant information** for users, but the allocation of expenses by function requires the use of judgement and can be arbitrary. An example of this classification follows.

	20X9 $'000
Revenue	X
Cost of sales	(X)
Gross profit	X
Other income	X
Distribution costs	(X)
Administrative expenses	(X)
Other expenses	(X)
Finance costs	(X)
Profit before tax	X
Income tax expense	(X)
Profit for the year	X

If an entity uses the function of expenses method, additional disclosure should be given on the nature of expenses, including depreciation, amortisation and employee expenses.

Exam alert

The usual method of presentation is expenses by function and this is the format likely to appear in your exam.

Section summary

IAS 1 requires all items of income and expense in a period to be shown in a **statement of comprehensive income**.

IAS 1 offers **two** possible formats for the income statement section or separate income statement - by function or by nature. Classification by function is more common.

5 Statement of changes in equity

Introduction

The statement of changes in equity presents the movements in an entity's capital and reserves balances. Changes in an entity's equity over the reporting period reflect the increase or decrease in its net assets, and therefore its wealth, for the period. This section covers the requirements in IAS 1 for this statement.

5.1 Statement of changes in equity example

This is the format of the statement of changes in equity as per IAS 1.

XYZ LIMITED

STATEMENT OF CHANGES IN EQUITY FOR THE YEAR ENDED 31 DECEMBER 20X9

	Share capital $'000	Retained earnings $'000	Available for sale financial assets $'000	Revaluation surplus $'000	Total equity $'000
Balance at 1 January 20X8	X	X	X	–	X
Changes in accounting policy	–	X	–	–	X
Restated balance	X	X	X	–	X
Changes in equity					
Dividends	–	X	–	–	X
Total comprehensive income for the year	–	X	X	X	X
Balance at 31 December 20X8	X	X	X	X	X
Changes in equity for 20X9					
Issue of share capital	X	–	–	–	X
Dividends	–	X	–	–	X
Total comprehensive income for the year	–	X	X	X	X
Transfer to retained earnings	–	X	–	(X)	–
Balance at 31 December 20X9	X	X	X	X	X

Section summary

IAS 1 requires a statement of changes in equity. This shows the movement in the equity section of the statement of financial position.

6 Notes to the financial statements

Introduction

In this final section we will learn about notes to the financial statements, including their function and presentation.

6.1 Structure

Notes to the financial statements provide more detailed analysis and narrative information about items in the financial statements and also give additional information, such as contingent liabilities and commitments.

Per IAS 1, the notes to the financial statements should perform the following functions:

(a) Provide information about the **basis on which the financial statements were prepared** and which **specific accounting policies** were chosen and applied to significant transactions/events

(b) Disclose any information, not shown elsewhere in the financial statements, which is **required by IFRSs**

(c) Show any additional information that is relevant to understanding which is not shown elsewhere in the financial statements

The way the notes are presented is important. They should be given in a **systematic manner** and **cross referenced** to other related information.

IAS 1 suggests a **certain order** for notes to the financial statements, which assists users when comparing the statements of different entities. The suggested order is as follows.

(a) A statement of **compliance** with IFRSs

(b) A summary of significant **accounting policies** applied

(c) **Supporting information** for items in each financial statement in the same order as each financial statement and line item is presented

(d) Other disclosures, eg:

    (i)   Contingent liabilities, commitments and other financial disclosures
    (ii)   Non-financial disclosures

The order of specific items may have to be varied occasionally, but a systematic structure is still required.

6.2 Presentation of accounting policies

The accounting policies section should describe the following.

(a) The **measurement basis** (or bases) used in preparing the financial statements

(b) The **other accounting policies** used, as required for a proper understanding of the financial statements

6.3 Other disclosures

An entity must also disclose in the notes:

(a) The amount of **dividends proposed or declared** before the financial statements were authorised for issue but not recognised as a distribution to owners during the period, and the amount per share

(b) The amount of any **cumulative preference dividends** not recognised.

Section summary

IAS 1 suggests a certain order for notes to the financial statements.

7   Approach to answering exam questions

Introduction

A methodical approach to answering questions on preparing financial statements will help you in the exam. In this section we summarise our recommended approach.

Exam alert

In Section C of your exam, you are likely to be asked to prepare at least two of the three main statements (statement of financial position, statement of comprehensive income or statement of changes in equity) for a total of 25 marks. You must therefore be very familiar with the format of each statement. Question practice is the best way to do this, our step-by-step approach will help you to answer questions in a methodical way.

Read the requirements of the question. Scan through the question detail.

Set up separate pages of paper for each of the following (if required in the question):
- A proforma statement of financial position
- A proforma statement of comprehensive income
- A proforma statement of changes in equity
- A page for workings.

Read the additional information given and highlight or mark any relevant caption in the trial balance that is going to change as a result of the additional information.

Transfer any unaffected figures in the trial balance from the question onto your proformas, tick the figures in the trial balance as you transfer them so that you know you have dealt with them.

Finally deal with the additional information using your workings page and transfer items to the financial statements as you work them out.

Work through the following example and then attempt the two questions at the end of this section, using the approach we recommend above.

Example: Preparing financial statements

USB Limited has the following trial balance at 31 December 20X9.

	Debit $'000	Credit $'000
Cash at bank	100	
Inventory at 1 January 20X9	2,200	
Administrative expenses	2,206	
Distribution costs	650	
Non-current assets at cost:		
Land	12,000	
Buildings	10,000	
Plant and equipment	1,400	
Motor vehicles	320	
Suspense		1,500
Accumulated depreciation		
Buildings		4,000
Plant and equipment		480
Motor vehicles		120
Retained earnings		12,360
Trade receivables	876	
Purchases	4,200	
Dividend paid	200	
Sales revenue		11,752
Trade payables		2,440
Share premium		500
$1 ordinary shares		1,000
	34,152	34,152

The following additional information is relevant.

(a)   Depreciation is to be provided as follows:

　　(i)   Buildings at 5% straight line, charged to administrative expenses.
　　(ii)   Plant and equipment at 20% on the reducing balance basis, charged to cost of sales.
　　(iii) Motor vehicles at 25% on the reducing balance basis, charged to distribution costs.

(b)   No final dividend is being proposed.

(c)   A customer has gone bankrupt owing $76,000. This debt is not expected to be recovered and an adjustment should be made. An allowance for receivables of 5% is to be set up.

(d)   1 million new ordinary shares were issued at $1.50 on 1 December 20X9. The proceeds have been left in a suspense account.

(e)   The land is to be revalued to $18,000,000.

(f)   Closing inventory figure is $1,600,000.

Required

Prepare in a form suitable for publication, the statement of comprehensive income for the year to 31 December 20X9, a statement of changes in equity and a statement of financial position at that date in accordance with the requirements of International Financial Reporting Standards. Ignore taxation. Notes to the financial statements are not required.

Solution

USB LIMITED
STATEMENT OF COMPREHENSIVE INCOME FOR THE YEAR ENDED 31 DECEMBER 20X9

	$'000
Revenue	11,752
Cost of sales (W2)	4,984
Gross profit	6,768
Administrative expenses (W3)	2,822
Distribution costs (650 + 50 (W1))	700
Profit for the year	3,246
Other comprehensive income	
Gain on revaluation of land	6,000
Total comprehensive income	9,246

USB LIMITED
STATEMENT OF CHANGES IN EQUITY FOR THE YEAR ENDED 31 DECEMBER 20X9

	Share capital $'000	Share premium $'000	Retained earnings $'000	Revaluation surplus $'000	Total $'000
Balance at 1 Jan 20X9	1,000	500	12,360	–	13,860
Total comprehensive income	–	–	3,246	6,000	9,246
Dividend paid	–	–	(200)	–	(200)
Share issue	1,000	500	–	–	1,500
Balance at 31 Dec 20X9	2,000	1,000	15,406	6,000	24,406

USB LIMITED
STATEMENT OF FINANCIAL POSITION AS AT 31 DECEMBER 20X9

	$'000	$'000
Non-current assets		
Property, plant and equipment (W1)	6,386	
Land (W1)	18,000	
		24,386
Current assets		
Inventory	1,600	
Trade receivables (876 – 76 – 40)	760	
Cash	100	
		2,460
Total assets		26,846
Equity and liabilities		
Equity		
Share capital		2,000
Retained earnings		15,406
Share premium		1,000
Revaluation surplus		6,000
Current liabilities		
Trade payables		2,440
Total equity and liabilities		26,846

Workings

1   *Depreciation*

	$'000
Buildings (10,000 × 5%)	500
Plant (1,400 – 480) × 20%	184
Motor vehicles (320 – 120) × 25%	50

Property, plant and equipment

	Cost	Acc Dep	Dep chg	NBV
	$'000	$'000	$'000	$'000
Buildings	10,000	4,000	500	5,500
Plant	1,400	480	184	736
Motor vehicles	320	120	50	150
	11,720	4,600	734	6,386

Land is to be revalued to $18m. When the land is revalued, a reserve of $18m – $12m = $6m is created and the increase in value is shown in other comprehensive income.

Tutorial note: revaluations of non-current assets are covered in Chapter 6 of this Study Text.

2   *Cost of sales*

	$'000
Opening inventory	2,200
Purchases	4,200
Depreciation on plant (W1)	184
Closing inventory	(1,600)
	4,984

3   *Administrative expenses*

	$'000
Per trial balance	2,206
Depreciation on buildings (W1)	500
Irrecoverable debt	76
Receivables allowance ((876 – 76) × 5%)	40
	2,822

Question 4.1   Financial statements I

Learning outcome C1(a)

The accountant of Wislon Co has prepared the following list of account balances as at 31 December 20X8

	$'000
50c ordinary shares (fully paid)	450
10% debentures (secured)	200
Retained earnings 1.1.X8	242
General reserve 1.1.X8	171
Land and buildings 1.1.X8(cost)	430
Plant and machinery 1.1.X8(cost)	830
Accumulated depreciation	
Buildings 1.1.X8	20
Plant and machinery 1.1.X8	222
Inventory 1.1.X8	190
Sales	2,695
Purchases	2,152
Ordinary dividend	15
Debenture interest	10
Wages and salaries	254
Light and heat	31
Sundry expenses	113
Suspense account	135
Trade accounts receivable	179
Trade accounts payable	195
Cash	126

Notes

(a)   Sundry expenses include $9,000 paid in respect of insurance for the year ending 1 September 20X9. Light and heat does not include an invoice of $3,000 for electricity for the three months ending 2 January 20X9 which was paid in February 20X9. Light and heat also includes $20,000 relating to salesmen's commission.

(b)   The suspense account is in respect of the following items.

	$'000
Proceeds from the issue of 100,000 ordinary shares	120
Proceeds from the sale of plant	300
	420
Less consideration for the acquisition of Mary & Co	285
	135

(c)   The net assets of Mary & Co were purchased on 3 March 20X8. Assets were valued as follows

	$'000
Available-for-sale financial assets	231
Inventory	34
	265

All the inventory acquired was sold during 20X8. The available-for-sale financial assets were still held by Wislon at 31 December 20X8. Goodwill has not been impaired in value.

(d)   The property was acquired some years ago. The buildings element of the cost was estimated at $100,000 and the estimated useful life of the assets was fifty years at the time of purchase. As at 31 December 20X8 the property is to be revalued at $800,000.

(e)   The plant which was sold had cost $350,000 and had a carrying amount of $274,000 as on 1 January 20X8. $36,000 depreciation is to be charged on plant and machinery for 20X8.

(f)   The management wish to provide for:

(i)   Debenture interest due
(ii)   A transfer to general reserve of $16,000
(iii)   Audit fees of $4,000

(g)   Inventory as at 31 December 20X8 was valued at $220,000 (cost).

Required

Prepare in a form suitable for publication the financial statements of Wislon Co as at 31 December 20X8 in accordance with International Financial Reporting Standards.

You do not need to produce notes to the financial statements. Ignore taxation.

Question 4.2

Learning outcome C1(a)

Atok Co compiles its financial statements to 30 June annually. At 30 June 20X9, the company's trial balance was as follows:

	$'000	$'000
Sales revenue		14,800
Purchases	8,280	
Inventory at 1 July 20X8	1,390	
Distribution costs	1,080	
Administration expenses	1,460	
Land at valuation	10,500	
Building: cost	8,000	
accumulated depreciation at 1 July 20X8		2,130
Plant and equipment: cost	12,800	
accumulated depreciation at 1 July 20X8		2,480
Trade receivables and payables	4,120	2,240
Cash at bank	160	
Ordinary shares of 50c each: as at 1 July 20X8		10,000
issued during year		4,000
Share premium account: as at 1 July 20X8		2,000
arising on shares issued during year		2,000
Revaluation surplus as at 1 July 20X8		3,000
Retained earnings		3,140
10% loan notes (redeemable 20Y8)		
(issued 1 April 20X9 with interest payable 31 March and 30		2,000
September each year)	47,790	47,790

The following matters remain to be adjusted for in preparing the financial statements for the year ended 30 June 20X9:

(a) Inventory at 30 June 20X9 amounted to $1,560,000 at cost. A review of inventory items revealed the need for some adjustments for two inventory lines.

    (i) Items which had cost $80,000 and which would normally sell for $120,000 were found to have deteriorated. Remedial work costing $20,000 would be needed to enable the items to be sold for $90,000.

    (ii) Some items sent to customers on sale or return terms had been omitted from inventory and included as sales in June 20X9. The cost of these items was $16,000 and they were included in sales at $24,000. In July 20X9 the items were returned in good condition by the customers.

(b) Depreciation is to be provided as follows:

    Buildings   2% per year on cost
    Plant and equipment   20% per year on cost

    80% of the depreciation is to be charged in cost of sales, and 10% each in distribution costs and administrative expenses.

(c) The land is to be revalued to $12,000,000. No change was required to the value of the buildings.

(d) Accruals and prepayments were:

	Accruals	Prepayments
	$'000	$'000
Distribution costs	190	120
Administrative expenses	70	60

Required

(a)   Prepare the company's statement of comprehensive income for the year ended 30 June 20X9 and statement of financial position as at that date for publication, complying with the provisions of International Financial Reporting Standards.

(b)   Prepare a statement of changes in equity for the year ending 30 June 20X9, complying with the provisions of International Financial Reporting Standards.

Notes to the financial statements are not required. Ignore taxation.

Section summary

Following our step-by-step approach to preparing financial statements will help you in the exam.

Chapter Roundup

✓   Financial statements should **present fairly** the financial position, financial performance and cash flows of an entity

✓   IAS 1 covers the **form and content** of financial statements. The main components are:

- Statement of financial position
- Statement of comprehensive income
- Statement of changes in equity
- Statement of cash flows
- Notes to the financial statements

✓   IAS 1 suggests a format for the statement of financial position and specifies various items which must be shown in the statement.

✓   An entity should present **current** and **non-current** assets as separate classifications in the statement of financial position.

✓   IAS 1 requires all items of income and expense in a period to be shown in a **statement of comprehensive income**.

✓   IAS 1 offers **two** possible formats for the income statement section or separate income statement – by function or by nature. Classification by function is more common.

✓   IAS 1 requires a **statement of changes in equity**. This shows the movement in the equity section of the statement of financial position.

✓   IAS 1 suggests a certain order for notes to the financial statements.

✓   Following our step-by-step approach to preparing financial statements will help you in the exam.

Quick Quiz

1   Financial statements provide users with information about the financial ...., financial .... and .... of an entity.

2   Which of the following are examples of current assets?

(a)   Property, plant and equipment
(b)   Prepayments
(c)   Cash equivalents
(d)   Manufacturing licences
(e)   Retained earnings

3   Provisions must be disclosed in the statement of financial position.

True   ☐

False   ☐

4   Which of the following must be disclosed on the face of the income statement?

(a)   Tax expense
(b)   Analysis of expenses
(c)   Net profit or loss for the period.

5   Where are revaluation gains shown in the financial statements?

Answers to Quick Quiz

1   Position, performance, cashflows

2   (b) and (c) only

3   True

4   (a) and (c) only. (b) may be shown in the notes.

5   In the statement of comprehensive income and the statement of changes in equity.

Answers to Questions

4.1   Financial statements I

WISLON CO
STATEMENT OF COMPREHENSIVE INCOME FOR THE YEAR ENDED 31 DECEMBER 20X8

	$'000	$'000
Revenue		2,695
Less cost of sales		
Opening inventory	190	
Purchases (2,152 + 34) (W5)	2,186	
Less closing inventory	(220)	
		2,156
Gross profit		539
Other income (profit on disposal of plant)		26
		565
Administrative expenses		
Wages, salaries and commission (254 + 20) (W2)	274	
Sundry expenses (113 – 6) (W1)	107	
Light and heat (31 – 20 + 3) (W2) (W1)	14	
Depreciation: buildings (W3)	2	
Plant	36	
Audit fees	4	
		437
Finance costs		(20)
Profit for the year		108
Other comprehensive income:		
Gain on property revaluation		392
Total comprehensive income for the year		500

WISLON CO
STATEMENT OF FINANCIAL POSITION AS AT 31 DECEMBER 20X8

	$'000	$'000
Assets		
Non-current assets		
Property, plant and equipment		
Property at valuation		800
Plant: cost (W4)	480	
Accumulated depreciation (W4)	(182)	
		298
Goodwill (W5)		20
Available-for-sale financial assets		231
Current assets		
Inventory	220	
Trade accounts receivable	179	
Prepayments (W1)	6	
Cash	126	
		531
Total assets		1,880

	$'000	$'000
Equity and liabilities		
Equity		
50c ordinary shares	500	
Share premium	70	
Revaluation surplus (W3)	392	
General reserve	187	
Retained earnings	319	
		1,468
Non-current liabilities		
10% loan stock (secured)		200
Current liabilities		
Trade accounts payable	195	
Accrued expenses (W1)	17	
		212
Total equity and liabilities		1,880

WISLON CO
STATEMENT OF CHANGES IN EQUITY
FOR THE YEAR ENDED 31 DECEMBER 20X8

	Share capital $'000	Share premium $'000	Retained earnings $'000	General reserve $'000	Revaluation Surplus $'000	Total $'000
Balance at 1.1.X8	450	–	242	171	-	863
Issue of share capital (W6)	50	70				120
Dividends			(15)			(15)
Total comprehensive income for the year			108		392	500
Transfer to reserve			(16)	16		
Balance at 31.12.X8	500	70	319	187	392	1,468

Note that the total comprehensive income is analysed into its components.

Workings

(1)   Normal adjustments are needed for accruals and prepayments (insurance, light and heat, debenture interest and audit fees). The debenture interest accrued is calculated as follows.

	$'000
Charge needed in income statement (10% × $200,000)	20
Amount paid so far, as shown in list of account balances	10
Accrual: presumably six months' interest now payable	10

The accrued expenses shown in the statement of financial position comprise:

	$'000
Debenture interest	10
Light and heat	3
Audit fee	4
	17

Prepayment

Insurance (sundry expenses) ($9,000 × 8/12) = $6,000

(2)   The misposting of $20,000 to light and heat is also adjusted, by reducing the light and heat expense, but charging $20,000 to salesmen's commission.

(3)   Depreciation on the building is calculated as $\dfrac{\$100,000}{50}$ = $2,000.

The carrying value of the property is then $430,000 – $20,000 – $2,000 = $408,000 at the end of the year. When the property is revalued a reserve of $800,000 – $408,000 = $392,000 is then created.

(4)   The profit on disposal of plant is calculated as proceeds $300,000 (per suspense account) less NBV $274,000, ie $26,000. The cost of the remaining plant is calculated at $830,000 – $350,000 = $480,000. The depreciation provision at the year end is:

	$'000
Balance 1.1.X8	222
Charge for 20X8	36
Less depreciation on disposals (350 – 274)	(76)
	182

(5)   Goodwill arising on the purchase of Mary & Co is:

	$'000
Consideration (per suspense account)	285
Assets at valuation	265
Goodwill	20

This is shown as an asset in the statement of financial position. The financial assets, being owned by Wislon at the year end, are also shown on the statement of financial position, whereas Mary's inventory, acquired and then sold, is added to the purchases figure for the year.

Tutorial note: goodwill and acquisitions are covered Section C of this Study Text.

(6)   The other item in the suspense account is dealt with as follows.

	$'000
Proceeds of issue of 100,000 ordinary shares	120
Less nominal value 100,000 × 50c	50
Excess of consideration over par value (= share premium)	70

Tutorial note: share issues are covered in Chapter 12 of this Study Text.

(7)   The transfer to general reserve increases it to $171,000 + $16,000 = $187,000.

4.2 Financial statements II

(a)   ATOK CO

STATEMENT OF COMPREHENSIVE INCOME FOR THE YEAR ENDED 30 JUNE 20X9

	$'000
Revenue (14,800 – 24) (W1)	14,776
Cost of sales (W1)	(10,280)
Gross profit	4,496
Distribution costs (1,080 + 272 + 190 – 120)	(1,422)
Administration expenses (1,460 + 272 + 70 – 60)	(1,742)
Finance cost (2,000 × 10% × 3/12)	(50)
Profit for the year	1,282
Other comprehensive income	
Gain on revaluation of land	1,500
Total comprehensive income for the year	2,782

ATOK CO

STATEMENT OF FINANCIAL POSITION AS AT 30 JUNE 20X9

	$'000	$'000
Assets		
Non current assets		
Property, plant and equipment (W3)		25,470
Current assets		
Inventories (W1)	1,566	
Receivables (4,120 + 120 + 60 – 24)	4,276	
Cash and cash equivalents	160	
		6,002
Total assets		31,472
Equity		
Share capital		14,000
Retained earnings		4,422
Share premium account		4,000
Revaluation surplus		4,500
		26,922
Non current liabilities		
10% loan notes 20Y8		2,000
Current liabilities		
Trade payables	2,240	
Accruals (190 + 70 + 50)	310	
Total current liabilities		2,250
Total equity and liabilities		31,472

(b)   ATOK CO

STATEMENT OF CHANGES IN EQUITY FOR THE YEAR ENDED 30 JUNE 20X9

	Share capital $'000	Share premium $'000	Revaluation surplus $'000	Retained earnings $'000	Total $'000
As at 1 July 20X8	10,000	2,000	3,000	3,140	18,1
Issue of shares	4,000	2,000	–	–	6,0
Total comprehensive income for the year	–	–	1,500	1,282	2,7
As at 30 June 20X9	14,000	4,000	4,500	4,422	26,9

Workings

1   *Cost of sales*

	$'000
Opening inventory	1,390
Purchases	8,280
	9,670
Closing inventories ((1,560 + 16 – 10) see below)	(1,566)
	8,104
Depreciation (W2)	2,176
Cost of sales	10,280

Inventory adjustments

(i)   Lower of cost ($80,000) and NRV ($90,000 – $20,000) = $70,000. Therefore $10,000 (80,000 – 70,000) adjustment.

(ii)   Inventory understated by $16,000

Sales overstated by $24,000

Tutorial note: inventories are covered in Chapter 11 of this Study Text.

2   *Depreciation*

	$'000
Buildings (8,000 @ 2%)	160
Plant (12,800 @ 20%)	2,560
	2,720

80% to cost of sales: 2,176. 10% to distribution and 10% to administration: 272

3   *Property, plant and equipment*

	$'000
Land and buildings (12,000 + 8,000 – 2,130 – 160)	17,710
Plant and equipment (12,800 – 2,480 – 2,560)	7,760
	25,470

Tutorial note: remember that land is not depreciated.

REPORTING FINANCIAL PERFORMANCE

 We first look at **IAS 18** which covers the recognition of revenue.

We then look at **IFRS 5** which deals with discontinued operations and non-current assets held for sale, before moving on to cover **IAS 8** which looks at accounting policies. IAS 8 also examines certain circumstances and transactions which require different treatment to normal profit or loss items.

In the final part of this chapter, we cover **IFRS 8** on segment reporting which requires publicly quoted entities to provide additional information on their results, breaking them down by segment.

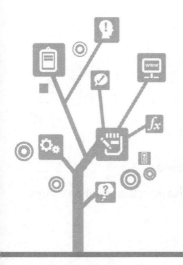

topic list	learning outcomes	syllabus references	ability required
1 IAS 18 *Revenue*	C2(a)	C2(i)	application
2 IFRS 5 *Non-current assets held for sale and discontinued operations*	C2(a)	C2(i),(v)	application
3 IAS 8 *Accounting policies, changes in accounting estimates and errors*	C2(a)	C2(i)	application
4 IFRS 8 *Operating segments*	C2(a)	C2(i)	application

1   IAS 18 *Revenue*

Introduction

Accruals accounting is based on the **matching of costs with the revenue they generate**. It is crucially important under this convention that we can establish the point at which revenue may be recognised so that the correct treatment can be applied to the related costs. The decision has a **direct impact on profit** since under the prudence concept it would be unacceptable to recognise the profit on sale until a sale had taken place in accordance with the criteria of revenue recognition.

There are two international standards which cover revenue: IAS 18 *Revenue* and IAS 11 *Construction contracts*. This section will look at IAS 18. IAS 11 is covered later in this Text.

1.1 IAS 18 *Revenue*

IAS 18 governs the recognition of revenue in specific (common) types of transaction. Generally, recognition should be when it is probable that **future economic benefits** will flow to the entity and when these benefits can be **measured reliably**.

Income, as defined by the IASB's *Framework* document, includes both revenues and gains. Revenue is income arising in the ordinary course of an entity's activities and it may be called different names, such as sales, fees, interest, dividends or royalties.

Exam skills

In the exam you should be able to apply the IAS, not just describe it.

1.2 Scope

IAS 18 covers the revenue from specific types of transaction or events.

- **Sale of goods** (manufactured products and items purchased for resale)
- **Rendering of services**
- Use by others of entity assets yielding **interest, royalties and dividends**

Interest, royalties and dividends are included as income because they arise from the use of an entity's assets by other parties.

1.3 Measurement of revenue

When a transaction takes place, the amount of revenue is usually decided by the **agreement of the buyer and seller**. The revenue is actually measured, however, as the **fair value of the consideration received**, which will take account of any trade discounts and volume rebates.

1.4 Recognition of revenue - sale of goods

IAS 18 specifies that revenue from the sale of goods should only be recognised when *all* the following conditions are satisfied.

(a)   The entity has transferred the **significant risks and rewards** of ownership of the goods to the buyer

(b)   The entity retains neither **continuing managerial involvement** to the degree usually associated with ownership, nor effective control over the goods sold

(c)   The amount of revenue can be **measured reliably**

(d)   It is probable that the **economic benefits** associated with the transaction will flow to the entity

(e)   The **costs incurred** or to be incurred in respect of the transaction can be measured reliably

The transfer of risks and rewards can only be decided by examining each transaction. Usually, the transfer occurs at the same time as either the **transfer of legal title**, or the **passing of possession** to the buyer – this is what happens when you buy something in a shop, but this is not always the case.

If **significant risks and rewards remain with the seller**, then the transaction is *not* a sale and revenue cannot be recognised. For example if the receipt of the revenue from a particular sale depends on the buyer receiving revenue from his own sale of the goods, then the significant risks and rewards associated with the goods have not been transferred to the buyer, and no revenue should be recognised by the seller.

Matching should take place, ie the revenue and expenses relating to the same transaction should be recognised at the same time. It is usually easy to estimate expenses at the date of sale (eg warranty costs, shipment costs, etc). Where they cannot be estimated reliably, then revenue cannot be recognised; any consideration which has already been received is treated as a liability.

1.5 Recognition of revenue – rendering of services   5/10

IAS 18 specifies that when the outcome of a transaction involving the rendering of services can be estimated reliably, the associated revenue should be recognised by reference to the **stage of completion of the transaction** at the end of the reporting period. The outcome of a transaction can be estimated reliably when *all* the following conditions are satisfied.

(a)   The amount of revenue can be **measured reliably**

(b)   It is probable that the **economic benefits** associated with the transaction will flow to the entity

(c)   The **stage of completion** of the transaction at the end of the reporting period can be measured reliably

(d)   The **costs incurred** for the transaction and the costs to complete the transaction can be measured reliably

There are various methods of determining the stage of completion of a transaction, depending on which is considered the most reliable. IAS 18 lists the following methods:

(a)   Surveys of work performed

(b)   Services performed to date as a percentage of total services to be performed; or

(c)   Costs incurred to date (that reflect services performed to date) as a percentage of estimated total costs.

For practical purposes, when services are performed by an indeterminate number of acts over a period of time, revenue should be recognised on a **straight line basis** over the period, unless there is evidence for the use of a more appropriate method. If one act is of more significance than the others, then the significant act should be carried out *before* revenue is recognised.

In uncertain situations, when the outcome of the transaction involving the rendering of services cannot be estimated reliably, the standard recommends a **no loss/no gain approach**. Revenue is recognised only to the extent of the expenses recognised that are recoverable.

1.6 Recognition of revenue - interest, royalties and dividends

When others use the entity's assets yielding interest, royalties and dividends for the entity, the revenue should be recognised when:

(a)   it is probable that the **economic benefits** associated with the transaction will flow to the entity; and

(b)   the amount of the revenue can be **measured reliably**.

The revenue is recognised on the following bases.

(a)   **Interest** is recognised using the effective interest method set out in IAS 39

(b)   **Royalties** are recognised on an accruals basis in accordance with the substance of the relevant agreement

(c)   **Dividends** are recognised when the shareholder's right to receive payment is established

1.7 Disclosure

The following items should be disclosed.

(a)   The **accounting policies** adopted for the recognition of revenue, including the methods used to determine the stage of completion of transactions involving the rendering of services

(b)   The amount of each **significant category of revenue** recognised during the period including revenue arising from:

   (i)   The sale of goods
   (ii)   The rendering of services
   (iii)   Interest
   (iv)   Royalties
   (v)   Dividends

(c)   The amount of revenue arising from **exchanges of goods or services** included in each significant category of revenue

Question 5.1   Revenue recognition

Learning outcome C2(a)

Given that prudence is the main consideration, explain under what circumstances, if any, revenue might be recognised at the following stages of a sale.

(a)   Goods are acquired by the business which it confidently expects to resell very quickly.
(b)   A customer places a firm order for goods.
(c)   Goods are delivered to the customer.
(d)   The customer is invoiced for goods.
(e)   The customer pays for the goods.
(f)   The customer's cheque in payment for the goods has been cleared by the bank.

Section summary

Revenue recognition is straightforward in most business transactions but some situations are more complicated. It is necessary to determine the **substance of each transaction** rather than the legal form.

IAS 18 *Revenue* is concerned with the recognition of revenues arising from:

-   the sale of goods
-   the rendering of services
-   the use by others of equity assets yielding interest, royalties and dividends

IAS 18 gives conditions which must be met for revenue to be recognised.

2   IFRS 5 *Non-current assets held for sale and discontinued operations*

Introduction

This section looks at IFRS 5 *Non-current assets held for sale and discontinued operations*. We first explore the background to the standard and then move on to examine the necessary presentation and disclosures.

2.1 Background

IFRS 5 is the result of a short-term convergence project with the US Financial Accounting Standards Board (FASB). It replaces IAS 35 *Discontinuing operations*.

IFRS 5 requires assets and groups of assets that are 'held for sale' to be **presented separately** in the statement of financial position and the results of discontinued operations to be presented separately in the statement of comprehensive income. This is required so that users of financial statements will be better able to make **projections** about the financial position, profits and cash flows of the entity.

KEY TERM

DISPOSAL GROUP: a group of assets to be disposed of, by sale or otherwise, together as a group in a single transaction, and liabilities directly associated with those assets that will be transferred in the transaction. (In practice a disposal group could be a subsidiary, a cash-generating unit or a single operation within an entity.)   *(IFRS 5)*

IFRS 5 does not apply to certain assets covered by other accounting standards:

(a)   Deferred tax assets (IAS 12)

(b)   Assets arising from employee benefits (IAS 19)

(c)   Financial assets (IAS 39)

(d)   Investment properties accounted for in accordance with the fair value model (IAS 40)

(e)   Agricultural and biological assets that are measured at fair value less estimated point of sale costs (IAS 41)

(f)   Insurance contracts (IFRS 4)

2.2 Classification of assets held for sale   5/11

A non-current asset (or disposal group) should be classified as **held for sale** if its carrying amount will be recovered **principally through a sale transaction** rather than **through continuing use**. A number of detailed criteria must be met:

(a)   The asset must be **available for immediate sale** in its present condition.

(b)   Its sale must be **highly probable** (ie, significantly more likely than not).

For the sale to be highly probable, the following must apply.

(a)   Management must be **committed** to a plan to sell the asset.

(b)   There must be an active programme to **locate a buyer.**

(c)   The asset must be marketed for sale at a **price that is reasonable** in relation to its current fair value.

(d)   The sale should be expected to take place **within one year** from the date of classification.

(e)   It is unlikely that significant changes to the plan will be made or that the plan will be withdrawn.

An asset (or disposal group) can still be classified as held for sale, even if the sale has not actually taken place within one year. However, the delay must have been **caused by events or circumstances beyond the entity's control** and there must be sufficient evidence that the entity is still committed to sell the asset or disposal group. Otherwise the entity must cease to classify the asset as held for sale.

If an entity acquires a disposal group (eg, a subsidiary) exclusively with a view to its subsequent disposal it can classify the asset as held for sale only if the sale is expected to take place within one year and it is highly probable that all the other criteria will be met within a short time (normally three months).

Question 5.2	Assets held for sale

Learning outcome C2(a)

On 1 December 20X3, a company became committed to a plan to sell a manufacturing facility and has already found a potential buyer. The company does not intend to discontinue the operations currently carried out in the facility. At 31 December 20X3 there is a backlog of uncompleted customer orders. The subsidiary will not be able to transfer the facility to the buyer until after it ceases to operate the facility and has eliminated the backlog of uncompleted customer orders. This is not expected to occur until spring 20X4.

Required

Can the manufacturing facility be classified as 'held for sale' at 31 December 20X3?

2.3 Measurement of assets held for sale   5/11

KEY TERMS

FAIR VALUE: the amount for which an asset could be exchanged, or a liability settled, between knowledgeable, willing parties in an arm's length transaction.

COSTS TO SELL: the incremental costs directly attributable to the disposal of an asset (or disposal group), excluding finance costs and income tax expense.

RECOVERABLE AMOUNT: the higher of an asset's fair value less costs to sell and its value in use.

VALUE IN USE: the present value of estimated future cash flows expected to arise from the continuing use of an asset and from its disposal at the end of its useful life.

A non-current asset (or disposal group) that is held for sale should be measured at the **lower of** its **carrying amount** and **fair value less costs to sell**. Fair value less costs to sell is equivalent to net realisable value.

An **impairment loss** should be recognised where fair value less costs to sell is lower than carrying amount. Note that this is an exception to the normal rule. IAS 36 *Impairment of assets* requires an entity to recognise an impairment loss only where an asset's recoverable amount is lower than its carrying value. Recoverable amount is defined as the higher of net realisable value and value in use. IAS 36 does not apply to assets held for sale.

Non-current assets held for sale **should not be depreciated**, even if they are still being used by the entity.

A non-current asset (or disposal group) that is **no longer classified as held for sale** (for example, because the sale has not taken place within one year) is measured at the **lower of**:

(a)   Its **carrying amount** before it was classified as held for sale, adjusted for any depreciation that would have been charged had the asset not been held for sale

(b)   Its **recoverable amount** at the date of the decision not to sell

2.4 Presentation of a non-current asset or disposal group classified as held for sale   5/11

Non-current assets and disposal groups classified as held for sale should be **presented separately** from other assets in the statement of financial position. The liabilities of a disposal group should be presented separately from other liabilities in the statement of financial position. Note that:

(a)   Assets and liabilities held for sale **should not be offset**.

(b)   The **major classes** of assets and liabilities held for sale should be **separately disclosed** either in the statement of financial position or in the notes.

2.5 Additional disclosures

In the period in which a non-current asset (or disposal group) has been either classified as held for sale or sold the following should be disclosed.

(a)   A **description** of the non-current asset (or disposal group)

(b)   A description of the **facts and circumstances** of the disposal

(c)   Any **gain or loss** recognised when the item was classified as held for sale

Where an asset previously classified as held for sale is **no longer held for sale**, the entity should disclose a description of the facts and circumstances leading to the decision and its effect on results.

2.6 Presenting discontinued operations   5/10, 5/11

KEY TERMS

DISCONTINUED OPERATION: a component of an entity that has either been disposed of, or is classified as held for sale, and:

(a)   Represents a separate major line of business or geographical area of operations

(b)   Is part of a single co-ordinated plan to dispose of a separate major line of business or geographical area of operations, or

(c)   Is a subsidiary acquired exclusively with a view to resale.

COMPONENT OF AN ENTITY: operations and cash flows that can be clearly distinguished, operationally and for financial reporting purposes, from the rest of the entity.

An entity should **present and disclose information** that enables users of the financial statements to evaluate the financial effects of **discontinued operations** and disposals of non-current assets or disposal groups.

An entity should disclose a **single amount** in the statement of comprehensive income comprising the total of:

(a)   The **post-tax profit or loss** of discontinued operations and

(b)   The post-tax gain or loss recognised on the **measurement to fair value less costs to sell** or on the disposal of the assets or disposal group(s) constituting the discontinued operation.

An entity should also disclose an **analysis** of this single amount into:

(a)   The revenue, expenses and pre-tax profit or loss of discontinued operations

(b)   The related income tax expense

(c)   The gain or loss recognised on the measurement to fair value less costs to sell or on the disposal of the assets or disposal group(s) constituting the discontinued operation

(d)   The related income tax expense

This may be presented either in the statement of comprehensive income or in the notes. If it is presented in the statement of comprehensive income it should be presented in a section identified as relating to discontinued operations, ie separately from continuing operations. This analysis is not required where the discontinued operation is a newly acquired subsidiary that has been classified as held for sale.

An entity should disclose the **net cash flows** attributable to the operating, investing and financing activities of discontinued operations. These disclosures may be presented either on the face of the statement of cash flows or in the notes.

Gains and losses on the remeasurement of a disposal group that is not a discontinued operation but is held for sale should be included in profit or loss from continuing operations.

Comparative information for the discontinued operation should also be presented.

Exam alert

You may be required to produce an income statement or statement of comprehensive income from a trial balance in an exam question for a company with discontinued operations.

2.7 Illustration

The following amended illustration is taken from the implementation guidance to IFRS 5. Profit for the period from discontinued operations would be analysed in the notes.

XYZ
INCOME STATEMENT
FOR THE YEAR ENDED 31 DECEMBER 20X2

	20X2 $'000	20X1 $'000
Continuing operations		
Revenue	X	X
Cost of sales	(X)	(X)
Gross profit	X	X
Other income	X	X
Distribution costs	(X)	(X)
Administrative expenses	(X)	(X)
Other expenses	(X)	(X)
Finance costs	(X)	(X)
Profit before tax	X	X
Income tax expense	(X)	(X)
Profit for the year from continuing operations	X	X
Discontinued operations		
Profit for the year from discontinued operations	X	X
Profit for the year	X	X

Note that if there were items of 'other comprehensive income' this would be shown as a full 'statement of comprehensive income' as per the format in the previous chapter.

Question 5.3	Discontinued operation

Learning outcome C2(a)

On 20 October 20X3 the directors of a parent company made a public announcement of plans to close a steel works. The closure means that the group will no longer carry out this type of operation, which until recently has represented about 10% of its total sales revenue. The works will be gradually shut down over a period of several months, with complete closure expected in July 20X4. At 31 December 20X3 output had been significantly reduced and some redundancies had already taken place. The cash flows, revenues and expenses relating to the steel works can be clearly distinguished from those of the subsidiary's other operations.

Required

How should the closure be treated in the financial statements for the year ended 31 December 20X3?

Section summary

IFRS 5 *Non-current assets held for sale and discontinued operations* requires assets 'held for sale' to be presented separately in the statement of financial position. The results of discontinued operations should be presented separately in the statement of comprehensive income.

3 IAS 8 *Accounting policies, changes in accounting estimates and errors*

Introduction

IAS 8 deals with accounting policies, the treatment of changes in accounting policies and of changes in accounting estimates, and errors.

3.1 Developing accounting policies

KEY TERM

ACCOUNTING POLICIES are the specific principles, bases, conventions, rules and practices adopted by an entity in preparing and presenting financial statements.

Accounting policies are determined by **applying the relevant IFRS or IAS**.

Where there is no applicable IFRS or IAS management should use its **judgement** in developing and applying an accounting policy that results in information that is **relevant** and **reliable**.

An entity must select and apply its accounting policies for a period **consistently** for similar transactions, other events and conditions, unless an IFRS or an IAS specifically requires or permits categorisation of items for which different policies may be appropriate. If an IFRS or an IAS requires or permits categorisation of items, an appropriate accounting policy must be selected and applied consistently to each category.

3.2 Changes in accounting policies   5/11

The same accounting policies are usually adopted from period to period, to allow users to analyse trends over time in profit, cash flows and financial position. **Changes in accounting policy will therefore be rare** and should be made only if required by one of three things:

(a)   A new statutory requirement

(b)   A new accounting standard

(c)   If the change will result in a **more appropriate presentation** of events or transactions in the financial statements of the entity.

The standard highlights two types of event **which do not constitute changes in accounting policy**.

(a)   Adopting an accounting policy for a **new type of transaction** or event not dealt with previously by the entity.

(b)   Adopting a **new accounting policy** for a transaction or event which has not occurred in the past or which was not material.

If a policy of revaluation of property, plant and equipment is adopted for the first time then this is treated as a revaluation under IAS 16 *Property, plant and equipment*, not as a change of accounting policy under IAS 8.

An example of a change in accounting policy is where inventory previously valued on a FIFO basis is now to be valued on a weighted average cost basis.

3.2.1 Applying a change in accounting policy

IAS 8 requires **retrospective application** of a change in accounting policy, *unless* it is **impracticable** to determine the cumulative amount of the adjustment.

RETROSPECTIVE APPLICATION means to apply a new accounting policy to transactions, other events and conditions as if that policy had always been applied.

KEY TERM

Applying a requirement is IMPRACTICABLE when the entity cannot apply it after making every reasonable effort to do so. It is impracticable to apply a change in an accounting policy retrospectively or to make a retrospective restatement to correct an error if one of the following apply.

(a)   The effects of the retrospective application or retrospective restatement are not determinable.

(b)   The retrospective application or retrospective restatement requires assumptions about what management's intent would have been in that period.

(c)   The retrospective application or retrospective restatement requires significant estimates of amounts and it is impossible to distinguish objectively information about those estimates that: provides evidence of circumstances that existed on the date(s) at which those amounts are to be recognised, measured or disclosed; and would have been available when the financial statements for that prior period were authorised for issue, from other information.   *(IAS 8)*

In other words, retrospective application means that all comparative information must be restated **as if the new policy had always been in force**, with amounts relating to earlier periods reflected in an adjustment to opening reserves of the earliest period presented. Comparative information should be restated unless it is impracticable to do so.

Prospective application is allowed only when it is impracticable to determine the cumulative effect of the change.

PROSPECTIVE APPLICATION of a change in accounting policy means to apply the new accounting policy to transactions, other events and conditions occurring after the date as at which the policy is changed.

KEY TERM

In other words, the new accounting policy is applied from the point it is adopted to transactions occurring from that date forwards. No adjustments are made for the treatment of transactions that occurred in the past under the old policy.

3.2.2 Disclosure of a change in accounting policy

Certain **disclosures** are required when a change in accounting policy has a material effect on the current period or any prior period presented, or when it may have a material effect in subsequent periods.

(a)   Reasons for the change

(b)   Nature of the change

(c)   Amount of the adjustment for the current period and for each period presented

(d)   Amount of the adjustment relating to periods prior to those included in the comparative information

(e)   The fact that comparative information has been restated or that it is impracticable to do so.

If an entity has chosen to change an accounting policy, rather than this being required by statute or accounting standards, an explanation of why the new policy provides more reliable and relevant information must be given.

An entity should also disclose information relevant to assessing the **impact of new IFRSs** on the financial statements where these have **not yet come into force.**

3.3 Changes in accounting estimates

3.3.1 What are accounting estimates?

Estimates arise in relation to business activities because of the **uncertainties inherent within them**. Judgements are made based on the most up to date information and the use of such estimates is a necessary part of the preparation of financial statements. It does *not* undermine their reliability. Here are some examples of accounting estimates.

* A necessary **doubtful debt provision**
* **Useful lives** of depreciable assets
* Provision for **obsolescence of inventory**

Where circumstances change or more information becomes available, the estimate may need to be revised.

3.3.2 Changes in accounting estimates

When an accounting estimate needs to be changed, the **effect of the change** should be included in the financial statements in the period it arises, and in future periods if the change affects both current and future periods.

An example of a change in accounting estimate which affects only the **current period** is a change in the doubtful debt estimate. However, a revision in the life over which an asset is depreciated would affect both the **current and future periods**, in the amount of the depreciation expense.

Reasonably enough, the effect of a change in an accounting estimate should be included in the **same expense classification** as was used previously for the estimate. This rule helps to ensure **consistency** between the financial statements of different periods.

The **materiality** of the change is also relevant. The nature and amount of a change in an accounting estimate that has a material effect in the current period (or which is expected to have a material effect in subsequent periods) should be disclosed. If it is not possible to quantify the amount, this impracticability should be disclosed.

3.4 Prior period errors

KEY TERM

PRIOR PERIOD ERRORS are omissions from, and misstatements in, the entity's financial statements for one or more prior periods arising from a failure to use, or misuse of, reliable information that:

(a)   Was available when financial statements for those periods were authorised for issue, and

(b)   Could reasonably be expected to have been obtained and taken into account in the preparation and presentation of those financial statements.

Such errors include the effects of mathematical mistakes, mistakes in applying accounting policies, oversights or misinterpretations of facts, and fraud.   *(IAS 8)*

3.4.1 Accounting treatment for prior period errors

Prior period errors should be corrected retrospectively.

This involves:

(a)   Either restating the comparative amounts for the prior period(s) in which the error occurred,

(b)   Or, when the error occurred before the earliest prior period presented, restating the opening balances of assets, liabilities and equity for that period

so that the financial statements are presented **as if the error had never occurred.**

Only where it is **impracticable** to determine the cumulative effect of an error on prior periods can an entity correct an error **prospectively.**

Various **disclosures** are required.

(a)   **Nature** of the prior period error

(b)   For each prior period, to the extent practicable, the **amount** of the correction

      (i)   For each financial statement line item affected

      (ii)   If IAS 33 applies, for basic and diluted earnings per share

(c)   The amount of the correction at the **beginning of the earliest prior** period presented

(d)   If **retrospective restatement is impracticable** for a particular prior period, the **circumstances** that led to the existence of that condition and a description of how and from when the error has been corrected. Subsequent periods need not repeat these disclosures

Question 5.4	Prior period error

Learning outcome C2(a)

During 20X7 Global discovered that certain items had been included in inventory at 31 December 20X6, valued at $4.2m, which had in fact been sold before the year end. The following figures for 20X6 (as reported) and 20X7 (draft) are available.

	20X6 $'000	20X7 (draft) $'000
Sales	47,400	67,200
Cost of goods sold	(34,570)	(55,800)
Profit before taxation	12,830	11,400
Income taxes	(3,880)	(3,400)
Net profit	8,950	8,000

Reserves at 1 January 20X6 were $13m. The cost of goods sold for 20X7 includes the $4.2m error in opening inventory. The income tax rate was 30% for 20X6 and 20X7.

Required

Prepare the income statement for 20X7, with the 20X6 comparative, and a reconciliation of opening and closing retained earnings for 20X6 and 20X7.

Section summary

IAS 8 deals with the treatment of changes in accounting estimates, changes in accounting policies and errors.

Accounting policies must comply with accounting standards and be applied **consistently**

Changes in accounting policy are applied **retrospectively**.

Changes in accounting estimates are **not** applied retrospectively.

Prior period errors will require **retrospective** correction if they are **material**.

4   IFRS 8 *Operating segments*

Introduction

Large entities produce a wide range of products and services, often in several different countries. Further information on how the overall results of entities are made up from each of these product or geographical areas will help the users of the financial statements assess the past performance of the entity, better understand its risks and returns, and make more informed judgments about the entity as a whole. This is the reason for **segment reporting.**

Segment reporting is covered by IFRS 8 *Operating segments*, which replaced IAS 14 *Segment reporting* in November 2006.

4.1 IFRS 8 *Operating segments*

IFRS 8 requires an entity to adopt the 'management approach' to reporting on the financial performance of its operating segments. This 'management approach' has two intended advantages:

(a)   It allows users of the financial statements to view operations through the eyes of management.

(b)   As it is based on information which is being collected anyway, it should not involve too much cost or time to prepare.

In the words of the Standard:

'An entity shall disclose information to enable users of its financial statements to evaluate the nature and financial effects of the business activities in which it engages and the economic environments in which it operates.'

IFRS 8 applies to listed companies only.

4.1.1 Operating segments   11/10, 5/11

KEY TERM

An OPERATING SEGMENT is a component of an entity:

(a)   that engages in business activities from which it may earn revenues and incur expenses

(b)   whose operating results are regularly reviewed by the entity's chief operating decision maker to make decisions about resources to be allocated to the segment and assess its performance, and

(c)   for which discrete financial information is available   *(IFRS 8)*

4.1.2 Determining reportable segments   5/11

An entity must report separate information about **each operating segment** that:

(a)   Has been identified as meeting the **definition of an operating segment**; and

(b) Exceeds any of the following thresholds:

(i) Segment **revenue** (internal and external) is **10% or more** of total revenue, or

(ii) Segment **profit or loss** is **10% or more** of all segments in profit (or all segments in loss if greater)

(iii) Segment **assets** are **10% or more** of total assets.

At least **75% of total external revenue** must be reported by operating segments. Where this is not the case, additional segments must be identified (even if they do not meet the 10% thresholds).

Two or more operating segments **below** the thresholds may be aggregated to produce a reportable segment if the segments have **similar economic characteristics** and the segments are similar in *each* of the following respects:

- The **nature of the products or services**
- The **nature of the production process**
- The **type or class of customer for their products or services**
- The **methods used to distribute their products or provide their services**, and
- If applicable, the **nature of the regulatory environment**

Operating segments that do not meet **any of the quantitative thresholds** may be reported separately if management believes that information about the segment would be useful to users of the financial statements.

Example: Operating segments

CTU Co has the following operating segments

Segment	Internal revenue $'000	External revenue $'000	Total revenue $'000
Car division	29	61	90
Bike division	–	45	45
Truck division	–	39	39
Tractor division	–	23	23
Van division	–	21	21
Digger division	–	17	15
	29	206	235

The reportable operating segments are the Car, Bike and Truck divisions as each of them has revenue of more than $23,500 (10% of the total revenue of $235,000).

These three divisions between them have external revenue of $145,000. This is less than 75% of the total external revenue (75% × $206,000 = $154,500) so the Tractor division is also a reportable segment. This brings external revenue generated by reportable segments to $168,000, so neither of the two remaining segments need to be reported on.

4.1.3 Decision tree to assist in identifying reportable segments

The following decision tree will assist in identifying reportable segments.

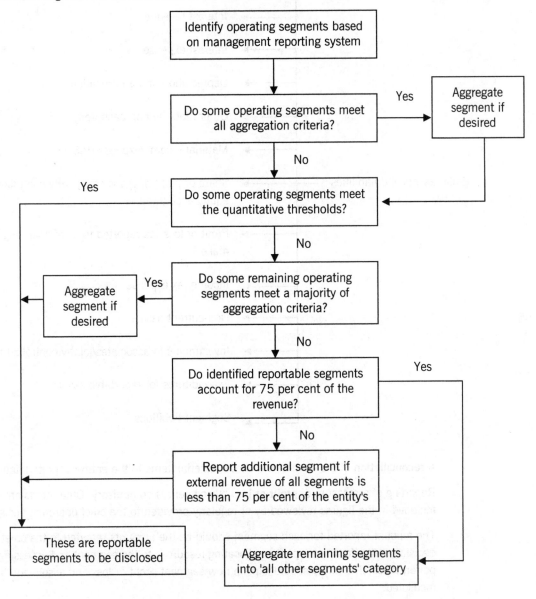

4.1.4 Disclosures

Disclosures required by the IFRS are extensive, and best learned by looking at the example and proforma, which follow the list of requirements given below.

Disclosure requirements:

(a)   Factors used to identify the entity's reportable segments
(b)   **Types of products and services** from which each reportable segment derives its revenues
(c)   Reportable segment revenues, profit or loss, assets, liabilities and other material items:

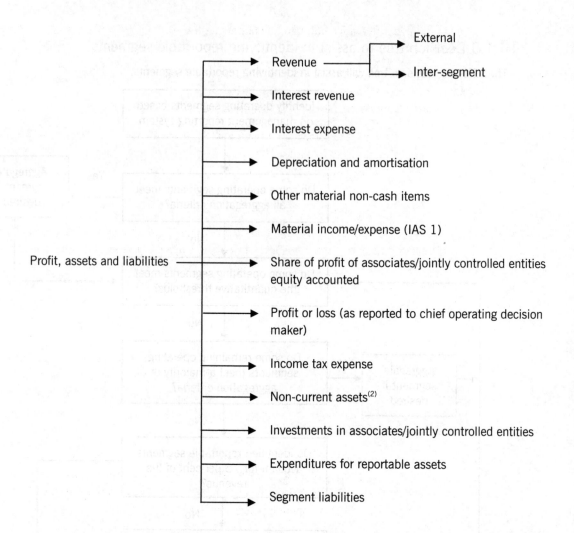

A **reconciliation** of the each of the above material items to the entity's reported figures is required.

Reporting of a measure of **profit or loss** by segment is compulsory. Other items are disclosed if included in the figures reviewed by or regularly provided to the chief operating decision maker.

The amount reported for each segment should be the amounts reported to the chief operating decision maker for the purpose of allocating resources to the segment and assessing its performance. The entity should explain how segment profit or loss and assets and liabilities are measured.

(d)   **External revenue** by each product and service (if reported basis is not products and services)

(e)   **Geographical information**:

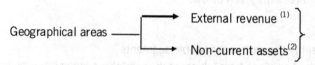

Notes

(1)   External revenue is allocated based on the customer's location.

(2)   Non-current assets excludes financial instruments, deferred tax assets, post-employment benefit assets, and rights under insurance contracts.

(f)   Information about **reliance on major customers** (ie those who represent more than 10% of external revenue), including:

     (i)   The percentage of revenue for each such customer
     (ii)   The total amount of revenues from each such customer
     (iii)   The identity of the segment or segments reporting the revenues.

The identity of the major customer or the amount of revenues that each segment reports from that customer does not need to be disclosed. Groups of entities under common control (including government controlled entities) are classified as a single customer for this purpose.

Exam alert

IFRS 8 was amended in April 2009 by the IASB's 2009 annual improvements project. Before the amendment, it was compulsory to disclose **total assets per segment.** The amendment changed IFRS 8 so that total assets per segment only needs to be disclosed if that figure is regularly provided to the chief operating decision maker. The CIMA Study System refers to the standard before the amendment, so watch out for this in your exam.

4.1.5 Disclosure example from IFRS 8

The following example is adapted from the IFRS 8 *Implementation Guidance*, which emphasises that this is for illustrative purposes only and that the information must be presented in the most understandable manner in the specific circumstances.

The hypothetical company does not allocate tax expense (tax income) or non-recurring gains and losses to reportable segments. In addition, not all reportable segments have material non-cash items other than depreciation and amortisation in profit or loss. The amounts in this illustration are assumed to be the amounts in reports used by the chief operating decision maker.

	Car parts $	Motor vessel $	Software $	Electronics $	Finance $	All other $	Totals $
Revenues from external customers	3,000	5,000	9,500	12,000	5,000	1,000[a]	35,500
Intersegment revenues	–	–	3,000	1,500	–	–	4,500
Interest revenue	450	800	1,000	1,500	–	–	3,750
Interest expense	350	600	700	1,100	–	–	2,750
Net interest revenue [b]	–	–	–	–	1,000	–	1,000
Depreciation and amortisation	200	100	50	1,500	1,100	–	2,950
Reportable segment profit	200	70	900	2,300	500	100	4,070
Other material non-cash items:							
Impairment of assets	–	200	–	–	–	–	200
Reportable segment assets	2,000	5,000	3,000	12,000	57,000	2,000	81,000
Expenditure for reportable segment non-current assets	300	700	500	800	600	–	2,900
Reportable segment liabilities	1,050	3,000	1,800	8,000	30,000	–	43,850

(a) Revenues from segments below the quantitative thresholds are attributable to four operating segments of the company. Those segments include a small property business, an electronics equipment rental business, a software consulting practice and a warehouse leasing operation. None of those segments has ever met any of the quantitative thresholds for determining reportable segments.

(b) The finance segment derives a majority of its revenue from interest. Management primarily relies on net interest revenue, not the gross revenue and expense amounts, in managing that segment. Therefore, as permitted by IFRS 8, only the net amount is disclosed.

4.1.6 Suggested proforma

Information about profit or loss, assets and liabilities

	Segment A	Segment B	Segment C	All other segments	Inter segment	Entity total
Revenue – external customers	X	X	X	X	–	X
Revenue – inter segment	X	X	X	X	X	–
	X	X	X	X	(X)	X
Interest revenue	X	X	X	X	(X)	X
Interest expense	(X)	(X)	(X)	(X)	X	(X)
Depreciation and amortisation	(X)	(X)	(X)	(X)	–	(X)
Other material non-cash items	X/(X)	X/(X)	X/(X)	X/(X)	X/(X)	X/(X)
Material income/expense (IAS 1)	X/(X)	X/(X)	X/(X)	X/(X)	X/(X)	X/(X)
Share of profit of associate/JVs	X	X	X	X	–	X
Segment profit before tax	X	X	X	X	(X)	X
Income tax expense	(X)	(X)	(X)	(X)	–	(X)
Unallocated items						X/(X)
Profit for the year						X
Segment assets	X	X	X	X	(X)	X
Investments in associate/JVs	X	X	X	X	–	X
Unallocated assets						X
Entity's assets						X
Expenditures for reportable assets	X	X	X	X	(X)	X
Segment liabilities	X	X	X	X	(X)	X
Unallocated liabilities						X
Entity's liabilities						X

Information about geographical areas

	Country of domicile	Foreign countries	Total
Revenue – external customers	X	X	X
Non-current assets	X	X	X

4.2 Key changes from IAS 14 *Segment reporting*

(a)   IFRS 8 **converges with US GAAP** by adopting the US reporting standard SFAS 131 *Disclosures about segments of an enterprise and related information*.

(b)   The managerial approach to identifying segments based on an internal organisation structure is used rather than the IAS 14 risk and returns approach.

(c)   There is no longer a requirement for more than 50% of revenue to be external for a segment to be reported separately.

(d)   **Revenue, profit and assets** for reportable segment testing are **no longer defined**. The basis used depends on the information reported to the chief operating decision maker.

(e)   The **level of compulsory segment disclosure** is **lower**, as only profit or loss are required figures. Other items are only disclosed if included in the figures reviewed by or regularly provided to the chief operating decision maker.

(f)   The **scope of disclosure is widened** to include finance income, finance cost and income tax expense (if the specified amounts are included in the measure of segment profit or loss reviewed by the chief operating decision maker).

(g)   New disclosures are required on **factors used to determine reportable segments** and types of products and services.

(h)   **Geographical disclosures** are required on a **country by country** basis if material.

(i)   There is no requirement to disclose capital expenditure on a geographical basis.

4.3 Advantages and disadvantages of the old and new segment definition approaches

	Advantages	Disadvantages
'Risks and Returns' approach (IAS 14)	• The information can be reconciled to the financial statements • It is a consistent method • The method helps to highlight the profitability, risks and returns of an identifiable segment	• The information may be commercially sensitive • The segments may include operations with different risks and returns
'Managerial' approach (IFRS 8)	• It is cost effective because the marginal cost of reporting segmental data will be low • Users can be sure that the segment data reflects the operational strategy of the business	• Segment determination is the responsibility of directors and is subjective • Management may report segments which are not consistent for internal reporting and control purposes making its usefulness questionable

4.4 Criticisms of IFRS 8

(a) Some commentators have criticized the 'management approach' as leaving segment identification **too much to the discretion of the entity.**

(b) The management approach may mean that financial statements of different entities are **not comparable.**

(c) Segment determination is the responsibility of directors and is **subjective.**

(d) Management may report segments which are **not consistent** for internal reporting and control purposes, making its usefulness questionable.

(e) For accounting periods beginning on or after 1 January 2005 listed entities within the EU are required to use adopted international standards in their consolidated financial statements. The **EU has not yet adopted IFRS 8** and until it does IAS 14 will continue to apply here. Some stakeholders believe the standard to be flawed due to the amount of discretion it gives to management.

(f) **Geographical information** has been **downgraded.** It could be argued that this **breaks the link between a company and its stakeholders.**

(g) There is **no defined measure** of segment profit or loss.

Question 5.5	Segment reporting

Learning outcome C2(a)

A company has three divisions all based in the UK. Their revenues, results and net assets are as below:

	$'000
Division A	
Sales to B	304,928
Other UK sales	57,223
Middle East export sales	406,082
Pacific fringe export sales	77,838
	846,071
Division B	
Sales to C	31,034
Export sales to Europe	195,915
	226,949
Division C	
Export sales to North America	127,003

	Division A $'000	Division B $'000	Division C $'000
Profit/(loss) before tax	162,367	18,754	(8,303)
Interest costs	3,459	6,042	527
Non-current assets	200,921	41,612	113,076
Current assets	121,832	39,044	92,338
Liabilities	16,959	6,295	120,841

Required

As far as the information permits, prepare the segment information required by IFRS 8.

Section summary

IFRS 8 is a **disclosure standard**, which is applicable to listed companies.

Segment reporting is necessary for a better understanding and assessment of:

- Past performance
- Risks and returns
- Informed judgements

IFRS 8 adopts the **managerial approach** to identifying segments.

IFRS 8 gives guidance on how segments should be **identified** and **what information should be disclosed** for each reportable segment.

IFRS 8 also sets out **requirements for related disclosures** about products and services, geographical areas and major customers.

Chapter Roundup

✓ **Revenue recognition** is straightforward in most business transactions but some situations are more complicated. It is necessary to determine the **substance of each transaction** rather than the legal form.

✓ IAS 18 *Revenue* is concerned with the recognition of revenues arising from:

- the sale of goods
- the rendering of services
- the use by others of equity assets yielding interest, royalties and dividends

✓ IAS 18 gives conditions which must be met for revenue to be recognised.

✓ IFRS 5 *Non-current assets held for sale and discontinued operations* requires assets 'held for sale' to be presented separately in the statement of financial position.

✓ The results of discontinued operations should be presented separately in the statement of comprehensive income.

✓ IAS 8 deals with the treatment of changes in accounting estimates, changes in accounting policies and errors.

✓ Accounting policies must comply with accounting standards and be applied **consistently**.

✓ Changes in accounting policy are applied **retrospectively**.

✓ Changes in accounting estimates are **not** applied retrospectively.

✓ Prior period errors will require **retrospective** correction if they are **material**.

✓ IFRS 8 is a **disclosure standard**, which is applicable to listed companies.

✓ **Segment reporting** is necessary for a better understanding and assessment of:

- Past performance
- Risks and returns
- Informed judgements

✓ IFRS 8 adopts the **managerial approach** to identifying segments.

✓ IFRS 8 gives guidance on how segments should be **identified** and **what information should be disclosed** for each reportable segment.

✓ IFRS 8 also sets out **requirements for related disclosures** about products and services, geographical areas and major customers.

Quick Quiz

1   How should a prior period error be corrected under IAS 8?

2   Give three circumstances when a change in accounting policy might be required.

3   IFRS 8 adopts the .... to identifying segments

4   A non-current asset is classified as held for sale if its carrying amount will be recovered principally through continuing use rather than through a sale transaction

      True ☐

      False ☐

5   Which of the following is not an accounting estimate?

      A   Prepaid rent
      B   Useful lives of depreciable assets
      C   A doubtful debt provision
      D   Restructuring provision

6   Prior period errors must be corrected prospectively.

      True ☐

      False ☐

7   What five conditions must be satisfied before revenue from the sale of goods can be recognised?

Answers to Quick Quiz

1   By adjusting the opening balance of retained earnings.

2   (a)   A new statutory requirement

      (b)   A new accounting standard

      (c)   If the change will result in a more appropriate presentation of events or transactions in the financial statements of the entity

3   Managerial approach

4   False

5   A

6   False

7   •   The entity has transferred the significant risks and rewards of ownership of the goods to the buyer

      •   The entity retains neither continuing managerial involvement to the degree usually associated with ownership, nor effective control over the goods sold

      •   The amount of revenue can be measured reliably

      •   It is probable that the economic benefits associated with the transaction will flow to the entity

      •   The costs incurred or to be incurred in respect of the transaction can be measured reliably

Answers to Questions

5.1 Revenue recognition

(a) A sale must never be recognised before the goods have even been ordered by a customer. There is no certainty about the value of the sale, nor when it will take place, even if it is virtually certain that goods will be sold.

(b) A sale must never be recognised when the customer places an order. Even though the order will be for a specific quantity of goods at a specific price, it is not yet certain that the sale transaction will go through. The customer may cancel the order, the supplier might be unable to deliver the goods as ordered or it may be decided that the customer is not a good credit risk.

(c) A sale will be recognised when delivery of the goods is made only when:

   (i) the sale is for cash, and so the cash is received at the same time; or
   (ii) the sale is on credit and the customer accepts delivery (eg by signing a delivery note).

(d) The critical event for a credit sale is usually the despatch of an invoice to the customer. There is then a legally enforceable debt, payable on specified terms, for a completed sale transaction.

(e) The critical event for a cash sale is when delivery takes place and when cash is received; both take place at the same time.

   It would be too cautious or 'prudent' to await cash payment for a credit sale transaction before recognising the sale, unless the customer is a high credit risk and there is a serious doubt about his ability or intention to pay.

(f) It would again be over-cautious to wait for clearance of the customer's cheques before recognising sales revenue. Such a precaution would only be justified in cases where there is a very high risk of the bank refusing to honour the cheque.

5.2 Assets held for sale

The facility will not be transferred until the backlog of orders is completed; this demonstrates that the facility is not available for immediate sale in its present condition. The facility cannot be classified as 'held for sale' at 31 December 20X3. It must be treated in the same way as other items of property, plant and equipment: it should continue to be depreciated and should not be separately disclosed.

5.3 Discontinued operation

Because the steel works is being closed, rather than sold, it cannot be classified as 'held for sale'. In addition, the steel works is not a discontinued operation. Although at 31 December 20X3 the group was firmly committed to the closure, this has not yet taken place and therefore the steel works must be included in continuing operations. Information about the planned closure could be disclosed in the notes to the financial statements.

5.4 Prior period error

INCOME STATEMENT

	20X6 $'000	20X7 $'000
Sales	47,400	67,200
Cost of goods sold (W1)	(38,770)	(51,600)
Profit before tax	8,630	15,600
Income tax (W2)	(2,620)	(4,660)
Profit for the year	6,010	10,940

RETAINED EARNINGS

	20X6 $'000	20X7 $'000
Opening retained earnings		
As previously reported	13,000	21,950
Correction of prior period error (4,200 – 1,260)	–	(2,940)
As restated	13,000	19,010
Profit for the year	6,010	10,940
Closing retained earnings	19,010	29,950

Workings

1 Cost of goods sold

	20X6 $'000	20X7 $'000
As stated in question	34,570	55,800
Inventory adjustment	4,200	(4,200)
	38,770	51,600

2 Income tax

	20X6 $'000	20X7 $'000
As stated in question	3,880	3,400
Inventory adjustment (4,200 × 30%)	(1,260)	1,260
	2,620	4,660

5.5 Segment reporting

Profit, assets and liabilities	*Division A* $'000	*Division B* $'000	*Division C* $'000	*Total* $'000
External revenue	541,143	195,915	127,003	864,061
Intersegment revenue	304,928	31,034		335,962
Interest expense	3,459	6,042	527	10,028
Segment profit (loss)	162,367	18,754	(8,303)	172,818
Segment assets	322,753	80,656	205,414	608,823
Segment liabilities	16,959	6,295	120,841	144,095

Information about geographical areas

	UK $'000	*Middle East* $'000	*Pacific fringe* $'000	*Europe* $'000	*N America* $'000	*Total* $'000
Revenues	57,223	406,082	77,838	195,915	127,003	864,061

Now try these questions from the Exam Question Bank

Number	Level	Marks	Time
Q13	Examination	5	9 mins

ACCOUNTING FOR
NON-CURRENT ASSETS

This chapter covers one of the important items on the statement of financial position, non-current assets. Intangible assets are covered later in Chapter 7. This chapter deals with IAS 16, IAS 36 and IAS 23.

IAS 16 should be familiar to you from your earlier studies, as should the mechanics of accounting for depreciation, revaluations of non-current assets and disposals of non-current assets. Some questions are given here for revision purposes.

IAS 36 on impairment is an important and very examinable standard.

IAS 23 deals with the treatment of funds used in self-constructed assets.

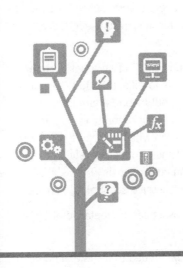

6

topic list	learning outcomes	syllabus references	ability required
1 Depreciation accounting	C2(a)	C2(ii)	application
2 IAS 16 *Property, plant and equipment*	C2(a)	C2(ii)	application
3 IAS 36 *Impairment of assets*	C2(a)	C2(v)	application
4 IAS 23 *Borrowing costs*	C2(a)	C2(viii)	application
5 Available-for-sale financial assets	C2(a)	C2(viii)	application

1 Depreciation accounting

Introduction

This section on deprecation of non-current assets should be familiar to you from your earlier studies. Make sure you can answer the questions in this section before moving on.

1.1 Non-current assets

Where assets held by an entity have a **limited useful life** to that entity it is necessary to apportion the value of an asset used in a period against the revenue it has helped to create. If an asset's life extends over more than one accounting period, it earns profits over more than one period. It is a **non-current asset**.

1.2 What is depreciation?

The need to depreciate non-current assets arises from the **accruals assumption**. If money is expended in purchasing an asset then the amount expended must at some time be charged against profits. If the asset is one which contributes to an entity's revenue over a number of accounting periods it would be inappropriate to charge any single period (eg the period in which the asset was acquired) with the whole of the expenditure. Instead, some method must be found of spreading the cost of the asset over its useful economic life.

This view of depreciation as a process of allocation of the cost of an asset over several accounting periods is the view adopted by IAS 16. It is worth mentioning here two **common misconceptions** about the purpose and effects of depreciation.

(a) It is sometimes thought that the carrying amount or 'net book value' (NBV) of an asset is equal to its net realisable value and that the object of charging depreciation is to reflect the fall in value of an asset over its life. This misconception is the basis of a common, but incorrect, argument which says that freehold properties (say) need not be depreciated in times when property values are rising. It is true that historical cost often gives a misleading impression when a property's NBV is much below its market value, but in such a case it is open to a business to incorporate a revaluation into its books, or even to prepare its accounts based on current costs. This is a separate problem from that of allocating the property's cost over successive accounting periods.

(b) Another misconception is that depreciation is provided so that an asset can be replaced at the end of its useful life. This is not the case.

    (i) If there is no intention of replacing the asset, it could then be argued that there is no need to provide for any depreciation at all.

    (ii) If prices are rising, the replacement cost of the asset will exceed the amount of depreciation provided.

1.3 Definitions

Depreciation accounting is governed by IAS 16 *Property, plant and equipment* which we will look at in Section 2 of this chapter. However, this section will deal with some of the IAS 16 definitions concerning depreciation.

DEPRECIATION is the result of systematic allocation of the depreciable amount of an asset over its useful life.

PROPERTY, PLANT AND EQUIPMENT are tangible items that:

- Are expected to be used during more than one period; and
- Are held for use in the production or supply of goods and service, for rental to others, or for administrative purposes

USEFUL LIFE is one of two things.

- The period over which an asset is expected to be available for use by an entity
- The number of production or similar units expected to be obtained from the asset by the entity.

DEPRECIABLE AMOUNT of a depreciable asset is the cost of an asset or other amount substituted for cost, less its residual value.   *(IAS 16)*

An 'amount substituted for cost' will normally be a **current market value** after a revaluation has taken place.

1.4 Requirements of IAS 16 for depreciation

IAS 16 requires the depreciable amount of a depreciable asset to be allocated on a **systematic basis** to each accounting period during the useful life of the asset.

One way of defining depreciation is to describe it as a means of **spreading the cost** of a non-current asset over its useful life, and so matching the cost against the full period during which it earns profits for the business.

There are situations where, over a period, an asset has **increased in value**, ie its current value is greater than the carrying value in the financial statements. You might think that in such situations it would not be necessary to depreciate the asset. The standard states, however, that this is irrelevant, and that depreciation should still be charged to each accounting period, based on the depreciable amount, irrespective of a rise in value.

An entity is required to begin depreciating an item of property, plant and equipment when it is available for use and to continue depreciating it until it is derecognised even if it is idle during the period.

Some assets require routine repairs and maintenance, however, depreciation should still be charged on these assets.

1.5 Useful life

The following factors should be considered when **estimating the useful life** of a depreciable asset.

- Expected **physical wear and tear**
- **Obsolescence**
- Legal or other **limits** on the use of the assets

Once decided, the useful life should be **reviewed at least every financial year end** and depreciation rates adjusted for the current and future periods, if expectations vary significantly from the original estimates. The effect of the change should be disclosed in the accounting period in which the change takes place.

The assessment of useful life requires **judgement** based on previous experience with similar assets or classes of asset. When a completely new type of asset is acquired (ie through technological advancement or through use in producing a brand new product or service) it is still necessary to estimate useful life, even though the exercise will be much more difficult.

The standard also points out that the physical life of the asset might be longer than its useful life to the entity in question. One of the main factors to be taken into consideration is the **physical wear and tear** the asset is likely to endure. This will depend on various circumstances, including the number of shifts for which the asset will be used, the entity's repair and maintenance programme and so on. Other factors to be considered include obsolescence (due to technological advances/improvements in production/reduction in demand for the product/service produced by the asset) and legal restrictions, eg length of a related lease.

Land and buildings are dealt with separately even when they are acquired together because land normally has an unlimited useful life and is therefore not depreciated. In contrast buildings do have a limited life and must be depreciated. Any increase in the value of land on which a building is standing will have no effect on the determination of the building's useful life.

1.6 Residual value

KEY TERM

The RESIDUAL VALUE is the net amount which the entity expects to obtain for an asset at the end of its useful life after deducting the expected costs of disposal.

In most cases the residual value of an asset is **likely to be immaterial**. If it is likely to be of any significant value, that value must be estimated at the date of purchase or any subsequent revaluation. The amount of residual value should be estimated based on the current situation with other similar assets, used in the same way, which are now at the end of their useful lives. Any expected costs of disposal should be offset against the gross residual value. If residual value happens to be greater than the carrying amount of the asset, then the depreciation charge would be nil.

1.7 Depreciation methods   5/10, 11/10, 5/11

There are various methods of allocating depreciation to accounting periods. An entity should choose the method which best reflects the way the future economic benefits arising from the asset will be consumed by the entity.

The depreciation method chosen should be reviewed at least every financial year end. If there has been a **significant change** in the way the entity uses the asset, the method of depreciation should be changed to reflect this. A change in the method of depreciation should be accounted for as a **change in accounting estimate under IAS 8**.

You should be familiar with the various **accepted methods of allocating depreciation, which are the straight line, reducing balance and machine hour methods,** and the relevant calculations and accounting treatments. These are revised in questions at the end of this section.

Depreciation is usually treated as an **expense**, but not where it is absorbed by the entity in the process of producing other assets. For example, depreciation of plant and machinery may be incurred in the production of goods for sale (inventory items). In such circumstances, the depreciation is included in the cost of the new assets produced.

Exam alert

Non-current assets are examined regularly. You should make sure you are able to calculate depreciation using the straight line, reducing balance and machine hours methods.

1.8 Disclosure

An accounting policy note should disclose the **valuation bases** used for determining the amounts at which depreciable assets are stated, along with the other accounting policies.

IAS 16 also requires the following to be disclosed for each major class of depreciable asset.

* **Depreciation methods** used
* **Useful lives** or the depreciation rates used
* **Gross amount** of depreciable assets and the related accumulated depreciation

Question 6.1

Depreciation I

Learning outcome C2(a)

A lorry bought for a business cost $17,000. It is expected to last for five years and then be sold for scrap for $2,000. Usage over the five years is expected to be:

Year 1   200 days
Year 2   100 days
Year 3   100 days
Year 4   150 days
Year 5   40 days

Required

Work out the depreciation to be charged each year under:

(a)   The straight line method
(b)   The reducing balance method (using a rate of 35%)
(c)   The machine hour method

Question 6.2

Depreciation II

Learning outcome C2(a)

(a)   What are the purposes of providing for depreciation?

(b)   In what circumstances is the reducing balance method more appropriate than the straight-line method? Give reasons for your answer.

Question 6.3

Depreciation III

Learning outcome C2(a)

A business purchased two rivet-making machines on 1 January 20X5 at a cost of $15,000 each. Each had an estimated life of five years and a nil residual value. The straight line method of depreciation is used.

Owing to an unforeseen slump in market demand for rivets, the business decided to reduce its output of rivets, and switch to making other products instead. On 31 March 20X7, one rivet-making machine was sold (on credit) to a buyer for $8,000.

Later in the year, however, it was decided to abandon production of rivets altogether, and the second machine was sold on 1 December 20X7 for $2,500 cash.

Prepare the machinery account, provision for depreciation of machinery account and disposal of machinery account for the accounting year to 31 December 20X7.

Section summary

The cost of a non-current asset, less its estimated residual value, is allocated fairly between accounting periods by means of depreciation. The provision for depreciation is both:

- Charged against profit
- Deducted from the value of the non-current asset in the statement of financial position

2 IAS 16 *Property, plant and equipment*

Introduction

This section looks at IAS 16 and the rules for recognition, derecognition and measurement. We will also cover what happens when an asset is revalued.

2.1 Application of IAS 16

This standard covers all aspects of accounting for property, plant and equipment. This represents the bulk of items which are **'tangible' non-current assets**.

2.2 Scope

IAS 16 should be followed when accounting for property, plant and equipment *unless* another international accounting standard requires a **different treatment**.

IAS 16 **does not apply** to the following.

(a)   Biological assets related to agricultural activity
(b)   Mineral rights and mineral reserves, such as oil, gas and other non-regenerative resources

However, the standard applies to property, plant and equipment used to develop these assets.

2.3 Definitions

The standard gives a large number of definitions.

KEY TERMS

PROPERTY, PLANT AND EQUIPMENT are tangible assets that:

- are held for use in the production or supply of goods or services, for rental to others, or for administrative purposes; and

- are expected to be used during more than one period.

COST is the amount of cash or cash equivalents paid or the fair value of the other consideration given to acquire an asset at the time of its acquisition or construction.

ENTITY-SPECIFIC VALUE is the present value of the cash flows an entity expects to arise from the continuing use of an asset and from its disposal at the end of its useful life, or expects to incur when settling a liability.

FAIR VALUE is the amount for which an asset could be exchanged between knowledgeable, willing parties in an arm's length transaction.

CARRYING AMOUNT is the amount at which an asset is recognised in the statement of financial position after deducting any accumulated depreciation and accumulated impairment losses.

An IMPAIRMENT LOSS is the amount by which the carrying amount of an asset exceeds its recoverable amount.

RECOVERABLE AMOUNT is the higher of an asset's fair value less costs to sell and its value in use. *(IAS 16)*

Exam skills

These definitions are important. Make sure you know them all for the exam.

2.4 Recognition

In this context, recognition simply means incorporation of the item in the business's accounts, in this case as a non-current asset. The recognition of property, plant and equipment depends on two criteria:

(a)   It is probable that **future economic benefits** associated with the asset will flow to the entity
(b)   The cost of the asset to the entity can be **measured reliably**

These recognition criteria apply to **subsequent expenditure** as well as costs incurred initially. There are no longer any separate criteria for recognising subsequent expenditure.

Property, plant and equipment can amount to **substantial amounts** in financial statements, affecting the presentation of the company's financial position and the profitability of the entity, through depreciation and also if an asset is wrongly classified as an expense and taken to profit or loss.

2.4.1 First criterion: future economic benefits

The **degree of certainty** attached to the flow of future economic benefits must be assessed. This should be based on the evidence available at the date of initial recognition (usually the date of purchase). The entity should thus be assured that it will receive the rewards attached to the asset and it will incur the associated risks, which will only generally be the case when the rewards and risks have actually passed to the entity. Until then, the asset should not be recognised.

2.4.2 Second criterion: cost measured reliably

It is generally easy to measure the cost of an asset as the **transfer amount on purchase**, ie what was paid for it. **Self-constructed assets** can also be measured easily by adding together the purchase price of all the constituent parts (labour, material etc) paid to external parties.

2.5 Separate items

Most of the time assets will be identified individually, but this will not be the case for **smaller items**, such as tools, dies and moulds, which are sometimes classified as inventory and written off as an expense.

Major components or spare parts, however, should be recognised as property, plant and equipment.

For very **large and specialised items**, an apparently single asset should be broken down into its composite parts. This occurs where the different parts have different useful lives and different depreciation rates are applied to each part, eg an aircraft, where the body and engines are separated as they have different useful lives.

2.6 Safety and environmental equipment

When such assets as these are acquired they will qualify for recognition where they enable the entity to **obtain future economic benefits** from related assets in excess of those it would obtain otherwise. The recognition will only be to the extent that the carrying amount of the asset and related assets does not exceed the total recoverable amount of these assets.

2.7 Initial measurement

Once an item of property, plant and equipment qualifies for recognition as an asset, it will initially be **measured at cost**.

2.7.1 Components of cost

The standard lists the components of the cost of an item of property, plant and equipment:

- **Purchase price**, less any trade discount or rebate

- **Import duties** and non-refundable purchase taxes

- **Directly attributable costs** of bringing the asset to working condition for its intended use, eg:
    - The cost of site preparation
    - Initial delivery and handling costs
    - Installation costs
    - Testing
    - Professional fees (architects, engineers)

- Initial estimate of the cost of dismantling and removing the asset and restoring the site on which it is located

IAS 16 provides **additional guidance on directly attributable** costs included in the cost of an item of property, plant and equipment.

(a)   These costs bring the asset to the location and working conditions necessary for it to be capable of operating in the manner intended by management, including those costs to test whether the asset is functioning properly.

(b)   These are determined after deducting the net proceeds from selling any items produced when bringing the asset to its location and condition.

The standard also states that income and related expenses of operations that are **incidental** to the construction or development of an item of property, plant and equipment should be **recognised** in profit or loss.

The following costs **will not be part of the cost** of property, plant or equipment unless they can be attributed directly to the asset's acquisition, or bringing it into its working condition.

- Administration and other general overhead costs
- Start-up
- Initial operating losses before the asset reaches planned performance

All of these will be recognised as an **expense** rather than an asset.

In the case of **self-constructed assets**, the same principles are applied as for acquired assets. If the entity makes similar assets during the normal course of business for sale externally, then the cost of the asset will be the cost of its production under IAS 2 *Inventories*. This also means that abnormal costs (wasted material, labour or other resources) are excluded from the cost of the asset. An example of a self-constructed asset is when a building company builds its own head office.

2.7.2 Exchanges of assets

IAS 16 specifies that exchanges of items of property, plant and equipment, regardless of whether the assets are similar, are measured at **fair value, unless the exchange transaction lacks commercial substance** or the fair value of neither of the assets exchanged can be **measured reliably**. If the acquired item is not measured at fair value, its cost is measured at the carrying amount of the asset given up.

2.7.3 Subsequent expenditure

Expenditure incurred in replacing or renewing a component of an item of property, plant and equipment must be **recognised in the carrying amount of the item**. The carrying amount of the replaced or renewed component must be derecognised. If part of an item of property, plant and equipment is depreciated separately, when it is replaced, the new part is treated as an acquisition and the replaced part is treated like a disposal.

A similar approach is also applied when an item of property, plant and equipment, such as an aircraft, has to undergo a major inspection to enable the continued use of the item, regardless of whether parts of the item are replaced. When each major inspection is performed, its cost is recognised in the carrying amount of the item of property, plant and equipment as a replacement (eg to the previous inspection) if the recognition criteria are met. Any remaining carrying amount of the previous inspection is derecognised. This occurs regardless of whether the cost of the previous inspection was identified in the transaction in which the item was acquired or constructed.

2.8 Measurement subsequent to initial recognition

The standard offers two possible treatments here, essentially a choice between keeping an asset recorded at **cost** or revaluing it to **fair value**.

(a)   **Cost model.** Carry the asset at its cost less accumulated depreciation and any accumulated impairment losses.

(b)   **Revaluation model.** Carry the asset at a revalued amount, being its fair value at the date of the revaluation less any subsequent accumulated depreciation and subsequent accumulated impairment losses. The revised IAS 16 makes clear that the **revaluation model is available only if the fair value of the item can be measured reliably**. Revaluations are considered below.

2.9 Impairment of asset values

An **impairment loss** should be treated in the same way as a **revaluation decrease** (ie the decrease should be **recognised as an expense**). However, a revaluation decrease (or impairment loss) should be charged directly against any related revaluation surplus to the extent that the decrease does not exceed the amount held in the revaluation surplus in respect of that same asset.

A **reversal of an impairment** loss should be treated in the same way as a **revaluation increase**, ie a revaluation increase should be recognised as income to the extent that it reverses a revaluation decrease or an impairment loss of the same asset previously recognised as an expense.

2.10 Retirements and disposals

When an asset is permanently **withdrawn from use, or sold or scrapped**, and no future economic benefits are expected from its disposal, it should be withdrawn from the statement of financial position.

Gains or losses are the difference between the net disposal proceeds and the carrying amount of the asset. They should be recognised as income or expense in profit or loss. This applies also to **revalued assets**.

2.11 Derecognition   5/10, 5/11

An entity is required to **derecognise the carrying amount** of an item of property, plant or equipment that it disposes of on the date the **criteria for the sale of goods** in IAS 18 *Revenue* would be met. This also applies to parts of an asset.

An entity cannot classify as revenue a gain it realises on the disposal of an item of property, plant and equipment.

2.12 Revaluations   5/10, 5/11

The **market value** of land and buildings usually represents fair value, assuming existing use and line of business. Such valuations are usually carried out by professionally qualified valuers.

In the case of **plant and equipment**, fair value can also be taken as **market value**. Where a market value is not available, however, depreciated replacement cost should be used. There may be no market value where types of plant and equipment are sold only rarely or because of their specialised nature (ie they would normally only be sold as part of an ongoing business).

The frequency of valuation depends on the **volatility of the fair values** of individual items of property, plant and equipment. The more volatile the fair value, the more frequently revaluations should be carried out. Where the current fair value is very different from the carrying value then a revaluation should be carried out.

Most importantly, when an item of property, plant and equipment is revalued, **the whole class of assets to which it belongs should be revalued.** A class is a grouping of assets of a similar nature, for example, land, buildings, motor vehicles etc.

All the items within a class should be **revalued at the same time**, to prevent selective revaluation of certain assets and to avoid disclosing a mixture of costs and values from different dates in the financial statements. A rolling basis of revaluation is allowed if the revaluations are kept up to date and the revaluation of the whole class is completed in a short period of time.

2.12.1 Accounting entries for a revaluation

When an asset is revalued, the double entry to account for it is:

DEBIT   Property, plant and equipment (statement of financial position)

CREDIT   Revaluation surplus (statement of financial position)

The revaluation surplus is part of owners' equity and so the credit to the revaluation surplus will be seen as **'other comprehensive income'** in the statement of comprehensive income. If the revaluation is reversing a previous decrease in value that was recognised as an expense, the increase in value should first be recognised as income up the value that was previously recognised as an expense, any excess is then taken to the revaluation surplus.

Example: Revaluation surplus

Binkie Co has an item of land carried in its books at $13,000. Two years ago a slump in land values led the company to reduce the carrying value from $15,000. This was taken as an expense in the income statement. There has been a surge in land prices in the current year, however, and the land is now worth $20,000.

Required

Account for the revaluation in the current year.

Solution

The double entry is:

DEBIT	Asset value (statement of financial position)	$7,000	
CREDIT	Income statement		$2,000
	Revaluation surplus		$5,000

Note: **the credit to the revaluation surplus will be shown under 'other comprehensive income'.**

The case is similar for a **decrease in value** on revaluation. Any decrease should be recognised as an expense, except where it offsets a previous increase taken as a revaluation surplus in owners' equity. Any decrease greater than the previous upwards increase in value must be taken as an expense in the profit or loss.

Example: Revaluation decrease

Let us simply swap round the example given above. The original cost was $15,000, revalued upwards to $20,000 two years ago. The value has now fallen to $13,000.

Required

Account for the decrease in value.

Solution

The double entry is:

DEBIT	Revaluation surplus	$5,000	
DEBIT	Income statement	$2,000	
CREDIT	Asset value (statement of financial position)		$7,000

There is a further complication when a **revalued asset is being depreciated**. As we have seen, an upward revaluation means that the depreciation charge will increase. Normally, a revaluation surplus is only realised when the asset is sold, but when it is being depreciated, part of that surplus is being realised as the asset is used. The amount of the surplus realised is the difference between depreciation charged on the revalued amount and the (lower) depreciation which would have been charged on the asset's original cost. **This amount can be transferred to retained (ie realised) earnings** as a direct transfer between reserves. It should *not* be put through the income statement.

Example: Revaluation and depreciation

Crinckle Co bought an asset for $10,000 at the beginning of 20X6. It had a useful life of five years. On 1 January 20X8 the asset was revalued to $12,000. The expected useful life has remained unchanged (ie three years remain).

Required

Account for the revaluation and state the treatment for depreciation from 20X8 onwards.

Solution

On 1 January 20X8 the carrying value of the asset is $10,000 – (2 × $10,000 ÷ 5) = $6,000. For the revaluation:

DEBIT	Asset value	$6,000	
CREDIT	Revaluation surplus		$6,000

The depreciation for the next three years will be $12,000 ÷ 3 = $4,000, compared to depreciation on cost of $10,000 ÷ 5 = $2,000. So each year, the extra $2,000 can be treated as part of the surplus which has become realised:

DEBIT	Revaluation surplus	$2,000	
CREDIT	Retained earnings		$2,000

This is a movement on owners' equity only, not an item in the income statement.

Exam skills

The transfer of excess depreciation to retained earnings is optional. Do not do this unless the question tells you to.

2.12.2 Tax effect of revaluations

The tax effect of revaluations must be recognised and disclosed in accordance with IAS 12 *Income taxes*. An increase in the value of property, plant and equipment resulting from a revaluation will usually increase the deferred tax balance associated with it. This increase in the deferred tax balance should be included in the same section of the statement of comprehensive income as the revaluation itself, ie through the other comprehensive income section.

2.12.3 Disposal of revalued items

When a revalued item is disposed of, the gain or loss on disposal is calculated as the sales proceeds less the carrying value of the asset at the date of disposal. This amount is recognised in profit or loss. The revaluation surplus associated with the asset that has been disposed of is transferred directly to retained earnings. This transfer will be seen in the statement of changes in equity.

Example: Revaluation and disposal

Dartford Inc bought an asset for $50,000 at the beginning of 20X3. It had a useful life of five years. On 1 January 20X4 the asset was revalued to $60,000, the useful life remained the same (ie 4 years remaining). On 31 December 20X4, the asset was sold for £63,000. (Note: Dartford does not transfer the excess depreciation to retained earnings.)

Required

Account for the disposal of the asset and show the double entries required.

Solution

On 1 January 20X4 the carrying value of the asset is $50,000 – ($50,000 ÷ 5) = $40,000

For the revaluation:

DEBIT	Asset cost ($60,000 – $50,000)	$10,000	
DEBIT	Accumulated depreciation	$10,000	
CREDIT	Revaluation surplus		$20,000

At 31 December 20X4, the carrying value of the asset is $60,000 – ($60,000 ÷ 4) = £45,000

The gain on disposal is therefore $63,000 - $45,000 = $18,000

To account for the disposal:

DEBIT	Cash	$63,000	
DEBIT	Accumulated depreciation	$15,000	
CREDIT	Asset value		$60,000
CREDIT	Gain on sale (income statement)		$18,000

To remove the associated revaluation surplus:

DEBIT	Revaluation surplus	$20,000	
CREDIT	Retained earnings		£20,000

This is a movement on owners' equity only, not an item in the income statement.

2.13 Disclosure

The standard has a long list of disclosure requirements, for each class of property, plant and equipment.

(a)   **Measurement bases** for determining the gross carrying amount (if more than one, the gross carrying amount for that basis in each category)

(b)   **Depreciation methods** used

(c)   **Useful lives** or depreciation rates used

(d)   **Gross carrying amount** and accumulated depreciation (aggregated with accumulated impairment losses) at the beginning and end of the period

(e)   **Reconciliation** of the carrying amount at the beginning and end of the period showing:

   (i)   Additions
   (ii)   Disposals and assets classified as 'held for sale' in accordance with IFRS 5
   (iii)   Acquisitions through business combinations
   (iv)   Increases/decreases during the period from revaluations and from impairment losses
   (v)   Impairment losses recognised in profit or loss
   (vi)   Impairment losses reversed in profit or loss
   (vii)   Depreciation

The financial statements should also disclose the following.

(a)   Existence and amounts of **restrictions on title**, and items pledged as security for liabilities

(b)   Amount of commitments to **acquisitions**

Revalued assets require further disclosures.

(a)   Basis used to revalue the assets

(b)   Effective date of the revaluation

(c)   Whether an independent valuer was involved

(d)   Carrying amount of each class of property, plant and equipment that would have been included in the financial statements had the assets not been revalued.

(e)   Revaluation surplus.

The following format (with notional figures) is commonly used to disclose non-current asset movements.

	Total $	Land and buildings $	Plant and equipment $
Cost or valuation			
At 1 January 20X4	50,000	40,000	10,000
Revaluation surplus	12,000	12,000	–
Additions in year	4,000	–	4,000
Disposals in year	(1,000)	–	(1,000)
At 31 December 20X4	65,000	52,000	13,000
Depreciation			
At 1 January 20X4	16,000	10,000	6,000
Charge for year	4,000	1,000	3,000
Eliminated on disposals	(500)	–	(500)
At 31 December 20X4	19,500	11,000	8,500
Carrying value			
At 31 December 20X4	45,500	41,000	4,500
At 1 January 20X4	34,000	30,000	4,000

Exam alert

You could be asked to produce a disclosure note for non-current assets in an exam question.

Question 6.4   IAS 16

Learning outcome C2(a)

(a)   In a statement of financial position prepared in accordance with IAS 16, what does carrying amount or NBV represent?

(b)   In a set of financial statements prepared in accordance with IAS 16, is it correct to say that the carrying value figure in a statement of financial position cannot be greater than the market (net realisable) value of the partially used asset as at the end of the reporting period? Explain your reasons for your answer.

Section summary

IAS 16 *Property, plant and equipment* provides the basic rules on **depreciation** including important definitions of depreciation, depreciable assets, useful life and depreciable amount.

When a non-current asset is **revalued**, depreciation is charged on the revalued amount.

When a non-current asset is **sold**, there is likely to be a profit or loss on disposal. This is the difference between the net sale price of the asset and its carrying value at the time of disposal.

3   IAS 36 *Impairment of assets*

Introduction

There is an established principle that assets should not be carried at above their recoverable amount. An entity should write down the carrying value of an asset to its recoverable amount if the carrying value of an asset is not recoverable in full. IAS 36 was published in June 1998 and was revised in March 2004. It puts in place a detailed methodology for carrying out impairment reviews and related accounting treatments and disclosures. We will look at the standard in this section.

3.1 Scope

IAS 36 applies to all tangible, intangible and financial assets except inventories, assets arising from construction contracts, deferred tax assets, assets arising under IAS 19 *Employee benefits* and financial assets within the scope of IAS 32 *Financial instruments, disclosure and presentation*. This is because those IASs already have rules for recognising and measuring impairment. Note also that IAS 36 does not apply to non-current assets held for sale, which are dealt with under IFRS 5 *Non-current assets held for sale and discontinued operations*.

KEY TERM

IMPAIRMENT: a fall in the value of an asset, so that its 'recoverable amount' is now less than its carrying value in the statement of financial position.   *(IAS 36)*

The basic principle underlying IAS 36 is relatively straightforward. If an asset's value in the accounts is higher than its realistic value, measured as its 'recoverable amount', the asset is judged to have suffered an impairment loss. It should therefore be reduced in value, by the amount of the **impairment loss**. The amount of the impairment loss should be **written off against profit** immediately (unless the asset has been revalued in which case the loss is treated as a revaluation decrease).

The main accounting issues to consider are therefore as follows.

(a)   How is it possible to **identify when** an impairment loss may have occurred?

(b)   How should the **recoverable amount** of the asset be measured?

(c)   How should an 'impairment loss' be **reported in the accounts**?

3.2 Identifying a potentially impaired asset

An entity should assess at the end of each reporting period whether there are any indications of impairment to any assets. The concept of **materiality** applies, and only material impairment needs to be identified.

If there are indications of possible impairment, the entity is required to make a formal estimate of the **recoverable amount** of the assets concerned.

IAS 36 suggests how **indications of a possible impairment** of assets might be recognised. The suggestions are based largely on common sense.

(a)   **External sources of information**

    (i)   A fall in the asset's market value that is significantly more than would normally be expected from passage of time or normal use.

    (ii)   Significant adverse changes in the technological, market, economic or legal environment in which the entity operates.

    (iii)   An increase in market interest rates or other market rates of return on investments likely to affect the discount rate used in calculating value in use.

    (iv)   The carrying amount of the entity's net assets being more than its market capitalisation.

(b)   **Internal sources of information**: evidence of obsolescence or physical damage, adverse changes in the use to which the asset is put, or the asset's economic performance

Even if there are no indications of impairment, the following assets must **always** be tested for impairment annually.

(a)   An intangible asset with an **indefinite useful life**

(b)   **Goodwill** acquired in a business combination

3.3 Measuring the recoverable amount of the asset

What is an asset's recoverable amount?

KEY TERM

The RECOVERABLE AMOUNT of an asset should be measured as the *higher value* of:

(a)   the asset's fair value less costs to sell; and

(b)   its value in use.   *(IAS 36)*

An asset's fair value less costs to sell is the amount net of selling costs that could be obtained from the sale of the asset. Selling costs include sales transaction costs, such as legal expenses.

(a)   If there is **an active market** in the asset, the net selling price should be based on the **market value**, or on the price of recent transactions in similar assets.

(b)   If there is **no active market** in the assets it might be possible to **estimate** a net selling price using best estimates of what 'knowledgeable, willing parties' might pay in an arm's length transaction.

Net selling price **cannot** be reduced, however, by including within selling costs any **restructuring or reorganisation expenses**, or any costs that have already been recognised in the accounts as liabilities.

The concept of **'value in use'** is very important.

KEY TERM

The VALUE IN USE of an asset is measured as the present value of future cash flows expected to be derived from an asset or cash-generating unit.

The cash flows used in the calculation should be **pre-tax cash flows** and a **pre-tax discount rate** should be applied to calculate the present value.

The calculation of **value in use** must reflect the following.

(a)   An estimate of the **future cash flows** the entity expects to derive from the asset
(b)   Expectations about **possible variations** in the amount and timing of future cash flows
(c)   The **time value of money**
(d)   The price for bearing the **uncertainty** inherent in the asset, and
(e)   **Other factors** that would be reflected in pricing future cash flows from the asset

Calculating a value in use therefore calls for estimates of future cash flows, and the possibility exists that an entity might come up with **over-optimistic estimates** of cash flows. The IAS therefore states the following.

(a)   Cash flow projections should be based on **'reasonable and supportable' assumptions**.

(b)   Projections of cash flows, normally up to a maximum period of five years, should be based on the most **recent budgets or financial forecasts**.

(c)   Cash flow projections beyond this period should be obtained by extrapolating short-term projections, using either a **steady or declining growth rate** for each subsequent year (unless a rising growth rate can be justified). The long term growth rate applied should not exceed the average long term growth rate for the product, market, industry or country, unless a higher growth rate can be justified.

3.4 Recognition and measurement of an impairment loss

The rule for **assets at historical cost** is:

KEY POINT

If the **recoverable amount** of an asset is **lower than the carrying amount,** the carrying amount should be **reduced** by the difference (ie the impairment loss) which should be charged as an **expense** in profit or loss.

The rule for **assets held at a revalued amount** (such as property revalued under IAS 16) is:

KEY POINT

The impairment loss is to be treated as a revaluation decrease under the relevant IAS.

In practice this means:

•   To the extent that there is a revaluation surplus held in respect of the asset, the impairment loss should be charged to revaluation surplus.

•   Any excess should be charged to profit or loss.

The IAS goes into quite a large amount of detail about the important concept of **cash-generating units**. As a basic rule, the recoverable amount of an asset should be calculated for the **asset individually**. However, there will be occasions when it is not possible to estimate such a value for an individual asset, particularly in the calculation of value in use. This is because cash inflows and outflows cannot be attributed to the individual asset.

KEY TERM

A CASH-GENERATING UNIT is the smallest identifiable group of assets for which independent cash flows can be identified and measured.

Question 6.5   Cash-generating unit

Learning outcome C2(a)

Can you think of some examples of how a cash-generating unit would be identified?

Example: Recoverable amount and carrying amount

Fourways Co is made up of four cash-generating units. All four units are being tested for impairment.

(a)   Property, plant and equipment and separate intangibles would be allocated to the cash-generating units as far as possible.

(b)   Current assets such as inventories, receivables and prepayments would be allocated to the relevant cash-generating units.

(c)   Liabilities (eg payables) would be deducted from the net assets of the relevant cash-generating units.

(d)   The net figure for each cash-generating unit resulting from this exercise would be compared to the relevant recoverable amount, computed on the same basis.

3.5 Goodwill and the impairment of assets

Goodwill acquired in a business combination (covered in chapter 7) does not generate cash flows independently of other assets. It must be **allocated** to each of the acquirer's **cash-generating units** (or groups of cash-generating units) that are expected to benefit from the synergies of the combination.

A cash-generating unit to which goodwill has been allocated is tested for impairment annually. The **carrying amount** of the unit, including goodwill, is **compared with the recoverable amount**. If the carrying amount of the unit exceeds the recoverable amount, the entity must recognise an impairment loss.

The annual impairment test may be performed at any time during an accounting period, but must be performed at the **same time every year**.

3.6 Corporate assets

Corporate assets are group or divisional assets such as a head office building, computer equipment or a research centre. Essentially, corporate assets are assets that do not generate cash inflows independently from other assets, hence their carrying amount cannot be fully attributed to a cash-generating unit under review.

In testing a cash-generating unit for impairment, an entity should identify all the corporate assets that relate to the cash-generating unit. Corporate assets will need to be allocated to cash-generating units on a reasonable and consistent basis.

3.7 Accounting treatment of an impairment loss

An impairment loss has occurred if the recoverable amount of an asset is less than its carrying amount in the statement of financial position. This loss should be **recognised immediately**:

(a)   The asset's **carrying amount** should be reduced to its recoverable amount in the statement of financial position.

(b)   The **impairment loss** should be recognised immediately in profit or loss (unless the asset has been revalued in which case the loss is treated as a revaluation decrease).

After reducing an asset to its recoverable amount, the **depreciation charge** on the asset should then be based on its new carrying amount, its estimated residual value (if any) and its estimated remaining useful life.

An impairment loss should be recognised for a **cash-generating unit** if (and only if) the recoverable amount for the cash-generating unit is less than the carrying amount in the statement of financial position for all the assets in the unit. When an impairment loss is recognised for a cash-generating unit, the loss should be allocated between the assets in the unit in the following order.

(a)   First, to the **goodwill** allocated to the cash-generating unit
(b)   Then to all other assets in the cash-generating unit, on a **pro rata basis**

In allocating an impairment loss, the carrying amount of an asset should not be reduced below the highest of:

(a)   Its fair value less costs to sell
(b)   Its value in use (if determinable)
(c)   Zero

Any remaining amount of an impairment loss should be recognised as a liability if required by other IASs.

Example: Impairment loss I

A company that extracts natural gas and oil has a drilling platform in the Caspian Sea. It is required by legislation of the country concerned to remove and dismantle the platform at the end of its useful life. Accordingly, the company has included an amount in its accounts for removal and dismantling costs, and is depreciating this amount over the platform's expected life.

The company is carrying out an exercise to establish whether there has been an impairment of the platform.

(a)   Its carrying amount in the statement of financial position is $3m.

(b)   The company has received an offer of $2.8m for the platform from another oil company. The bidder would take over the responsibility (and costs) for dismantling and removing the platform at the end of its life.

(c)   The present value of the estimated cash flows from the platform's continued use is $3.3m.

(d)   The carrying amount in the statement of financial position for the provision for dismantling and removal is currently $0.6m.

What should be the value of the drilling platform in the statement of financial position, and what, if anything, is the impairment loss?

Solution

Fair value less costs to sell   = $2.8m

Value in use   = PV of cash flows from use less the carrying amount of the
                                     provision/liability = $3.3m – $0.6m = $2.7m

Recoverable amount   = Higher of these two amounts, ie $2.8m

Carrying value   = $3m

Impairment loss   = $0.2m

The carrying value should be reduced to $2.8m

Example: Impairment loss II

A company has acquired another business for $4.5m: tangible assets are valued at $4.0m and goodwill at $0.5m.

An asset with a carrying value of $1m is destroyed in a terrorist attack. The asset was not insured. The loss of the asset, without insurance, has prompted the company to estimate whether there has been an impairment of assets in the acquired business and what the amount of any such loss is. The recoverable amount of the business (a single cash-generating unit) is measured as $3.1m.

Solution

There has been an impairment loss of $1.4m ($4.5m – $3.1m).

The impairment loss will be recognised in profit or loss. The loss will be allocated between the assets in the cash-generating unit as follows.

(a)   A loss of $1m can be attributed directly to the uninsured asset that has been destroyed.
(b)   The remaining loss of $0.4m should be allocated to goodwill.

The carrying value of the assets will now be $3m for tangible assets and $0.1m for goodwill.

3.8 Disclosure

IAS 36 calls for substantial disclosure about impairment of assets. The information to be disclosed includes the following.

(a)   For each class of assets, the amount of **impairment losses recognised** and the amount of any **impairment losses recovered** (ie reversals of impairment losses)

(b)   For each individual asset or cash-generating unit that has suffered a **significant impairment loss**, details of the nature of the asset, the amount of the loss, the events that led to recognition of the loss, whether the recoverable amount is fair value price less costs to sell or value in use, and if the recoverable amount is value in use, the basis on which this value was estimated (eg the discount rate applied)

Section summary

The main aspects of IAS 36 to consider are:

* Indications of impairment of assets
* Measuring recoverable amount, as net selling price or value in use
* Measuring value in use
* Cash-generating units
* Accounting treatment of an impairment loss, for individual assets and cash-generating units

4   IAS 23 *Borrowing costs*

Introduction

IAS 23 looks at the treatment of borrowing costs, particularly where the related borrowings are applied to the construction of certain assets. These are what are usually called 'self-constructed assets', where an entity builds its own inventory or non-current assets over a substantial period of time.

4.1 Definitions

Only two definitions are given by the standard:

KEY TERMS

BORROWING COSTS. Interest and other costs incurred by an entity in connection with the borrowing of funds.

QUALIFYING ASSET. An asset that necessarily takes a substantial period of time to get ready for its intended use or sale.

(IAS 23)

4.2 Capitalisation

IAS 23 requires that all eligible borrowing costs must be **capitalised**. Eligible borrowing costs are those borrowing costs which are directly attributable to the acquisition, construction or production of a qualifying asset. These are the borrowing costs that **would have been avoided** had the expenditure on the qualifying asset not been made.

4.2.1 Interest rate

Where specific borrowings have been used to finance the acquisition, construction or production of an asset, it is straightforward to work out the borrowing costs eligible for capitalisation. The interest rate applicable will be that associated with the specific borrowings.

Once the relevant borrowings which relate to a specific asset are identified, then the **amount of borrowing costs available for capitalisation** will be the actual borrowing costs incurred on those borrowings during the period, *less* any investment income on the temporary investment of those borrowings. It would not be unusual for some or all of the funds to be invested before they are actually used on the qualifying asset.

Example: Borrowing costs

On 1 January 20X6 Stremans Co borrowed $1.5m to finance the production of two assets, both of which were expected to take a year to build. Work started during 20X6. The loan facility was drawn down and incurred on 1 January 20X6, and was utilised as follows, with the remaining funds invested temporarily.

	Asset A	Asset B
	$'000	$'000
1 January 20X6	250	500
1 July 20X6	250	500

The loan rate was 9% and Stremans Co can invest surplus funds at 7%.

Required

Calculate the borrowing costs which may be capitalised for each of the assets and consequently the cost of each asset as at 31 December 20X6.

Solution

	Asset A $	Asset B $
Borrowing costs		
To 31 December 20X6 ($500,000/$1,000,000 × 9%)	45,000	90,000
Less investment income		
To 30 June 20X6 ($250,000/$500,000 × 7% × 6/12)	(8,750)	(17,500)
	36,250	72,500
Cost of assets		
Expenditure incurred	500,000	1,000,000
Borrowing costs	36,250	72,500
	536,250	1,072,500

Where no specific borrowings have been used, but the entity has used its general borrowings to finance an asset, the entity must work out an interest rate at which borrowing costs can be capitalised. This is known as the **capitalisation rate** and is calculated as the weighted average of the entity's borrowing costs in the period. This capitalisation rate is applied to the expenditure on the asset to calculate the borrowings costs that can be capitalised.

4.2.2 Period of capitalisation

Three events or transactions must be taking place for capitalisation of borrowing costs to be started.

(a) Expenditure on the asset is being incurred
(b) Borrowing costs are being incurred
(c) Activities are in progress that are necessary to prepare the asset for its intended use or sale

If active development is **interrupted for any extended periods,** capitalisation of borrowing costs should be suspended for those periods. Once substantially all the activities necessary to prepare the qualifying asset for its intended use or sale are complete, then capitalisation of borrowing costs should cease.

Question 6.6 — Borrowing costs

Learning outcomes C2(a)

Acruni Co had the following loans in place at the beginning and end of 20X6.

	1 January 20X6 $m	31 December 20X6 $m
10% Bank loan repayable 20X8	120	120
9.5% Bank loan repayable 20X9	80	80
8.9% debenture repayable 20X7	–	150

The 8.9% debenture was issued to fund the construction of a qualifying asset (a piece of mining equipment), construction of which began on 1 July 20X6.

On 1 January 20X6, Acruni Co began construction of a qualifying asset, a piece of machinery for a hydro-electric plant, using existing borrowings. Expenditure drawn down for the construction was: $30m on 1 January 20X6, $20m on 1 October 20X6.

Required

Calculate the borrowing costs that can be capitalised for the hydro-electric plant machine.

4.2.3 Disclosure

The following should be disclosed in the financial statements in relation to borrowing costs.

(a)   Amount of borrowing costs capitalised during the period
(b)   Capitalisation rate used to determine the amount of borrowing costs eligible for capitalisation

Section summary

IAS 23 looks at the treatment of borrowing costs, particularly where the related borrowings are applied to the **construction of certain assets.**

5 Available-for-sale financial assets

Introduction

This section looks very briefly at available-for-sale financial assets.

5.1 Available-for-sale financial assets

The non-current asset section of the statement of financial position includes a category for **available-for-sale financial assets**. These are investments in equity and other shares in other entities, as categorised by IAS 39.

This designation does not mean that they are held for the purpose of selling them. It simply means that they are available for sale. They are carried at fair value, which will probably be open market value.

Any increase in the value of these assets should go to the **revaluation surplus** in the statement of financial position. The gain will also be shown as **'other comprehensive income'** in the statement of comprehensive income as a **'gain on available-for-sale financial assets'**.

Exam alert

In your exam, you are most likely to encounter available-for-sale financial assets as a small part of a section C question. The examiner may call them 'available-for-sale investments'.

Section summary

Available-for-sale financial assets are carried at fair value in the statement of financial position.

Chapter Roundup

✓   The cost of a non-current asset, less its estimated residual value, is allocated fairly between accounting periods by means of depreciation. The provision for depreciation is both:

- Charged against profit
- Deducted from the value of the non-current asset in the statement of financial position.

✓   IAS 16 Property, plant and equipment provides the basic rules on depreciation, including important definitions of depreciation, depreciable assets, useful life and depreciable amount.

✓   When a non-current asset is revalued, depreciation is charged on the revalued amount.

✓   When a non-current asset is sold, there is likely to be a profit or loss on disposal. This is the difference between the net sale price of the asset and its carrying value at the time of disposal.

✓   The main aspects of IAS 36 to consider are:

- Indications of impairment of assets
- Measuring recoverable amount, as net selling price or value in use
- Measuring value in use
- Cash-generating unit
- Accounting treatment of an impairment loss, for individual assets and cash-generating units

✓   IAS 23 looks at the treatment of borrowing costs, particularly where the related borrowings are applied to the construction of certain assets.

✓   Available-for-sale financial assets are carried at fair value in the statement of financial position.

Quick Quiz

1   Define depreciation.

2   Which of the following elements can be included in the production cost of a non-current asset?

A   Purchase price
B   Architect's fees
C   Import duties
D   Installation costs

3   Market value can usually be taken as fair value. True or false?

4   Define impairment.

5   Any increase in the value of available for-sale financial assets should go to the .... surplus.

Answers to Quick Quiz

1   The result of the systematic allocation of the depreciable amount of an asset over its useful life.
2   All of them.
3   True
4   A fall in value of an asset, so that its 'recoverable amount' is less than its carrying value.
5   Revaluation

Answers to Questions

6.1 Depreciation I

(a) Under the straight line method, depreciation for each of the five years is:

$$\text{Annual depreciation} = \frac{\$(17,000 - 2,000)}{5} = \$3,000$$

(b) Under the reducing balance method, depreciation for each of the five years is:

Year	Depreciation	
1	35% × $17,000	= $5,950
2	35% × ($17,000 − $5,950) = 35% × $11,050	= $3,868
3	35% × ($11,050 − $3,868) = 35% × $7,182	= $2,514
4	35% × ($7,182 − $2,514) = 35% × $4,668	= $1,634
5	Balance to bring book value down to $2,000 = $4,668 − $1,634 − $2,000	= $1,034

(c) Under the machine hour method, depreciation for each of the five years is calculated as follows.

Total usage (days) = 200 + 100 + 100 + 150 + 40 = 590 days

$$\text{Depreciation per day} = \frac{\$(17,000 - 2,000)}{590} = \$25.42$$

Year	Usage (days)	Depreciation ($) (days × $25.42)
1	200	5,084.00
2	100	2,542.00
3	100	2,542.00
4	150	3,813.00
5	40	1,016.80
		14,997.80

Note. The answer does not come to exactly $15,000 because of the rounding carried out at the 'depreciation per day' stage of the calculation.

6.2 Depreciation II

(a) The accounts of a business try to recognise that the cost of a non-current asset is gradually consumed as the asset wears out. This is done by gradually writing off the asset's cost to profit or loss over several accounting periods. This process is known as depreciation, and is an example of the accruals assumption. IAS 16 *Property, plant and equipment* requires that depreciation should be allocated on a systematic basis to each accounting period during the useful life of the asset.

With regard to the accrual principle, it is fair that the profits should be reduced by the depreciation charge; this is not an arbitrary exercise. Depreciation is not, as is sometimes supposed, an attempt to set aside funds to purchase new non-current assets when required. Depreciation is not generally provided on freehold land because it does not 'wear out' (unless it is held for mining etc).

(b) The reducing balance method of depreciation is used instead of the straight line method when it is considered fair to allocate a greater proportion of the total depreciable amount to the earlier years and a lower proportion to the later years on the assumption that the benefits obtained by the business from using the asset decline over time.

In favour of this method it may be argued that it links the depreciation charge to the costs of maintaining and running the asset. In the early years these costs are low and the depreciation charge is high, while in later years this is reversed.

6.3 Depreciation III

MACHINERY ACCOUNT

20X7		$	20X7		$
1 Jan	Balance b/f	30,000	31 Mar	Disposal of machinery account	15,000
			1 Dec	Disposal of machinery account	15,000
		30,000			30,000

ACCUMULATED DEPRECIATION OF MACHINERY

20X7		$	20X7		$
31 Mar	Disposal of machinery account*	6,750	1 Jan	Balance b/f	12,000
1 Dec	Disposal of machinery account**	8,750	31 Dec	Income statement***	3,500
		15,500			15,500

*   Depreciation at date of disposal = $6,000 + $750

**   Depreciation at date of disposal = $6,000 + $2,750

***   Depreciation charge for the year = $750 + $2,750

DISPOSAL OF MACHINERY

20X7		$	20X7		$
31 Mar	Machinery account	15,000	31 Mar	Account receivable (sale price)	8,000
1 Dec	Machinery account	15,000	31 Mar	Provision for depreciation	6,750
			1 Dec	Cash (sale price)	2,500
			1 Dec	Provision for depreciation	8,750
			31 Dec	Income statement (loss on disposal)	4,000
		30,000			30,000

You should be able to calculate that there was a loss on the first disposal of $250, and on the second disposal of $3,750, giving a total loss of $4,000.

Workings

1   At 1 January 20X7, accumulated depreciation on the machines will be:

2 machines × 2 years × $\dfrac{\$15,000}{5}$ per machine pa = $12,000, or $6,000 per machine

2   Monthly depreciation is $\dfrac{\$3,000}{12}$ = $250 per machine per month

3   The machines are disposed of in 20X7.

(a)   On 31 March – after 3 months of the year. Depreciation for the year on the machine = 3 months × $250 = $750.

(b)   On 1 December – after 11 months of the year. Depreciation for the year on the machine = 11 months × $250 = $2,750

6.4 IAS 16

(a) In simple terms the carrying value of an asset is the cost of an asset less the 'accumulated depreciation', that is all depreciation charged so far. It should be emphasised that the main purpose of charging depreciation is to ensure that profits are fairly reported. Thus depreciation is concerned with the statement of comprehensive income rather than the statement of financial position. In consequence the carrying value in the statement of financial position can be quite arbitrary. In particular, it does not necessarily bear any relation to the market value of an asset and is of little use for planning and decision making.

An obvious example of the disparity between carrying value and market value is found in the case of buildings, which may be worth considerably more than their carrying value.

(b) Carrying value can in some circumstances be higher than market value (net realisable value). IAS 16 *Property, plant and equipment* states that the carrying value of an asset cannot be greater than its 'recoverable amount'. However 'recoverable amount' as defined in IAS 16 is the amount recoverable from further use. This may be higher than the market value.

This makes sense if you think of a specialised machine which could not fetch much on the secondhand market but which will produce goods which can be sold at a profit for many years.

6.5 Cash-generating unit

Here are two possibilities.

(a) A mining company owns a private railway that it uses to transport output from one of its mines. The railway now has no market value other than as scrap, and it is impossible to identify any separate cash inflows with the use of the railway itself. Consequently, if the mining company suspects an impairment in the value of the railway, it should treat the mine as a whole as a cash-generating unit, and measure the recoverable amount of the mine as a whole.

(b) A bus company has an arrangement with a town's authorities to run a bus service on four routes in the town. Separately identifiable assets are allocated to each of the bus routes, and cash inflows and outflows can be attributed to each individual route. Three routes are running at a profit and one is running at a loss. The bus company suspects that there is an impairment of assets on the loss-making route. However, the company will be unable to close the loss-making route, because it is under an obligation to operate all four routes, as part of its contract with the local authority. Consequently, the company should treat all four bus routes together as a cash-generating unit, and calculate the recoverable amount for the unit as a whole.

6.6 Borrowing costs

Capitalisation rate $\quad$ = weighted average rate = $(10\% \times \dfrac{120}{120+80}) + (9.5\% \times \dfrac{80}{120+80}) = 9.8\%$

Borrowing costs $\quad$ = ($30m × 9.8%) + ($20m × 9.8% × 3/12)

$\qquad\qquad\quad$ = $3.43m

Now try this question from the Exam Question Bank	Number	Level	Marks	Time
	Q17	Examination	5	9 mins

INTANGIBLE NON-CURRENT ASSETS

We begin our examination of intangible non-current assets with a discussion of a revised IAS on the subject **(IAS 38)**.

Goodwill and its treatment is a controversial area, as is the accounting for items similar to goodwill, such as brands. Goodwill is very important in **group accounts** which we will cover later in this text.

In Section 3 we look in more detail at the IAS 38 provisions covering research and development.

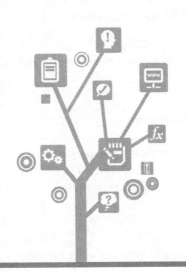

topic list	learning outcomes	syllabus references	ability required
1 IAS 38 *Intangible assets*	C2(a)	C2(iv)	application
2 Goodwill	C2(a)	C2(iv)	application
3 Research and development	C2(a)	C2(iii)	application

1   IAS 38 *Intangible assets*

Introduction

This section covers IAS 38 *Intangible assets* which was originally published in September 1998. It has been revised to reflect changes introduced by IFRS 3 *Business combinations*.

1.1 The objectives of the standard

(a)   To establish the criteria for when intangible assets may or should be **recognised**
(b)   To specify how intangible assets should be **measured**
(c)   To specify the **disclosure requirements** for intangible assets

It applies to all intangible assets with certain **exceptions**: deferred tax assets (IAS 12), leases that fall within the scope of IAS 17, financial assets, insurance contracts, assets arising from employee benefits (IAS 19), non-current assets held for sale and mineral rights and exploration and extraction costs for minerals etc (although intangible assets used to develop or maintain these rights are covered by the standard). It does *not* apply to goodwill acquired in a business combination, which is dealt with under IFRS 3 *Business combinations.*

1.2 Definition of an intangible asset

The definition of an intangible asset is a key aspect of the standard, because the rules for deciding whether or not an intangible asset may be **recognised** in the accounts of an entity are based on the definition of what an intangible asset is.

KEY TERM

An INTANGIBLE ASSET is an **identifiable** non-monetary asset without physical substance. The asset must be:

(a)   **Controlled** by the entity as a result of events in the past, and
(b)   Something from which the entity expects **future economic benefits** to flow.

Examples of items that might be considered as intangible assets include computer software, patents, copyrights, motion picture films, customer lists, franchises and fishing rights. IAS 38 gives a significant amount of guidance on the definition of an intangible asset. This is covered in the sections below.

1.2.1 Intangible asset: must be identifiable

An intangible asset must be identifiable in order to distinguish it from goodwill. With non-physical items, there may be a problem with '**identifiability**'.

(a)   If an intangible asset is **acquired separately through purchase**, there may be a transfer of a legal right that would help to make an asset identifiable.

(b)   An intangible asset may be identifiable if it is **separable**, ie if it could be rented or sold separately. However, 'separability' is not an essential feature of an intangible asset.

1.2.2 Intangible asset: must be controlled by the entity

Another element of the definition of an intangible asset is that it must be under the control of the entity as a result of a past event. The entity must therefore be able to enjoy the future economic benefits from the asset, and prevent the access of others to those benefits. A **legally enforceable right** is evidence of such control, but is not always a *necessary* condition.

(a)   Control over **technical knowledge or know-how** only exists if it is protected by a **legal right**.

(b)   The skill of employees, arising out of the benefits of **training costs**, is most unlikely to be recognisable as an intangible asset, because an entity does not control the future actions of its staff.

(c)   Similarly, **market share and customer loyalty** cannot normally be intangible assets, since an entity cannot control the actions of its customers.

1.2.3 Intangible asset: expected future economic benefits

An item can only be recognised as an intangible asset if economic benefits are expected to flow in the future from ownership of the asset. Economic benefits may come from the **sale** of products or services, or from a **reduction in expenditures** (cost savings).

1.3 Recognition of intangible assets

Intangible assets can be **internally generated** or can be **purchased**, either separately or as part of a business combination.

An item should be recognised as an intangible asset if it **fully meets the definition** in IAS 38 and if:

(a)   It is **probable** that the **future economic benefits** that are attributable to the asset will **flow to the entity, and**

(b)   The **cost of the asset can be measured reliably**.

Management has to exercise its judgement in assessing the degree of certainty attached to the flow of economic benefits to the entity. External evidence is best.

1.3.1 Purchased intangible assets

How the cost of an intangible asset is measured depends on whether it was purchased or internally generated.

If an intangible asset is **purchased separately**, its cost can usually be measured reliably as its purchase price (including incidental costs of purchase such as legal fees, and any costs incurred in getting the asset ready for use).

When an intangible asset is acquired as **part of a business combination** (ie an acquisition or takeover), the cost of the intangible asset is its **fair value** at the date of the acquisition. **Quoted market prices** in an active market provide the most reliable estimate of the fair value. If no active market exists for an intangible asset, its fair value is the amount that the entity would have paid for the asset, at the acquisition date, in an arm's length transaction between knowledgeable and willing parties, on the basis of the best information available. In determining this amount, an entity should consider the outcome of recent transactions for similar assets. There are techniques for estimating the fair values of unique intangible assets (such as brand names) and these may be used to measure an intangible asset acquired in a business combination.

IFRS 3 *Business combinations* explains that when the fair value of intangible assets acquired in business combinations can be measured reliably, they should be **recognised separately** from goodwill.

In accordance with IAS 20, intangible assets acquired by way of government grant and the grant itself may be recorded initially either at cost (which may be zero) or fair value.

1.3.2 Internally generated intangible assets

It can be difficult to determine whether an internally generated intangible asset meets the IAS 38 recognition criteria. For example, in some cases, the cost of an internally generated intangible asset is difficult to distinguish from the cost of running day-to-day operations.

Therefore IAS 38 provides additional guidance for the recognition of internally generated intangible assets by classifying the generation of the asset into a **research phase** or a **development phase**.

1.3.3 Internally generated goodwill

IAS 38 does **not permit the recognition** of **internally generated goodwill** as its cost cannot be reliably measured.

1.4 Other expenditure

All expenditure related to an intangible asset which does not meet the criteria for recognition either as an identifiable intangible asset or as goodwill arising on an acquisition should be **expensed as incurred**. The IAS gives examples of such expenditure.

- Start up costs
- Training costs

- Advertising costs
- Business relocation costs

Prepaid costs for services, for example advertising or marketing costs for campaigns that have been prepared but not launched, can still be recognised as a **prepayment**.

If tangible asset costs have been expensed in previous financial statements, they may not be recognised as part of the cost of an asset in the future.

1.5 Measurement of intangible assets subsequent to initial recognition

IAS 38 allows two methods of measurement for intangible assets after they have been first recognised.

(a)   The **cost model** or **'amortised cost'**: an intangible asset should be **carried at its cost**, less any accumulated depreciation and less any accumulated impairment losses. Expenditure on an intangible asset subsequent to initial recognition rarely meets the definition of an intangible asset in IAS 38 and is usually expensed.

(b)   The **revaluation model** allows an intangible asset to be carried at a revalued amount, which is its **fair value** at the date of revaluation, less any subsequent accumulated amortisation and any subsequent accumulated impairment losses. Note that:

(i)   The fair value must be able to be measured reliably with reference to an **active market** in that type of asset.

(ii)   The **entire class** of intangible assets of that type must be revalued at the same time (to prevent selective revaluations).

(iii)   If an intangible asset in a class of revalued intangible assets cannot be revalued because there is **no active market** for this asset, the asset should be carried at its **cost less any accumulated amortisation and impairment losses**.

(iv)   Revaluations should be made with such **regularity** that the carrying amount does not differ from that which would be determined using fair value at the end of the reporting period.

KEY POINT

This treatment is **not** available for the **initial recognition** of intangible assets. This is because the cost of the asset must be reliably measured.

The guidelines state that there **will not usually be an active market** in an intangible asset; therefore the revaluation model will usually not be available. For example, although copyrights, publishing rights and film rights can be sold, each has a unique sale value. In such cases, revaluation to fair value would be inappropriate. A fair value might be obtainable however for assets such as fishing rights or quotas or taxi cab licences.

Where an intangible asset is revalued upwards to a fair value, the amount of the revaluation should be credited directly to equity under the heading of a **revaluation surplus**. The increase will be shown as a gain in other comprehensive income in the statement of comprehensive income.

However, if a revaluation surplus is a **reversal of a revaluation decrease** that was previously charged against income, the increase can be recognised as income in profit or loss for the year.

Where the carrying amount of an intangible asset is revalued downwards, the amount of the **downward revaluation** should be charged as an expense against income, unless the asset has previously been revalued upwards. A revaluation decrease should be first charged against any previous revaluation surplus in respect of that asset.

Question 7.1	Revaluation

Learning outcome C2(a)

An intangible asset is measured by a company at fair value. The asset was revalued by $400 in 20X3, and there is a revaluation surplus of $400 in the statement of financial position. At the end of 20X4, the asset is valued again, and a downward valuation of $500 is required.

Required

State the accounting treatment for the downward revaluation.

When the revaluation model is used, and an intangible asset is revalued upwards, the cumulative revaluation **surplus may be transferred to retained earnings** when the surplus is eventually realised. The surplus would be realised when the asset is disposed of. However, the surplus may also be realised over time as the **asset is used** by the entity. The amount of the surplus realised each year is the difference between the amortisation charge for the asset based on the revalued amount of the asset, and the amortisation that would be charged on the basis of the asset's historical cost. The realised surplus in such cases should be transferred from revaluation surplus directly to retained earnings, and should not be taken through profit or loss.

1.6 Useful life

An entity should **assess** the useful life of an intangible asset, which may be **finite or indefinite**. An intangible asset has an indefinite useful life when there is **no foreseeable limit** to the period over which the asset is expected to generate net cash inflows for the entity.

Many factors are considered in determining the useful life of an intangible asset, including: expected usage; typical product life cycles; technical, technological, commercial or other types of obsolescence; the stability of the industry; expected actions by competitors; the level of maintenance expenditure required; and legal or similar limits on the use of the asset, such as the expiry dates of related leases. Computer software and many other intangible assets normally have short lives because they are susceptible to technological obsolescence. However, uncertainty does not justify choosing a life that is unrealistically short.

The useful life of an intangible asset that arises from **contractual or other legal rights** should not exceed the period of the rights, but may be shorter depending on the period over which the entity expects to use the asset.

1.7 Amortisation period and amortisation method

An intangible asset with a finite useful life should be amortised over its **expected useful life**.

(a)   Amortisation should start when the asset is **available for use**.

(b)   Amortisation should cease at the earlier of the date that the asset is classified **as held for sale** in accordance with IFRS 5 *Non-current assets held for sale and discontinued operations* and the date that the asset is **derecognised**.

(c)   The amortisation method used should reflect the **pattern in which the asset's future economic benefits are consumed**. If such a pattern cannot be predicted reliably, the straight line method should be used.

(d)   The amortisation charge for each period should normally be recognised **in profit or loss**.

The **residual value** of an intangible asset with a finite useful life is **assumed to be zero** unless a third party is committed to buying the intangible asset at the end of its useful life or unless there is an active market for that type of asset (so that its expected residual value can be measured) and it is probable that there will be a market for the asset at the end of its useful life.

The useful life and the amortisation method used for an intangible asset with a finite useful life should be **reviewed at each financial year-end**. Any changes to useful life or amortisation method should be accounted for as a **change in accounting estimate** in accordance with IAS 8.

1.8 Intangible assets with indefinite useful lives

An intangible asset with an indefinite useful life **should not be amortised**. IAS 36 *Impairment of assets* requires that such an asset is tested for impairment at least annually.

The useful life of an intangible asset that is not being amortised should be **reviewed each year** to determine whether it is still appropriate to assess its useful life as indefinite. Reassessing the useful life of an intangible asset as finite rather than indefinite is an indicator that the asset may be impaired and therefore it should be tested for impairment.

Question 7.2	Useful life

Learning outcome C2(a)

It may be difficult to establish the useful life of an intangible asset, and judgement will be needed. Consider how to determine the useful life of a *purchased* brand name.

1.9 Disposals/retirements of intangible assets

An intangible asset should be eliminated from the statement of financial position when it is disposed of or when there is no further expected economic benefit from its future use. On disposal the gain or loss arising from the **difference between the net disposal proceeds and the carrying amount** of the asset should be taken to profit or loss as a gain or loss on disposal (ie treated as income or expense).

1.10 Disclosure requirements

The standard has fairly extensive disclosure requirements for intangible assets. The financial statements should disclose the **accounting policies** for intangible assets that have been adopted.

For **each class of intangible assets**, disclosure is required of the following.

*   The **method of amortisation** used

*   The **useful life** of the assets or the amortisation rate used

*   The **gross carrying amount**, the **accumulated amortisation** and the **accumulated impairment losses** as at the beginning and the end of the period

- A **reconciliation of the carrying amount** as at the beginning and at the end of the period (additions, retirements/disposals, revaluations, impairment losses, impairment losses reversed, amortisation charge for the period, net exchange differences, other movements)

- The carrying amount of **internally-generated intangible assets**

The financial statements should also disclose the following.

- In the case of intangible assets that are assessed as having an indefinite useful life, the carrying amounts and the reasons supporting that assessment

- For intangible assets acquired by way of a **government grant** and initially recognised at fair value, the **fair value initially recognised**, the **carrying amount**, and the accounting treatment for subsequent remeasurements

- The carrying amount, nature and remaining amortisation period of any intangible asset that is **material to the financial statements of the entity as a whole**

- The existence (if any) and amounts of intangible assets whose **title is restricted** and of intangible assets that have been **pledged as security** for liabilities

- The amount of any **commitments for the future acquisition of intangible assets**

Where intangible assets are accounted for at revalued amounts, disclosure is required of the following.

- The **effective date of the revaluation** (by class of intangible assets)

- The **carrying amount** of revalued intangible assets

- The carrying amount that would have been shown (by class of assets) **if the cost model had been used**, and the amount of amortisation that would have been charged

- The amount of any **revaluation surplus** on intangible assets, as at the beginning and end of the period, and movements in the surplus during the year (and any restrictions on the distribution of the balance to shareholders)

- The methods and significant assumptions applied in estimating fair values.

The financial statements should also disclose the amount of research and development expenditure that has been charged as an expense of the period.

Section summary

- An intangible asset should be recognised if, and only if, it is probable that future economic benefits will flow to the entity and the cost of the asset can be measured reliably.

- An asset is initially recognised at cost and subsequently carried either at cost or revalued amount.

- Costs that do not meet the recognition criteria should be expensed as incurred.

- An intangible asset with a finite useful life should be amortised over its useful life. An intangible asset with an indefinite useful life should not be amortised.

2 Goodwill

Introduction

This section looks at both internally generated and purchased goodwill.

2.1 Internally generated goodwill

Goodwill is **created by good relationships** between a business and its customers.

(a)   By building up a **reputation** (by word of mouth perhaps) for high quality products or high standards of service

(b)   By **responding promptly and helpfully** to queries and complaints from customers

(c)   Through the **personality of the staff** and their attitudes to customers

The value of goodwill to a business might be **extremely significant**. However, **internally generated goodwill** is *not* included in the accounts of a business at all, and we should not expect to find an amount for internally generated goodwill in the company's statement of financial position.

KEY POINT

Internally generated goodwill may **not** be recognised as an asset.

IAS 38 deliberately precludes the recognition of internally generated goodwill because it is not an identifiable resource with a cost that is capable of being reliably measured. Therefore any costs associated with generating goodwill in this way are recognised as an expense as they are incurred in the statement of comprehensive income.

On reflection, we might agree with this omission of internally generated goodwill from the accounts of a business:

(a)   The goodwill is **inherent** in the business but it has not been paid for, and it does not have an 'objective' value. We can guess at what such goodwill is worth, but such guesswork would be a matter of individual opinion, and not based on hard facts.

(b)   Goodwill **changes** from day to day. One act of bad customer relations might damage goodwill and one act of good relations might improve it. Staff with a favourable personality might retire or leave to find another job, to be replaced by staff who need time to find their feet in the job, etc. Since goodwill is continually changing in value, it cannot realistically be recorded in the accounts of the business.

2.2 Purchased goodwill

When an entity purchases another entity, it may generally pay more than the sum total of the assets and liabilities in the entity's financial statements. This is because it expects to generate future economic benefits from the acquisition which are over and above the price paid. The excess amount paid represents the **goodwill** inherent in the business and is known as **purchased goodwill**.

2.2.1 IFRS 3 *Business combinations*

The treatment of purchased goodwill in a business combination is dealt with by IFRS 3 *Business combinations*.

(a)   IFRS 3 defines goodwill as 'an asset representing the future economic benefits arising from other assets acquired in a business combination that are not individually identified and separately recognised'.

(b)   Goodwill is calculated as the difference between the **purchase consideration** and the **fair value** of the identifiable assets and liabilities acquired.

As a result of this calculation, purchased goodwill can therefore be **positive** or **negative**.

Positive goodwill is recognised as an intangible non-current asset in the statement of financial position. After recognition, positive goodwill is measured **at the original amount less any accumulated impairment losses**. It is **not amortised**. Instead it is tested for impairment at least annually, in accordance with IAS 36 *Impairment of assets*.

Negative goodwill acquired in a business combination in effect means that the buyer has got a '**bargain purchase**' as they have paid less for the entity than the fair value of its identifiable assets and liabilities. Negative goodwill could be thought of as a discount on the purchase price. As this is unusual, IFRS 3 requires that the purchaser checks to make sure that the acquired assets and liabilities are correctly identified and valued and that goodwill calculation is correct. Negative goodwill should be **credited to profit or loss** in the year of acquisition.

Goodwill acquired in a business combination is an important part of group accounting which is covered later in this Study Text.

Section summary

If a business has **goodwill**, it means that the value of the business as a going concern is greater than the value of its identifiable net assets. The valuation of goodwill is extremely subjective and fluctuates constantly. For this reason internally generated goodwill is **not** shown as an asset in the statement of financial position.

Purchased positive goodwill arising on a business combination is recognised as an intangible asset under the requirements of **IFRS 3**. It must then be reviewed for impairment annually.

Purchased negative goodwill is credited to profit or loss in the year of acquisition.

3   Research and development

Introduction

As we saw above, it can be difficult to determine whether an internally generated intangible asset meets the IAS 38 recognition criteria. IAS 38 provides additional guidance on when these assets should be recognised by classifying the generation of the asset into a research phase or a development phase. This guidance will be the focus of this section.

3.1 Definitions

The following definitions are given by IAS 38.

KEY TERMS

RESEARCH is original and planned investigation undertaken with the prospect of gaining new scientific or technical knowledge and understanding.

DEVELOPMENT is the application of research findings or other knowledge to a plan or design for the production of new or substantially improved materials, devices, products, processes, systems or services prior to the commencement of commercial production or use.

Although we will concentrate on costs incurred in research and development as defined above, IAS 38 broadens the application to include costs incurred in a **research phase** or **development phase** of an **internal project.**

3.2 Research phase

KEY POINT

Research costs cannot be recognised as an intangible asset and must be **charged to profit or loss** in the year they are incurred.

Research costs by definition do not meet the criteria for recognition under IAS 38. This is because, at the research stage of a project, it cannot be certain that probable future economic benefits will flow to the entity from the project. There is too much uncertainty about the likely success or otherwise of the project. Research costs that have been recognised as an expense cannot be subsequently recognised as an asset in a later period.

Examples of research activities include:

- Activities aimed at obtaining new knowledge
- The search for applications of research findings or other knowledge
- The search for product or process alternatives
- The formulation and design of possible new or improved product or process alternatives.

3.3 Development phase   5/10

Development activities tend to be much further advanced than the research stage. Where the entity can demonstrate that it is probable that future economic benefits will flow to the entity from the project, the entity may be able to recognise an intangible asset.

Development activities include:

- The design, construction and testing of pre-production prototypes and models

- The design of tools, jigs, moulds and dies involving new technology

- The design, construction and operation of a pilot plant that is not of a scale economically feasible for commercial production

- The design, construction and testing of a chosen alternative for new/improved materials.

3.3.1 Recognition of development costs as an intangible asset

Development expenditure must be recognised as an intangible asset (sometimes called 'deferred development expenditure') if, and only if, the business can demonstrate **all** of the criteria in IAS 38 have been met.

Exam skills

The recognition criteria can be summarised by the mnemonic **PIRATE** which makes it easier to learn for your exam.

The recognition criteria are as follows.

The entity must demonstrate:

- **P** – how the intangible asset will generate **Probable** future economic benefits. (This is demonstrated by the existence of an external market or by how the asset will be useful to the business if it is to be used internally.)

- **I** – its **Intention** to complete the intangible asset and use or sell it

- **R** – the availability of adequate technical, financial and other **Resources** to complete the development and to use or sell the intangible asset

- **A** – its **Ability** to use or sell the intangible asset

- **T** – the **Technical** feasibility of completing the intangible asset so that it will be available for use or sale

- **E** – its ability to measure reliably the **Expenditure** attributable to the intangible asset during its development.

Exam alert

You should memorise these criteria as they are very likely to be examined.

The development costs of a project recognised as an intangible asset should not exceed the amount that it is probable will be **recovered from related future economic benefits**, after deducting further development costs, related production costs, and selling and administrative costs directly incurred in marketing the product.

IAS 38 **prohibits** the recognition of **internally generated brands, mastheads, publishing titles and customer lists** and similar items as intangible assets. These all fail to meet one or more (in some cases all) of the definition and recognition criteria and in some cases are probably indistinguishable from internally generated goodwill.

3.4 Cost of an internally generated intangible asset

The costs allocated to an internally generated intangible asset should be only costs that can be **directly attributed** or allocated on a reasonable and consistent basis to creating, producing or preparing the asset for its intended use. IAS 38 lists the following which may form part of the cost of an intangible asset:

(a) **Salaries, wages** and other employment related costs of personnel arising from the generation of the intangible asset

(b) Costs of **materials and services** consumed in generating the intangible asset

(c) **Overhead costs** that were incurred to generate the intangible asset, such as the depreciation of property, plant and equipment

(d) **Other direct costs**, such as the amortisation of patents and licences that are used to generate the intangible asset or fees to register a legal right.

Interest may also be included as an element of cost. IAS 23 *Borrowing costs* specifies criteria for this.

IAS 38 specifically **excludes** the following costs from being recognised as part of the cost:

(a) **Selling** and **administrative** costs
(b) Costs to train staff to operate the asset.

The cost of an internally generated intangible asset is the sum of the permitted **expenditure incurred from the date when** the intangible asset **first meets the recognition criteria**. If, as often happens, considerable costs have already been recognised as expenses before management could demonstrate that the criteria have been met, this earlier expenditure should not be retrospectively recognised at a later date as part of the cost of an intangible asset.

| Question 7.3 | Intangible asset |

Learning outcome C2(a)

Doug Co is developing a new production process. During 20X3, expenditure incurred was $100,000, of which $90,000 was incurred before 1 December 20X3 and $10,000 between 1 December 20X3 and 31 December 20X3. Doug Co can demonstrate that, at 1 December 20X3, the production process met the criteria for recognition as an intangible asset. The recoverable amount of the know-how embodied in the process is estimated to be $50,000.

How should the expenditure be treated?

3.5 Amortisation of development costs   11/10, 5/11

Once capitalised as an intangible asset, development costs must be **amortised** and recognised as an expense to match the costs with the related revenue or cost savings. This must be done on a systematic basis, so as to reflect the pattern in which the related economic benefits are recognised.

It is unlikely to be possible to **match exactly** the economic benefits obtained with the costs which are held as an asset simply because of the nature of development activities. The entity should consider either:

(a)　　the revenue or other benefits from the sale/use of the product/process; *or*

(b)　　the period of time over which the product/process is expected to be sold/used.

KEY POINT

If the pattern cannot be determined reliably, the straight-line method should be used.

The amortisation will begin when the **asset is available for use**.

3.6 Impairment of development costs　　　　　　　　　　　　5/11

As with all assets, impairment is a possibility, but perhaps even more so in cases such as this. Impairments of intangible assets are covered by IAS 36 *Impairment of assets*. The development costs should be **written down** to the extent that the unamortised balance (taken together with further development costs, related production costs, and selling and administrative costs directly incurred in marketing the product) is no longer probable of being recovered from the expected future economic benefit.

3.7 Disclosure

For **each class of intangible assets** (including development costs), IAS 38 requires the following disclosures.

* The **method of amortisation** used

* The **useful life** of the assets or the amortisation rate used

* The **gross carrying amount**, the **accumulated amortisation** and the **accumulated impairment losses** as at the beginning and the end of the period

* A **reconciliation of the carrying amount** as at the beginning and at the end of the period (additions, retirements/disposals, revaluations, impairment losses, impairment losses reversed, amortisation charge for the period, net exchange differences, other movements)

* The carrying amount of **internally-generated intangible assets**

Question 7.4	Research and development I

Learning outcome C2(a)

Y Co is a research company which specialises in developing new materials and manufacturing processes for the furniture industry. The company receives payments from a variety of manufacturers, which pay for the right to use the company's patented fabrics and processes.

Research and development costs for the year ended 30 September 20X5 can be analysed as follows.

　　　　　　　　　　　　　　　　　　　　　　　　　　　　　　　　　　$

Project A　　　　　　　　　　　　　　　　　　　　　　　　　280,000

New flame-proof padding. Expected to cost a total of $400,000 to complete development. Expected total revenue $2,000,000 once work completed - probably late 20X6. Customers already placed advanced orders for the material after seeing demonstrations of its capabilities earlier in the year.

Project B　　　　　　　　　　　　　　　　　　　　　　　　　150,000

New colour-fast dye. Expected to cost a total of $3,000,000 to complete. The dye is being developed as a cheaper replacement for a dye already used in Y Co's most successful product, cost savings of over $10,000,000 are expected from its use. Although Y has demonstrated that the dye is a viable product, and has the intention to finish developing it, the completion date is currently uncertain because external funding will have to be obtained before the development work can be completed.

Project C   110,000

Investigation of new adhesive recently developed in aerospace industry. If this proves
effective then Y Co may well generate significant income because it will be used in place
of existing adhesives.

Explain how the three research projects A, B and C will be dealt with in Y Co's statement of
comprehensive income and statement of financial position.

In each case, explain your proposed treatment in terms of IAS 38 *Intangible assets*.

Question 7.5   Research and development II

Learning outcome C2(a)

Y Co had the following balances relating to deferred development expenditure at 30 September 20X4:

	$
Deferred development expenditure (cost)	1,250,000
Amortisation	(125,000)
Carrying value at 30 September 20X4	1,125,000

The existing deferred development expenditure is being amortised over 10 years on a straight line basis.

Show how these balances and the research and development costs in the previous question will be
disclosed in the accounts of Y Co at 30 September 20X5.

Show extracts from the:

(a)   Income statement
(b)   Statement of financial position
(c)   Notes to the financial statements

Section summary

If the criteria laid down by IAS 38 are satisfied, development costs should be capitalised as an intangible
asset. They are then amortised, beginning from the time when the development project is available for
use.

Chapter Roundup

✓ An intangible asset should be recognised if, and only if, it is probable that future economic benefits will flow to the entity and the cost of the asset can be measured reliably.

✓ An asset is initially recognised at cost and subsequently carried either at cost or revalued amount.

✓ Costs that do not meet the recognition criteria should be expensed as incurred.

✓ An intangible asset with a finite useful life should be amortised over its useful life. An intangible asset with an indefinite useful life should not be amortised.

✓ If a business has goodwill, it means that the value of the business as a going concern is greater than the value of its identifiable net assets. The valuation of goodwill is extremely subjective and fluctuates constantly. For this reason internally generated goodwill is not shown as an asset in the statement of financial position.

✓ Purchased positive goodwill arising on a business contribution is recognised as an intangible asset under the requirements of IFRS 3. It must then be reviewed for impairment annually.

✓ Purchased negative goodwill is credited to profit or loss in the year of acquisition.

✓ If the criteria laid down by IAS 38 are satisfied, development costs may be capitalised as an intangible asset. They are then amortised, beginning from the time when the development project is available for use.

Quick Quiz

1 Intangible assets can only be recognised in a company's accounts if:

- It is probable that .... will flow to the entity
- The cost can be ....

2 What are the criteria which must be met before development expenditure can be recognised as an intangible asset?

3 Research costs must be expensed. True or false?

4 How is goodwill calculated under IFRS 3?

5 The following statements relate to intangible assets.

    1 An intangible asset should be amortised on a systematic basis over the asset's useful life.

    2 Internally generated goodwill may be carried in the statement of financial position if the value can be determined with reasonable certainty.

    3 Internally generated brands can never be recognised as intangible assets.

    Which of the above statements are consistent with IAS 38 *Intangible Assets*?

    A   1 and 2 only
    B   1 and 3 only
    C   2 only
    D   3 only

Answers to Quick Quiz

1   Future economic benefits. Measured reliably.

2   **PIRATE** criteria:

Probable economic benefits will be generated by the intangible asset

Intention to complete the intangible asset and use or sell it

Resources (technical, financial) adequate to complete the development and to use or sell

Ability to use or sell the intangible asset

Technical feasibility of completing the intangible asset

Expenditure can be measured reliably.

3   True

4   Goodwill is calculated as the difference between the purchase consideration and the fair value of the identifiable assets and liabilities acquired

5   B   Internally generated goodwill can not be recognised as an intangible asset as its cost cannot be reliably measured.

Answers to Questions

7.1 Revaluation

In this example, the downward valuation of $500 can first be set against the revaluation surplus of $400. The revaluation surplus will be reduced to nil and a charge of $100 made as an expense in 20X4.

7.2 Useful life

Factors to consider would include the following.

(a)   Legal protection of the brand name and the control of the entity over the (illegal) use by others of the brand name (ie control over pirating)

(b)   Age of the brand name

(c)   Status or position of the brand in its particular market

(d)   Ability of the management of the entity to manage the brand name and to measure activities that support the brand name (eg advertising and PR activities)

(e)   Stability and geographical spread of the market in which the branded products are sold

(f)   Pattern of benefits that the brand name is expected to generate over time

(g)   Intention of the entity to use and promote the brand name over time (as evidenced perhaps by a business plan in which there will be substantial expenditure to promote the brand name)

7.3 Intangible asset

At the end of 20X3, the production process is recognised as an intangible asset at a cost of $10,000. This is the expenditure incurred since the date when the recognition criteria were met, that is 1 December 20X3. The $90,000 expenditure incurred before 1 December 20X3 is expensed, because the recognition criteria were not met. It will never form part of the cost of the production process recognised in the statement of financial position.

7.4 Research and development I

Project A

This project meets the criteria in IAS 38 for development expenditure to be recognised as an asset. These are as follows.

(a)   **P** – how the intangible asset will generate **probable** future economic benefits: Customers have already placed advanced orders for the final product after development

(b)   **I** – its **intention** to complete the intangible asset and use to sell it: Y Co intends to finish development of the product by late 20X6 and then sell the right to use it to customers

(c)   **R** – the availability of adequate technical, financial and other **resources** to complete the development and to use or sell the intangible asset: Adequate resources to exist, the project seems to be in the late stages of development

(d)   **A** – its **ability** to use or sell the intangible asset: Customers have already placed advanced orders for the final product, so Y Co's ability to use the asset is clear

(e)   **T** – the **technical** feasibility of completing the intangible asset so that it will be available for use or sale: the capabilities of the product were demonstrated to customers, so the technical feasibility is assured

(f)   **E** – its ability to measure reliably the **expenditure** attributable to the intangible asset during its development: Y Co has a reliable estimation of costs to date and to complete.

Hence the costs of $280,000 incurred to date should be capitalised as an intangible asset in the statement of financial position. Once the material is ready for use, the intangible asset should be amortised over its useful life.

Project B

This project meets most of the criteria discussed above which would enable the costs to be carried forward, however, it fails on the availability of adequate resources to complete the project. As such, the costs cannot be capitalised and should be expensed to the income account.

Once funding is obtained the situation can then be reassessed and future costs may be capitalised.

Project C

This is a research project according to IAS 38, ie original and planned investigation undertaken with the prospect of gaining new scientific or technical knowledge or understanding.

There is no certainty as to its ultimate success or commercial viability and therefore it cannot be considered to be a development project. IAS 38 therefore requires that costs be written off as incurred.

7.5 Research and development II

(a)   INCOME STATEMENT (EXTRACT)

	$
Research expenditure (Project C)	110,000
Development costs (Project B)	150,000
Amortisation of capitalised development costs	125,000

(b)   STATEMENT OF FINANCIAL POSITION (EXTRACT)

	$
Non-current assets	
Intangible assets – deferred development expenditure (1,125 – 125 + 280)	1,280,000

(c)   NOTE TO THE FINANCIAL STATEMENTS

Note X - *Deferred development costs*

	$
Cost	
Balance b/f	1,250,000
Additions during year (Project A)	280,000
Balance c/f	1,530,000
Amortisation	
Balance b/f	125,000
Charge during year	125,000
Balance c/f	250,000
Carrying value at 30 September 20X5	1,280,000
Carrying value at 30 September 20X4	1,125,000

Now try this question from the Exam Question Bank	Number	Level	Marks	Time
	Q18	Examination	5	9 mins

IAS 17: LEASES

This is an **important practical** subject. Leasing transactions are extremely common, especially in recent years where there has been considerable growth in leasing agreements, for example **hire purchase agreements** in the UK. IAS 17 *Leases* standardises the accounting treatment and disclosure of assets held under lease.

In this chapter we look at the characteristics of operating and finance leases according to IAS 17, and how to account for both of these in the lessees' financial statements.

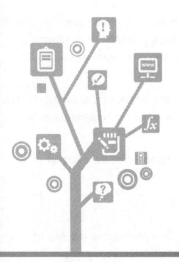

topic list	learning outcomes	syllabus references	ability required
1 Characteristics of leases	C2(a)	C2(xi)	comprehension
2 Accounting for leases	C2(a)	C2(xi)	application

1 Characteristics of leases

Introduction

This section examines the characteristics of operating and finance leases according to IAS 17, and how to distinguish between them.

1.1 The need for IAS 17

Before the introduction of IAS 17, there was widespread abuse in the use of lease accounting by companies. These companies 'owned' an asset and 'owed' a debt for its purchase, but showed neither the asset nor the liability on the statement of financial position because the lease agreement for the asset was made to look like a rental agreement. The substance of the transaction was in fact for the purchase of an asset on credit.

This is called 'off-balance sheet financing' and was used by companies to make their financial statements look better by reducing the level of borrowing shown on the statement of financial position.

IAS 17 was introduced to combat the abuse of lease accounting in this way by basing the accounting treatment of a leasing arrangement on the **substance of the transaction rather than its strict legal form**.

IAS 17 was issued in December 1997 and revised in December 2003.

1.2 What is a lease?

Where goods are acquired other than on immediate cash terms, arrangements have to be made in respect of the future payments on those goods. In the simplest case of **credit sales**, the purchaser is allowed a period of time (say one month) to settle the outstanding amount and the normal accounting procedure in respect of receivables/payables will be adopted.

In a leasing transaction there is a **contract** between the lessor and the lessee for the hire of an asset. The lessor retains legal ownership but conveys to the lessee the right to use the asset for an agreed period of time in return for specified rentals.

In this chapter the **user** of an asset will often be referred to simply as the **lessee**, and the **supplier** as the **lessor**.

IAS 17 defines a lease and recognises two types.

KEY TERMS

LEASE. An agreement whereby the lessor conveys to the lessee in return for a payment or a series of payments the **right to use an asset** for an agreed period of time.

FINANCE LEASE. A lease that transfers substantially all the **risks and rewards** incident to ownership of an asset. Title may or may not eventually be transferred.

OPERATING LEASE. A lease other than a finance lease.   *(IAS 17)*

1.3 Operating leases

Operating leases do not really pose an accounting problem. The lessee pays amounts periodically to the lessor and these are **charged to the income statement**. The lessor treats the leased asset as a non-current asset and depreciates it in the normal way. Rentals received from the lessee are credited to the income statement in the lessor's books.

1.4 Finance leases

For assets held under **finance leases** the accounting treatment described above for operating leases would not disclose the reality of the situation. If a **lessor** leases out an asset on a finance lease, the asset will probably never be seen on the lessor's premises or used in his business again. It would be inappropriate for a lessor to record such an asset as a non-current asset. In reality, what the lessor owns is a **stream of cash flows receivable** from the lessee. **The asset is an amount receivable rather than a non-current asset.**

Similarly, a **lessee** may use a finance lease to fund the 'acquisition' of a major asset which he will then use in his business perhaps for many years. **The substance of the transaction is that the lessee has acquired a non-current asset**, and this is reflected in the accounting treatment prescribed by IAS 17, even though in law the lessee never becomes the owner of the asset.

1.4.1 Characteristics of a finance lease

A **finance lease** is a lease that transfers substantially all the **risks and rewards** of ownership of an asset to the lessee. Deciding whether a lease is an operating lease or a finance lease requires judgment and can often be complex. The lease arrangement as a whole needs to be looked at to determine who has the significant risks and rewards associated with owning the asset.

IAS 17 gives examples of situations that individually or in combination would normally lead to a lease being classified as a finance lease:

(a)   At the inception of the lease the **present value of the minimum lease payments** amounts to at least substantially all of the **fair value** of the **leased asset.** The present value should be calculated by using the **interest rate implicit in the lease.**

(b)   The **lease term** is for the major part of the **economic life** of the asset even if title is not transferred to the lessee.

(c)   The lease **transfers ownership** of the asset to the lessee by the end of the lease term.

(d)   The lease includes an **option** for the lessee **to purchase** the asset at a price **sufficiently below fair value** and it is reasonably certain at the inception of the lease that the lessee will exercise the option.

(e)   The leased assets are so **specialised** that only the lessee can use them without major modifications.

IAS 17 also gives additional indicators of situations that could lead to a lease being classified as a finance lease:

- If the lessee can cancel the lease, he must bear any losses suffered by the lessor associated with the cancellation

- The lessee has the ability to continue the lease for a secondary period at a rent that is substantially lower than market rent

- Gains or losses due to fluctuation in the fair value of the residual value of the asset accrue to the lessee

There are some key definitions in IAS 17 that are relevant.

KEY TERMS

MINIMUM LEASE PAYMENTS. The payments over the lease term that the lessee is required to make.

INTEREST RATE IMPLICIT IN THE LEASE

The discount rate that, at the inception of the lease, causes the aggregate present value of the:

(a)   Minimum lease payments
(b)   Unguaranteed residual value

To be equal to the sum of:

(a)   The fair value of the leased asset

(b)   Any initial direct costs of the lessor

LEASE TERM. The non-cancellable period for which the lessee has contracted to lease the asset together with any further terms for which the lessee has the option to continue to lease the asset, with or without further payment, when at the inception of the lease it is reasonably certain that the lessee will exercise the option.

ECONOMIC LIFE is either the:

(a)   Period over which an asset is expected to be economically usable by one or more users, or

(b)   Number of production or similar units expected to be obtained from the asset by one or more users.

USEFUL LIFE is the estimated remaining period, from the beginning of the lease term over which the economic benefits embodied in the asset are expected to be consumed by the entity.

Exam skills

In your exam, you may be required to comment or decide on whether a lease is an operating lease or a finance lease. You should use the characteristics given in IAS 17 to assess the lease and work out what the accounting treatment should be.

1.4.2 Leases of land and buildings

Under IAS 17 the land and buildings elements of a lease of land and buildings are **considered separately** for the purposes of lease classification. A lease of land is normally treated as an operating lease, unless title is expected to pass at the end of the lease term. A lease of buildings will be treated as a finance lease if it satisfies the requirements for a finance lease given above. The minimum lease payments are allocated between the land and buildings elements in proportion to the relative fair values of the leasehold interests in the land and the buildings. If the value of the land is immaterial, classification will be according to the buildings.

If payments cannot be reliably allocated, the entire lease is classified as a finance lease, unless both elements are operating leases, in which case the entire lease is classified as an operating lease.

Section summary

Under IAS 17, a lease of assets can either be a **finance lease** or an **operating lease.**

A finance lease is a lease that transfers substantially all the **risks and rewards** of ownership to the lessee.

An operating lease is a lease other than a finance lease.

IAS 17 gives examples of situations that indicate that an agreement is a finance lease.

Leases of land are usually classified as operating leases.

2 Accounting for leases

Introduction

This section explains the accounting treatment of a lease in the books of the lessee.

Exam skills

You are not required to know the accounting treatment of a lease in the books of the lessor as CIMA has stated that this is not in the syllabus for F1.

2.1 Accounting for operating leases

The accounting treatment for an operating lease in the books of the lessee is straightforward.

KEY POINT

Operating lease payments are treated as an **expense** of the entity and should be **charged to profit or loss** on a systematic (normally **straight line**) basis over the lease term.

2.1.1 Operating lease incentives   5/10

Where the lessee is offered an incentive such as a **rent-free period** or **cashback incentive**, this is effectively a **discount**, which will be spread over the period of the operating lease in accordance with the accruals principle. For instance, if a company entered into a 4-year operating lease but was not required to make any payments until year 2, the total payments to be made over years 2-4 should be charged evenly over years 1-4.

Where a cashback incentive is received, the total amount payable over the lease term, less the cashback, should be charged evenly over the term of the lease. This can be done by crediting the cashback received to deferred income and releasing it to profit or loss over the lease term.

2.1.2 Operating lease disclosures

IAS 17 requires the following disclosures by lessees in respect of **operating leases**.

The total of future minimum lease payments under non-cancellable operating leases for each of the following periods:

* Not later than one year
* Later than one year and not later than five years
* Later than five years

This disclosure note is required because, although operating leases do not give rise to a liability on the statement of financial position, they are non-cancellable and so they do entail a future financial commitment, which should be disclosed.

IAS 17 also requires a general description of the entity's significant lease arrangements and the amount of lease payments recognised as an expense in the period.

2.2 Accounting for finance leases   5/11

IAS 17 requires that, when an asset changes hands under a **finance lease, lessor and lessee should account for the transaction as though it were a credit sale.** In the lessee's books therefore:

DEBIT   Property, plant and equipment   *to capitalise the asset*
CREDIT   Finance lease liability   *to recognise the lease liability*

The amount to be recorded in this way is the **lower of** the **fair value of the leased asset** and the **present value of the minimum lease payments**. This will generally be the purchase price of the asset. The result of this double entry is that the lessee has recognised a liability which equates to the capital cost of the asset.

The asset should be **depreciated** over the shorter of:

- The lease term
- The asset's useful life

If there is **reasonable certainty of eventual ownership** of the asset, then it should be depreciated over its **useful life**.

2.2.1 Lease payments   5/10, 5/11

The substance of a finance lease arrangement is that the lessee takes ownership of an asset and then pays for that asset in instalments. This same effect could have been achieved if the entity had taken a loan with a bank and used the loan to purchase the asset from the lessor. In effect then, the lease payments are similar to loan repayments and therefore they include an element of **interest** and an element of **capital repayment**.

The accounting problem is to decide what proportion of each instalment paid by the lessee represents interest (finance charge in the income statement), and what proportion represents a repayment of the capital. The aim is that the finance charge should reduce over the lease term in line with the outstanding liability.

There are three apportionment methods you may encounter:

- The straight line method
- The actuarial method
- The sum-of-the-digits method

Exam skills

An examination question will always make it clear which method should be used. If you are given an interest rate, you will be expected to use the actuarial method. If not, use the sum-of-the-digits method.

The **straight line method** is simple but does not provide a constant rate of interest. The interest amount is simply allocated equally over the lease periods. You are not likely to be asked to use this method in the exam, but you should know about it.

The **actuarial method** is the best and most scientific method. It derives from the common-sense assumption that the interest charged by a lessor company will equal the rate of return desired by the company, multiplied by the amount of capital it has invested.

(a)   At the beginning of the lease the capital invested is equal to the fair value of the asset (less any initial deposit paid by the lessee).

(b)   This amount reduces as each instalment is paid. It follows that the interest accruing is greatest in the early part of the lease term, and gradually reduces as capital is repaid.

Later in this section, we will look at a simple example of the actuarial method.

Exam skills

If you are required to use the actuarial method in the exam, you will be given the interest rate.

The **sum-of-the-digits** method approximates to the actuarial method, splitting the total interest (without reference to a rate of interest) in such a way that the greater proportion falls in the earlier years. The procedure is as follows.

Assign a digit to each instalment. The digit 1 should be assigned to the final instalment, 2 to the penultimate instalment and so on.

Add the digits. A quick method of adding the digits is to use the formula $\frac{n(n+1)}{2}$ where n is the number of instalments. If there are twelve instalments, then the sum of the digits will be 78. For this reason, the sum of the digits method is sometimes called the **rule of 78**.

Calculate the interest charge included in each instalment. Do this by multiplying the total interest accruing over the lease term by the fraction:

$$\frac{\text{Digit applicable to the instalment}}{\text{Sum of the digits}}$$

Later in this section, we will look at a simple example of the sum-of-the-digits method.

2.2.2 Accounting entries

Once the interest has been calculated using one of these methods, the capital element of the lease repayment can be calculated (capital element = lease payment – interest element). The double entries to record the interest and the lease payment are as follows.

To record the interest:

DEBIT   Finance charge (with the calculated interest element)
CREDIT   Accruals

To record the lease payment:

DEBIT   Finance lease liability (with the calculated capital element)
DEBIT   Accruals (with the calculated interest element)
CREDIT   Cash (with the lease payment)

At the end of the year, the balance on the finance lease liability account will represent the outstanding capital liability. This liability should be split into current and non-current liabilities. Future interest/finance charges are not part of this figure because the capital could be paid off at any time, thus avoiding these charges.

The following example shows how to account for a finance lease using the actuarial and sum-of-the-digits methods of interest allocation described above.

Example: Finance lease accounting

On 1 January 20X0 Bacchus Co, wine merchants, buys a small bottling and labelling machine from Silenus Co under a finance lease. The cash price of the machine was $7,710 while the amount to be paid was $10,000. The agreement required the immediate payment of a $2,000 deposit with the balance being settled at $2,000 per annum *in arrears* commencing on 31 December 20X0. The charge of $2,290 represents interest of 15% per annum, calculated on the remaining balance of the liability during each accounting period. Depreciation on the plant is to be provided for at the rate of 20% per annum on a straight line basis assuming a residual value of nil. At the end of the lease, ownership will pass to Bacchus Co.

Required

Show the breakdown of each instalment between interest and capital, using the sum-of-the-digits method and the actuarial method.

Use the breakdown calculated for the **actuarial method** to give the following statement of financial position extracts relating to the machine as at 31 December each year from 20X0 to 20X3:

(a)   Non-current assets: machine at net book value
(b)   Current liabilities: obligation under finance lease
(c)   Non-current liabilities: obligation under finance lease

Solution

In this example, enough detail is given to use either the sum-of-the-digits method or the actuarial method. In an examination question, you would normally be directed to use one method specifically.

Sum-of-the-digits method

Each instalment is allocated a digit as follows.

Instalment	Digit
1st (20X0)	4
2nd (20X1)	3
3rd (20X2)	2
4th (20X3)	1
	10

Or using the formula, $\frac{4 \times 5}{2} = 10$.

The $2,290 interest charges can then be apportioned.

		$
1st instalment	$2,290 × 4/10	916
2nd instalment	$2,290 × 3/10	687
3rd instalment	$2,290 × 2/10	458
4th instalment	$2,290 × 1/10	229
		2,290

The breakdown is then as follows.

	1st instalment $	2nd instalment $	3rd instalment $	4th Instalment $
Interest	916	687	458	229
Capital repayment (balance)	1,084	1,313	1,542	1,771
	2,000	2,000	2,000	2,000

The workings for the finance lease can then be calculated as follows.

	Balance $
Cash price of machine	7,710
Deposit	(2,000)
Capital balance at 1.1.X0	5,710
Interest	916
1st instalment	(2,000)
Capital balance at 31.12.X0	4,626
Interest	687
2nd instalment	(2,000)
Capital balance at 31.12.X1	3,313
Interest	458
3rd instalment	(2,000)
Capital balance at 31.12.X2	1,771
Interest	229
4th instalment	(2,000)
Capital balance at 31.12.X3	–

Actuarial method

The instalments in this example are paid in **arrears**, therefore interest is calculated as 15% of the outstanding balance at the beginning of each year, ie *before* the lease payment has been made.

	Balance $
Cash price of machine	7,710
Deposit	(2,000)
Capital balance at 1.1.X0	5,710
Interest (5,710 × 15%)	856
1st instalment	(2,000)
Capital balance at 31.12.X0	4,566
Interest (4,566 × 15%)	685
2nd instalment	(2,000)
Capital balance at 31.12.X1	3,251
Interest (3,251 × 15%)	488
3rd instalment	(2,000)
Capital balance at 31.12.X2	1,739
Interest (1,739 × 15%)	261
4th instalment	(2,000)
Capital balance at 31.12.X3	–

The journal entries at 1 January 20X0 will be:

(a) To record the asset and initial finance lease liability

DEBIT	Property, plant and equipment	$7,710	
CREDIT	Finance lease liability: Silenus		$7,710

(b) To record the deposit payment

DEBIT	Finance lease liability: Silenus	$2,000	
CREDIT	Cash		$2,000

Entries at 31 December 20X0 will be:

(c) To record the interest element

DEBIT	Finance charge	$856	
CREDIT	Accruals		$856

(d) To record the annual lease payment

DEBIT	Finance lease liability: Silenus	$1,144	
DEBIT	Accruals	$856	
CREDIT	Cash		$2,000

The statement of financial position extracts are as follows.

(a) *Non-current assets: machine at net book value (Note.* Eventual ownership is certain.)

		$
At 31.12.X0	Machine at cost	7,710
	Accumulated depreciation (7,710 × 1/5)	1,542
	Carrying amount	6,168
At 31.12.X1	Machine at cost	7,710
	Accumulated depreciation (7,710 × 2/5)	3,084
	Carrying amount	4,626
At 31.12.X2	Machine at cost	7,710
	Accumulated depreciation (7,710 × 3/5)	4,626
	Carrying amount	3,084
At 31.12.X3	Machine at cost	7,710
	Accumulated depreciation (7,710 × 4/5)	6,168
	Carrying amount	1,542

(b) Current liabilities: obligation under finance lease

	$
At 31.12.X0	1,315
At 31.12.X1	1,512
At 31.12.X2	1,739
At 31.12.X3	–

When lease payments are paid in arrears, the easiest way to calculate the current liabilities balance is to first identify the non-current liability, which is simply the capital balance outstanding in the following year, and deduct this from the capital balance outstanding at the current year end.

For example:

Current liability at 31.12.X0   = total capital balance at 31.12.X0 – total capital balance at 31.12.X1

= $4,566 - $3,251

= $1,315

(c) Non-current liabilities: obligation under finance lease

	$
At 31.12.X0	3,251
At 31.12.X1	1,739
At 31.12.X2	–
At 31.12.X3	–

Notice that when lease payments are made in arrears, the year end liability is **all capital**. Any interest which has accrued during the year has been settled by the instalment paid in that year, because the instalment is paid in arrears.

2.2.3 Payments in advance or in arrears

It is important to note whether payments are made **in advance** or **in arrears** because it has an effect on the mechanics of the calculation you will perform and on the year end liability.

In the sum-of-the-digits method of allocating interest, payments made in arrears mean that the number of finance periods is equal to the number of instalments paid. But if payments are made in advance, the number of finance periods is the number of instalments minus one. This is because the lease liability is extinguished one period earlier if repayments are made in advance as opposed to in arrears, and so it is not necessary to allocate interest to that final period.

When lease payments are made **in advance**, the first payment made repays capital only as no time has yet elapsed for interest to accrue. At the end of each accounting period, the year end liability will include capital and interest that has accrued to date but which has not yet been paid.

Question 8.1	Sum-of-the-digits method

Learning outcome C2(a)

Dundas Co purchased a machine under a finance lease on 1 January 20X6. The lease is for 4 years with instalments of $2,000 to be paid **in advance** on 1 January each year. The fair value of the machine was $6,500. its useful life is 6 years, and its residual value is nil. Dundas will depreciate the machine on a straight line basis.

In apportioning interest to respective accounting periods, the company uses the 'sum-of-the-digits' method.

Required

Show the following statement of financial position extracts relating to the machine as at each year end from 31 December 20X6 to 31 December 20X9.

(a)   Non-current assets: machine at net book value
(b)   Current liabilities: obligation under finance lease
(c)   Non-current liabilities: obligation under finance lease

---

Exam alert

When doing lease calculations, you must highlight the **answer** to the question. Many students can do the calculation correctly but struggle to select the correct answer to the question from their workings.

2.2.4 Finance lease disclosure requirements

IAS 17 requires the following disclosures by lessees, in respect of **finance leases**.

- The **net carrying amount** at the end of the reporting period for each class of asset

- A **reconciliation** between the total of minimum lease payments at the end of the reporting period, and their present value. In addition, an entity should disclose the total of minimum lease payments at the end of the reporting period, and their present value, for each of the following periods:

  - Not later than one year
  - Later than one year and not later than five years
  - Later than five years

- **Contingent rents** recognised in income for the period

- Total of **future minimum sublease payments** expected to be received under non-cancellable subleases at the end of the reporting period

- A **general description** of the lessee's significant leasing arrangements including, but not limited to, the following:

  - The basis on which contingent rent payments are determined

  - The existence and terms of renewal or purchase options and escalation clauses

  - Restrictions imposed by lease arrangements, such as those concerning dividends, additional debt, and further leasing

IAS 17 encourages (but does not require) further disclosures, as appropriate.

Example: Lessee disclosures

These disclosure requirements will be illustrated for Bacchus Co (above example). Assume that Bacchus Co makes up its accounts to 31 December and uses the actuarial method to apportion finance charges.

Solution

The company's accounts for the first year of the lease, the year ended 31 December 20X0, would include the information given below.

STATEMENT OF FINANCIAL POSITION AS AT 31 DECEMBER 20X0 (EXTRACTS)

	$	$
Non-current assets		
Assets held under finance leases		
Plant and machinery at cost	7,710	
Less accumulated depreciation (20% × $7,710)	1,542	
		6,168
Current liabilities		
Obligations under finance leases (4,566 - 3,251)		1,315
Non-current liabilities		
Obligations under finance leases		3,251

INCOME STATEMENT FOR THE YEAR ENDED 31 DECEMBER 20X0

	$
Interest payable and similar charges	
Interest on finance leases	856

Section summary

- You must learn (through repeated practice) how to apply the actuarial and sum-of-the-digits methods of interest allocation.

- You must also learn the disclosure requirements of IAS 17.

Chapter Roundup

✓   Under IAS 17, a lease of assets can either be a finance lease or an operating lease.

✓   A finance lease is a lease that transfers substantially all the risks and rewards of ownership to the lessee.

✓   An operating lease is a lease other than a finance lease.

✓   IAS 17 gives examples of situations that indicate that an agreement is a finance lease.

✓   Leases of land are usually classified as operating leases.

✓   You must learn (through repeated practice) how to apply the actuarial and sum-of-the-digits methods of interest allocation.

✓   You must also learn the disclosure requirements of IAS 17.

Quick Quiz

1   (a)   .... leases transfer substantially all the risks and rewards of ownership.

     (b)   .... leases are usually short-term rental agreements with the lessor being responsible for the repairs and maintenance of the asset.

2   A business acquires an asset under a finance lease. What is the double entry?

3   What is the formula to calculate each period's interest using sum of the digits?

4   List the disclosures required under IAS 17 for lessees.

5   A lorry has an expected useful life of six years. It is acquired under a four year finance lease and will probably be kept for its entire six year life. Over which period should it be depreciated?

6   A company leases a photocopier under an operating lease which expires in June 20X2. Its office is leased under an operating lease due to expire in January 20X3. How should past and future operating leases be disclosed in its 31 December 20X1 accounts?

Answers to Quick Quiz

1   (a)   Finance
     (b)   Operating

2   DEBIT   Asset account
     CREDIT   Lessor account

3    $\dfrac{\text{Digit applicable to the instalment}}{\text{Sum of the digits}} \times \text{Total interest charge}$

4   See Para 2.2.4.

5   As eventual ownership of the lorry is reasonably certain, it should be depreciated over its six year useful life.

6   The total operating lease rentals charged though the income statement should be disclosed. The payments committed to should be disclosed, analysing them between those falling due in the next year and the second to fifth years.

Answers to Questions

8.1 Sum-of-the-digits method

	$
Fair value of machine at 1.1.X6	6,500
1st instalment at 1.1.X6	(2,000)
	4,500
Interest 20X6 (W)	750
Balance at 31.12.X6	5,250
2nd Instalment paid at 1.1.X7	(2,000)
	3,250
Interest 20X7 (W)	500
Balance at 31.12.X7	3,750
3rd Instalment paid at 1.1.X8	(2,000)
	1,750
Interest 20X8 (W)	250
Balance at 31.12.X8	2,000
4th Instalment paid at 1.1.X8	(2,000)
Balance at 31.12.X9	–

Note that because the lease payments are made **in advance**, the lease payment for each year is deducted from the outstanding capital balance **before** the interest is added on. It is particularly important to set your calculation up this way when using the actuarial method of allocating interest so that you calculate the interest on the correct capital balance.

Working
Finance charge

	$
Total lease payments	8,000
Fair value of machine	(6,500)
Finance charge	1,500

Number of finance periods = total number of repayments − 1 = 3

Sum of the digits = 3 + 2 + 1 = 6

Interest charge 20X6 = $1,500 \times \dfrac{3}{6}$	750
Interest charge 20X7 = $1,500 \times \dfrac{2}{6}$	500
Interest charge 20X8 = $1,500 \times \dfrac{1}{6}$	250
	1,500

(a)   Non-current assets: machine at net book value

		$
At 31.12.X6	Machine at cost	6,500
	Accumulated depreciation	(1,625)
	Carrying amount	4,875
At 31.12.X7	Machine at cost	6,500
	Accumulated depreciation	(3,250)
	Carrying amount	3,250
At 31.12.X8	Machine at cost	6,500
	Accumulated depreciation	(4,875)
	Carrying amount	1,625
At 31.12.X9	Machine at cost	6,500
	Accumulated depreciation	(6,500)
	Carrying amount	–

Working

Annual depreciation charge on a straight-line basis $= \dfrac{\$6,500}{4} = \$1,625$ per year

(b)   Current liabilities: obligation under finance lease

	$
At 31.12.X6*	2,000
At 31.12.X7	2,000
At 31.12.X8	2,000
At 31.12.X9	–

*Note. The interest element ($750) of the current liability can also be shown separately as interest payable. Similarly for the following years.

Notice how the year end liability includes capital *and* interest that has accrued to date but which has not yet been paid. This is because the lease payments are made *in advance*, so they are made before any interest has accrued. Look back at the example in the chapter and compare the two answers to make sure you see the difference when payments are made in arrears and when they are made in advance.

(c)   Non-current liabilities: obligation under finance lease

	$
At 31.12.X6 (5,250 – 2,000)	3,250
At 31.12.X7 (3,750 – 2,000)	1,750
At 31.12.X8 (2,000 – 2000)	–
At 31.12.X9	–

Now try this question from the Exam Question Bank	Number	Level	Marks	Time
	Q14	Examination	5	9 mins

STATEMENTS OF CASH FLOWS

The importance of the distinction between cash and profit and the scant attention paid to this by the income statement has resulted in the development of statements of cash flows.

This chapter adopts a systematic approach to the preparation of statements of cash flows in examinations; you should learn this method and you will then be equipped for any problems in the exam itself.

The third section of the chapter looks at the information which is provided by statements of cash flows and how it should be analysed.

topic list	learning outcomes	syllabus references	ability required
1 IAS 7 *Statement of cash flows*	C1(a)	C1(ii)	application
2 Preparing a statement of cash flows	C1(a)	C1(ii)	application
3 Interpretation of statements of cash flows	C1(a)	C1(ii)	application

1   IAS 7 *Statement of cash flows*

Introduction

In this section we look at why statements of cash flows are useful. We also cover the required presentation of a statement of cash flows as per IAS 7.

Exam alert

The November 2010 and May 2011 exams contained a Section C question on the preparation of a statement of cash flows. In November 2010, the examiner commented that some candidates 'didn't really know what they were doing, suggesting that some had been question spotting and had not prepared for statements of cash flow'. Make sure you work carefully through this chapter and attempt the practice questions in the Practice and Revision Kit as this topic can, and will, be examined.

1.1 Cash flow and profit

It has been argued that 'profit' does not always give a useful or meaningful picture of a company's operations. Readers of a company's financial statements might even be **misled by a reported profit figure**.

(a)   Shareholders might believe that if a company makes a profit after tax, of say, $100,000 then this is the amount which it could afford to **pay as a dividend**. Unless the company has **sufficient cash** available to stay in business and also to pay a dividend, the shareholders' expectations would be wrong.

(b)   Employees might believe that if a company makes profits, it can afford to **pay higher wages** next year. This opinion may not be correct: the ability to pay wages depends on the **availability of cash**.

(c)   Survival of a business entity depends not so much on profits as on its **ability to pay its debts when they fall due**. Such payments might include 'revenue' items such as material purchases, wages, interest and taxation etc, but also capital payments for new non-current assets and the repayment of loan capital when this falls due (for example on the redemption of debentures).

From these examples, it may be apparent that a company's performance and prospects depend not so much on the 'profits' earned in a period, but more realistically on liquidity or **cash flows**.

1.2 Funds flow and cash flow

Some countries, either currently or in the past, have required the disclosure of additional statements based on **funds flow** rather than cash flow. However, the definition of 'funds' can be very vague and such statements often simply require a rearrangement of figures already provided in the statement of financial position and income statement. By contrast, a statement of cash flows is unambiguous and provides information which is additional to that provided in the rest of the accounts. It also lends itself to organisation by activity and not by classification in the statement of financial position.

Statements of cash flows are frequently given as an **additional statement**, supplementing the statement of financial position, statement of comprehensive income and related notes. The group aspects of statements of cash flows (and certain complex matters) have been excluded as they are beyond the scope of your syllabus.

1.3 Objective of IAS 7

The aim of IAS 7 is to provide information to users of financial statements about an entity's **ability to generate cash and cash equivalents**, as well as indicating the cash needs of the entity. The statement of cash flows provides *historical* information about cash and cash equivalents, classifying cash flows between operating, investing and financing activities.

1.4 Scope

A statement of cash flows should be presented as an **integral part** of an entity's financial statements. All types of entity can provide useful information about cash flows as the need for cash is universal, whatever the nature of their revenue-producing activities. Therefore **all entities are required by the standard to produce a statement of cash flows.**

1.5 Benefits of cash flow information

The use of statements of cash flows is very much **in conjunction** with the rest of the financial statements. Users can gain further appreciation of the change in net assets, of the entity's financial position (liquidity and solvency) and the entity's ability to adapt to changing circumstances by affecting the amount and timing of cash flows. Statements of cash flows **enhance comparability** as they are not affected by differing accounting policies used for the same type of transactions or events.

Cash flow information of a historical nature can be used as an indicator of the amount, timing and certainty of future cash flows. Past forecast cash flow information can be **checked for accuracy** as actual figures emerge. The relationship between profit and cash flows can be analysed as can changes in prices over time.

1.6 Definitions

The standard gives the following definitions, the most important of which are **cash** and **cash equivalents**.

KEY TERMS

CASH comprises cash on hand and demand deposits.

CASH EQUIVALENTS are short-term, highly liquid investments that are readily convertible to known amounts of cash and which are subject to an insignificant risk of changes in value.

CASH FLOWS are inflows and outflows of cash and cash equivalents.

OPERATING ACTIVITIES are the principal revenue-producing activities of the entity and other activities that are not investing or financing activities.

INVESTING ACTIVITIES are the acquisition and disposal of non-current assets and other investments not included in cash equivalents.

FINANCING ACTIVITIES are activities that result in changes in the size and composition of the contributed equity capital and borrowings of the entity.   *(IAS 7)*

1.7 Cash and cash equivalents

The standard expands on the definition of cash equivalents: they are not held for investment or other long-term purposes, but rather to meet short-term cash commitments. To fulfil the above definition, an investment's **maturity date should normally be three months from its acquisition date**. It would usually be the case then that equity investments (ie shares in other companies) are *not* cash equivalents. An exception would be where preferred shares were acquired with a very close maturity date.

Loans and other borrowings from banks are classified as financing activities. In some countries, however, **bank overdrafts** are repayable on demand and are treated as part of an entity's total cash management system. In these circumstances an overdrawn balance will be included in cash and cash equivalents. Such banking arrangements are characterised by a balance which fluctuates between overdrawn and credit.

Movements between different types of cash and cash equivalent are not included in cash flows. The investment of surplus cash in cash equivalents is part of cash management, not part of operating, investing or financing activities.

1.8 Presentation of a statement of cash flows

IAS 7 requires statements of cash flows to report cash flows during the period classified by **operating, investing and financing activities.**

Example: Simple statement of cash flows

Flail Co commenced trading on 1 January 20X1 with a medium-term loan of $21,000 and a share issue which raised $35,000. The company purchased non-current assets for $21,000 cash, and during the year to 31 December 20X1 entered into the following transactions.

(a)   Purchases from suppliers were $19,500, of which $2,550 was unpaid at the year end.
(b)   Wages and salaries amounted to $10,500, of which $750 was unpaid at the year end.
(c)   Interest on the loan of $2,100 was fully paid in the year and a repayment of $5,250 was made.
(d)   Sales revenue was $29,400, including $900 receivables at the year end.
(e)   Interest on cash deposits at the bank amounted to $75.
(f)   A dividend of $4,000 was proposed as at 31 December 20X1.

You are required to prepare a statement of cash flows for the year ended 31 December 20X1.

Solution

FLAIL CO
STATEMENT OF CASH FLOWS
FOR THE YEAR ENDED 31 DECEMBER 20X1

	$	$
Cash flows from operating activities		
Cash received from customers ($29,400 – $900)	28,500	
Cash paid to suppliers ($19,500 – $2,550)	(16,950)	
Cash paid to and on behalf of employees ($10,500 – $750)	(9,750)	
Interest paid	(2,100)	
Interest received	75	
Net cash flow from operating activities		(225)
Investing activities		
Purchase of non-current assets		(21,000)
Financing activities		
Issue of shares	35,000	
Proceeds from medium-term loan	21,000	
Repayment of medium-term loan	(5,250)	
Net cash flow from financing activities		50,750
Net increase in cash and cash equivalents		29,525
Cash and cash equivalents at 1 January 20X1		–
Cash and cash equivalents at 31 December 20X1		29,525

Note that the dividend is only proposed and so there is no related cash flow in 20X1.

1.9 Presentation

The manner of presentation of cash flows from operating, investing and financing activities **depends on the nature of the entity**. By classifying cash flows between different activities in this way users can see the impact on cash and cash equivalents of each one, and their relationships with each other. We can look at each in more detail.

1.9.1 Operating activities

This is perhaps the key part of the statement of cash flows because it shows whether, and to what extent, companies can **generate cash from their operations**. It is these operating cash flows which must, in the end pay for all cash outflows relating to other activities, ie paying loan interest, dividends and so on.

Most of the components of cash flows from operating activities will be those items which **determine the net profit or loss of the entity**, ie they relate to the main revenue-producing activities of the entity. The standard gives the following as examples of cash flows from operating activities.

(a) Cash receipts from the sale of goods and the rendering of services
(b) Cash receipts from royalties, fees, commissions and other revenue
(c) Cash payments to suppliers for goods and services
(d) Cash payments to and on behalf of employees

Certain items may be included in the net profit or loss for the period which do *not* relate to operational cash flows, for example the profit or loss on the sale of a piece of plant will be included in net profit or loss, but the cash flows will be classed as **investing**.

1.9.2 Investing activities

The cash flows classified under this heading show the extent of new investment in **assets which will generate future profit and cash flows**. The standard gives the following examples of cash flows arising from investing activities.

(a) Cash payments to acquire property, plant and equipment, intangibles and other non-current assets, including those relating to capitalised development costs and self-constructed property, plant and equipment

(b) Cash receipts from sales of property, plant and equipment, intangibles and other non-current assets

(c) Cash payments to acquire shares or debentures of other entities

(d) Cash receipts from sales of shares or debentures of other entities

(e) Cash advances and loans made to other parties

(f) Cash receipts from the repayment of advances and loans made to other parties

1.9.3 Financing activities

This section of the statement of cash flows shows the share of cash which the entity's capital providers have claimed during the period. This is an indicator of **likely future interest and dividend payments**. The standard gives the following examples of cash flows which might arise under these headings.

(a) Cash proceeds from issuing shares

(b) Cash payments to owners to acquire or redeem the entity's shares

(c) Cash proceeds from issuing debentures, loans, notes, bonds, mortgages and other short or long-term borrowings

(d) Principal repayments of amounts borrowed under finance leases

Item (d) needs more explanation. Where the reporting entity owns an asset held under a finance lease, the amounts to go in the statement of cash flows under financing activities are repayments of the **principal (capital)** rather than the **interest**.

Example: Finance lease rental

The notes to the financial statements of Hayley Co show the following in respect of obligations under finance leases.

Year ended 30 June	20X5 $'000	20X4 $'000
Amounts payable within one year	12	8
Within two to five years	110	66
	122	74
Less finance charges allocated to future periods	(14)	(8)
	108	66

Interest paid on finance leases in the year to 30 June 20X5 amounted to $6,000. Additions to property, plant and equipment acquired under finance leases were shown in the non-current asset note at $56,000.

Required

Calculate the capital repayment to be shown in the statement of cash flows of Hayley Co for the year to 30 June 20X5.

Solution

OBLIGATIONS UNDER FINANCE LEASES

	$'000		$'000
Capital repayment (bal fig)	14	Bal 1.7.X4	66
Bal 30.6.X5	108	Additions	56
	122		122

1.10 Reporting cash flows from operating activities

The standard offers a choice of method for this part of the statement of cash flows.

(a) **Direct method:** disclose major classes of gross cash receipts and gross cash payments

(b) **Indirect method:** net profit or loss is adjusted for the effects of transactions of a non-cash nature, any deferrals or accruals of past or future operating cash receipts or payments, and items of income or expense associated with investing or financing cash flows

Exam alert

You are required to know about the direct method but the indirect method is easier and is more likely to be examined.

1.10.1 Using the direct method

There are different ways in which the **information about gross cash receipts and payments** can be obtained. The most obvious way is simply to extract the information from the accounting records. This may be a laborious task, however, and the indirect method below may be easier. The example and question above used the direct method.

1.10.2 Using the indirect method   11/10, 5/11

This method is undoubtedly **easier** from the point of view of the preparer of the statement of cash flows. The net profit or loss for the period is adjusted for the following.

(a)   Changes during the period in inventories, operating receivables and payables
(b)   Non-cash items, eg depreciation, provisions, profits/losses on the sales of assets
(c)   Other items, the cash flows from which should be classified under investing or financing activities.

A **proforma** of such a calculation, taken from the IAS, is as follows and this method may be more common in the exam. (The proforma has been amended to reflect changes to IFRS.)

	$
Cash flows from operating activities	
Net profit before taxation	X
Adjustments for:	
Depreciation	X
Profit (loss) on disposal of a non-current asset	X
Investment income	(X)
Interest expense	X̲
Operating profit before working capital changes	X
Increase in trade and other receivables	(X)
Decrease in inventories	X
Decrease in trade payables	(X̲)
Cash generated from operations	X
Interest paid	(X)
Income taxes paid	(X̲)
Net cash from operating activities	X̲

It is important to understand why **certain items are added and others subtracted**. Note the following points.

(a)   Depreciation is not a cash expense, but is deducted in arriving at profit. It makes sense, therefore, to eliminate it by adding it back.

(b)   By the same logic, a loss on a disposal of a non-current asset (arising through underprovision of depreciation) needs to be added back and a profit deducted.

(c)   An increase in inventories means less cash – so cash has been spent on buying inventories.

(d)   An increase in receivables means the company's debtors have not paid as much, and therefore there is less cash.

(e)   If payables are paid, causing the payables figure to decrease, the business has less cash.

1.10.3 Indirect versus direct

The direct method is encouraged where the necessary information is not too costly to obtain, but IAS 7 does not require it. In practice, therefore, the direct method is rarely used. It is not obvious that businesses in practice are right in favouring the indirect method. It could be argued that companies ought to monitor their cash flows carefully enough on an ongoing basis to be able to use the direct method at minimal extra cost.

A proforma for the direct method is given below.

	$'000	$'000
Cash flows from operating activities		
Cash receipts from customers	X	
Cash paid to suppliers and employees	(X̲)	
Cash generated from operations	X	
Interest paid	(X)	
Income taxes paid	(X̲)	
Net cash from operating activities		X̲

194   9: Statements of cash flows   PART B SINGLE COMPANY FINANCIAL ACCOUNTS

1.11 Interest and dividends

Cash flows from interest and dividends received and paid should each be **disclosed separately**. Each should be classified in a consistent manner from period to period as either operating, investing or financing activities.

Dividends paid by the entity can be classified in **one of two ways**.

(a)   As a **financing cash flow**, showing the cost of obtaining financial resources.

(b)   As a component of **cash flows from operating activities** so that users can assess the entity's ability to pay dividends out of operating cash flows.

1.12 Taxes on income

Cash flows arising from taxes on income should be **separately disclosed** and should be classified as cash flows from operating activities *unless* they can be specifically identified with financing and investing activities.

Taxation cash flows are often **difficult to match** to the originating underlying transaction, so most of the time all tax cash flows are classified as arising from operating activities.

Example of a statement of cash flows

In the next section we will look at the procedures for preparing a statement of cash flows. First, look at this **example**, adapted from the example given in the standard (which is based on a group and therefore beyond the scope of your syllabus).

Direct method

STATEMENT OF CASH FLOWS (DIRECT METHOD)
YEAR ENDED 31 DECEMBER 20X7

	$m	$m
Cash flows from operating activities		
Cash receipts from customers	30,330	
Cash paid to suppliers and employees	(27,600)	
Cash generated from operations	2,730	
Interest paid	(270)	
Income taxes paid	(900)	
Net cash from operating activities		1,560
Cash flows from investing activities		
Purchase of property, plant and equipment	(900)	
Proceeds from sale of equipment	20	
Interest received	200	
Dividends received	200	
Net cash used in investing activities		(480)
Cash flows from financing activities		
Proceeds from issuance of share capital	250	
Proceeds from long-term borrowings	250	
Dividends paid*	(1,290)	
Net cash used in financing activities		(790)
Net increase in cash and cash equivalents		290
Cash and cash equivalents at beginning of period		120
Cash and cash equivalents at end of period		410

* This could also be shown as an operating cash flow

Indirect method

STATEMENT OF CASH FLOWS (INDIRECT METHOD)
YEAR ENDED 31 DECEMBER 20X7

	$m	$m
Cash flows from operating activities		
Net profit before taxation	3,570	
Adjustments for:		
Depreciation	450	
Investment income	(500)	
Interest expense	400	
Operating profit before working capital changes	3,920	
Increase in trade and other receivables	(500)	
Decrease in inventories	1,050	
Decrease in trade payables	(1,740)	
Cash generated from operations	2,730	
Interest paid	(270)	
Income taxes paid	(900)	
Net cash from operating activities		1,560
Cash flows from investing activities		
Purchase of property, plant and equipment	(900)	
Proceeds from sale of equipment **	20	
Interest received	200	
Dividends received	200	
Net cash used in investing activities		(480)
Cash flows from financing activities		
Proceeds from issuance of share capital	250	
Proceeds from long-term borrowings	250	
Dividends paid*	(1,290)	
Net cash used in financing activities		(790)
Net increase in cash and cash equivalents		290
Cash and cash equivalents at beginning of period		120
Cash and cash equivalents at end of period		410

*   This could also be shown as an operating cash flow
**   The equipment was disposed of at its NBV, so no profit or loss arose.

Section summary

Statements of cash flows are a useful addition to the financial statements of companies because it is recognised that accounting profit is not the only indicator of a company's performance.

IAS 7 requires cash flows during the period to be classified by **operating, investing and financing activities**.

Cash flows from operating activities can be reported using the **direct** or **indirect method**.

2 Preparing a statement of cash flows   11/10, 5/11

Introduction

This section will teach you how to prepare a statement of cash flows. This is an important skill for your exam.

2.1 Working capital adjustments

In essence, preparing a statement of cash flows is very straightforward. You should therefore simply learn the format and apply the steps noted in the example below. Note that the following items are treated in a way that might seem confusing, but the treatment is logical if you **think in terms of cash**.

(a) **Increase in inventory** is treated as **negative** (in brackets). This is because it represents a cash **outflow**; cash is being spent on inventory.

(b) An **increase in receivables** would be treated as **negative** for the same reasons; more receivables means less cash.

(c) By contrast an **increase in payables is positive** because cash is being retained and not used to settle accounts payable. There is therefore more of it.

Example: Preparation of a statement of cash flows

Kane Co's income statement for the year ended 31 December 20X2 and statements of financial position at 31 December 20X1 and 31 December 20X2 were as follows.

KANE CO
INCOME STATEMENT FOR THE YEAR ENDED 31 DECEMBER 20X2

	$'000	$'000
Sales		720
Raw materials consumed	70	
Staff costs	94	
Depreciation	118	
Loss on disposal of property, plant and equipment	18	
		300
Operating profit		420
Interest payable		28
Profit before tax		392
Taxation		124
Profit for the year		268

Note: Total dividends paid during the year were $66,000.

KANE CO
STATEMENTS OF FINANCIAL POSITION AS AT 31 DECEMBER

	20X2		20X1	
	$'000	$'000	$'000	$'000
Assets				
Property, plant and equipment				
Cost	1,596		1,560	
Depreciation	318		224	
		1,278		1,336
Current assets				
Inventory	24		20	
Trade receivables	76		58	
Bank	48		56	
		148		134
Total assets		1,426		1,470
Equity and liabilities				
Share capital	360		340	
Share premium	36		24	
Retained earnings	716		514	
		1,112		878
Non-current liabilities				
Long-term loans		200		500
Current liabilities				
Trade payables	12		6	
Taxation	102		86	
		114		92
		1,426		1,470

During the year, the company paid $90,000 for a new piece of machinery.

Required

Prepare a statement of cash flows for Kane Co for the year ended 31 December 20X2 in accordance with the requirements of IAS 7, using the indirect method.

Solution

 Set out the proforma statement of cash flows with the headings required by IAS 7. You should leave plenty of space. Ideally, use three or more sheets of paper, one for the main statement, one for the notes and one for your workings. It is essential to know the formats well.

 Begin with the **cash flows from operating activities** as far as possible. When preparing the statement from statements of financial position, you will usually have to calculate such items as depreciation, loss on sale of non-current assets, profit for the year and tax paid. Note that you may not be given the tax charge in the income statement. You will then have to assume that the tax paid in the year is last year's year-end provision and calculate the charge as the balancing figure.

 Calculate the cash flow figures for purchase or sale of non-current assets, issue of shares and repayment of loans if these are not already given to you (as they may be).

 You will now be able to complete the statement by slotting in the figures given or calculated.

KANE CO

STATEMENT OF CASH FLOWS FOR THE YEAR ENDED 31 DECEMBER 20X2

	$'000	$'000
Net cash flow from operating activities		
Profit before tax	392	
Depreciation charges	118	
Interest expense	28	
Loss on sale of property, plant and equipment	18	
Increase in inventories	(4)	
Increase in receivables	(18)	
Increase in payables	6	
Cash generated from operations	540	
Interest paid	(28)	
Dividends paid	(66)	
Tax paid (86 + 124 – 102)	(108)	
Net cash flow from operating activities		338
Cash flows from investing activities		
Payments to acquire property, plant and equipment	(90)	
Receipts from sales of property, plant and equipment (W)	12	
Net cash flows from investing activities		(78)
Cash outflow from financing activities		
Issues of share capital (360 + 36 – 340 – 24)	32	
Long-term loans repaid (500 – 200)	(300)	
Net cash outflow from financing activities		(268)
Decrease in cash and cash equivalents		(8)
Cash and cash equivalents at 1.1.X2		56
Cash and cash equivalents at 31.12.X2		48

Working: property, plant and equipment

COST

	$'000		$'000
At 1.1.X2	1,560	At 31.12.X2	1,596
Purchases	90	Disposals (balance)	54
	1,650		1,650

ACCUMULATED DEPRECIATION

	$'000		$'000
At 31.1.X2	318	At 1.1.X2	224
Depreciation on disposals (balance)	24	Charge for year	118
	342		342

	$'000
Carrying value of disposals	30
Net loss reported	(18)
Proceeds of disposals	12

Question 9.1

Statement of cash flows

Learning outcome C1(a)

Set out below are the financial statements of Emma Co. You are the financial controller, faced with the task of implementing IAS 7 *Statement of cash flows*.

EMMA CO
INCOME STATEMENT FOR THE YEAR ENDED 31 DECEMBER 20X2

	$'000
Sales revenue	2,553
Cost of sales	1,814
Gross profit	739
Distribution costs	125
Administrative expenses	264
Operating profit	350
Interest received	25
Interest paid	75
Profit before taxation	300
Taxation	140
Profit for the year	160

EMMA CO
STATEMENTS OF FINANCIAL POSITION AS AT 31 DECEMBER

	20X2 $'000	20X1 $'000
Assets		
Non-current assets		
Property, plant and equipment	380	305
Intangible assets	250	200
Investments	–	25
Current assets		
Inventories	150	102
Receivables	390	315
Short-term investments (highly liquid)	50	–
Cash in hand	2	1
Total assets	1,222	948
Equity and liabilities		
Equity		
Share capital ($1 ordinary shares)	200	150
Share premium account	160	150
Revaluation surplus	100	91
Retained earnings	260	180
Non-current liabilities		
Long-term loan	170	50
Current liabilities		
Trade payables	127	119
Bank overdraft	85	98
Taxation	120	110
Total equity and liabilities	1,222	948

The following information is available.

(a) The proceeds of the sale of non-current asset investments amounted to $30,000.

(b) Fixtures and fittings, with an original cost of $85,000 and a net book value of $45,000, were sold for $32,000 during the year.

(c) The following information relates to property, plant and equipment.

	31 December 20X2 $'000	20X1 $'000
Cost	720	595
Accumulated depreciation	340	290
Carrying value	380	305

(d)   50,000 $1 ordinary shares were issued during the year at a premium of 20c per share.

(e)   Dividends totalling $80,000 were paid in 20X2.

Required

Prepare a statement of cash flows for the year to 31 December 20X2 using the indirect method in accordance with IAS 7.

Exam skills

Remember that every item in the statement of financial position will have some impact on the statement of cash flows. It will either appear in the statement or be part of an adjustment. When you are doing a question, you should check back through the statement of financial position and make sure everything is accounted for.

Section summary

You need to be aware of the **format** of the statement of cash flows as laid out in **IAS 7**. Setting out the format is an essential first stage in preparing the statement, so this format must be learnt.

3 Interpretation of statements of cash flows

Introduction

Here we briefly cover how to analyse a statement of cash flows. We then look at some advantages of cash flow accounting.

3.1 Uses of the statement of cash flows

IAS 7 *Statement of cash flows* was introduced on the basis that it would provide better, more comprehensive and more useful information than what was already shown in the financial statements. So what kind of information does the statement of cash flows, along with its notes, provide?

Some of the main areas where IAS 7 should provide information not found elsewhere in the financial statements are as follows.

(a)   The **relationships between profit and cash** can be seen clearly and analysed accordingly.

(b)   **Cash equivalents** are highlighted, giving a better picture of the liquidity of the company.

(c)   **Financing inflows and outflows must be shown, rather than simply passed through reserves**.

One of the most important things to realise at this point is that it is wrong to try to assess the health or predict the death of a reporting entity solely on the basis of a single indicator. When analysing cash flow data, the **comparison should not just be between cash flows and profit, but also between cash flows over a period of time** (say three to five years).

Cash is not synonymous with profit on an annual basis, but you should also remember that the 'behaviour' of profit and cash flows will be very different. **Profit is smoothed out** through accruals, prepayments, provisions and other accounting conventions. This does not apply to cash, so the **cash flow figures** are likely to be **'lumpy'** in comparison. You must distinguish between this 'lumpiness' and the trends which will appear over time.

The **relationship between profit and cash flows will vary constantly**. Note that healthy companies do not always have reported profits exceeding operating cash flows. Similarly, unhealthy companies can have operating cash flows well in excess of reported profit. The value of comparing them is in determining the extent to which earned profits are being converted into the necessary cash flows.

Profit is not as important as the extent to which a company can **convert its profits into cash on a continuing basis.** This process should be judged over a period longer than one year. The cash flows should be compared with profits over the same periods to decide how successfully the reporting entity has converted earnings into cash.

When **analysing** a statement of cash flows, you should bear in mind that it is not difficult to distort cash balances in the short term. For example, the cash balance at the year end could be improved by delaying payments of suppliers or the replenishing of inventories until after the year end.

3.2 The advantages of cash flow accounting

The advantages of cash flow accounting are as follows.

(a) Survival in business depends on the **ability to generate** cash. Cash flow accounting directs attention towards this critical issue.

(b) Cash flow is **more comprehensive** than 'profit' which is dependent on accounting conventions and concepts.

(c) Suppliers and lenders are more interested in an entity's ability to repay them than in its profitability. Whereas 'profits' might indicate that cash is likely to be available, cash flow accounting is more direct with its message.

(d) Cash flow reporting provides a better means of **comparing the results** of different companies than traditional profit reporting.

(e) Cash flow reporting **satisfies the needs of all users** better.

   (i) For **management**, it provides the sort of information on which decisions should be taken: (in management accounting, 'relevant costs' to a decision are future cash flows); traditional profit accounting does not help with decision-making.

   (ii) For **shareholders and auditors**, cash flow accounting can provide a satisfactory basis for stewardship accounting.

   (iii) As described previously, the information needs of **creditors and employees** will be better served by cash flow accounting.

(f) Cash flow forecasts are **easier to prepare**, as well as more useful, than profit forecasts.

(g) They can in some respects be **audited more easily** than accounts based on the accruals concept.

(h) The accruals concept is confusing, and cash flows are **more easily understood**.

(i) Cash flow accounting should be both retrospective, and also include a forecast for the future. This is of **great information value** to all users of accounting information.

(j) **Forecasts** can subsequently be **monitored** by the publication of variance statements which compare actual cash flows against the forecast.

Section summary

Note that you may be expected to analyse or interpret a statement of cash flows.

Chapter Roundup

✓   **Statements of cash flows** are a useful addition to the financial statements of companies because it is recognised that accounting profit is not the only indicator of a company's performance.

✓   IAS 7 requires cash flows during the period to be classified by operating, investing and financing activities.

✓   Cash flows from operating activities can be reported using the direct or indirect method.

✓   You need to be aware of the **format** of the statement as laid out in **IAS 7**. Setting out the format is an essential first stage in preparing the statement, so this format must be learnt.

✓   Note that you may be expected to **analyse** or **interpret** a statement of cash flows.

Quick Quiz

1   What is the aim of a statement of cash flows?

2   The standard headings in IAS 7 *Statement of cash flows* are:

- O.................... a.....................
- I.................... a.....................
- F.................... a.....................
- Net.................... in C.................... and ....

3   Cash equivalents are current asset investments which will mature or can be redeemed within three months of the year end. True or false?

4   Why are you more likely to encounter the indirect method as opposed to the direct method?

5   List five advantages of cash flow accounting.

6   List the steps that should be followed to prepare a statement of cash flows.

Answers to Quick Quiz

1   To indicate an entity's ability to generate cash and cash equivalents.

2   - Operating activities
- Investing activities
- Financing activities
- Net increase (decrease) in cash and cash equivalents

3   False. See the definition in paragraph 1.6 if you are not sure about this.

4   The indirect method utilises figures which appear in the financial statements. The figures required for the direct method may not be readily available.

5   See paragraph 3.2.

6   •   Set out the proforma statement of cash flows

      •   Complete the reconciliation of profit before tax to net cash from operating activities

      •   Calculate cash flow figures for purchase or sale of non-current assets, issue of shares and repayment of loans

      •   Insert figures given or calculated into statement of cash flows

 # Answers to Questions

9.1 Statement of cash flows

EMMA CO
STATEMENT OF CASH FLOWS FOR THE YEAR ENDED 31 DECEMBER 20X2

	$'000	$'000
Net cash flows from operating activities		
Profit before tax	300	
Depreciation charge (W1)	90	
Net interest charge	50	
Loss on sale of property, plant and equipment (45 – 32)	13	
Profit on sale of non-current asset investments (30 – 25)	(5)	
(Increase)/decrease in inventories	(48)	
(Increase)/decrease in receivables	(75)	
Increase/(decrease) in payables	8	
Cash generated from operating activities	333	
Interest received	25	
Interest paid	(75)	
Dividends paid	(80)	
Tax paid (110 + 140 – 120)	(130)	
Net cash flows from operating activities		73
Cash flows from investing activities		
Payments to acquire property, plant and equipment (W2)	(201)	
Payments to acquire intangible non-current assets	(50)	
Receipts from sales of property, plant and equipment	32	
Receipts from sale of non-current asset investments	30	
Net cash outflow from investing activities		(189)
Cash flows from financing activities		
Issue of share capital	60	
Long-term loan	120	
Net cash flows from financing		180
Increase in cash and cash equivalents		64
Net cash and cash equivalents at 1.1 X2		(97)
Cash and cash equivalents at 31.12.X2		(33)

Workings

1   Depreciation charge

	$'000	$'000
Depreciation at 31 December 20X2		340
Depreciation 31 December 20X1	290	
Depreciation on assets sold (85 – 45)	40	
		250
Charge for the year		90

2   Purchase of property, plant and equipment

PROPERTY, PLANT AND EQUIPMENT

	$'000		$'000
1.1.X2 Balance b/d	595	Disposals	85
Revaluation (100 − 91)	9		
Purchases (bal fig)	201	31.12.X2 Balance c/d	720
	805		805

Now try these questions from the Exam Question Bank

Number	Level	Marks	Time
Q20	Examination	30	54 mins
Q21	Examination	30	54 mins

MISCELLANEOUS STANDARDS

IAS 37 and IAS 10 are very important as they can affect many items in the accounts. Students sometimes get them confused with each other, so make sure you learn all the relevant definitions and understand the standard accounting treatment.

Related party disclosures are important to users of accounts. Make sure you understand why. You must also know what constitutes a related party.

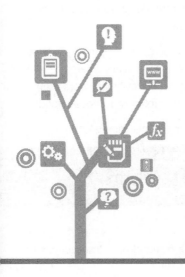

topic list	learning outcomes	syllabus references	ability required
1 IAS 37 *Provisions, contingent liabilities and contingent assets*	C2(a)	C2(x)	application
2 IAS 10 *Events after the reporting period*	C2(a)	C2(ix)	application
3 IAS 24 *Related party disclosures*	C2(a)	C2(vii)	application

1 IAS 37 *Provisions, contingent liabilities and contingent assets*

Introduction

This long section introduces provisions, contingent liabilities and contingent assets. You will need to be able to recognise these in a given scenario.

1.1 Dealing with uncertainty

Financial statements must include **all the information necessary for an understanding of the company's financial position**. Provisions, contingent liabilities and contingent assets are 'uncertainties' that must be accounted for consistently if we are to achieve this understanding.

1.2 Objective

IAS 37 *Provisions, contingent liabilities and contingent assets* aims to ensure that appropriate **recognition criteria** and **measurement bases** are applied to provisions, contingent liabilities and contingent assets and that **sufficient information** is disclosed in the **notes** to the financial statements to enable users to understand their nature, timing and amount.

1.3 Provisions

You will be familiar with provisions (allowances) for depreciation and doubtful debts from your earlier studies. The provisions addressed by IAS 37 are, however, rather different.

Before IAS 37, there was no accounting standard dealing with provisions. Companies wanting to show their results in the most favourable light used to make large 'one off' provisions in years where a high level of underlying profit was generated. These provisions, often known as 'big bath' provisions, were then available to shield expenditure in future years when perhaps the underlying profits were not as good.

In other words, provisions were used for **profit smoothing**. Profit smoothing is misleading.

KEY POINT

The key aim of IAS 37 is to ensure that provisions are made only where there are valid grounds for them. IAS 37 views a provision as a **liability**.

KEY TERMS

A PROVISION is a liability of uncertain timing or amount.

A LIABILITY is an obligation of an entity to transfer economic benefits as a result of past transactions or events.   *(IAS 37)*

The IAS distinguishes provisions from other liabilities such as trade payables and accruals. This is on the basis that for a provision there is **uncertainty** about the timing or amount of the future expenditure. While uncertainty is clearly present in the case of certain accruals the uncertainty is generally much less than for provisions.

1.4 Recognition

IAS 37 states that a provision should be **recognised** as a liability in the financial statements when all three of the following conditions can be met:

- An entity has a **present obligation** (legal or constructive) as a result of a past event
- It is probable that a **transfer of economic benefits** will be required to settle the obligation
- A **reliable estimate** can be made of the obligation

LEARNING MEDIA

1.4.1 Meaning of obligation

It is fairly clear what a legal obligation is: it is one which arises from a contract, legislation or from any other operation of law. However, you may not know what a **constructive obligation** is.

KEY TERM

IAS 37 defines a CONSTRUCTIVE OBLIGATION as

An obligation that derives from an entity's actions where:

- by an established pattern of past practice, published policies or a sufficiently specific current statement the entity has indicated to other parties that it will accept certain responsibilities; and

- as a result, the entity has created a valid expectation on the part of those other parties that it will discharge those responsibilities.

Question 10.1	Recognising a provision

Learning outcome C2(a)

In which of the following circumstances might a provision be recognised?

(a)   On 13 December 20X9 the board of an entity decided to close down a division. The accounting date of the company is 31 December. Before 31 December 20X9 the decision was not communicated to any of those affected and no other steps were taken to implement the decision.

(b)   The board agreed a detailed closure plan on 20 December 20X9 and details were given to customers and employees.

(c)   A company obliged to incur clean up costs for environmental damage (that has already been caused).

(d)   A company intends to carry out future expenditure to operate in a particular way in the future.

1.4.2 Probable transfer of economic benefits

For the purpose of the IAS, a transfer of economic benefits is regarded as **'probable'** if the event is **more likely than not** to occur. This appears to indicate a probability of more than 50%. However, the standard makes it clear that where there are a number of similar obligations the probability should be based on considering the population as a whole, rather than one single item. Often it will be a matter of judgement to determine the probability of an event occurring and hence its accounting treatment.

Example: Transfer of economic benefits

If a company has entered into a warranty obligation then the probability of transfer of economic benefits may well be extremely small in respect of one specific item. However, when considering the population as a whole the probability of some transfer of economic benefits is quite likely to be much higher. If there is a **greater than 50% probability** of some transfer of economic benefits then a **provision** should be made for the **expected amount**.

1.5 Measurement of provisions

5/11

KEY POINT

The amount recognised as a provision should be the **best estimate** of the expenditure required to settle the present obligation at the end of the reporting period.

The estimates will be determined by the **judgement** of the entity's management supplemented by the experience of similar transactions. If the provision relates to just one item, the best estimate of the expenditure will be the most likely outcome.

LEARNING MEDIA

When a provision is needed that involves a lot of items (for example, a warranty provision, where each item sold has a warranty attached to it), then the provision is calculated using the **expected value approach**. The expected value approach takes each possible outcome (ie the amount of money that will need to be paid under each circumstance) and weights it according to the probability of that outcome happening. This is illustrated in the following question.

Question 10.2 Warranty provision

Learning outcome C2(a)

Parker Co sells goods with a warranty under which customers are covered for the cost of repairs of any manufacturing defect that becomes apparent within the first six months of purchase. The company's past experience and future expectations indicate the following pattern of likely repairs.

% of goods sold	Defects	Cost of repairs $m
75	None	–
20	Minor	1.0
5	Major	4.0

What provision should be made for warranty claims?

1.6 Provisions: other issues

1.6.1 Discounting

Where the effect of the **time value of money** is material, the amount of a provision should be the **present value** of the expenditure required to settle the obligation. An appropriate **discount** rate should be used.

The discount rate should be a **pre-tax rate** that reflects current market assessments of the time value of money. **The discount rate(s) should not reflect risks for which future cash flow estimates have been adjusted.**

Exam alert

It is unlikely (but not impossible) that you will be expected to perform a calculation involving discounting in your exam. But you should be aware of the principle.

1.6.2 Future events

Future events which are reasonably expected to occur (eg new legislation, changes in technology) may affect the amount required to settle the enterprise's obligation and should be taken into account.

1.6.3 Expected disposal of assets

Gains from the expected disposal of assets should not be taken into account in measuring a provision.

1.6.4 Reimbursements

Some or all of the expenditure needed to settle a provision may be expected to be recovered from a third party. If so, the **reimbursement should be recognised only when it is virtually certain that reimbursement will be received if the entity settles the obligation.**

(a) The reimbursement should be treated as a separate asset, and the amount recognised should not be greater than the provision itself.

(b) The provision and the amount recognised for reimbursement may be netted off in profit or loss.

1.6.5 Changes in provisions

Provisions should be reviewed at the end of each reporting period and adjusted to reflect the current best estimate. If it is no longer probable that a transfer of economic benefits will be required to settle the obligation, the provision should be reversed.

1.6.6 Use of provisions

A provision should be used only for expenditures for which the provision was originally recognised. Setting expenditures against a provision that was originally recognised for another purpose would conceal the impact of two different events.

1.6.7 Future operating losses

Provisions should not be recognised for future operating losses. They do not meet the definition of a liability and the general recognition criteria set out in the standard.

1.6.8 Onerous contracts

If an entity has a contract that is onerous, the present obligation under the contract **should be recognised and measured** as a provision. An example might be vacant leasehold property.

KEY TERM

An ONEROUS CONTRACT is a contract entered into with another party under which the unavoidable costs of fulfilling the terms of the contract exceed any revenues expected to be received from the goods or services supplied or purchased directly or indirectly under the contract and where the entity would have to compensate the other party if it did not fulfil the terms of the contract.

1.7 Examples of possible provisions   11/10

It is easier to see what IAS 37 is driving at if you look at examples of those items which are possible provisions under this standard. Some of these we have already touched on.

(a) **Warranties**. These are argued to be genuine provisions as on past experience it is probable, ie more likely than not, that some claims will emerge. The provision must be estimated, however, on the basis of the class as a whole and not on individual claims. There is a clear legal obligation in this case.

(b) **Major repairs**. In the past it has been quite popular for companies to provide for expenditure on a major overhaul to be accrued gradually over the intervening years between overhauls. Under IAS 37 this is no longer be possible as IAS 37 holds that this is a mere intention to carry out repairs, not an obligation. The entity can always sell the asset in the meantime. The only solution is to treat major assets such as aircraft, ships, furnaces etc as a series of smaller assets where each part is depreciated over different lives. Thus any major overhaul may be argued to be replacement and therefore capital rather than revenue expenditure.

(c) **Self insurance**. A number of companies have created a provision for self insurance based on the expected cost of making good fire damage etc instead of paying premiums to an insurance company. Under IAS 37 this provision is no longer justifiable as the entity has no obligation until a fire or accident occurs. No obligation exists until that time.

(d) **Environmental contamination**. If the company has an environment policy such that other parties would expect the company to clean up any contamination or if the company has broken current environmental legislation then a provision for environmental damage must be made.

(e)   **Decommissioning or abandonment costs**. When an oil company initially purchases an oilfield it is put under a legal obligation to decommission the site at the end of its life. Prior to IAS 37 most oil companies set up the provision gradually over the life of the field so that no one year would be unduly burdened with the cost.

IAS 37, however, insists that a legal obligation exists on the initial expenditure on the field and therefore a liability exists immediately. This would appear to result in a large charge to profit and loss in the first year of operation of the field. However, the IAS takes the view that the cost of purchasing the field in the first place is not only the cost of the field itself but also the costs of putting it right again. Thus all the costs of abandonment may be capitalised.

(f)   **Restructuring**. This is considered in detail below.

1.8 Provisions for restructuring   5/10

One of the main purposes of IAS 37 was to target abuses of provisions for restructuring. Accordingly, IAS 37 lays down **strict criteria** to determine when such a provision can be made.

KEY TERM

IAS 37 defines a RESTRUCTURING as:

A programme that is planned and is controlled by management and materially changes either:

- the scope of a business undertaken by an entity; or
- the manner in which that business is conducted.

The IAS gives the following **examples** of events that may fall under the definition of restructuring.

- The **sale or termination** of a line of business
- The **closure of business locations** in a country or region or the **relocation** of business activities from one country region to another
- **Changes in management structure**, for example, the elimination of a layer of management
- **Fundamental reorganisations** that have a material effect on the **nature and focus** of the entity's operations

The question is whether or not an entity has an obligation - legal or constructive - at the end of the reporting period:

- An entity must have a **detailed formal plan** for the restructuring.
- It must have **raised a valid expectation** in those affected that it will carry out the restructuring by starting to implement that plan or announcing its main features to those affected by it

KEY POINT

A mere management decision is not normally sufficient. Management decisions may sometimes trigger off recognition, but only if earlier events such as negotiations with employee representatives and other interested parties have been concluded subject only to management approval.

Where the restructuring involves the **sale of an operation** then IAS 37 states that no obligation arises until the entity has entered into a **binding sale agreement**. This is because until this has occurred the entity will be able to change its mind and withdraw from the sale even if its intentions have been announced publicly.

1.8.1 Costs to be included within a restructuring provision

The IAS states that a restructuring provision should include only the **direct expenditures** arising from the restructuring, which are those that are both:

- **Necessarily entailed** by the restructuring; and
- Not associated with the **ongoing activities** of the entity.

The following costs should specifically **not** be included within a restructuring provision.

- **Retraining** or relocating continuing staff
- **Marketing**
- **Investment in new systems** and distribution networks

1.8.2 Disclosure

Disclosures for provisions fall into two parts.

- Disclosure of details of the **change in carrying value** of a provision from the beginning to the end of the year
- Disclosure of the **background** to the making of the provision and the uncertainties affecting its outcome

1.9 Contingent liabilities

Now that you understand provisions it will be easier to understand contingent assets and liabilities.

KEY TERM

IAS 37 defines a CONTINGENT LIABILITY as:

- A possible obligation that arises from past events and whose existence will be confirmed only by the occurrence or non-occurrence of one or more uncertain future events not wholly within the entity's control; or
- A present obligation that arises from past events but is not recognised because:

  - It is not probable that a transfer of economic benefits will be required to settle the obligation; or

  - The amount of the obligation cannot be measured with sufficient reliability.

As a rule of thumb, probable means **more than 50%** likely. **If an obligation is probable, it is not a contingent liability** - instead, a **provision is needed.**

1.9.1 Treatment of contingent liabilities

KEY POINT

Contingent liabilities **should not be recognised in financial statements** but they **should be disclosed,** unless the possibility of an outflow of economic benefits is **remote**.

The required disclosures are:

- A brief description of the nature of the contingent liability
- An estimate of its financial effect
- An indication of the uncertainties that exist
- The possibility of any reimbursement

1.10 Contingent assets

KEY TERM

IAS 37 defines a CONTINGENT ASSET as:

A possible asset that arises from past events and whose existence will be confirmed by the occurrence of one or more uncertain future events not wholly within the entity's control.

1.10.1 Treatment of contingent assets

KEY POINT

A contingent asset **must not be recognised as an asset** in the statement of financial position. Instead it should be **disclosed in the notes to the accounts** if it is **probable** that the economic benefits associated with the asset will flow to the entity.

A brief description of the contingent asset should be provided along with an estimate of its likely financial effect.

If the flow of economic benefits associated with the contingent asset becomes **virtually certain**, it should then be recognised as an asset in the statement of financial position as it is no longer a contingent asset.

1.10.2 'Let out'

IAS 37 permits reporting entities to avoid disclosure requirements relating to provisions, contingent liabilities and contingent assets if they would be expected to **seriously prejudice** the position of the entity in dispute with other parties. However, this should only be employed in **extremely rare** cases. Details of the general nature of the provision/contingencies must still be provided, together with an explanation of why it has not been disclosed.

1.11 IAS 37 flow chart

You must practise the questions below to get the hang of IAS 37. But first, study the flow chart, taken from IAS 37, which is a good summary of its requirements.

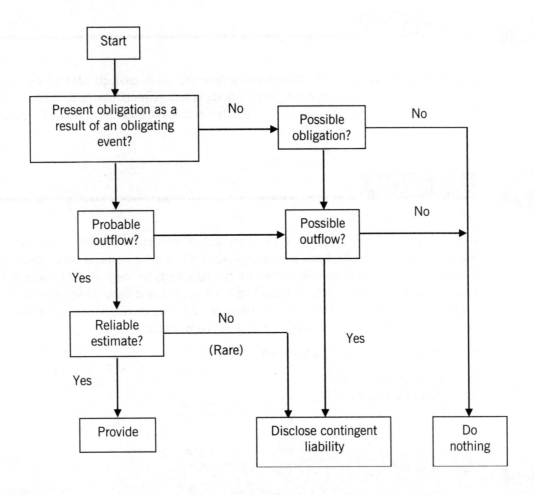

 Exam skills

If you learn this flow chart you should be able to deal with most questions you are likely to meet in an exam.

Question 10.3	Provide or not? (I)

Learning outcome C2(a)

During 20X0 Smack Co gives a guarantee of certain borrowings of Pony Co, whose financial condition at that time is sound. During 20X1, the financial condition of Pony Co deteriorates and at 30 June 20X1 Pony Co files for protection from its creditors.

What accounting treatment is required:

(a)   At 31 December 20X0?
(b)   At 31 December 20X1?

Question 10.4   Provide or not? (II)

Learning outcome C2(a)

Warren Co gives warranties at the time of sale to purchasers of its products. Under the terms of the warranty the manufacturer undertakes to make good, by repair or replacement, manufacturing defects that become apparent within a period of three years from the date of the sale. Should a provision be recognised?

Question 10.5   Provide or not? (III)

Learning outcome C2(a)

After a wedding in 20X0 ten people became seriously ill, possibly as a result of food poisoning from products sold by Callow Co. Legal proceedings are started seeking damages from Callow but it disputes liability. Up to the date of approval of the financial statements for the year to 31 December 20X0, Callow's lawyers advise that it is probable that it will not be found liable. However, when Callow prepares the financial statements for the year to 31 December 20X1 its lawyers advise that, owing to developments in the case, it is probable that it will be found liable.

What is the required accounting treatment:

(a)   At 31 December 20X0?
(b)   At 31 December 20X1?

Section summary

- The objective of IAS 37 is to ensure that appropriate recognition criteria and measurement bases are applied to provisions and contingencies and that sufficient information is disclosed.

- IAS 37 seeks to ensure that provisions are **only recognised** when a **measurable obligation** exists. It includes detailed rules that can be used to ascertain when an obligation exists and how to measure the obligation.

- IAS 37 attempts to **eliminate 'profit smoothing'**.

2 IAS 10 *Events after the reporting period*   11/10

Introduction

In this section we cover the reporting requirements where an event occurs after the end of the reporting period. In some instances, the financial statements will need to be amended for such an event.

2.1 Purpose of IAS 10

The financial statements are significant indicators of a company's success or failure. It is important, therefore, that they include all the information necessary for an understanding of the company's position.

IAS 10 *Events after the reporting period* requires the provision of additional information in order to facilitate such an understanding. IAS 10 deals with events **after** the end of the reporting period which may affect the position at the end of the reporting period.

2.2 Definitions

The standard gives the following definition.

KEY TERM

EVENTS OCCURRING AFTER THE END OF THE REPORTING PERIOD are those events, both favourable and unfavourable, that occur between the end of the reporting period and the date on which the financial statements are authorised for issue. Two types of events can be identified.

- Those that provide evidence of conditions that existed at the end of the reporting period – *adjusting events after the reporting period*
- Those that are indicative of conditions that arose after the end of the reporting period – *non-adjusting events after the reporting period*   *(IAS 10)*

2.3 Adjusting events

KEY POINT

An adjusting event is one which **provides evidence of conditions that existed at the end of the reporting period**. IAS 10 requires the entity to adjust amounts recognised in its financial statements to reflect these adjusting events.

An **example** of additional evidence which becomes available after the end of the reporting period is where a **customer goes bankrupt, thus confirming that the trade account receivable balance at the year end is uncollectable.**

In relation to **going concern**, the standard states that, where operating results and the financial position have deteriorated after the end of the reporting period, it may be necessary to reconsider whether the going concern assumption is appropriate in the preparation of the financial statements.

Other examples of **adjusting events** are:

- Evidence of a permanent diminution in property value prior to the year end
- Sale of inventory after the end of the reporting period for less than its carrying value at the year end
- Insolvency of a customer with a balance owing at the year end
- Amounts received or paid in respect of legal or insurance claims which were in negotiation at the year end
- Determination after the year end of the sale or purchase price of assets sold or purchased before the year end
- Evidence of a permanent diminution in the value of a long-term investment prior to the year end
- Discovery of error or fraud which shows that the financial statements were incorrect

2.4 Non-adjusting events

KEY POINT

A non-adjusting event is one which is **indicative of conditions that arose after the end of the reporting period**. Non-adjusting events do not require adjustment of items in the financial statements.

The standard gives the following examples of events which are non-adjusting:

- Acquisition of, or disposal of, a subsidiary after the year end
- Announcement of a plan to discontinue an operation
- Major purchases and disposals of assets
- Destruction of a production plant by fire after the end of the reporting period
- Announcement or commencing implementation of a major restructuring
- Share transactions after the end of the reporting period
- Litigation commenced after the end of the reporting period

But note that, while they may be non-adjusting, events that are **material** should be disclosed in the notes to the financial statements.

2.5 Dividends

Dividends on equity shares should only be included as a liability in the financial statements if they have been declared before the end of the reporting period. Those dividends declared by the entity after the end of the reporting period should not be recognised as a liability at the end of the reporting period, but should be disclosed in the notes to the financial statements.

2.6 Disclosures

The following **disclosure requirements** are given **for events** which occur after the end of the reporting period which do not require adjustment. If disclosure of events occurring after the end of the reporting period is required, the following information should be provided.

(a)   The nature of the event
(b)   An estimate of the financial effect, or a statement that such an estimate cannot be made

The financial statements should also state the date on which they were authorised for issue.

Question 10.6	Adjusting or not?

Learning outcome C2(a)

State whether the following events occurring after the end of the reporting period require an adjustment to the assets and liabilities of the financial statements.

(a)   Purchase of an investment
(b)   A change in the rate of corporate tax, applicable to the previous year
(c)   An increase in pension benefits
(d)   Losses due to fire
(e)   A bad debt suddenly being paid
(f)   The receipt of proceeds of sales or other evidence concerning the net realisable value of inventory
(g)   A sudden decline in the value of property held as a long-term asset

Section summary

IAS 10 deals with **events occurring after the reporting period**. It distinguishes between **adjusting** and **non-adjusting** events and gives examples.

3   IAS 24 *Related party disclosures*   11/10

Introduction

This section introduces the area of related parties. We will look at what a related party is, what disclosures are required and why.

3.1 Why was a standard needed?

In the absence of information to the contrary, it is assumed that a reporting entity has **independent discretionary power** over its resources and transactions and pursues its activities independently of the interests of its individual owners, managers and others. Transactions are presumed to have been undertaken on an **arm's length basis**, ie on terms such as could have obtained in a transaction with an external party, in which each side bargained knowledgeably and freely, unaffected by any relationship between them.

These assumptions may not be justified when **related party relationships** exist, because the requisite conditions for competitive, free market dealings may not be present. Whilst the parties may endeavour to achieve arm's length bargaining the very nature of the relationship may preclude this occurring.

3.2 Objective

The objective of IAS 24 is to ensure that an entity's financial statements contain the disclosures necessary to draw attention to the possibility that its financial position and profit or loss may have been affected by the existence of related parties and by transactions and outstanding balances with such parties.

3.3 Definitions

The following important definitions are given in the standard:

KEY TERM

Under the standard a party is a RELATED PARTY if:

(a)   Directly or indirectly the party

    (i)   Controls, is controlled by, or is under common control with, the entity (this includes parents, subsidiaries, fellow subsidiaries)

    (ii)   Has an interest in the entity that gives it significant influence over the entity; or

    (iii)   Has joint control over the entity

(b)   The party is an associate of the entity

(c)   The party is a joint venture in which the entity is a venturer

(d)   The party is a member of the key management personnel of the entity or its parent

(e)   The party is a close member of the family of any individual referred to in (a) or (d)

(f)   The party is an entity that is controlled, jointly controlled or significantly influenced by, or a significant proportion of whose voting rights are held by, any individual referred to in (d) or (e)

(g)   The party is a post-employment benefit plan for the benefit of employees of the entity, or of any entity that is a related party of the entity

KEY TERMS

RELATED PARTY TRANSACTION. A transfer of resources, services or obligations between related parties, regardless of whether a price is charged.

KEY MANAGEMENT PERSONNEL. Those persons having authority and responsibility for planning, directing and controlling the activities of the entity, directly or indirectly, including any director of that entity.

KEY POINT

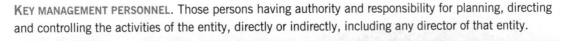
In summary, a party is related to an entity if it has **control** or the ability to exercise **significant influence** over the entity.

You should note that significant influence is presumed when an investor owns 20% or more of the voting power of the entity, unless it can be clearly shown that this is not the case. Therefore any investor owning 20% or more of the voting rights will be presumed to be a related party.

Exam alert

Although IAS 24 includes parents, subsidisaries, associates, joint ventures and post-employment benefit plans as related parties, CIMA has stated that they are outside the scope of the F1 syllabus.

3.4 Exclusions

IAS 24 states that the following are not necessarily related parties:

(a)   Two entities simply because they have a director or other member of key management personnel in common

(b)   Two venturers simply because they share control over a joint venture

(c)   (i)   Providers of finance
           (ii)   Trade unions
           (iii)   Public utilities; and
           (iv)   Government departments and agencies

(d)   A customer, supplier, franchisor, distributor or general agent with whom the entity transacts a significant volume of business, merely by virtue of the resulting economic dependence. (In other words, this is not designated as *significant influence*.)

3.5 Disclosures

(a)   **Relationships between parents and subsidiaries** are to be disclosed irrespective of whether any transactions have taken place.

(b)   **Key management personnel compensation** is to be disclosed in total and for each of:

           (i)   short-term employee benefits (eg wages, salaries, social security contributions)
           (ii)   post-employment benefits such as pensions
           (iii)   other long-term employee benefits (eg bonuses, profit sharing, long service leave)
           (iv)   termination benefits
           (v)   share-based payments.

(c)   **Transactions between related parties** require disclosure of the nature of the relationship as well as information about the transaction and any outstanding balances necessary for an understanding of the potential effect of the relationship on the financial statements. As a minimum, disclosure should include:

           (i)   amount of the transaction(s)

           (ii)   amount of any outstanding balances (including terms and conditions attached to them and any guarantees given and received)

           (iii)   any provisions or expenses in respect of doubtful debts due from related parties.

Disclosure that related party transactions were made on terms equivalent to transactions that occur at arm's length should only be given if such terms can be substantiated.

3.6 Transactions

The standard gives the following examples of transactions that are disclosed if they are with a related party:

(a)   Purchases or sales of goods
(b)   Purchases or sales of property and other assets
(c)   Rendering or receiving of services
(d)   Leases
(e)   Transfers of research and development
(f)   Transfers under licence agreement
(g)   Transfers under finance arrangements (such as loans)
(h)   Provisions of guarantees or collateral; and
(i)   Settlement of liabilities on behalf of the entity, or by the entity on behalf of another party

Exam alert

A question on IAS 24 may simply be on what constitutes a related party. Make sure you know this and are able to provide examples.

Section summary

IAS 24 is primarily a **disclosure standard**. It is concerned with improving the quality of information provided by published accounts.

Chapter Roundup

✓   The objective of IAS 37 is to ensure that appropriate recognition criteria and measurement bases are applied to provisions and contingencies and that sufficient information is disclosed.

✓   IAS 37 seeks to ensure that provisions are **only recognised** when a **measurable obligation** exists. It includes detailed rules that can be used to ascertain when an obligation exists and how to measure the obligation.

✓   IAS 37 attempts to **eliminate 'profit smoothing'**.

✓   IAS 10 deals with **events occurring after the reporting period**. It distinguishes between adjusting and non-adjusting events and gives examples.

✓   **IAS 24** is primarily a **disclosure standard**. It is concerned with improving the quality of information provided by published accounts.

Quick Quiz

1   A customer goes bankrupt after the end of the reporting period and his debt must be written off. Is this an adjusting or non-adjusting event according to IAS 10?

     Adjusting event   ☐

     Non-adjusting event   ☐

2   Inventory is lost in a fire after the end of the reporting period. Is this an adjusting or non-adjusting event according to IAS 10?

     Adjusting event   ☐

     Non-adjusting event   ☐

3   A provision is a .... of .... timing or amount.

4   A programme is undertaken by management which converts the previously wholly owned chain of restaurants they ran into franchises. Is this restructuring?

5   Define contingent asset and contingent liability.

6   Banks lending money to a company are deemed related parties by IAS 24. Is this statement true or false?

     True   ☐

     False   ☐

Answers to Quick Quiz

1   Adjusting

2   Non-adjusting

3   Liability, uncertain

4   Yes. The manner in which the business is conducted has changed.

5   Refer to paragraphs 1.9 and 1.10

6   False (see Para 3.4).

Answers to Questions

10.1 Recognising a provision

(a)   No provision would be recognised as the decision has not been implemented.

(b)   A provision would be made in the 20X9 financial statements.

(c)   A provision for such costs is appropriate.

(d)   No present obligation exists and under IAS 37 no provision would be appropriate. This is because the entity could avoid the future expenditure by its future actions, maybe by changing its method of operation.

10.2 Warranty provision

Parker Co should use expected values to calculate the provision.

(75% × $nil) + (20% × $1.0m) + (5% × $4.0m) = $400,000.

10.3 Provide or not? (I)

(a)   **At 31 December 20X0**: There is a present obligation as a result of a past obligating event. The obligating event is the giving of the guarantee, which gives rise to a legal obligation. However, at 31 December 20X0 no transfer of economic benefits is probable in settlement of the obligation.

No provision is recognised. The guarantee is disclosed as a contingent liability unless the probability of any transfer is regarded as remote.

(b)   **At 31 December 20X1**: As above, there is a present obligation as a result of a past obligating event, namely the giving of the guarantee. At 31 December 20X1 it is probable that a transfer of economic events will be required to settle the obligation. A provision is therefore recognised for the best estimate of the obligation.

10.4 Provide or not? (II)

Warren Co **cannot avoid** the cost of repairing or replacing all items of product that manifest manufacturing defects in respect of which warranties are given before the end of the reporting period, and a provision for the cost of this should therefore be made.

Warren Co is obliged to repair or replace items that fail within the entire warranty period. Therefore, in respect of **this year's sales**, the obligation provided for at the end of the reporting period, should be the cost of making good items for which defects have been notified but not yet processed, **plus** an estimate of costs in respect of the other items sold for which there is sufficient evidence that manufacturing defects **will** manifest themselves during their remaining periods of warranty cover.

10.5 Provide or not? (III)

(a)   At 31 December 20X0

On the basis of the evidence available when the financial statements were approved, there is no obligation as a result of past events. No provision is recognised. The matter is disclosed as a contingent liability unless the probability of any transfer is regarded as remote.

(b)   At 31 December 20X1

On the basis of the evidence available, there is a present obligation. A transfer of economic benefits in settlement is probable. A provision is recognised for the best estimate of the amount needed to settle the present obligation.

10.6 Adjusting or not?

(b), (e) and (f) require adjustment.

Now try these questions from the Exam Question Bank	Number	Level	Marks	Time
	Q19	Examination	5	9 mins
	Q22	Examination	5	9 mins

INVENTORIES AND CONSTRUCTION CONTRACTS

You have encountered inventory and its valuation in your earlier studies. Inventory and short term work-in-progress valuation has a direct impact on a company's gross profit and it can often be a material item in a company's accounts. This is therefore an important subject area. If you have any doubts about accounting for inventories and methods of inventory valuation you would be advised to go back to your earlier study material and revise this topic.

Section 1 of this chapter goes over some of this ground again, concentrating on the effect of IAS 2. Section 2 goes on to discuss a new area, construction contracts, which are effectively long-term work in progress. You should find this topic fairly logical as long as you work through the examples and question carefully.

topic list	learning outcomes	syllabus references	ability required
1 Inventories and short-term WIP (IAS 2)	C2(a)	C2(vi)	application
2 IAS 11 *Construction contracts*	C2(a)	C2(viii)	application

1   Inventories and short-term WIP (IAS 2)

Introduction

In this section we develop the knowledge on inventories you have accumulated in previous papers. We will examine IAS 2 (revised) *Inventories,* specifically how the value of inventory should be measured and disclosed.

1.1 Valuing inventory

In most businesses the value put on inventory is an important factor in the determination of profit. Inventory valuation is, however, a highly subjective exercise and consequently there is a wide variety of different methods used in practice.

1.2 IAS 2 (revised) *Inventories*

IAS 2 lays out the required accounting treatment for inventories (sometimes called stocks) under the historical cost system. The major area of contention is the cost **value of inventory** to be recorded. This is recognised as an asset of the entity until the related revenues are recognised (ie the item is sold) at which point the inventory is recognised as an expense (ie cost of sales). Part or all of the cost of inventories may also be expensed if a write-down to **net realisable value** is necessary. The IAS also provides guidance on the cost formulas that are used to assign costs to inventories.

1.3 Definitions

The standard gives the following important definition.

KEY TERM

INVENTORIES are assets:

- Held for sale in the ordinary course of business;

- In the process of production for such sale; or

- In the form of materials or supplies to be consumed in the production process or in the rendering of services.

Inventories can **include** any of the following.

- **Goods purchased and held for resale**, eg goods held for sale by a retailer, or land and buildings held for resale

- **Finished goods** produced

- **Work in progress** being produced

- Materials and supplies awaiting use in the production process (**raw materials**)

1.4 Measurement of inventories

KEY POINT

Inventories should be measured at the **lower** of **cost** and **net realisable value.**

1.5 Cost of inventories

The cost of inventories will consist of all:

(a)   **Costs of purchase**
(b)   **Costs of conversion**
(c)   **Other costs** incurred in bringing the inventories to their **present location** and **condition**

1.5.1 Costs of purchase

The standard lists the following as comprising the costs of purchase of inventories:

(a)   **Purchase price** *plus*

(b)   **Import duties** and other taxes *plus*

(c)   Transport, handling and any other costs **directly attributable** to the acquisition of finished goods, services and materials *less*

(d)   **Trade discounts**, rebates and other similar amounts

1.5.2 Costs of conversion

Costs of conversion of inventories consist of two main parts.

(a)   Costs **directly related** to the units of production, eg direct materials, direct labour

(b)   Fixed and variable **production overheads** that are incurred in converting materials into finished goods, allocated on a systematic basis.

You may have come across the terms 'fixed production overheads' or 'variable production overheads' elsewhere in your studies. The standard defines them as follows.

KEY TERMS

FIXED PRODUCTION OVERHEADS are those indirect costs of production that remain relatively constant regardless of the volume of production, eg the cost of factory management and administration.

VARIABLE PRODUCTION OVERHEADS are those indirect costs of production that vary directly, or nearly directly, with the volume of production, eg indirect materials and labour.   *(IAS 2)*

The standard emphasises that fixed production overheads must be allocated to items of inventory on the basis of the **normal capacity of the production facilities**. This is an important point.

(a)   **Normal capacity** is the expected achievable production based on the average over several periods/seasons, under normal circumstances.

(b)   The above figure should take account of the capacity lost through **planned maintenance**.

(c)   If it approximates to the normal level of activity then the **actual level of production** can be used.

(d)   **Low production** or **idle plant** will *not* result in a higher fixed overhead allocation to each unit.

(e)   **Unallocated overheads** must be recognised as an **expense** in the period in which they were incurred.

(f)   When production is **abnormally high**, the fixed production overhead allocated to each unit will be reduced, so avoiding inventories being stated at more than cost.

(g)   The allocation of variable production overheads to each unit is based on the **actual use** of production facilities.

1.5.3 Other costs

Any other costs should only be recognised if they are incurred in bringing the inventories to their **present location and condition**. Borrowing costs can be included in the cost of inventory provided the requirements of IAS 23 *Borrowing costs* are met.

The standard lists types of cost which **would not be included** in cost of inventories. Instead, they should be recognised as an **expense** in the period they are incurred.

*   **Abnormal amounts** of wasted materials, labour or other production costs

*   **Storage costs** (except costs which are necessary in the production process before a further production stage)

*   **Administrative overheads** not incurred to bring inventories to their present location and condition

*   **Selling costs**

1.6 Determining cost

Cost of inventories should be assigned by **specific identification** of their individual costs for items that are not ordinarily interchangeable (ie identical or very similar) and for goods or services produced and segregated for **specific projects**. Specific identification of cost means that specific costs are attributed to identified items of inventory. However, calculating costs on an individual item basis could be onerous. For convenience, IAS 2 allows the use of cost estimation techniques, such as the **standard cost method** or the **retail method**, provided that the results approximate cost.

(a)   **Standard costs** take into account **normal** levels of materials and supplies, labour, efficiency and capacity utilisation. They are regularly reviewed and revised if necessary to ensure they appropriately resemble actual costs.

(b)   The **retail method** is often used in the retail industry for measuring inventories of large numbers of rapidly changing items with similar margins for which it is impracticable to use other costing methods. The cost of the inventory is determined by reducing the sales value of the inventory by the percentage gross margin.

1.6.1 Interchangeable items

Where inventories consist of a large number of interchangeable (ie identical or very similar) items, it will be virtually impossible to determine costs on an individual item basis. Therefore IAS 2 allows the following cost estimation techniques.

(a)   **FIFO** (first in, first out). Using this technique, we assume that components are used in the order in which they are received from suppliers. The components issued are deemed to have formed part of the oldest consignment still unused and are costed accordingly.

(b)   **Weighted Average Cost.** As purchase prices change with each new consignment, the average price of components in inventory is constantly changed. Each component in inventory at any moment is assumed to have been purchased at the average price of all components in inventory at that moment. Under the weighted average cost method, a recalculation can be made after each purchase, **or alternatively only at the period end**.

The same technique should be used by the entity for all inventories that have a similar nature and use.

Note that the LIFO formula (last in, first out) is **not permitted** by the revised IAS 2.

1.7 Net realisable value (NRV)

KEY TERM

NET REALISABLE VALUE is the estimated selling price in the ordinary course of business less the estimated costs of completion and the estimated costs necessary to make the sale.

As we noted earlier, a key principle in IAS 2 is that inventories should be carried at the lower of cost and NRV.

We can identify the principal situations in which **NRV is likely to be less than cost**, ie where there has been:

(a)   An **increase in costs** or a **fall in selling price**

(b)   A **physical deterioration** in the condition of inventory

(c)   **Obsolescence** of products

(d)   A decision as part of the company's marketing strategy to manufacture and sell products at a **loss**

(e)   **Errors in production or purchasing**

1.8 Disclosure

The financial statements should disclose the following.

(a)   **Accounting policies** adopted in measuring inventories, including the cost formula used

(b)   **Total carrying amount of inventories** and the carrying amount in classifications appropriate to the entity

(c)   **Carrying amount** of inventories carried at NRV.

Question 11.1	Inventory valuation

Learning outcomes C2(a)

You are the accountant at Water Pumps Co, and you have been asked to calculate the valuation of the company's inventory at cost at its year end of 30 April 20X5.

Water Pumps manufactures a range of pumps. The pumps are assembled from components bought by Water Pumps (the company does not manufacture any parts).

The company does not use a standard costing system, and work in progress and finished goods are valued as follows.

(a)   Material costs are determined from the product specification, which lists the components required to make a pump.

(b)   The company produces a range of pumps. Employees record the hours spent on assembling each type of pump, this information is input into the payroll system which prints the total hours spent each week assembling each type of pump. All employees assembling pumps are paid at the same rate and there is no overtime.

(c)   Overheads are added to the inventory value in accordance with IAS 2 *Inventories*. The financial accounting records are used to determine the overhead cost, and this is applied as a percentage based on the direct labour cost.

For direct labour costs, you have agreed that the labour expended for a unit in work in progress is half that of a completed unit.

The draft accounts show the following materials and direct labour costs in inventory.

	Raw materials	Work in progress	Finished goods
Materials ($)	74,786	85,692	152,693
Direct labour ($)		13,072	46,584

The costs incurred in April, as recorded in the financial accounting records, were as follows.

	$
Direct labour	61,320
Selling costs	43,550
Depreciation and finance costs of production machines	4,490
Distribution costs	6,570
Factory manager's wage	2,560
Other production overheads	24,820
Purchasing and accounting costs relating to production	5,450
Other accounting costs	7,130
Other administration overheads	24,770

For your calculations assume that all work in progress and finished goods were produced in April 20X5 and that the company was operating at a normal level of activity.

Required

Calculate the value of overheads which should be added to work in progress and finished goods in accordance with IAS 2 *Inventories*.

Note. You should include details and a description of your workings and all figures should be calculated to the nearest $.

Section summary

Inventories should be measured at the **lower** of **cost** and **net realisable value.**

The cost of inventories includes the **costs of purchase**, **costs of conversion** and **other costs** incurred in bringing the inventories to their present location and condition.

The cost of inventories that are not interchangeable can be estimated using the **standard cost** method or the **retail method**.

The cost of interchangeable inventories should be measured using **FIFO** (first in, first out) or **Weighted Average Cost**. LIFO (last in, first out) is not allowed under IAS 2.

Net realisable value is the estimated selling price less the estimated costs of completion and the estimated costs necessary to make the sale.

2 IAS 11 *Construction contracts*

Introduction

In this section we introduce construction contracts. We will look at the required treatments and disclosures under IAS 11. Make sure that you work through and understand all the examples.

2.1 The need for IAS 11

Imagine that you are the accountant at a construction company. Your company is building a large tower block that will house offices, under a contract with an investment company. It will take three years to build the block and over that time you will obviously have to pay for building materials, wages of workers on the building, architects' fees and so on. You will receive periodic payments from the investment company at various predetermined stages of the construction. How do you decide, in each of the three years, **what to include as income and expenditure** for the contract in the statement of comprehensive income?

This is the problem tackled by IAS 11 *Construction contracts*.

Example: Construction contract

A numerical example might help to illustrate the problem. Suppose that a contract is started on 1 January 20X5, with an estimated completion date of 31 December 20X6. The final contract price is $1,500,000. In the first year, to 31 December 20X5:

(a) Costs incurred amounted to $600,000.

(b) Half the work on the contract was completed.

(c) Certificates of work completed have been issued, to the value of $750,000. (*Note*. It is usual, in a construction contract, for a qualified person such as an architect or engineer to inspect the work completed, and if it is satisfactory, to issue certificates. This will then be the notification to the customer that progress payments are now due to the contractor. Progress payments are commonly the amount of valuation on the work certificates issued, minus a precautionary retention of 10%).

(d) It is estimated with reasonable certainty that further costs to completion in 20X6 will be $600,000.

What is the contract profit in 20X5, and what entries would be made for the contract at 31 December 20X5 if:

(a) Profits are deferred until the completion of the contract?
(b) A proportion of the estimated revenue and profit is credited to the profit or loss in 20X5?

Solution

(a) If profits were deferred until the completion of the contract in 20X6, the revenue and profit recognised on the contract in 20X5 would be nil, and the value of work in progress on 31 December 20X5 would be $600,000. IAS 11 takes the view that this policy is unreasonable, because in 20X6, the total profit of $300,000 would be recorded. Since the contract revenues are earned throughout 20X5 and 20X6, a profit of nil in 20X5 and $300,000 in 20X6 would be contrary to the accruals concept of accounting.

(b) **It is fairer to recognise revenue and profit throughout the duration of the contract.**

As at 31 December 20X5 revenue of $750,000 should be matched with cost of sales of $600,000 in the statement of comprehensive income, leaving an attributable profit for 20X5 of $150,000.

The only entry in the statement of financial position as at 31 December 20X5 is a receivable of $750,000 recognising that the company is owed this amount for work done to date. No balance remains for work in progress, the whole $600,000 having been recognised in cost of sales.

2.2 What is a construction contract?

A contract which needs IAS 11 treatment does not have to last for a period of more than one year. The main point is that the contract activity **starts in one financial period and ends in another**, thus creating the problem: to which of two or more periods should contract income and costs be allocated? In fact the definition given in the IAS of a construction contract is very straightforward.

CONSTRUCTION CONTRACT. A contract specifically negotiated for the construction of an asset or a combination of assets that are closely interrelated or interdependent in terms of their design, technology and function or their ultimate purpose or use. *(IAS 11)*

The standard differentiates between fixed price contracts and cost plus contracts.

FIXED PRICE CONTRACT. A contract in which the contractor agrees to a fixed contract price, or a fixed rate per unit of output, which in some cases is subject to cost escalation clauses.

COST PLUS CONTRACT. A construction contract in which the contractor is reimbursed for allowable or otherwise defined costs, plus a percentage of these costs or a fixed fee. *(IAS 11)*

Construction contracts may involve the building of one asset, eg a bridge, or a series of interrelated assets eg an oil refinery. They may also include **rendering of services** (eg architects) or restoring or demolishing an asset.

2.3 Combining and segmenting construction contracts

The standard lays out the factors which determine whether the construction of a **series of assets** under one contract should be treated as several contracts.

- **Separate proposals** are submitted for each asset
- **Separate negotiations** are undertaken for each asset; the customer can accept/reject each individually
- **Identifiable costs and revenues** can be separated for each asset

There are also circumstances where a **group of contracts** should be treated as **one single construction contract**.

- The group of contracts are negotiated as a **single package**
- Contracts are **closely interrelated**, with an overall profit margin
- The contracts are performed **concurrently** or **in a continuous sequence**

2.4 Contract revenue

Contract revenue will be the **amount specified in the contract**, subject to variations in the contract work, incentive payments and claims *if* these will probably give rise to revenue and *if* they can be reliably measured. The result is that contract revenue is measured at the **fair value** of received or receivable revenue.

The standard elaborates on the types of uncertainty, which depend on the outcome of future events, that affect the **measurement of contract revenue**.

- An **agreed variation** (increase/decrease)
- **Cost escalation clauses** in a fixed price contract (increase)
- **Penalties** imposed due to delays by the contractor (decrease)
- **Number of units** varies in a contract for fixed prices per unit (increase/decrease)

In the case of any variation, claim or incentive payment, two factors should be assessed to determine whether contract revenue should be recognised.

(a) Whether it is **probable** that the customer will accept the variation/claim, or that the contract is sufficiently advanced that the performance criteria will be met

(b) Whether the amount of the revenue can be **measured reliably**

2.5 Contract costs

Contract costs consist of:

- Costs relating **directly** to the contract

- Costs attributable to general contract activity which can be **allocated** to the contract, such as insurance, cost of design and technical assistance not directly related to a specific contract and construction overheads

- Any other costs which can be **charged to the customer** under the contract, which may include general administration costs and development costs

Costs that **relate directly** to a specific contract include the following.

- **Site labour costs**, including site supervision
- Costs of **materials** used in construction
- **Depreciation** of plant and equipment used on the contract
- Costs of **moving** plant, equipment and materials to and from the contract site
- Costs of **hiring** plant and equipment
- Costs of **design and technical assistance** that are directly related to the contract
- Estimated costs of **rectification and guarantee work**, including expected warranty costs
- **Claims from third parties**

General contract activity costs should be **allocated systematically and rationally**, and all costs with similar characteristics should be treated **consistently**. The allocation should be based on the **normal level** of construction activity.

Some costs **cannot be attributed** to contract activity and so the following should be **excluded** from construction contract costs.

- **General administration costs** (unless reimbursement is specified in contract)
- **Selling costs**
- **R&D** (unless reimbursement is specified in contract)
- **Depreciation** of idle plant and equipment not used on any particular contract

2.6 Recognition of contract revenue and expenses

KEY POINT

When the outcome of a contract can be **estimated reliably**, the contract revenue and costs can be recognised according to the **stage of completion** of the contract.

This is often known as the **percentage of completion method**.

If a **loss** is predicted on a contract, then it should be **recognised immediately**.

A reliable estimate of the outcome of a construction contract can only be made when **certain conditions** have been met, and these conditions will be different for fixed price and cost plus contracts.

- **Fixed price contracts**

  - Probable that economic benefits of the contract will flow to the entity

  - Total contract revenue can be reliably measured

  - Stage of completion at the period end and costs to complete the contract can be reliably measured

  - Costs attributable to the contract can be identified clearly and be reliably measured (actual costs can be compared to previous estimates)

- **Cost plus contracts**

  - Probable that economic benefits of the contract will flow to the entity

  - Costs attributable to the contract (whether or not reimbursable) can be identified clearly and be reliably measured

The **percentage of completion method** is an application of the **accruals assumption**. Contract revenue is matched to the contract costs incurred in reaching the stage of completion, so revenue, costs and profit are attributed to the proportion of work completed.

We can **summarise** the treatment as follows.

- Recognise **contract revenue** as revenue in the accounting periods in which the work is performed

- Recognise **contract costs** as an expense in the accounting period in which the work to which they relate is performed

- Any **expected excess** of total contract costs over total contract revenue (ie a loss) should be recognised as an expense immediately

- Any costs incurred which relate to **future activity** should be recognised as an asset if it is probable that they will be recovered (often called contract work in progress, ie amounts due from the customer)

- Where amounts have been recognised as contract revenue, but their **collectability** from the customer becomes doubtful, such amounts should be recognised as an expense, not a deduction from revenue

2.7 When can reliable estimates be made?

IAS 11 only allows contract revenue and costs to be recognised when the outcome of the contract can be predicted, ie when it is probable that the economic benefits attached to the contract will flow to the entity. IAS 11 states that this can only be when a contract has been agreed which establishes the following.

- The **enforceable rights** of each party in respect of the asset to be constructed
- The **consideration** that is to be exchanged
- **Terms and manner of settlement**

In addition, the entity should have an **effective internal financial budgeting and reporting system**, in order to review and revise the estimates of contract revenue and costs as the contract progresses.

2.8 Determining the stage of completion

How should you decide on the stage of completion of any contract? IAS 11 gives three methods which are commonly used:

(a) Proportion of contract costs incurred for work carried out to date

$$\frac{\text{Costs to date}}{\text{Total estimated costs}}$$

(b) Surveys of work carried out

$$\frac{\text{Work certified}}{\text{Contract price}}$$

(c) Physical proportion of the contract work completed

Example: Stage of completion

Centrepoint Co have a fixed price contract to build a tower block. The initial amount of revenue agreed is $220m. At the beginning of the contract on 1 January 20X6 our initial estimate of the contract costs is $200m. At the end of 20X6 our estimate of the total costs has risen to $202m.

During 20X7 the customer agrees to a variation which increases expected revenue from the contract by $5m and causes additional costs of $3m. At the end of 20X7 there are materials stored on site for use during the following period which cost $2.5m.

We have decided to determine the stage of completion of the contract by calculating the proportion that contract costs incurred for work to date bear to the latest estimated total contract costs. The contract costs incurred at the end of each year were 20X6: $52.52m, 20X7: $154.2m (including materials in store), 20X8 $205m.

Required

Calculate the stage of completion for each year of the contract and show how revenues, costs and profits will be recognised in each year.

Solution

We can summarise the financial data for each year end during the construction period as follows.

	20X6 $'000	20X7 $'000	20X8 $'000
Initial amount of revenue agreed in the contract	220,000	220,000	220,000
Variation	–	5,000	5,000
Total contract revenue	220,000	225,000	225,000
Contract costs incurred to date	52,520	154,200	205,000
Contract costs to complete	149,480	50,800	–
Total estimated contract costs	202,000	205,000	205,000
Estimated profit	18,000	20,000	20,000
Stage of completion	**26%**	**74%**	**100%**

The stage of completion has been calculated using the formula:

$$\frac{\text{Costs to date}}{\text{Total estimated costs}}$$

The stage of completion in 20X7 is calculated by deducting the $2.5m of materials held for the following period from the costs incurred up to that year end, ie $154.2m – $2.5m = $151.7m.

$$\frac{\$151.7m}{\$205m} = 74\%$$

Revenue, expenses and profit will be recognised in profit or loss as follows.

	To date $'000	Recognised in prior years $'000	Recognised in current year $'000
20X6 Revenue ($220m × 26%)	57,200		
Costs ($202m × 26%)	52,520		
	4,680		
20X7 Revenue ($225m × 74%)	166,500	57,200	109,300
Costs ($205m × 74%)	151,700	52,520	99,180
	14,800	4,680	10,120
20X8 Revenue ($225m × 100%)	225,000	166,500	58,500
Costs ($205m × 100%)	205,000	151,700	53,300
	20,000	14,800	5,200

You can see from the above example that, when the stage of completion is determined using the contract costs incurred to date, only contract costs reflecting the work to date should be included in costs incurred to date:

- Exclude costs relating to **future activity**, eg cost of materials delivered but not yet used
- Exclude payments made to subcontractors **in advance** of work performed

2.9 Outcome of the contract cannot be predicted reliably

When the contract's outcome cannot be predicted reliably the following treatment should be followed.

- Only recognise revenue to the extent of contract costs incurred which are expected to be **recoverable**

- Recognise contract costs as an **expense** in the period they are incurred

This **no profit/no loss approach** reflects the situation near the beginning of a contract, ie the outcome cannot be reliably estimated, but it is likely that costs will be recovered.

Contract costs which **cannot be recovered** should be recognised as an expense straight away. IAS 11 lists the following situations where this might occur.

- The contract is **not fully enforceable**, ie its validity is seriously questioned
- The completion of the contract is subject to the outcome of **pending litigation or legislation**
- The contract relates to properties which will probably be **expropriated or condemned**
- The customer is **unable to meet its obligations** under the contract
- The contractor **cannot complete** the contract or in any other way meet its obligations under the contract

Where these **uncertainties cease to exist,** contract revenue and costs should be recognised as normal, ie by reference to the stage of completion.

2.10 Recognition of expected losses

Any loss on a contract should be **recognised as soon as it is foreseen**. The loss will be the amount by which total expected contract revenue is exceeded by total expected contract costs. The loss amount is not affected by whether work has started on the contract, the stage of completion of the work or profits on other contracts (unless they are related contracts treated as a single contract).

 Exam skills

The treatment of expected losses is very important and students often miss it. An exam question may give you a contract on which a loss is expected. **The first thing you should do when you attempt a question on construction contracts is to work out whether the contract is overall profit or loss making.**

2.11 Summary of accounting treatment

The following summarises the accounting treatment for construction contracts in the financial statements – **make sure that you understand it.**

2.11.1 Statement of comprehensive income   5/10

(a)   **Revenue and costs**

Sales revenue and associated costs should be recorded in the income statement section as the contract activity progresses:

(i)   Include a proportion of total contract value as sales revenue in the income statement. The proportion is based on the stage of completion of the contract.

(ii)   The costs incurred in reaching that stage of completion are matched with this sales revenue, resulting in the reporting of results which can be attributed to the proportion of work completed.

(b)   **Profit recognised in the contract**

(i)   If the contract is expected to be profitable overall, then profit related to the proportion of work carried out should be recognised.

(ii)   If the contract is expected to be loss making overall, then all of the loss must be recognised as soon as it is anticipated.

The effect in the income statement can be summarised as follows:

	$
Revenue recognised	X
Costs recognised	(X)
Recognised profit/loss	X/(X)

2.11.2 Statement of financial position

(a)   **Gross amount due from/to customers**

	$
Costs incurred	X
Recognised profits less recognised losses	X
	X
Less: progress billings to date	(X)
Amount recognised as an asset/(liability)	X/(X)

Gross amounts due from customers should be recognised as a current asset and gross amounts due to customers should be recognised as a current liability.

Exam alert

In your exam, make sure you state clearly whether the amount you have calculated is a current asset or current liability.

(b)   **Trade receivables**

	$
Progress billings to date	X
Less: cash received to date	(X)
	X

Work through the following example to make sure you understand how the accounting works.

Example: Construction contracts

Haggrun Co has two contracts in progress, the details of which are as follows.

	Happy $'000	Grumpy $'000
Total contract price	300	300
Costs incurred to date	90	150
Estimated costs to completion	135	225
Progress payments invoiced and received	116	116

Required

Show extracts from the statement of comprehensive income and the statement of financial position for each contract, assuming they are both:

(a)   40% complete; and

(b)   36% complete.

Solution

Tutorial note: Before doing any other workings, you should calculate whether each contract is expected to be profit or loss making overall.

Happy contract

	$'000
Final contract price	300
Less: costs to date	(90)
estimated future costs	(135)
Estimated final profit	75

Grumpy contract

	$'000
Final contract price	300
Less: costs to date	(150)
estimated future costs	(225)
Estimated final loss	(75)

Tutorial note: Now we can go on to calculate the amounts that should be recognised in the financial statements.

Happy contract (profit making)

(a)   *40% complete*

Statement of comprehensive income

	$'000
Revenue (300 × 40%)	120
Cost of sales (balancing figure)	(90)
Profit to date (75 × 40%)	30

Statement of financial position

	$'000
Costs incurred	90
Recognised profits less recognised losses	30
	120
Less: progress billings to date	(116)
Amount due from customers	4

Amount due from customers is an **asset of $4,000** which should be recognised in current assets.

(b)   *36% complete*

Statement of comprehensive income

	$'000
Revenue (300 × 36%)	108
Cost of sales (balancing figure)	(81)
Profit to date (75 × 36%)	27

	$'000
Statement of financial position	
Costs to date	90
Recognised profits less recognised losses	27
	117
Less: progress billings to date	(116)
Amount due from customers	1

Amount due from customers is an **asset of $1,000** which should be recognised in current assets.

Grumpy contract (loss making)

(a)   *40% complete*

Statement of comprehensive income

	$'000
Revenue (300 × 40%)	120
Cost of sales (balancing figure)	(195)
Recognised loss*	(75)

* *Remember that the whole of the expected loss is recognised as soon as it is anticipated.*

Statement of financial position

	$'000
Costs to date	150
Recognised profits less recognised losses	(75)
	75
Less: progress billings to date	(116)
Amounts due to customers	(41)

Amount due to customers is a **liability of $41,000** which should be recognised in current liabilities.

(b)   *36% complete*

Statement of comprehensive income

	$'000
Revenue (300 × 36%)	108
Cost of sales (balancing figure)	(183)
Recognised loss*	(75)

* *Remember that the whole of the expected loss is recognised as soon as it is anticipated.*

Statement of financial position

	$'000
Costs to date	150
Recognised profits less recognised losses	(75)
	75
Progress billings	(116)
Amount due to customers	(41)

Amount due to customers is a **liability of $41,000** which should be recognised in current liabilities.

Question 11.2	Construction contracts

Learning outcomes C2(a)

The main business of Santolina Co is construction contracts. At the end of September 20X3 there is an uncompleted contract on the books, details of which are as follows.

Date commenced	1.4.X1
Expected completed date	23.12.X3

Santolina Co calculates the stage of completion of contracts using the value of work certified as a proportion of total contract value.

	$
Final contract price	290,000
Costs to 30.9.X3	210,450
Value of work certified to 30.9.X3	230,000
Progress billings to 30.9.X3	210,000
Cash received to 30.9.X3	194,000
Estimated costs to completion at 30.9.X3	20,600

Required

Prepare calculations showing the amounts to be included in the income statement and the statement of financial position at 30 September 20X3 in respect of the above contract.

2.12 Changes in estimates

The effect of any change in the estimate of contract revenue or costs or the outcome of a contract should be accounted for as a **change in accounting estimate** under IAS 8 *Accounting policies, changes in accounting estimates and errors*.

Example: Changes in estimates

The example below shows the effect of a change in estimate of costs on the figures that appear in the statement of comprehensive income and statement of financial position.

Battersby Co enters into a three-year contract.

Estimated revenue = $20,000
Estimated total cost = $16,000.

However, during Year 2, management revises its estimate of total costs incurred and thus the outcome of the contract. As a result, during Year 2, a loss is recognised on the contract for the year, even though the contract will still be profitable overall.

	Year 1 $	Year 2 $	Year 3 $
Estimated revenue	20,000	20,000	20,000
Estimated total cost	16,000	18,000	18,000
Estimated total profit	4,000	2,000	2,000
Cost incurred to date	$8,000	$13,500	$18,000
Percentage of completion	50%	75%	100%
Recognised profit/(loss) to date	$2,000	($500)	$500
Cumulative recognised profit	$2,000	$1,500	$2,000

Progress billings of $8,000, $8,000 and $4,000 are made on the last day of each year and are received in the first month of the following year. The asset/liability at the end of each year is:

Gross amounts due to/from customers	Year 1 $	Year 2 $	Year 3 $
Costs incurred	8,000	13,500	18,000
Recognised profits	2,000	2,000	2,500
(Recognised losses)	–	(500)	(500)
Less: progress billings to date	(8,000)	(16,000)	(20,000)
Amount recognised as an asset/(liability)	2,000	(1,000)	–

In addition, at each year end, the entity recognises a **trade receivable** for the amount outstanding at the end of the year of $8,000, $8,000 and $4,000.

2.13 Disclosures

The following should be disclosed under IAS 11.

- Contract revenue recognised as **revenue in the period**
- **Methods used** to determine the **contract revenue**
- **Methods used** to determine **stage of completion** of contracts which are in progress

For **contracts in progress** at the end of the reporting period, show the following.

- **Total costs incurred** and recognised profits (less recognised losses) to date
- **Advances** received
- **Retentions** (progress billings not paid until the satisfaction of certain conditions)

Amounts owed by customers and to sub-contractors for contract work must be **shown gross as an asset and a liability respectively**. These are determined by comparing the total costs incurred plus recognised profits to the sum of recognised losses and progress billings, as you will see in the question below.

Any **contingent gains or losses**, eg due to warranty costs, claims, penalties or possible losses, should be disclosed in accordance with IAS 37 *Provisions, contingent liabilities and contingent assets*.

Example: IAS 11 disclosures

Suppose that Tract Ore Co finishes its first year of operations in which all contract costs were paid in cash and all progress billings and advances were received in cash. For contracts W, X and Z only:

(a) contract costs include costs of materials purchased for use in the contract which have not been used at the period end; and

(b) customers have advanced sums to the contractor for work not yet performed.

The relevant figures for all contracts at the end of Tract Ore's first year of trading are as follows.

	V $m	W $m	X $m	Y $m	Z $m	Total $m
Contract revenue recognised	37.7	135.2	98.8	52.0	14.3	338.0
Contract expenses recognised	28.6	117.0	91.0	65.0	14.3	315.9
Expected losses recognised	–	–	–	10.4	7.8	18.2
Recognised profits less recognised losses	9.1	18.2	7.8	(23.4)	(7.8)	3.9
Contract costs incurred in the period	28.6	132.6	117.0	65.0	26.0	369.2
Contract expenses recognised	28.6	117.0	91.0	65.0	14.3	315.9
Contract expenses that relate to						
future activity recognised as an asset	–	15.6	26.0	–	11.7	53.3
Contract revenue	37.7	135.2	98.8	52.0	14.3	338.0
Progress billings	26.0	135.2	98.8	46.8	14.3	321.1
Unbilled contract revenue	11.7	–	–	5.2	–	16.9
Advances	–	20.8	5.2	–	6.5	32.5

Required

Show the figures that should be disclosed under IAS 11.

Solution

Following IAS 11, the required disclosures would be as follows.

	$m
Contract revenue recognised in the period	338.0
Contract costs incurred and recognised profits (less recognised losses) to date (W)	373.1
Advances received	32.5
Gross amount due from customers for contract work: asset (W)	57.2
Gross amount due to customers for contract work: liability (W)	(5.2)

Workings

These amounts are calculated as follows.

	V $m	W $m	X $m	Y $m	Z $m	Total $m
Contract costs incurred	28.6	132.6	117.0	65.0	26.0	369.2
Recognised profits less recognised losses	9.1	18.2	7.8	(23.4)	(7.8)	3.9
	37.7	150.8	124.8	41.6	18.2	373.1
Less: progress billings to date	26.0	135.2	98.8	46.8	14.3	321.1
Due from customers	11.7	15.6	26.0		3.9	57.2
Due to customers				(5.2)		(5.2)

2.14 IAS 11 example

This example is given in the appendix to IAS 11. Work through it and make sure you understand it.

Example: IAS 11 example

A construction contractor has a fixed price contract to build a bridge. The initial amount of revenue agreed in the contract is $9,000. The contractor's initial estimate of contract costs is $8,000. It will take three years to build the bridge. By the end of year 1, the contractor's estimate of contract costs has increased to $8,050.

In year 2, the customer approves a variation resulting in an increase in contract revenue of $200 and estimated additional contract costs of $150. At the end of year 2, costs incurred include $100 for standard materials stored on site to be used in year 3 to complete the project.

The contractor determines the **stage of completion** of the contract by calculating the proportion that contract costs incurred for work performed to date bear to the latest estimated total contract costs. A summary of the financial data during the construction period is as follows:

	Year 1 $	Year 2 $	Year 3 $
Initial amount of revenue agreed in contract	9,000	9,000	9,000
Variation	–	200	200
Total contract revenue	9,000	9,200	9,200
Contract costs incurred to date	2,093	6,168	8,200
Contract costs to complete	5,957	2,023	–
Total estimated contract costs	8,050	8,200	8,200
Estimated profit	950	1,000	1,000
Stage of completion	26%	74%	100%

The stage of completion for year 2 (74%) is determined by excluding from contract costs incurred for work performed to date the $100 of standard materials stored at the site for use in year 3.

The amounts of revenue, expenses and profit recognised in the statement of comprehensive income in the three years are as follows:

	To date	Recognised in prior years	Recognised in current year
	$	$	$
Year 1			
Revenue (9,000 × 26%)	2,340	–	2,340
Expenses (8,050 × 26%)	2,093	–	2,093
Profit	247	–	247
Year 2			
Revenue (9,200 × 74%)	6,808	2,340	4,468
Expenses (8,200 × 74%)	6,068	2,093	3,975
Profit	740	247	493
Year 3			
Revenue (9,200 × 100%)	9,200	6,808	2,392
Expenses	8,200	6,068	2,132
Profit	1,000	740	260

Here is another example illustrating the disclosures required under IAS 11.

Example: Construction contract disclosures

A contractor has five contracts in progress at the end of year 1 as follows:

	A	B	C	D	E	Total
	$	$	$	$	$	$
Contract revenue recognised	145	520	380	200	55	1,300
Contract expenses recognised	110	450	350	250	55	1,215
Expected losses recognised	–	–	–	40	30	70
Recognised profits less recognised losses	35	70	30	(90)	(30)	15
Contract costs incurred in the period	110	510	450	250	100	1,420
Contract costs incurred recognised as expenses	110	450	350	250	55	1,215
Contract costs relating to future activity (WIP)	–	60	100	–	45	205
Contract revenue (as above)	145	520	380	200	55	1,300
Progress billings	100	520	380	180	55	1,235
Unbilled contract revenue	45	–	–	20	–	65
Advances	–	80	20	–	25	125

The amounts to be disclosed in accordance with IAS 11 are as follows:

	$
Contract revenue recognised as revenue in the period	1,300
Contract costs incurred and recognised profits less recognised losses to date	1,435
Advances received	125
Gross amount due from customers for contract work (asset)	220
Gross amounts due to customers for contract work (liability)	(20)

These amounts are calculated as follows:

	A	B	C	D	E	Total
	$	$	$	$	$	$
Contract costs incurred	110	510	450	250	100	1,420
Recognised profits less recognised losses	35	70	30	(90)	(30)	15
	145	580	480	160	70	1,435
Progress billings	100	520	380	180	55	1,235
Due from customers	45	60	100	–	15	220
Due to customers	–	–	–	(20)	–	(20)

Note that where you are dealing with a single construction contract, there will be *either* a gross amount due to customers *or* a gross amount due from customers. In the above example we are dealing with more than one contract and, instead of showing a net balance of $200 due from customers, the standard requires the asset and the liability are shown separately.

Section summary

The rules for calculating accounting entries on **construction contracts** can be summarised as follows.

- When the outcome of a construction contract can be **estimated reliably**, contract revenue and contract costs shall be recognised as revenue and expenses respectively by reference to the stage of completion of the contract.

- When it is probable that total contract costs will exceed total contract revenue, the expected loss shall be **recognised as an expense immediately**.

Chapter Roundup

✓ Inventories should be measured at the **lower of cost and net realisable value**.

✓ The cost of inventories includes the **costs of purchase**, **costs of conversion** and other costs incurred in bringing the inventories to their present location and condition.

✓ The cost of inventories that are not interchangeable can be estimated using the **standard cost** method or the **retail method**.

✓ The cost of interchangeable inventories should be measured using **FIFO** (first in, first out) or **Weighted Average Cost**. LIFO (last in, first out) is not allowed under IAS 2.

✓ **Net realisable value** is the estimated selling price less the estimated costs of completion and the estimated costs necessary to make the sale.

✓ The rules for calculating accounting entries on **construction contracts** can be summarised as follows.

- When the outcome of a construction contract can be **estimated reliably**, contract revenue and contract costs shall be recognised as revenue and expenses respectively by reference to the **stage of completion** of the contract.

- When it is probable that total contract costs will exceed total contract revenue, the expected loss shall be **recognised as an expense immediately**.

Quick Quiz

1 Net realisable value = Selling price **less** .... **less** ....

2 Which inventory costing method is allowed under IAS 2?

   (a) FIFO (b) LIFO

3 Any expected loss on a construction contract must be recognised, in full, in the year it was identified. Is this true or false?

4 What are the three methods that IAS 11 gives for calculating the stage of completion of a contract?

5 Which items in the statement of comprehensive income and statement of financial position are potentially affected by construction contracts?

Answers to Quick Quiz

1 Net realisable value = selling price **less** costs to completion **less** costs necessary to make the sale.

2 (a) FIFO. LIFO is not allowed.

3 True

4 (a) Proportion of contract costs incurred for work carried out to date

$$\frac{\text{Costs to date}}{\text{Total estimated costs}}$$

   (b) Surveys of work carried out

$$\frac{\text{Work certified}}{\text{Contract price}}$$

   (c) Physical proportion of the contract work completed

5   Statement of comprehensive income: revenue and cost of sales.

Statement of financial position: current assets, current liabilities.

 Answers to Questions

11.1 Inventory valuation

Calculation of overheads for inventory

Production overheads are as follows.

	$
	$
Depreciation/finance costs	4,490
Factory manager's wage	2,560
Other production overheads	24,820
Accounting/purchase costs	5,450
	37,320

Direct labour = $61,320

$$\therefore \text{ Production overhead rate} = \frac{37,320}{61,320} = 60.86\%$$

Inventory valuation

	Raw materials $	WIP $	Finished goods $	Total $
Materials	74,786	85,692	152,693	313,171
Direct labour	–	13,072	46,584	59,656
Production overhead (at 60.86% of labour)	–	7,956	28,351	36,307
	74,786	106,720	227,628	409,134

Variable overheads will be included in the cost of inventory.

11.2 Construction contracts

Tutorial note: you should first determine whether the contract is profitable or loss making

	$
Final contract price	290,000
Less: costs to date	(210,450)
estimated future costs	(20,600)
Estimated final profit	58,950

$$\text{Stage of completion} = \frac{\text{Work certified}}{\text{Total contract price}} = \frac{230,000}{290,000} = 79.3\%$$

Amounts recognised in the income statement at 30 September 20X3:

	$
Revenue recognised (work certified)	230,000
Costs recognised (balancing figure)	(183,253)
Recognised profit (79.3% × 58,950)	46,747

Amounts recognised in the statement of financial position at 30 September 20X3:

	$
Costs incurred	210,450
Recognised profits	46,753
	257,203
Less: progress billings to date	(210,000)
Gross amount due from customers (asset)	47,203

Recognise an asset in the statement of financial position under current assets:

Gross amounts due from customers $47,203

Now try these questions from the Exam Question Bank	Number	Level	Marks	Time
	Q12	Examination	10	18 mins
	Q16	Examination	5	9 mins

CAPITAL TRANSACTIONS AND FINANCIAL INSTRUMENTS

The treatment of share issues is an important accounting topic and is covered in this chapter. Financial instruments are a complex area but you are only required to know the rules governing share capital transactions.

topic list	learning outcomes	syllabus references	ability required
1 The issue and forfeiture of shares	C2(b)	C2(xii)	comprehension
2 Purchase of own shares	C2(b)	C2(xii)	comprehension
3 Financial instruments	C2(b)	C2(xii)	comprehension

1 The issue and forfeiture of shares

Introduction

In this section we look at how shares are issued in the UK. We then cover the accounting treatment for the issue of shares. Work carefully through the examples in this chapter.

1.1 Ordinary versus preference shares

There are two types of shares most often encountered: **preference shares** and **ordinary shares**.

1.1.1 Preference shares

KEY TERM

PREFERENCE SHARES are shares which confer certain preferential rights on their holder.

Preference shares carry the right to a final dividend which is expressed as a percentage of their par value: eg a 6% $1 preference share carries a right to an annual dividend of 6c. Preference dividends have priority over ordinary dividends; in other words, if the managers of a company wish to pay a dividend (which they are not obliged to do) they must pay any preference dividend first. Otherwise, no ordinary dividend may be paid. Preference shares are sometimes called **non-equity shares**.

The rights attaching to preference shares are set out in the company's constitution. They may vary from company to company and country to country, but typically:

(a)   Preference shareholders have a **priority right** over ordinary shareholders to a return of their capital if the company goes into liquidation.

(b)   Preference shares do not **carry a right to vote**.

(c)   If the preference shares are **cumulative**, it means that before a company can pay an ordinary dividend it must not only pay the current year's preference dividend, but must also make good any arrears of preference dividends unpaid in previous years.

In recent years, preference shares have become unpopular with both shareholders and companies. From the shareholders perspective, preferences shares are higher risk than making loans, and have less dividend potential than ordinary shares. From the entity's perspective, preference dividends are not tax deductable (similarly with ordinary dividends) and so are a more expensive source of finance than obtaining bank loans or issuing bonds.

1.1.2 Ordinary shares

Ordinary shares are by far the most common type of shares. They carry no right to a fixed dividend but are entitled to all profits left after payment of any preference dividend. Generally, however, only a part of such remaining profits is distributed, the rest being kept in reserve.

KEY TERM

ORDINARY SHARES are shares which are not preferred with regard to dividend payments. Thus a holder only receives a dividend after fixed dividends have been paid to preference shareholders.

The amount of ordinary dividends fluctuates although there is a general expectation that it will increase from year to year. Should the company be wound up, any surplus not distributed is shared between the ordinary shareholders. Ordinary shares normally carry **voting rights**.

Ordinary shareholders are thus the effective **owners** of a company. They own the 'equity' of the business, and any reserves of the business belong to them. Ordinary shareholders are sometimes referred to as **equity shareholders**. It should be emphasised, however, that the precise rights attached to preference and ordinary shares may vary; the distinctions noted above are generalisations.

Dividends paid to ordinary shareholders are shown in the statement of changes in equity. Remember that dividends must be declared before the end of the reporting period if they are to be recognised in the financial statements. Any dividends declared after this date and before the financial statements are authorised for issue are disclosed in the notes in accordance with IAS 1 *Presentation of financial statements*.

1.2 Authorised versus issued share capital

Financial statements refer to **authorised** and **issued** share capital.

(a)   **Authorised (or legal) capital** is the maximum amount of share capital that a company is empowered to issue. The amount of authorised share capital varies from company to company, and can change by agreement. For example, a company's authorised share capital might be 5,000,000 ordinary shares of $1 each. This would then be the maximum number of shares it could issue, unless the maximum were to be changed by agreement.

(b)   **Issued capital** is the par amount of share capital that has been issued to shareholders. The amount of issued capital cannot exceed the amount of authorised capital. Continuing the example above, the company with authorised share capital of 5,000,000 ordinary shares of $1 might have issued 4,000,000 shares. This would leave it the option to issue 1,000,000 more shares at some time in the future. When share capital is issued, shares are allotted to shareholders. The term 'allotted' share capital means the same thing as issued share capital.

1.3 IAS 1 requirements

IAS 1 requires entities to give a detailed note about their share capital structure. This note is important for shareholders as it shows the rights attached to the different classes of shares and allows shareholders to assess how their interests will be affected by a new issue of shares or a change in the share capital structure.

IAS 1 requires the following disclosure to be given in either in the statement of financial position or the statement of changes in equity, or in the notes:

(a)   For each class of share capital:

   (i)   The number of shares **authorised**

   (ii)   The number of shares **issued** and fully paid, and issued but not fully paid

   (iii)   **Par value** per share, or that the shares have no par value

   (iv)   A **reconciliation** of the **number of shares** outstanding at the beginning and at the end of the period

   (v)   The **rights, preferences and restrictions** attaching to that class including restrictions on the distribution of dividends and the repayment of capital

   (vi)   Shares in the entity held by the entity or by its subsidiaries or associates

   (vii)   Shares reserved for issue under options and contracts for the sale of shares, including terms and amounts

(b)   A description of the nature and purpose of each reserve within equity.

IAS 1 also requires the disclosure of the amount of cumulative preference dividends not recognised in the financial statements.

1.4 Share issues

A company can increase its share capital by means of a **share issue**. Here we will look at the specific accounting entries necessary for such an issue, including where a share premium account is required (when the price of the share is greater than its nominal value).

KEY POINT

Local rules and procedures may vary – below the UK rules are given.

1.5 General rules and procedures

KEY TERM

As a general rule, if a company issues ordinary shares for cash it must first offer them to its existing ordinary shareholders in proportion to their shareholdings. This is called a RIGHTS ISSUE because members may obtain new shares in right of their existing holdings.

If they do not accept the shares within 21 days, the company may then offer the shares to non-members. A private company may, by the terms of its memorandum or articles, permanently exclude the members' right of pre-emption (as just described). A public company may authorise its directors (by special resolution) to allot ordinary shares for cash without first offering the shares to members.

When a company issues shares it must obtain consideration at least equal in value to the **nominal value** of the shares (to issue shares **at par value** means to obtain equal value): shares cannot be issued at a discount. The entire consideration does not have to be received at the time of allotment, and the holder of such **partly-paid shares** is liable to pay the balance. Usually the company may make a 'call' for the balance or any part of it under a procedure laid down in the articles whenever the directors decide to do so. When a call has been made the capital is 'called-up' to that extent, and when the shareholders pay the call it is 'paid-up' to that extent (including in each case previous amounts due or paid). If the company goes into liquidation the liquidator is entitled to call up any balance outstanding.

KEY TERMS

Although a company may not allot shares for a consideration of less value than the nominal value of the shares, it is free to obtain a consideration of greater value. The excess of the consideration over the nominal value of the shares is SHARE PREMIUM which must be credited to a SHARE PREMIUM ACCOUNT as part of the equity and reserves of the entity.

Except when a **rights issue** is made to existing members, it is generally considered to be the duty of directors to obtain the highest possible price for the shares, and so to maximise the premium (if any). A rights issue is an issue of shares to existing shareholders. The shares are offered for cash but at a discount to the current market price, and are offered to shareholders in proportion to their existing holdings. For instance a '1 for 4' issue means that a shareholder can buy one new share for each four that he currently holds.

The **share premium account** may be repaid to members (or otherwise eliminated) under a reduction of share capital authorised by the court, but it may not be distributed as dividend because it is a **non-distributable reserve**. It may, however, be applied in the following ways:

(a)   Issuing fully paid bonus shares to the members (explained below).

(b)   Writing off:

(i)   Preliminary expenses of company formation
(ii)   Share or loan stock issue expenses (including commissions and discounts)

(c)   In certain circumstances, paying any premium payable when the company redeems redeemable shares or debentures.

KEY TERM

In issuing shares a company may capitalise available reserves (normally the share premium account) instead of requiring its members to pay cash for new shares. This procedure, called making a BONUS ISSUE of shares, is only permitted to the extent that the articles provide for it (and the correct procedure must be observed).

Since reserves (which in some cases might be distributed as dividends) are part of the shareholders' funds, the effect is to convert them into permanent capital. The members pay for their additional shares by forgoing whatever rights they had to the reserves. Any reserve may be reclassified in this way, including a share premium account or other statutory reserve.

Examples of the treatment for both **bonus issues** and **rights issues** are given towards the end of this section.

1.6 Accounting for an issue of shares for cash

If share subscription monies are payable in instalments, journal entries are made initially to **application and allotment accounts** and **call accounts**. Balances on these accounts are eventually transferred to share capital and share premium accounts.

KEY POINT

Issue costs for ordinary shares are not an expense of the entity and should be deducted from a reserve, usually the share premium account.

Occasionally (though rarely nowadays) a shareholder may fail to pay amounts due on allotment or on a call. If the entity's articles of association allow, the company may (after due warning) confiscate the shares without refund of any amounts paid to date. The shares are not cancelled but their called up value is transferred from share capital account to a **forfeited shares account** (the share premium account is not affected) until they are reissued. Forfeited shares may be reissued at any price provided that the total amount received (from both applicants) is not less than the par value of the shares.

1.7 Accounting entries for a share issue　　　　　　　　　　5/10

The following procedure is followed for the issue and forfeiture of shares.

(a)　**Application**: where potential shareholders apply for shares in the company and send cash to cover the amount applied for.

DEBIT　　Bank
CREDIT　Application and allotment account
Application proceeds

(b)　**Allotment and issue**: the company allocates ('allots' or formally issues) shares to the successful applicants and if the share issue has been oversubscribed, returns cash to unsuccessful applicants.

DEBIT　　Application and allotment account
CREDIT　Bank
Money returned to unsuccessful applicants

DEBIT　　Application and allotment account
CREDIT　Share capital
CREDIT　Share premium
Issue of shares

(c)　**Call**: where the purchase price is payable in instalments, the company will call for instalments on their due dates of payment.

DEBIT　　Call account
CREDIT　Share capital
Call of final instalment owed

DEBIT　　Bank
CREDIT　Call account
Cash receipts banked

(d)   **Forfeiture**: if a shareholder fails to pay a call, his shares may be forfeited without the need to return the money he has paid. These shares represent an investment in the company's own shares before they are re-issued to other shareholders.

DEBIT   Investment: own shares (or forfeit account)
CREDIT   Call account
Forfeited shares

DEBIT   Bank
CREDIT   Investment: own shares (or forfeit account)
CREDIT   Share premium account
Shares re-issued, any excess funds (ie more than needed to clear the forfeit account) go to share premium.

Example: Accounting for an issue of shares for cash

Ibex wished to issue 500,000 $1 ordinary shares, 60c (including 10c premium) per share payable on application, 20c on allotment and the final 30c on call, four months later. The prospectus was published and applications for 600,000 shares were received. The directors rejected 'small' applicants for a total of 100,000 shares and allotted the remainder. Show the journal entries involved in respect of the issue, assuming that all cheques were banked on receipt.

Solution

JOURNAL ENTRIES

(a)   DEBIT   Bank $360,000
         CREDIT   Application and allotment account $360,000
         Being amounts received on application

(b)   DEBIT   Application and allotment account $60,000
         CREDIT   Bank $60,000
         Being return of application money to unsuccessful subscribers

(c)   DEBIT   Application and allotment account $400,000
         CREDIT   Share capital account $350,000
         CREDIT   Share premium account $50,000
         Being allotment of shares

(At this stage the total of the balances on the share capital account and share premium account shows the total amount receivable on **application and allotment** (ie 80c per share 80c x 500,000 = $400,000), while the debit balance on the application and allotment account records how much of that amount is still outstanding.)

(d)   DEBIT   Bank $100,000
         CREDIT   Application and allotment account $100,000
         Being receipt of amounts due on allotment

(This entry closes the application and allotment account.)

(e)   DEBIT   Call account $150,000
         CREDIT   Share capital account $150,000
         Being the amount of the call on shares to make them fully paid

(The share capital account is credited with the full amount due on the call, and the call account records the actual receipt of the money.)

(f)   DEBIT   Bank $150,000
         CREDIT   Call account $150,000
         Being receipt of call money due

If, in the example, instead of rejecting some share applicants, shares had been allotted on a proportional basis, each subscriber would have received five-sixths of the number of shares applied for. There would therefore be no need for entry (b) above, and each subscriber's surplus application money would be applied to the amount due from him or her on allotment. Entry (c) above would remain the same, but entry (d) would be:

DEBIT	Bank	$40,000	
CREDIT	Application and allotment account		$40,000

Being receipt of amounts due on allotment

Now assume that after the call was made the money due on 10,000 of the shares was not received. The directors of Ibex (after due notice) forfeited the shares and subsequently reissued them at a price of 75c each. The journal entries (a) to (e) above would remain the same, but the subsequent entries would be:

(g)

DEBIT	Bank	$147,000	
CREDIT	Call account		$147,000

Being receipt of call money

(If a statement of financial position were drawn up at this stage, the debit balance on call account, being the $3,000 still receivable, would be shown as called up share capital not paid.)

(h)

DEBIT	Investments: own shares *	$3,000	
CREDIT	Call account		$3,000

Being the forfeiture of the shares. (The shares are now held by the company ready for re-issue.)

When the shares are reissued the journal entries made are as follows.

(i)

DEBIT	Bank	$7,500	
CREDIT	Investments: own shares *		$7,500

Being proceeds of reissue of shares

(j)

DEBIT	Investments: own shares*	$4,500	
CREDIT	Share premium account		$4,500

Being transfer of the premium on the reissued shares to share premium account.

(This is an additional premium obtained on the reissue of shares and is the excess of reissue price over the unpaid calls: 10,000 @ 45c.)

* OR a forfeiture account

The combined example may be worked in ledger account form.

BANK ACCOUNT

	$		$
Application & allotment a/c	360,000	Application & allotment a/c	60,000
Application & allotment a/c	100,000	Balance c/d	554,500
Call a/c	147,000		
Investments: own shares	7,500		
	614,500		614,500

APPLICATION AND ALLOTMENT ACCOUNT

	$		$
Bank (100,000 @ 60c)	60,000	Bank (600,000 @ 60c)	360,000
Ordinary share capital a/c:		Bank (500,000 @ 20c)	100,000
(500,000 @ 70c)	350,000		
Share premium a/c:			
(500,000 @ 10c)	50,000		
	460,000		460,000

SHARE CAPITAL ACCOUNT: $1 ORDINARY SHARES

	$		$
Balance c/d	500,000	Application & allotment a/c	350,000
		Call a/c	150,000
	500,000		500,000

SHARE PREMIUM ACCOUNT

	$		$
Balance	54,500	Application & allotment a/c	50,000
		Investments: own shares	4,500
	54,500		54,500

CALL ACCOUNT

	$		$
Ordinary share capital a/c		Bank (490,000 @ 30c)	147,000
(500,000 @ 30c)	150,000	Investments : own shares	3,000
	150,000		150,000

INVESTMENTS: OWN SHARES

	$		$
Call a/c	3,000	Bank (10,000 @ 75c)	7,500
Share premium account	4,500		
	7,500		7,500

Ibex statements of financial position would be as follows.

(a)   **After the call (but before forfeiture)**

	$
Current assets	
Receivables: called up share capital not paid	3,000
Cash at bank	547,000
	550,000
Equity	
Called up share capital: 500,000 $1 ordinary shares	500,000
Share premium account	50,000
	550,000

(b)   **After the forfeiture (but before reissue)**

	$
Current assets	
Investments: own shares	3,000
Cash at bank	547,000
	550,000
Equity	
Called up share capital: 500,000 $1 ord shares	500,000
Share premium account	50,000
	550,000

(c)   **After the reissue**

	$
Current assets	
Cash at bank	554,500
Equity	
Called up share capital: 500,000 $1 ord shares fully paid	500,000
Share premium account	54,500
	554,500

Question 12.1

Learning outcome C2(b)

Haggot Co issued 50,000 $1 shares at $1.20 per share. Monies due were as follows.

On application   50c including premium
On allotment   30c
Call   40c

Applications were received amounting to $30,000 (ie for 60,000 shares).

At the call, 1,000 shares were forfeited. These were subsequently reissued for $1.10 cash.

Required

Write up the relevant ledger accounts for the above issue.

1.8 Bonus issue of shares

KEY POINT

A **bonus issue of shares** is an issue of shares to existing shareholders in proportion to their existing share holdings which is paid for by capitalising existing reserves. No new cash is received by the entity for the new shares.

Example: Bonus issues

BUBBLES CO
STATEMENT OF FINANCIAL POSITION (EXTRACT)

	$'000	$'000
Equity		
Share capital		
$1 ordinary shares (fully paid)		1,000
Share premium	500	
Retained earnings	2,000	
		2,500
		3,500

Bubbles decided to make a '3 for 2' bonus issue (ie 3 new shares for every 2 already held).

The double entry is as follows.

		$'000	$'000
DEBIT	Share premium	500	
	Retained earnings	1,000	
CREDIT	Ordinary share capital		1,500

After the issue the statement of financial position is as follows.

	$'000
Equity	
Share capital	
$1 ordinary shares (fully paid)	2,500
Retained earnings	1,000
	3,500

1,500,000 new ('bonus') shares are issued to existing shareholders, so that if Mr X previously held 20,000 shares he will now hold 50,000. The total value of his holding should theoretically remain the same however, since the net assets of the company remain unchanged and his share of those net assets remains at 2% (50,000/2,500,000; previously 20,000/1,000,000).

1.9 Rights issue of shares

KEY POINT

A **rights issue of shares** is an issue of shares for cash to existing shareholders, in proportion to their existing holdings, at a discount to the current market price.

Example: Rights issues

Bubbles (from the example above) decides to make a rights issue, shortly after the bonus issue. The terms are '1 for 5 @ $1.20' (one new share for every five already held, at a price of $1.20). Assuming that all shareholders take up their rights (which they are not obliged to) the double entry is as follows.

		$'000	$'000
DEBIT	Cash	600	
CREDIT	Ordinary share capital		500
CREDIT	Share premium		100

Mr X who previously held 50,000 shares will now hold 60,000, and the value of his holding should increase (theoretically at least) because the net assets of the company will increase. The new statement of financial position will show:

	$'000	$'000
Equity		
Share capital		
$1 ordinary shares		3,000
Share premium	100	
Retained earnings	1,000	
		1,100
		4,100

The increase in funds of $600,000 represents the cash raised from the issue of 500,000 new shares at a price of $1.20 each.

Section summary

Ordinary shares (or equity shares) give the shareholder voting rights and the right to participate in the residual profits of the entity.

Preference shares do not usually carry voting rights and are usually non-equity, but do have the right to a fixed dividend.

Shares may be issued to existing shareholders via a **rights issue** or a **bonus issue**. Alternately they can be issued to new shareholders at market value.

A **rights issue** is where an entity issues shares for cash to its existing shareholders in proportion to their existing holdings at a discount to the current market price.

A **bonus issue** is where an entity issues free shares to its existing shareholders in proportion to their existing holdings. No cash is received for the shares, instead existing reserves are capitalised as consideration.

Share issue costs for ordinary shares should be deducted from a reserve, usually the share premium account. They are not an expense of the entity.

2 Purchase of own shares

Introduction

In this section we look at how and why a company might purchase its own shares.

2.1 Reduction of capital

Limited liability companies may be permitted to cancel unissued shares and in that way reduces their **authorised** share capital. That change does not alter the financial position of any company.

If a limited liability company wishes to **reduce its issued share capital** (and incidentally its authorised capital of which the issued capital is part) it may do so provided that certain conditions are met (set by national legislation). For example:

(a)   It must have the power to do so in its **articles** of association
(b)   It must pass a **special resolution**
(c)   It must obtain **confirmation** of the reduction **from the court**

Requirement (a) is usually a matter of procedure. Articles usually contain the necessary power. If not, the company in general meeting would first pass a special resolution to alter the articles appropriately and then proceed to pass a special resolution to reduce the capital.

There are various basic methods of reducing share capital. Three of the most common are discussed here.

(a)   **Extinguish or reduce liability on partly paid shares**. A company may have issued $1 (par) shares 75c paid up. The outstanding liability of 25c per share may be eliminated altogether by reducing each share to 75c (par) fully paid or some intermediate figure, eg 80c (par) 75c paid. Nothing is returned to the shareholders but the company gives up a claim against them for money which it could call up whenever needed.

(b)   **Cancel paid up share capital which has been lost or which is no longer represented by available assets.** Suppose that the issued shares are $1 (par) fully paid but the net assets now represent a value of only 50c per share. The difference is probably matched by a debit balance on the retained reserves. The company could reduce the par value of its $1 shares to 50c (or some intermediate figure) and apply the amount to write off the debit balance wholly or in part. It would then be able to resume payment of dividends out of future profits without being obliged to make good past losses. The resources of the company are not reduced by this procedure of part cancellation of nominal value of shares but it avoids having to rebuild lost capital by retaining profits.

(c)   **Pay off part of the paid up share capital out of surplus assets.** The company might repay to shareholders, say, 30c in cash per $1 share by reducing the par value of the share to 70c. This reduces the assets of the company by 30c per share.

2.2 Role of court in reduction of capital

In many countries the sanction of the court (or equivalent) may be required for a redemption of shares or reduction in capital. The purpose here is for the protection of the business's creditors (payables). The reduction in capital must not put at risk a company's ability to pay its debts. If it did so, then shareholders would be favoured over creditors for distributions from the company. Creditors may be allowed to petition the court against the proposed transaction, but the company may be able to override this by paying off its creditors. The details will vary from country to country.

2.3 Share premium account

Whenever a company obtains for its shares a consideration in excess of their par value, it must usually transfer the excess to a share premium account (capital in excess of par account). The general rule is that the **share premium account is subject to the same restrictions as share capital**. However, it may be possible to make a bonus issue using the share premium account (reducing share premium in order to increase issued share capital).

There may be an **exemption** from the general rules on setting up a share premium account, in certain circumstances where new shares are issued as consideration for the acquisition of shares in another company.

Examples of the **other likely permitted uses of share premium** are to pay:

(a)   Capital expenses such as preliminary expenses of forming the company
(b)   A discount on the issue of shares or debentures
(c)   A premium (if any) paid on redemption of debentures

Some companies may also be able to use a share premium account in purchasing or redeeming their own shares out of capital. It must be emphasised that these rules will vary from country to country according to national legislation.

2.4 Purchase by a company of its own shares

When a company repurchases its own shares, this should normally be financed in one of two ways:

(a)   **Out of the proceeds of a new issue of shares.** This is often done when companies need to repay redeemable shares, wish to tidy up their capital structure (ie redeem certain classes of shares and replace with one new class), or wish to reduce the amount of committed dividends that are required to be paid by redeeming preference shares with high dividend rates and replacing with preference shares with lower dividend rates.

(b)   **Out of distributable profits.** One way to preserve reserves for creditor protection is to prevent companies from repurchasing shares except by transferring a sum equal to the par value of shares purchased from distributable profit reserves to a non-distributable reserve, which here we will call the '**capital redemption reserve**'. This reduction in distributable reserves is an example of the **capitalisation of profits**, where previously distributable profits become undistributable.

Such regulations prevent companies from reducing their share capital investment so as to put creditors of the company at risk. This excess of non-distributable over distributable reserves is often referred to as the "creditor's buffer."

Exam alert

Unless you are told otherwise in an exam question, you should assume that any share redemption that is not financed by a new share issue is made from distributable profits and will require a transfer to a capital redemption reserve.

Example: Capitalisation of profits

Suppose, for example, that Muffin Co decided to repurchase and cancel $100,000 of its ordinary share capital. A statement of financial position of the company is currently as follows.

	$	$
Assets		
Cash		100,000
Other assets		300,000
		400,000
Equity and liabilities		
Equity		
Ordinary shares	130,000	
Retained earnings	150,000	
		280,000
Liabilities		
Trade accounts payable		120,000
		400,000

Now if Muffin were able to repurchase the shares without making any transfer from retained earnings to a capital redemption reserve, the effect of the share redemption on the statement of financial position would be as follows.

	$
Assets	
Non-cash assets	300,000
Equity and liabilities	
Equity	
Ordinary shares	30,000
Retained earnings	150,000
	180,000
Liabilities	
Trade accounts payable	120,000
	300,000

In this example, the company would still be able to pay dividends out of profits of up to $150,000. If it did, the creditors of the company would be highly vulnerable, financing $120,000 out of a total of $150,000 assets of the company.

The regulations prevent such extreme situations arising. On repurchase of the shares, Muffin would have been required to transfer $100,000 from its retained earnings to a non-distributable reserve, called here a capital redemption reserve. The effect of the repurchase of shares on the statement of financial position would have been:

	$	$
Assets		
Non-cash assets		300,000
Equity and liabilities		
Equity		
Ordinary shares		30,000
Reserves		
Distributable (retained earnings)	50,000	
Non-distributable (capital redemption reserve)	100,000	
		180,000
Liabilities		
Trade accounts payable		120,000
		300,000

The maximum distributable profits are now $50,000. If Muffin paid all these as a dividend, there would still be $250,000 of assets left in the company, just over half of which would be financed by non-distributable equity capital.

2.4.1 Premium on repurchase of shares

If there is any premium on the repurchase of shares, it may be the rule that **the premium must be paid out of distributable profits**, except that if the shares were issued at a premium, then any premium payable on their repurchase may be paid out of the proceeds of a new share issue made for the purpose, up to an amount equal to the lesser of:

(a)   The aggregate premiums received on issue of the shares; and

(b)   The balance on the share premium account (including premium on issue of the new shares).

This may seem complicated, but it makes logical sense. A numerical example might help.

Example: Repurchase of shares

Suppose that Jingle Co intends to repurchase 10,000 shares of $1 each at a premium of 5 cents per share. The repurchase must be financed in one of the following ways.

(a)   Jingle Co could purchase its own shares wholly out of distributable profits. It must then transfer to the capital redemption reserve an amount equal to the par value of the shares repurchased. The accounting entries would be as follows.

		$	$
DEBIT	Share capital account	10,000	
	Retained earnings (premium on repurchase)	500	
CREDIT	Cash		10,500
DEBIT	Retained earnings	10,000	
CREDIT	Capital redemption reserve		10,000

(b)   Jingle Co could purchase its shares wholly or partly out of the proceeds of a new share issue. It must transfer to the capital redemption reserve an amount by which the par value of the shares repurchased exceeds the *aggregate* proceeds from the new issue (ie par value of new shares issued plus share premium). The premium of $500 must be paid out of distributable profits. The accounting entries would be as follows.

		$	$
DEBIT	Share capital account (repurchased shares)	10,000	
	Retained earnings (premium)	500	
CREDIT	Cash (repurchase of shares)		10,500
DEBIT	Cash (from new issue)	10,000	
CREDIT	Share capital account		10,000

No credit to the capital redemption reserve is necessary because there is no decrease in the creditors' buffer.

(c)   Jingle Co may finance the repurchase out of a combination of a new share issue and distributable profits. Imagine the repurchase in the same example as in (b) were made by issuing 5,000 new $1 shares at par, and paying $5,500 out of distributable profits. The accounting entries would be as follows.

		$	$
DEBIT	Share capital account (repurchased shares)	10,000	
	Retained earnings (premium)	500	
CREDIT	Cash (repurchase of shares)		10,500
DEBIT	Cash (from new issue)	5,000	
CREDIT	Share capital account		5,000
DEBIT	Retained earnings	5,000	
CREDIT	Capital redemption reserve		5,000

(d)   Jingle Co could purchase its shares out of the proceeds of a new share issue (as the shares to be repurchased were issues at a premium). Assuming a new issue of 10,000 $1 shares at a premium of 8c per share, the accounting entries would be as follows.

		$	$
DEBIT	Cash (from new issue)	10,800	
CREDIT	Share capital account		10,000
	Share premium account		800
DEBIT	Share capital account (repurchased shares)	10,000	
	Share premium account	300	
	Retained earnings	200	
CREDIT	Cash (repurchase of shares)		10,500

No capital redemption reserve is required, as in (b) above. The repurchase is financed entirely by a new issue of shares.

Question 12.2
Purchase of own shares

Learning outcome C2(b)

Set out below is the summarised statement of financial position of A Co at 30 June 20X5.

	A $'000
Net assets	<u>520</u>
Equity	
Called up share capital $1 ordinary shares	300
Share premium account	60
Retained earnings	<u>160</u>
	<u>520</u>

On 1 July 20X5 A Co purchased and cancelled 50,000 of its own ordinary shares as follows.

A Co purchased its own shares at 150c each. The shares were originally issued at a premium of 20c. The repurchase was partly financed by the issue at par of 5,000 new shares of $1 each.

Required

Prepare the summarised statement of financial position of A Co at 1 July 20X5 immediately after the above transactions have been effected.

Exam skills

You must be able to carry out **simple calculations** showing the amounts to be transferred to the **capital redemption reserve** on purchase of own shares, and how the amount of any **premium** on redemption would be treated.

2.5 Treasury shares
11/10

In the above examples, the entity repurchased its own shares and then cancelled them. However, if an entity repurchases its own shares and does not cancel them by the end of the reporting period, they are referred to as '**treasury shares**'. Treasury shares are shown in the statement of financial position as a deduction from equity. These **treasury shares** can then be re-issued in the future or issued as part of an employee share scheme.

Example: Treasury shares

For instance, a company has 500,000 $1 shares in issue and $200,000 in share premium. It reacquires 100,000 shares for $1.40.

The shares re-acquired are classified as treasury shares and presented as follows:

	$'000
Share capital: $1 shares fully paid	500
Share premium	200
	<u>700</u>
Treasury shares	(<u>140</u>)
	<u>560</u>

2.6 Commercial reasons for altering capital structure

These include the following.

- Greater **security of finance**
- Better **image** for third parties
- A **'neater' statement of financial position**
- **Borrowing repaid** sooner
- **Cost of borrowing** reduced

2.7 Redeemable preference shares

We have been dealing up to now with the repurchase or redemption of **ordinary** shares. The rules and the necessary accounting for redemption of **redeemable preference shares** are quite different. IAS 32 classifies a redeemable preference share as a **liability**, not an equity instrument. This is explained in the next section on **financial instruments**.

Section summary

An entity that wishes to repurchase its own shares will usually have to do so using the proceeds of a new share issue or by capitalising distributable profits in a 'capital redemption reserve' in order to preserve the creditor's buffer.

Shares which an entity has repurchased but not cancelled are called **treasury shares**. These are shown as a deduction from equity in the statement of financial position.

3   Financial instruments

Introduction

This section looks at financial instruments and the rules in IAS 32 and IAS 39. These standards were introduced to provide guidance on the recognition, measurement and disclosure of financial instruments in order to improve comparability across different sets of financial statements.

3.1 IAS 32 and IAS 39

(a)   IAS 32 *Financial instruments: Presentation* deals with:

     (i)   The classification of financial instruments between liabilities and equity

     (ii)   Presentation of certain compound instruments

(b)   IAS 39 *Financial instruments: Recognition and measurement* deals with:

     (i)   Recognition and derecognition

     (ii)   The measurement of financial instruments

3.2 Definitions

The most important definitions are common to both standards.

KEY TERMS

FINANCIAL INSTRUMENT Any contract that gives rise to both a financial asset of one entity and a financial liability or equity instrument of another entity.

FINANCIAL ASSET. Any asset that is:

(a)   Cash

(b)   An equity instrument of another entity

(c)   A contractual right to receive cash or another financial asset from another entity; or to exchange financial instruments with another entity under conditions that are potentially favourable to the entity

FINANCIAL LIABILITY. Any liability that is a contractual obligation:

(a)   To deliver cash or another financial asset to another entity; or

(b)   To exchange financial instruments with another entity under conditions that are potentially unfavourable

EQUITY INSTRUMENT. Any contract that evidences a residual interest in the assets of an entity after deducting all of its liabilities.   *(IAS 32 and IAS 39)*

3.3 Assets and liabilities

Examples of **financial assets** include:

(a)   Trade receivables
(b)   Options
(c)   Shares (when used as an investment)

Examples of **financial liabilities** include:

(a)   Trade payables
(b)   Loans payable
(c)   Redeemable preference (non-equity) shares

3.4 Liabilities and equity

The main thrust of IAS 32 is that financial instruments should be presented according to their **substance, not merely their legal form**. In particular, entities which issue financial instruments should classify them (or their component parts) as **either financial liabilities, or equity**.

The classification of a financial instrument as a liability or as equity depends on the following.

•   The **substance of the contractual arrangement** on initial recognition
•   The definitions of a **financial liability** and an **equity instrument**

How should a **financial liability be distinguished from an equity instrument**? The critical feature of a **liability** is an **obligation** to transfer economic benefit. Therefore a financial instrument is a financial liability if there is a **contractual obligation** on the issuer either to deliver cash or another financial asset to the holder or to exchange another financial instrument with the holder under potentially unfavourable conditions to the issuer.

The financial liability exists **regardless of the way in which the contractual obligation will be settled**. The issuer's ability to satisfy an obligation may be restricted, eg by lack of access to foreign currency, but this is irrelevant as it does not remove the issuer's obligation or the holder's right under the instrument.

Where the above critical feature is *not* met, then the financial instrument is an **equity instrument**. IAS 32 explains that although the holder of an equity instrument may be entitled to a *pro rata* share of any distributions out of equity, the issuer does *not* have a contractual obligation to make such a distribution.

Although substance and legal form are often **consistent with each other**, this is not always the case. In particular, a financial instrument may have the legal form of equity, but in substance it is in fact a liability – eg a redeemable preference share.

3.5 IAS 32 and redeemable (or cumulative) preference shares

Many entities issue **preference shares** which must be **redeemed** by the issuer for a fixed (or determinable) amount at a fixed (or determinable) future date. Alternatively, the holder may have the right to require the issuer to redeem the shares at or after a certain date for a fixed amount. In such cases, the issuer has an **obligation**. Therefore the instrument is a **financial liability** and should be classified as such. The issuer will also have an obligation to the holder of a preference share if the share is **cumulative**. In this case the issuer is obliged to pay the dividend each year, and the preference share will be classified as a liability. Preference shares which are non-cumulative and non-redeemable will be classified as equity.

The classification of the financial instrument is made when it is **first recognised** and this classification will continue until the financial instrument is removed from the entity's statement of financial position.

3.6 Measurement of financial instruments: IAS 39

Financial instruments are initially measured at the **fair value** of the consideration given or received (ie, **cost**) **plus** (in most cases) **transaction costs** that are **directly attributable** to the acquisition or issue of the financial instrument.

The **exception** to this rule is where a financial instrument is designated as **at fair value through profit or loss**. In this case, **transaction costs** are **not** added to fair value at initial recognition.

The fair value of the consideration is normally the transaction price or market price. If market prices are not reliable, the fair value may be **estimated** using a valuation technique (for example, by discounting cash flows).

3.7 IAS 39 and redeemable preference shares

An entity which issues redeemable preference shares must account for the transaction according to IAS 39. Redeemable preference shares are classified as a **financial liability**. Payment of **dividends** on redeemable preference shares is treated as if it were payment of the **finance charge on a redeemable loan**.

3.8 Accounting for finance charges

How is the finance charge on a financial instrument calculated? It can be measured as the difference between the amount paid or received for the instrument, including any transaction costs, and all amounts received or paid subsequent to that – interest or dividends, amount payable or receivable on maturity. This amount must then be allocated over the life of the instrument.

IAS 39 prescribes the **effective interest method** of allocating the finance charge (or the interest receivable, in the case of the purchaser) over the life of the liability.

KEY TERM

The EFFECTIVE INTEREST RATE is the rate that exactly discounts estimated future cash payments or receipts through the expected life of the financial instrument.   (*IAS 39*)

Example: Allocation of interest receivable

On 1 January 20X1 Abacus Co purchases a debt instrument for its fair value of $1,000. The debt instrument is due to mature on 31 December 20X5. The instrument has a principal amount of $1,250 and carries fixed interest of 4.72% paid annually.

How should Abacus Co account for the debt instrument over its five year term?

Solution

The interest receivable will be calculated as follows.

	$
Interest:	
5 years × $59 (1,250 × 4.72%)	295
Amount at maturity	1,250
Purchase cost	(1,000)
Interest receivable	545

This interest receivable must be allocated over the five year term. Here the effective interest rate is 10%.

So the allocation would be as follows.

Year	Financial asset at beginning of year	Interest income for year (10%)	Interest received during year	Financial asset at end of year
	$	$	$	$
20X1	1,000	100	(59)	1,041
20X2	1,041	104	(59)	1,086
20X3	1,086	109	(59)	1,136
20X4	1,136	113	(59)	1,190
20X5	1,190	119	(59)	1,250

Each year the carrying amount of the financial asset is increased by the interest income for the year (DR Asset/CR Interest receivable) and reduced by the interest actually received during the year (DR Cash/CR Asset).

As Abacus was the **purchaser** of the financial instrument, we were dealing with **interest receivable**, rather than finance charge.

Now we will take the example of a finance charge.

Example: Allocation of finance charge

On 1 January 20X1 Abacus Co also issues 20 million $1 5% preference shares redeemable at par after 4 years. Issue costs are $2 million. The finance charge is calculated as follows.

	$m
Receipt from issue (20m – 2m)	18
Dividend payable over 4 years (20 × 5% ×4)	(4)
Payable on redemption	(20)
Finance charge	(6)

The effective interest rate is approximately 8% and the allocation is as follows.

Year	Statement of financial position liability $m	Finance charge for year 8% $m	Dividends paid $m	Statement of financial position liability $m
20X1	18.00	1.44	(1)	18.44
20X2	18.44	1.48	(1)	18.92
20X3	18.92	1.52	(1)	19.44
20X4	19.44	1.55	(1)	19.99

So by the redemption date the carrying value of the liability has been increased from the amount originally received ($18m) to the amount needed to redeem the shares ($20m).

Exam skills

If you were required to calculate finance charges or interest receivable on a financial instrument in the exam, you would be told the effective interest rate.

3.9 Convertible debt

Some financial instruments contain both a liability and an equity element, and are known as **compound instruments**. IAS 32 requires the component parts of a compound instrument to be **classified separately**, according to the substance of the contractual arrangement and the definitions of a financial liability and an equity instrument.

One of the most common types of compound instrument is **convertible debt**. This creates a primary financial liability of the issuer and grants an option to the holder of the instrument to convert it into an equity instrument (usually ordinary shares) of the issuer. This is the economic equivalent of the issue of conventional debt plus a warrant to acquire shares in the future.

Although in theory there are several possible ways of calculating the split, IAS 32 requires the following method:

(a)   Calculate the value for the liability component.
(b)   Deduct this from the instrument as a whole to leave a residual value for the equity component.

The reasoning behind this approach is that an entity's equity is its residual interest in its assets amount after deducting all its liabilities. The **sum of the carrying amounts** assigned to liability and equity will always be equal to the carrying amount that would be ascribed to the instrument **as a whole**.

Example: convertible debt

Rathbone Co issues 2,000 convertible bonds at the start of 20X2. The bonds have a three year term, and are issued at par with a face value of $1,000 per bond, giving total proceeds of $2m. Interest is payable annually in arrears at a nominal annual interest rate of 6%. Each bond is convertible at any time up to maturity into 250 ordinary shares.

When the bonds are issued, the prevailing market interest rate for similar debt without conversion options is 9%. Using this interest rate, the present value of a similar $2m loan without a conversion option is $1.544m and the present value of the interest payments on this same loan is $0.304m.

Required

What is the value of the equity component in the bond?

Solution

The liability component is valued first, and the **difference** between the proceeds of the bond issue and the fair value of the liability is assigned to the **equity component**. The present value of the liability component, which has been given in the question, is calculated using a discount rate of 9%, the market interest rate for similar bonds having no conversion rights.

	$m
Present value of the principal	1.544
Present value of the interest	0.304
Total liability component	1.848
Equity component (balancing figure)	0.152
Proceeds of the bond issue	2.000

The split between the liability and equity components remains the same throughout the term of the instrument, even if there are changes in the **likelihood of the option being exercised.** This is because it is not always possible to predict how a holder will behave. The issuer continues to have an obligation to make future payments until conversion, maturity of the instrument or some other relevant transaction takes place.

3.10 Disclosures

Disclosures for financial instruments are covered by IFRS 7 *Financial Instruments: Disclosures*. The two main categories of disclosure required by IFRS 7 are:

(a)   Information about the significance of financial instruments
(b)   Information about the nature and extent of risks arising from financial instruments.

IFRS 7 came into force in January 2007.

Section summary

- IAS 32 and IAS 39 deal with **financial instruments**. IAS 32 deals with presentation. IAS 39 sets out principles for recognising and measuring financial assets and liabilities.

- Financial instruments must be classified as **financial assets**, **financial liabilities** or **equity**.

- The substance of the financial instrument is more important than its **legal form**.

- The critical feature of a financial liability is the **contractual obligation to deliver cash** or another financial instrument.

- **Redeemable preference shares** are classified as a **financial liability**.

- **Convertible debt** has the characteristics of both an equity instrument and a financial liability and should be **split into its component parts**.

Chapter Roundup

- ✓ **Ordinary shares** (or equity shares) give the shareholder voting rights and the right to participate in the residual profits of the entity.

- ✓ **Preference shares** do not usually carry voting rights and are usually non-equity, but do have the right to a fixed dividend.

- ✓ Shares may be issued to existing shareholders via a **rights issue** or a **bonus issue**. Alternately they can be issued to new shareholders at market value.

- ✓ A **rights issue** is where an entity issues shares for cash to its existing shareholders in proportion to their existing holdings at a discount to the current market price.

- ✓ A **bonus issue** is where an entity issues free shares to its existing shareholders in proportion to their existing holdings. No cash is received for the shares, instead existing reserves are capitalised as consideration.

- ✓ Share issue costs for ordinary shares should be deducted from a reserve, usually the **share premium account**. They are not an expense of the entity.

- ✓ An entity that wishes to repurchase its own shares will usually have to do so using the proceeds of a new share issue or by capitalising distributable profits in a '**capital redemption reserve**' in order to preserve the creditor's buffer.

- ✓ Shares which an entity has repurchased but not cancelled are called **treasury shares**. These are shown as a deduction from equity in the statement of financial position.

- ✓ IAS 32 and IAS 39 deal with **financial instruments**. IAS 32 deals with presentation and disclosure. IAS 39 sets out principles for recognising and measuring financial assets and liabilities.

- ✓ Financial instruments must be classified as **financial assets, financial liabilities** or **equity**.

- ✓ The **substance** of the financial instrument is more important than its **legal form**.

- ✓ The critical feature of a financial liability is the **contractual obligation to deliver cash** or another financial instrument.

- ✓ **Redeemable preference** shares are classified as a **financial liability**.

- ✓ **Convertible debt** has the characteristics of both an equity instrument and a financial liability and should be **split into its component parts**.

Quick Quiz

1   Issue costs on ordinary shares are treated as an expense of the entity. True or false?

2   In a share issue, the excess of the consideration over the nominal value of the shares is known as ....which must be credited to a ....as part of the equity and reserves of the entity.

3   A company can redeem shares out of which sources of funds?

   (i)   Distributable profits
   (ii)   Proceeds of new shares
   (iii)   The share premium account

   A   All three
   B   (i) and (ii)
   C   (ii) and (iii)
   D   (i) and (iii)

4   How are redeemable preference shares accounted for by the entity that issues them?

5   Define a financial instrument.

6   How should convertible debt be accounted for in the financial statements?

Answers to Quick Quiz

1   False. Share issue costs for ordinary shares are not an expense of the entity. They should be deducted from a reserve, usually the share premium account.

2   Share premium, share premium account.

3   B

4   As a financial liability. Payment of dividends on redeemable preference shares is treated as if it were payment of the finance charge on a loan.

5   Any contract that gives rise to both a financial asset of one entity and a financial liability or equity instrument of another entity.

6   Convertible debt should be split into its two components: a debt component and an equity component. The fair value of the debt component should be measured as the fair value of similar debt without a conversion option. The fair value of the equity component is calculated as the difference between the fair value of the whole instrument and the fair value of the debt component.

Answers to Questions

12.1 Issue of shares

APPLICATION AND ALLOTMENT A/C

	$		$
Bank	5,000	Bank	30,000
Share capital	30,000	Bank	15,000
Share premium	10,000		
	45,000		45,000

BANK

	$		$
App & allot a/c	30,000	App & allot a/c	5,000
App & allot a/c	15,000		
Call	19,600		
Forfeit	1,100	C/d	60,700
	65,700		65,700

SHARE CAPITAL

	$		$
		App & allot	30,000
C/d	50,000	Call	20,000
	50,000		50,000

SHARE PREMIUM

	$		$
		App & allot a/c	10,000
C/d	10,700	Investments : own shares	700
	10,700		10,700

CALL A/C

	$		$
Share capital	20,000	Bank	19,600
		Forfeit	400
	20,000		20,000

INVESTMENT IN OWN SHARES

	$		$
Call a/c	400	Bank	1,100
Share premium	700		
	1,100		1,100

12.2 Purchase of own shares

	$	$
Cost of redemption (repurchase) (50,000 × $1.50)		75,000
Premium on redemption (50,000 × 50c)		25,000
No premium arises on the new issue.		
Distributable profits		
Retained earnings before redemption		160,000
Premium on redemption (must come out of distributable		
profits, no premium on new issue)		(25,000)
		135,000
Remainder of redemption costs	50,000	
Proceeds of new issue 5,000 × $1	(5,000)	
Remainder out of distributable profits		(45,000)
Balance on retained earnings		90,000
Transfer to capital redemption reserve		
Par value of shares redeemed		50,000
Proceeds of new issue		(5,000)
Balance to capital redemption reserve		45,000

STATEMENT OF FINANCIAL POSITION AS AT 1 JULY 20X5

	$'000
Total assets	450
Equity and liabilities	
Ordinary shares	255
Share premium	60
Capital redemption reserve	45
	360
Retained earnings	90
	450

<table>
<tr><td rowspan="2">**Now try these questions from the Exam Question Bank**</td><td>**Number**</td><td>**Level**</td><td>**Marks**</td><td>**Time**</td></tr>
<tr><td>Q15</td><td>Examination</td><td>30</td><td>54 mins</td></tr>
<tr><td></td><td>Q23</td><td>Examination</td><td>5</td><td>9 mins</td></tr>
</table>

GROUP FINANCIAL STATEMENTS

Part C

INTRODUCTION TO GROUP ACCOUNTING

Consolidation is an important area of your syllabus.

The key to consolidation questions in the examination is to adopt a logical approach and to practise as many questions as possible.

In this chapter we will look at the major definitions in consolidation. These matters are fundamental to your comprehension of group accounts, so make sure you can understand them and then **learn them**.

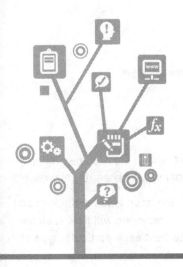

topic list	learning outcomes	syllabus references	ability required
1 Group accounts	C1(b)	C1(iii)	application

1 Group accounts

Introduction

Many large businesses consist of several companies controlled by one central or administrative company. Together these companies are called a group. The controlling company, called the parent or holding company, will own some or all of the shares in the other companies, called subsidiaries. There are many reasons for businesses to operate as groups including for the goodwill associated with the names of the subsidiaries and for tax or legal purposes.

IFRS requires that the results of a group should be presented as a whole, in a set of group or 'consolidated' financial statements. This chapter and those following will teach you the principles and mechanics of preparing a set of consolidated financial statements. In this first section, we look at the accounting standards which govern group accounting as well as some important definitions.

Exam alert

Group accounting is a significant part of your syllabus and has featured on all the exam papers so far. The specimen exam paper asked for the preparation of a consolidated statement of financial position for 20 marks in Section C and the May 2010 paper required the preparation of both a consolidated statement of financial position *and* a consolidated statement of comprehensive income for 20 marks in Section C. The November 2010 and May 2011 papers did not contain a Section C question on consolidation, but group accounting concepts featured heavily in Sections A and B.

1.1 Accounting standards

We will be looking at three accounting standards in this and the next three chapters.

- IAS 27 *Consolidated and separate financial statements*
- IFRS 3 *Business combinations*
- IAS 28 *Investments in associates*

These standards are all concerned with different aspects of group accounts, but there is some overlap between them, particularly between IFRS 3 and IAS 27. These two standards have been recently revised.

In this and the next chapter we will concentrate on IAS 27, which covers the basic group definitions and consolidation procedures of a parent-subsidiary relationship. First of all, however, we will look at all the important definitions involved in group accounts, which **determine how to treat each particular type of investment** in group accounts.

1.2 Definitions   11/10

We will look at some of these definitions in more detail later, but they are useful here in that they give you an overview of all aspects of group accounts.

KEY TERMS

- CONTROL. The power to govern the financial and operating policies of an entity so as to obtain benefits from its activities.   *(IFRS 3, IASs 27, 28)*

- SUBSIDIARY. An entity that is controlled by another entity (known as the parent). *(IASs 27, 28)*

- PARENT. An entity that has one or more subsidiaries.   *(IAS 27)*

- GROUP. A parent and all its subsidiaries.   *(IAS 27)*

- ASSOCIATE. An entity, including an unincorporated entity such as a partnership, in which an investor has significant influence and which is neither a subsidiary nor a joint venture of the investor.   *(IAS 28)*

- SIGNIFICANT INFLUENCE is the power to participate in the financial and operating policy decisions of an investee or an economic activity but is not control or joint control over those policies.*(IAS 28)*

- CONSOLIDATED FINANCIAL STATEMENTS. The financial statements of a group presented as those of a single economic entity.   *(IAS 27)*

We can summarise the different types of investment and the required accounting for them as follows.

Investment	Criteria	Required treatment in group accounts
Subsidiary	Control	Full consolidation
Associate	Significant influence	Equity accounting (see Chapter 16)
Investment which is none of the above	Asset held for accretion of wealth	As for single company accounts per IAS 39

As the level of investment increases, the amount of financial information given about the investment in the group accounts also increases. This makes sense as a larger investment will have a bigger effect on the financial results and financial position of the investing entity.

1.3 Investments in subsidiaries

The important point in determining whether an investment is a subsidiary is **control**. In most cases, control will involve the holding company or parent owning a majority of the ordinary shares in the subsidiary (to which normal voting rights are attached). There are circumstances, however, when the parent may own only a minority of the voting power in the subsidiary, *but* the parent still has control.

IAS 27 states that control can usually be assumed to exist when the parent **owns more than half (ie over 50%) of the voting power** of an entity *unless* it can be clearly shown that **such ownership does not constitute control** (these situations will be very rare).

What about situations where this ownership criterion does not exist? IAS 27 lists the following situations where control exists, even when the parent owns only 50% or less of the voting power of an entity.

(a)   The parent has power over more than 50% of the voting rights by virtue of **agreement with other investors**

(b)   The parent has power to **govern the financial and operating policies** of the entity by statute or under an agreement

(c)   The parent has the power to **appoint or remove a majority of members of the board of directors** (or equivalent governing body)

(d)   The parent has power to cast a **majority of votes at meetings of the board of directors**

IAS 27 also states that a parent loses control when it loses the power to govern the financial and operating policies of an investee. Loss of control can occur without a change in ownership levels. This may happen if a subsidiary becomes subject to the control of a government, court administrator or regulator (for example, in bankruptcy).

IAS 27 describes the nature of control in some detail because in the past, entities have tried to evade the requirements to consolidate entities by creating complicated ownership structures.

Exam alert

In your F1 exam, CIMA has stated that the holding company or parent will own 100% of the ordinary shares in the subsidiary and therefore have control.

You will cover the situation where the parent owns less than 100% of ordinary shares but still has control in F2 *Financial Management.*

1.3.1 Accounting treatment of subsidiaries in group accounts

Where a parent has one or more subsidiaries, IAS 27 requires the parent to present **consolidated financial statements** (also referred to as **group accounts**), in which the accounts of the parent and subsidiaries are combined and presented **as a single entity**. This presentation means that the substance, rather than the legal form, of the relationship between parent and subsidiaries will be presented.

1.4 Investments in associates

An investment in an associate is something less than a subsidiary, but more than a simple investment. The key criterion here is **significant influence**. This is defined as the 'power to participate', but *not* to 'control' (which would make the investment a subsidiary).

Significant influence can be determined by the holding of voting rights (usually attached to shares) in the entity. IAS 28 states that if an investor holds **20% or more** of the voting power of the investee, it can be presumed that the investor has significant influence over the investee, *unless* it can be clearly shown that this is not the case. Any **potential voting rights** should be taken into account in assessing whether the investor has significant influence over the investee.

Significant influence can be presumed *not* to exist if the investor holds **less than 20%** of the voting power of the investee, unless it can be demonstrated otherwise.

The **existence of significant influence** is evidenced in one or more of the following ways.

(a)   Representation on the **board of directors** (or equivalent) of the investee
(b)   Participation in the **policy making process**
(c)   **Material transactions** between investor and investee
(d)   Interchange of management personnel
(e)   Provision of essential technical information

1.4.1 Accounting treatment of associates in group accounts

IAS 28 requires the use of the **equity method** of accounting for investments in associates. This method will be explained in detail in Chapter 16.

Question 13.1	Treatments

Learning outcome C1(b)

Earlier in this section, we gave you a table showing the required treatment in group accounts for different investments. See if you can write out this table from memory before moving on.

1.5 Content of group accounts

It is important to note at this point that consolidated financial statements are an *additional* set of financial statements that are produced. They do not replace the individual financial statements of the parent or its subsidiaries. The group itself has no legal form, the group accounts are produced to satisfy accounting standards and in some countries, legal requirements.

Consolidated financial statements are issued to the shareholders of the parent and provide information to those shareholders on all the companies controlled by the parent.

Most parent companies present their own individual accounts and their group accounts in a single **package**. The package typically comprises the following.

- **Parent company financial statements**, which will include 'investments in subsidiary undertakings' as an asset in the statement of financial position, and income from subsidiaries (dividends) in the statement of comprehensive income

- **Consolidated statement of financial position**

- **Consolidated statement of comprehensive income** (or separate income statement)

- **Consolidated statement of cash flows**

1.6 Accounting for subsidiaries and associates in the parent's separate financial statements

A parent company will produce its own single company financial statements. In these statements, investments in subsidiaries and associates are shown as **investments** under non-current assets in the statement of financial position. The investments should be either accounted for at cost or in accordance with IAS 39.

1.7 Exemption from preparing group accounts

A parent **need not present** consolidated financial statements if and only if all of the following hold:

(a)   The parent is itself a **wholly-owned subsidiary** or it is a **partially owned subsidiary** of another entity and its other owners, including those not otherwise entitled to vote, have been informed about, and do not object to, the parent not presenting consolidated financial statements

(b)   Its securities are **not publicly traded**

(c)   It is **not in the process of issuing securities** in public securities markets; and

(d)   The **ultimate or intermediate parent** publishes consolidated financial statements that comply with International Financial Reporting Standards

A parent that does not present consolidated financial statements must comply with the IAS 27 rules on separate financial statements.

Section summary

IFRS requires that the results of a group should be presented as a whole, in a set of group or 'consolidated' financial statements.

The definition of a subsidiary is based on a 'control' relationship, which is assumed if the parent owns at least 50% of the equity shares in the entity.

The definition of an associate is based on the ability of the investing entity to exercise significant influence.

The different types of investment and the required accounting for them is summarised as follows.

Investment	Criteria	Required treatment in group accounts
Subsidiary	Control (> 50% rule)	Full consolidation (IAS 27)
Associate	Significant influence (20%+ rule)	Equity accounting (IAS 28)
Investment which is none of the above	Asset held for accretion of wealth	As for single company accounts (IAS 39)

IAS 27 includes some specific exemptions from the preparation of consolidated financial statements.

Chapter Roundup

✓ IFRS requires that the results of a group should be presented as a whole, in a set of group or 'consolidated' financial statements.

✓ The definition of a subsidiary is based on a 'control' relationship, which is assumed if the parent owns at least 50% of the equity shares in the entity.

✓ The definition of an associate is based on the ability of the investing entity to exercise significant influence.

✓ The different types of investment and the required accounting for them is summarised as follows.

Investment	Criteria	Required treatment in group accounts
Subsidiary	Control (> 50% rule)	Full consolidation (IAS 27)
Associate	Significant influence (20% + rule)	Equity accounting (IAS 28)
Investment which is none of the above	Asset held for accretion of wealth	As for single company accounts (IAS 39)

✓ IAS 27 includes some specific exemptions from the preparation of consolidated financial statements.

Quick Quiz

1 Define a 'subsidiary'.

2 What accounting treatment does IAS 27 require of a parent company?

3 When is a parent exempted from preparing consolidated financial statements?

4 According to IAS 27, in a parent-subsidiary relationship, when can control normally be assumed to exist?

5 How should an investment in a subsidiary be accounted for in the separate financial statements of the parent?

Answers to Quick Quiz

1 An entity that is controlled by another entity.

2 Consolidated financial statements must be prepared whereby the accounts of parent and subsidiary are combined and presented as a single entity.

3 When the parent is itself a wholly owned subsidiary, or a partially owned subsidiary and the non-controlling interests do not object.

4 IAS 27 states that control can usually be assumed to exist when the parent owns more than half (ie over 50%) of the voting power of an entity *unless* it can be clearly shown that such ownership does not constitute control.

5 As an investment in the non-current assets section of the statement of financial position, measured at cost or in accordance with IAS 39.

CONSOLIDATED STATEMENT OF FINANCIAL POSITION

This chapter introduces the **basic procedures** required in consolidation and gives a formal step plan for carrying out a statement of financial position consolidation.

This step procedure should be useful to you as a starting guide for answering any question, but remember that you cannot rely on it to answer the question for you. Each question must be approached and **answered on its own merits**. Examiners often put small extra or different problems in because, as they are always reminding students, it is not possible to 'rote-learn' consolidation.

The **method of consolidation** shown here uses schedules for workings rather than the ledger accounts used in some other texts. This is because we believe that ledger accounts lead students to 'learn' the consolidation journals without thinking about what they are doing - always a dangerous practice in consolidation questions.

There are plenty of questions and examples in this chapter – work through *all* of them carefully.

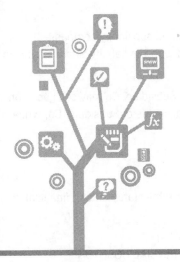

14

topic list	learning outcomes	syllabus references	ability required
1 IAS 27 Summary of consolidation procedures	C1(c)	C1(iii)	application
2 Dividends paid by a subsidiary	C1(c)	C1(iii)	application
3 Goodwill arising on consolidation	C1(c),(d)	C1(iii)	application
4 Intra-group trading	C1(c)	C1(iii)	application
5 Intra-group sales of non-current assets	C1(c)	C1(iii)	application
6 Fair values in acquisition accounting	C1(c),(d)	C1(iii)	application
7 Approach to answering exam questions	C1(c),(d)	C1(iii)	application

1   IAS 27 Summary of consolidation procedures

Introduction

How are consolidated financial statements prepared? IAS 27 lays out the basic procedures and we will consider these in the rest of this chapter.

Exam alert

You must know how to prepare a consolidated statement of financial position. The specimen exam paper and the May 2010 exam paper both required the preparation of a consolidated statement of financial position in Section C.

1.1 Basic procedure

The preparation of a consolidated statement of financial position, in a very simple form, consists of two procedures.

(a)   Take the individual accounts of the parent company and each subsidiary and **cancel out items** which appear as an asset in one company and a liability in another.

(b)   Add together all the uncancelled assets and liabilities throughout the group on a line by line basis.

Items requiring cancellation may include the following.

(a)   The asset **'shares in subsidiary companies'** (also called 'investment in subsidiary companies') which appears in the parent company's accounts will be matched with the liability 'share capital' in the subsidiaries' accounts.

(b)   There may be **intra-group trading** within the group. For example, Subsidiary Co may sell goods on credit to Parent Co. Parent Co would then be a receivable in the accounts of Subsidiary Co, while Subsidiary Co would be a payable in the accounts of Parent Co.

Example: basic consolidation procedure

Parent Co has just bought 100% of the shares of Subsidiary Co. Below are the statements of financial position of both companies just before consolidation.

PARENT CO STATEMENT OF FINANCIAL POSITION	$'000	SUBSIDIARY CO STATEMENT OF FINANCIAL POSITION	$'000
Assets			
Investment in subsidiary*	50	Receivables	20
Receivables	30	Cash	30
	80		50
Equity and liabilities			
Share capital	80	Share capital*	50
	80		50

* Cancelling items

The consolidated statement of financial position will appear as follows.

PARENT AND SUBSIDIARY
CONSOLIDATED STATEMENT OF FINANCIAL POSITION

	$'000
Receivables (30 + 20)	50
Cash	30
	80
Share capital**	80
	80

**Note. This is the parent company's share capital only. The subsidiary's has been cancelled.

Example: basic consolidation procedure with intra-group trading

P Co regularly sells goods to its one subsidiary company, S Co, which it has owned since S Co's incorporation. The statement of financial position of the two companies on 31 December 20X6 are given below.

STATEMENTS OF FINANCIAL POSITION AS AT 31 DECEMBER 20X6

	P Co $	S Co $
Assets		
Non-current assets		
Property, plant and equipment	35,000	45,000
Investment in 40,000 $1 shares in S Co at cost	40,000	
	75,000	
Current assets		
Inventories	16,000	12,000
Receivables: S Co	2,000	
Other	6,000	9,000
Cash at bank	1,000	
Total assets	100,000	66,000
Equity and liabilities		
Equity		
40,000 $1 ordinary shares		40,000
70,000 $1 ordinary shares	70,000	
Retained earnings	16,000	19,000
	86,000	59,000
Current liabilities		
Bank overdraft		3,000
Payables: P Co		2,000
Payables: Other	14,000	2,000
Total equity and liabilities	100,000	66,000

Required

Prepare the consolidated statement of financial position of the P group at 31 December 20X6.

Solution

The cancelling items are:

(a) P Co's asset 'investment in shares of S Co' ($40,000) cancels with S Co's liability 'share capital' ($40,000)

(b) P Co's asset 'receivables: S Co' ($2,000) cancels with S Co's liability 'payables: P Co' ($2,000).

The remaining assets and liabilities are added together to produce the following consolidated statement of financial position.

P GROUP CONSOLIDATED STATEMENT OF FINANCIAL POSITION AS AT 31 DECEMBER 20X6

	$	$
Assets		
Non-current assets		
Property, plant and equipment (35 + 45)		80,000
Current assets		
Inventories (16 + 12)	28,000	
Receivables (6 + 9)	15,000	
Cash at bank	1,000	
		44,000
Total assets		124,000
Equity and liabilities		
Equity		
70,000 $1 ordinary shares (P Co only)	70,000	
Retained earnings (16 + 19)	35,000	
		105,000
Current liabilities		
Bank overdraft	3,000	
Payables (14 + 2)	16,000	
		19,000
Total equity and liabilities		124,000

Note the following.

(a)   P Co's bank balance is **not netted off** with S Co's bank overdraft. To offset one against the other would be less informative and would conflict with the principle that assets and liabilities should not be netted off.

(b)   The share capital in the consolidated statement of financial position is the **share capital of the parent company alone**. This must *always* be the case, no matter how complex the consolidation, because the share capital of subsidiary companies must *always* be a wholly cancelling item.

1.2 Part cancellation

An item may appear in the statements of financial position of a parent company and its subsidiary, but not at the same amounts.

(a)   The parent company may have acquired **shares in the subsidiary** at a price **greater or less than their par value**. The asset will appear in the parent company's accounts at cost, while the liability will appear in the subsidiary's accounts at par value. This raises the issue of **goodwill**, which is dealt with later in this chapter.

(b)   The intra-group trading balances may not be equal to each other because of **goods or cash in transit**.

(c)   One company may have **issued loan stock** of which a **proportion only** is taken up by the other company.

The following question illustrates the techniques needed to deal with items (b) and (c) above. The procedure is to **cancel as far as possible**. The remaining uncancelled amounts will appear in the consolidated statement of financial position.

(a)   **Uncancelled loan stock** will appear as a **liability of the group**.

(b)   **Uncancelled balances on intra-group accounts** represent **goods or cash in transit**, which will appear in the consolidated statement of financial position.

Question 14.1

Learning outcome C1(c)

The statements of financial position of P Co and of its subsidiary S Co have been made up to 30 June. P Co has owned all the ordinary shares and 40% of the loan stock of S Co since its incorporation.

P CO STATEMENT OF FINANCIAL POSITION AS AT 30 JUNE

	$	$
Assets		
Non-current assets		
Property, plant and equipment	120,000	
Investment in S Co, at cost		
80,000 ordinary shares of $1 each	80,000	
$20,000 of 12% loan stock in S Co	20,000	
		220,000
Current assets		
Inventories	50,000	
Receivables	40,000	
Current account with S Co	18,000	
Cash	4,000	
		112,000
Total assets		332,000
Equity and liabilities		
Equity		
Ordinary shares of $1 each, fully paid	100,000	
Retained earnings	95,000	
		195,000
Non-current liabilities		
10% loan stock		75,000
Current liabilities		
Payables	47,000	
Taxation	15,000	
		62,000
Total equity and liabilities		332,000

S CO STATEMENT OF FINANCIAL POSITION AS AT 30 JUNE

	$	$
Assets		
Property, plant and equipment		100,000
Current assets		
Inventories	60,000	
Receivables	30,000	
Cash	6,000	
		96,000
Total assets		196,000
Equity and liabilities		
Equity		
80,000 ordinary shares of $1 each, fully paid	80,000	
Retained earnings	28,000	
		108,000
Non-current liabilities		
12% loan stock		50,000
Current liabilities		
Payables	16,000	
Taxation	10,000	
Current account with P Co	12,000	
		38,000
Total equity and liabilities		196,000

The difference on current accounts arises because of goods in transit.

Required

Prepare the consolidated statement of financial position of the P group.

Section summary

- The basic procedure of consolidation combines the financial statements of a parent and its subsidiaries on a **line by line** basis by adding together like items.

- Items which appear as an asset in one company and a liability in another are **cancelled out**.

- The asset **'shares in subsidiary companies'** (also called 'investment in subsidiary companies') which appears in the parent company's accounts will be cancelled with the liability **'share capital'** in the subsidiaries' accounts.

- If an item appears in the statements of financial position of a parent company and its subsidiary at different amounts, the procedure is to **cancel as far as possible**. The remaining uncancelled amounts will appear in the consolidated statement of financial position.

2 Dividends paid by a subsidiary

Introduction

This brief section covers how to treat dividends paid by a subsidiary company during the year.

When a subsidiary company pays a **dividend** during the year the accounting treatment is not difficult. Suppose S Co, a 100% subsidiary of P Co, pays a dividend of $1,000 on the last day of its accounting period. Its total reserves before paying the dividend stood at $5,000.

(a) The parent company receives $1,000 of the dividend, debiting cash and crediting profit or loss. This will be cancelled on consolidation.

(b) The remaining balance of retained earnings in S Co's statement of financial position ($4,000) will be consolidated in the normal way.

Section summary

Dividends paid from a subsidiary to a parent company are **cancelled** on consolidation.

3 Goodwill arising on consolidation   5/10, 11/10, 5/11

Introduction

In the examples we have looked at so far the cost of shares acquired by the parent company has always been equal to the par value of those shares. This is seldom the case in practice and we must now consider some more complicated examples.

3.1 Goodwill arising on consolidation

In this section, we will examine what happens when a parent company pays more than the par value of the shares it is acquiring in a subsidiary entity. We will do this through the following example.

Example: Goodwill arising on consolidation

P Co purchased all of the share capital (40,000 $1 shares) of S Co for $60,000. The statements of financial position of P Co and S Co prior to the acquisition are as follows.

STATEMENTS OF FINANCIAL POSITION AS AT 31.12.X1

	P Co $'000	S Co $'000
Non-current assets		
Property, plant and equipment	100	40
Cash at bank	60	
Total assets	160	40
Equity and liabilities		
Share capital	160	40
Total equity and liabilities	160	40

The carrying amount of S Co's property, plant and equipment is the same as the market value at the acquisition date.

First we will examine the entries made by the parent company in its own statement of financial position when it acquires the shares.

The entries in P Co's books would be:

DEBIT	Investment in S Co	$60,000	
CREDIT	Bank		$60,000

So P Co's statement of financial position will look as follows:

	P Co $'000
Non-current assets	
Property, plant and equipment	100
Investment in S Co	60
Total assets	160
Equity and liabilities	
Share capital	160
Total equity and liabilities	160

Next we will look at the group accounts.

Now when the directors of P Co agree to pay $60,000 for a 100% investment in S Co they must believe that, in addition to its non-current assets of $40,000, S Co must also have **intangible assets** worth $20,000. This amount of $20,000 paid over and above the value of the tangible assets acquired is called the **goodwill arising on consolidation** (sometimes **premium on acquisition**).

Following the normal cancellation procedure the $40,000 share capital in S Co's statement of financial position should be cancelled against $40,000 of the 'investment in S Co' in the statement of financial position of P Co. This would leave a $20,000 debit uncancelled in the parent company's accounts and this $20,000 would appear in the consolidated statement of financial position under the caption 'Intangible non-current assets: goodwill arising on consolidation', as follows.

P GROUP CONSOLIDATED STATEMENT OF FINANCIAL POSITION AS AT 31.12.X1

	$'000
Non-current assets	
Property, plant and equipment (100 + 40)	140
Intangible non-current assets: goodwill arising on consolidation	20
Total assets	160

Equity and liabilities	$'000
Share capital (P Co only)	160
Total equity and liabilities	160

3.2 Reminder: what is goodwill?

As we saw in our earlier studies on intangible assets and IAS 38, goodwill is created by good relationships between a business and its customers. The goodwill inherent in a business will include intangibles such as a good reputation, a well known brand or a valuable customer list. IAS 38 prohibits the recognition of internally generated goodwill.

However, when goodwill arises on consolidation, as we have seen in the example above, IFRS 3 requires the goodwill to be recognised as an intangible asset in the consolidated financial statements.

IFRS 3 defines goodwill as 'an asset representing the future economic benefits arising from other assets acquired in a business combination that are not individually identified and separately recognised'.

3.3 Measurement and treatment of goodwill

Goodwill arising on consolidation is calculated in accordance with IFRS 3 as the difference between the **purchase consideration** and the **fair value** of the identifiable assets acquired and liabilities assumed.

As a result of this calculation, the goodwill can therefore be **positive** or **negative**.

Positive goodwill is recognised as an intangible non-current asset in the statement of financial position. After recognition, positive goodwill is measured **at the original amount less any accumulated impairment losses**. It is **not amortised**. Instead it is tested for impairment at least annually, in accordance with IAS 36 *Impairment of assets*.

Negative goodwill acquired in a business combination in effect means that the buyer has got a '**bargain purchase**' as they have paid less for the entity that the fair value of its identifiable assets and liabilities. Negative goodwill could be thought of as a discount on the purchase price. As this is unusual, IFRS 3 requires that the purchaser checks to make sure that the acquired assets and liabilities are correctly identified and valued and that the goodwill calculation is correct. Negative goodwill should be **credited to profit or loss** in the year of acquisition.

3.4 Goodwill and pre-acquisition profits

Up to now we have assumed that S Co had no retained earnings when it was acquired and therefore we have not had to deal with any profits made by S Co before P Co took ownership of it. Assuming instead that S Co was purchased sometime after incorporation and had earned profits of $8,000 in the period before acquisition, its statement of financial position just before the purchase would look as follows.

S CO STATEMENT OF FINANCIAL POSITION	$
Total assets	48,000
Share capital	40,000
Retained earnings	8,000
	48,000

If P Co now purchases all the shares in S Co it will acquire total assets worth $48,000 at a cost of $60,000. Clearly in this case S Co's intangible assets (goodwill) are being valued at $12,000. Any earnings retained by the subsidiary **prior to its acquisition** by the parent company must be **incorporated in the cancellation** process so as to arrive at a figure for goodwill arising on consolidation. In other words, not only S Co's share capital, but also its **pre-acquisition** retained earnings, must be cancelled against the asset 'investment in S Co' in the accounts of the parent company. The uncancelled balance of $12,000 appears in the consolidated statement of financial position as goodwill.

The consequence of this is that **any pre-acquisition retained earnings of a subsidiary company are not aggregated with the parent company's retained earnings** in the consolidated statement of financial position. The figure of consolidated retained earnings comprises the retained earnings of the parent company plus the **post-acquisition retained earnings only of subsidiary companies**. The post-acquisition retained earnings are simply retained earnings now *less* retained earnings at acquisition.

Other reserves, such as the **revaluation surplus**, are treated in the same way as retained earnings.

Example: goodwill and pre-acquisition profits

Sing Co acquired the ordinary shares of Wing Co on 31 March 20X1 when the statements of financial position of each company were as follows.

STATEMENTS OF FINANCIAL POSITION AS AT 31 MARCH 20X1

	SING CO $	WING CO $
Assets		
Non-current assets		
Investment in 50,000 shares of Wing Co at cost	80,000	-
Current assets	40,000	60,000
Total assets	120,000	60,000
Equity and liabilities		
Equity		
Ordinary shares of $1 each	75,000	50,000
Retained earnings	45,000	10,000
Total equity and liabilities	120,000	60,000

Required

Prepare the consolidated statement of financial position as at 31 March 20X1.

Solution

The technique to adopt here is to produce a new working: 'Goodwill'. A proforma working is set out below.

Goodwill

	$	$
Consideration transferred		X
Less net value of identifiable assets acquired and liabilities assumed:		
Ordinary share capital	X	
Share premium	X	
Retained earnings at acquisition	X	
		(X)
Goodwill		X

Applying this to our example the working will look like this.

	$	$
Consideration transferred*		80,000
Less net value of identifiable assets acquired and liabilities assumed:		
Ordinary share capital	50,000	
Retained earnings at acquisition	10,000	
		(60,000)
Goodwill		20,000

*This is the cost of the investment in Sing Co's statement of financial position.

SING GROUP
CONSOLIDATED STATEMENT OF FINANCIAL POSITION AS AT 31 MARCH 20X1

	$
Assets	
Non-current assets	
Goodwill arising on consolidation (W)	20,000
Current assets (40,000 + 60,000)	100,000
	120,000
Equity	
Ordinary shares (Sing Co only)	75,000
Retained earnings*	45,000
	120,000

* Retained earnings of Sing Co plus *post-acquisition* retained earnings of Wing Co. At this point, ie the date of acquisition, all Wing Co's retained earnings are *pre-acquisition*.

Example: goodwill and pre-acquisition profits continued

Suppose that a year has passed and you now wish to prepare the consolidated statement of financial position for the Sing group as at 31 March 20X2. The individual statements of financial position are as follows.

STATEMENTS OF FINANCIAL POSITION AS AT 31 MARCH 20X2

	SING CO $	WING CO $
Assets		
Non-current assets		
Investment in 50,000 shares of Wing Co at cost	80,000	-
Current assets	50,000	80,000
Total assets	130,000	80,000
Equity and liabilities		
Equity		
Ordinary shares of $1 each	75,000	50,000
Retained earnings	55,000	30,000
Total equity and liabilities	130,000	80,000

Required

Prepare the consolidated statement of financial position as at 31 March 20X2.

Solution

You can see from the individual statements of financial position that Wing Co has generated profits of $20,000 since being owned by Sing Co as the retained earnings balance has increased from $10,000 on acquisition to $30,000 at 31 March 20X2. These profits belong to the group and should be consolidated. The technique to adopt here is to produce a new working: *Retained earnings*. A proforma working is set out below.

Retained earnings

	P Co $	S Co $
Per question	X	X
Pre-acquisition retained earnings		(X)
		X
Post-acquisition retained earnings of S Co	X	
Group retained earnings	X	

Applying this to our example the working will look like this.

Retained earnings

	SING CO $	WING CO $
Per question	55,000	30,000
Pre-acquisition retained earnings		(10,000)
		20,000
Post-acq'n ret'd earnings of Wing Co	20,000	
Group retained earnings	75,000	

The goodwill calculation will be the same as before as it is based on the net assets of Wing Co at the **acquisition date**.

SING GROUP
CONSOLIDATED STATEMENT OF FINANCIAL POSITION AS AT 31 MARCH 20X2

Assets	$
Non-current assets	
Goodwill arising on consolidation	20,000
Current assets (50,000 + 80,000)	130,000
	150,000
Equity and liabilities	
Ordinary shares (Sing Co only)	75,000
Retained earnings (see working above)	75,000
	150,000

Exam alert

A question in the May 2010 exam included a subsidiary with a debit balance on retained earnings at acquisition. Don't be put off by this, just insert the *negative* amount of retained earnings into the goodwill calculation and into the retained earnings working.

3.5 Forms of consideration

The consideration paid by the parent for the shares in the subsidiary can take different forms and this will affect the calculation of goodwill. Here are some examples.

3.5.1 Contingent consideration

IFRS 3 requires the acquisition-date **fair value** of contingent consideration to be recognised as part of the consideration for the acquiree. The fair value of contingent consideration should reflect both the discounted present value of the amount due and the likelihood of it being paid.

Example: Contingent consideration

P Co acquired 100% of S Co's $100m share capital on 1 January 20X6 for a cash payment of $150m and a further payment of $50m on 31 March 20X7 provided that S Co's post acquisition profits have exceeded an agreed amount by that date. The further payment due on 31 March 20X7 was considered to have a fair value of $30m at the acquisition date.

The further payment is 'contingent consideration' as its payment is contingent on the post acquisition profits of S Co exceeding the agreed amount. In P Co's consolidated financial statements for the year to 31 December 20X6, the fair value of the contingent consideration, $30m, will be added to the amount paid to acquire S Co.

3.5.2 Deferred consideration

An agreement may be made that part of the consideration for the combination will be paid at a future date. This consideration should be discounted to its present value using the acquiring entity's cost of capital.

Example: Deferred consideration

The parent acquired 100% of the subsidiary's 80m $1 shares on 1 January 20X7. It paid $3.50 per share and agreed to pay a further $108m on 1 January 20X8.

The parent company's cost of capital is 8%.

The cost of the combination will be as follows:

	$m
80m shares × $3.50	280
Deferred consideration:	
$108m × 1/1.08	100
Total consideration	380

At 31 December 20X7, $8m will be charged to finance costs, being the unwinding of the discount on the deferred consideration.

3.5.3 Share exchange

Sometimes the consideration paid in a business combination will be in the form of equity shares. As with other forms of consideration, the equity shares must be measured at **fair value**.

For shares that are quoted on a stock exchange, the fair value is the published share price on the date of the acquisition, except in rare circumstances. For shares that are unquoted, the fair value is calculated by reference to the proportional interest in the fair value of the acquirer or proportional interest in the fair value of the acquiree, whichever is more clearly evident.

Example: Share exchange

P Co has acquired all of the share capital of S Co (12,000 $1 shares) by issuing 5 of its own $1 shares for every 4 shares in S Co. The market value of P Co's shares is $6 at the date of acquisition.

The cost of the combination is calculated as:

12,000 × 5/4 × $6 = $90,000

This is credited to the share capital and share premium of P Co as follows:

	DR	CR
Investment in subsidiary	90,000	
Share capital ($12,000 × 5/4)		15,000
Share premium ($12,000 × 5/4 × 5)		75,000

3.5.4 Expenses and issue costs

All expenses incurred in a business combination are written off as incurred. This includes finder's fees advisory, legal, accounting, valuation and other professional or consulting fees and general administrative costs.

Section summary

- The amount that the parent pays **over and above** the value of identifiable assets and liabilities acquired in the subsidiary is called **goodwill**. Goodwill arising on consolidation is subject to an annual **impairment review**.

- **Pre-acquisition retained earnings** of a subsidiary company are **not aggregated** with the parent company's retained earnings on consolidation.

- Consideration transferred when a parent acquires a subsidiary could be in the form of cash or shares. Consideration can be **contingent**, **deferred** or in the form of a **share exchange**.

4 Intra-group trading   5/10, 5/11

Introduction

Remember that consolidated financial statements present the accounts of the parent and subsidiary as a single entity. Therefore the effects of any trading that has happened between the two entities must be eliminated. This section covers how to deal with this situation in a consolidation question.

4.1 Unrealised profit

Any receivable/payable balances outstanding between the companies are cancelled on consolidation. No further problem arises if all such intra-group transactions are **undertaken at cost**, without any mark-up for profit.

However, each company in a group is a separate trading entity and may wish to treat other group companies in the same way as any other customer. In this case, a company (say A Co) may buy goods at one price and sell them at a higher price to another group company (B Co). The accounts of A Co will quite properly include the profit earned on sales to B Co; and similarly B Co's statement of financial position will include inventories at their cost to B Co, ie at the amount at which they were purchased from A Co.

This gives rise to two problems.

(a)   Although A Co makes a profit as soon as it sells goods to B Co, the group does not make a sale or achieve a profit until an outside customer buys the goods from B Co.

(b)   Any purchases from A Co which remain unsold by B Co at the year end will be included in B Co's inventory. Their value in the statement of financial position will be their cost to B Co, which is not the same as their cost to the group.

The objective of consolidated accounts is to present the financial position of several connected companies as that of a single entity, the group. This means that **in a consolidated statement of financial position the only profits recognised should be those earned by the group** in providing goods or services to outsiders. Similarly, inventory in the consolidated statement of financial position should be valued at cost to the group.

Suppose that a holding company P Co buys goods for $1,600 and sells them to its subsidiary S Co for $2,000. The goods are in S Co's inventory at the year end and appear in S Co's statement of financial position at $2,000. In this case, P Co will record a profit of $400 in its individual accounts, but from the group's point of view the figures are:

Cost	$1,600
External sales	NIL
Closing inventory at cost	$1,600
Profit/loss	NIL

If we add together the figures for retained earnings and inventory in the individual statements of financial position of P Co and S Co the resulting figures for consolidated retained earnings and consolidated inventory will each be overstated by $400. A **consolidation adjustment** is therefore necessary as follows.

DEBIT   Group retained earnings
CREDIT   Group inventory (statement of financial position)

with the amount of **profit unrealised** by the group. We call this the '**provision for unrealised profit**' or PUP, as it is a provision against inventory for the unrealised profit generated by the intra-group sale.

Exam skills

If the sale is from the **parent to the subsidiary**, you should **debit the parent's retained earnings** with the unrealised profit in the retained earnings working. If the sale is from the **subsidiary to the parent**, you should **debit the subsidiary's retained earnings** with the unrealised profit in the retained earnings working.

Although this seems like an unnecessary complication at this level in your studies, it will become much more important at F2 where you will be dealing with subsidiaries that are not 100% owned.

Exam skills

You will probably have to calculate the unrealised profit given either a gross profit margin or a mark-up on cost. Remember that:

- **Mark-up** is the profit as a percentage of **cost**
- **Gross profit margin** is the profit as a percentage of **sales**

Question 14.2	Unrealised profit

Learning outcome C1(c)

P Co acquired all the shares in S Co one year ago when the retained earnings of S Co stood at $10,000. Draft statements of financial position for each company are as follows.

	P Co		S Co	
	$	$	$	$
Assets				
Non-current assets				
Property, plant and equipment	80,000			40,000
Investment in S Co at cost	46,000			
		126,000		
Current assets				
Trade receivables	30,000		25,000	
Inventories	10,000		5,000	
		40,000		30,000
Total assets		166,000		70,000
Equity and liabilities				
Equity				
Ordinary shares of $1 each	100,000		30,000	
Retained earnings	45,000		22,000	
		145,000		52,000
Current liabilities		21,000		18,000
Total equity and liabilities		166,000		70,000

BPP
LEARNING MEDIA

During the year S Co sold goods to P Co for $50,000, the profit to S Co being 20% of selling price. At the end of the reporting period, 25% of these goods remained unsold in the inventories of P Co. At the same date, P Co owed S Co $12,000 for goods bought and this debt is included in the trade payables of P Co and the receivables of S Co. The goodwill arising on consolidation has been impaired. The amount of the impairment is $1,500.

Required

Prepare a draft consolidated statement of financial position for the P group.

Section summary

- In a consolidated statement of financial position, the only profits recognised should be those **earned by the group** in providing goods or services to outsiders.

- Inventory in the consolidated statement of financial position should be valued at **cost to the group**.

- Consolidation adjustments are necessary to **remove unrealised profits** in the group.

5 Intra-group sales of non-current assets

Introduction

As well as engaging in trading activities with each other, group companies may on occasion wish to **transfer non-current assets**. In this section we will look at how this affects the consolidation process.

5.1 Accounting treatment

In their individual accounts the companies concerned will treat the transfer just like a sale between unconnected parties: the selling company will record a profit or loss on sale, while the purchasing company will record the asset at the amount paid to acquire it, and will use that amount as the basis for calculating depreciation.

On consolidation, the usual **'group entity' principle applies**. The consolidated statement of financial position must show assets at their cost to the group, and any depreciation charged must be based on that cost. Two consolidation adjustments will usually be needed to achieve this.

(a)   An adjustment to alter retained earnings and non-current assets cost so as to remove any element of unrealised profit or loss. This is similar to the adjustment required in respect of unrealised profit in inventory.

(b)   An adjustment to alter retained earnings and accumulated depreciation is made so that consolidated depreciation is based on the asset's cost to the group.

In practice, these steps are combined so that the retained earnings of the entity making the unrealised profit are debited with the unrealised profit less the additional depreciation.

The double entry is as follows.

DEBIT   Group retained earnings
CREDIT   Group non-current assets

with the profit on disposal, less the additional depreciation.

Example: intra-group sales of non-current assets

P Co owns 100% of S Co and on 1 January 20X1 S Co sells plant with a carrying amount of $10,000 to P Co for $12,500. The companies make up accounts to 31 December 20X1 and the balances on their retained earnings at that date are:

P Co after charging depreciation of 10% on plant	$27,000
S Co including profit on sale of plant	$18,000

Required

Show the working for consolidated retained earnings.

Solution

Retained earnings

	P Co $	S Co $
Per question	27,000	18,000
Adjustment (intra-group sale of plant*)		(2,250)
		15,750
Group share of post-acq'n ret'd earnings: S Co	15,750	
Group retained earnings	42,750	

* The asset is written down to cost and depreciation on the 'profit' element is removed. So the group profit for the year is reduced by ($2,500 – ($2,500 ×10%)) = $2,250. The adjustment is recorded against S Co's retained earnings because S Co made the sale.

Section summary

The consolidated statement of financial position must show **non-current assets** at their **cost to the group** and any depreciation charged must be based on that cost.

6 Fair values in acquisition accounting

Introduction

In this section we look at what fair value is and the adjustments necessary for consolidation.

6.1 Fair value on acquisition   11/10, 5/11

Remember that goodwill arising on consolidation is calculated as the difference between the **purchase consideration** and the **fair value** of the identifiable assets and liabilities acquired. The fair value of the identifiable assets and liabilities is therefore very important. Until now we have calculated goodwill as the difference between the consideration transferred and the **book value** of net assets acquired by the group, assuming that book value is equal to fair value. However, in a real transaction, and in your exam, this is unlikely to be the case.

6.2 What is fair value?

Fair value is defined as follows by IFRS 3 and various other standards – it is an important definition.

KEY TERM

FAIR VALUE. The amount for which an asset could be exchanged, or a liability settled, between knowledgeable, willing parties in an arm's length transaction.   (*IFRS 3*)

6.3 IFRS 3 fair value principles

IFRS 3 requires that the acquiree's identifiable assets and liabilities should be recognised at fair value at the date of acquisition.

IFRS 3 sets out **general principles** for arriving at the fair values of a subsidiary's assets and liabilities. The acquirer should recognise the acquiree's identifiable assets, liabilities and contingent liabilities at the acquisition date only if they satisfy the following criteria.

(a)   In the case of an **asset** other than an intangible asset, it is **probable** that any associated **future economic benefits** will flow to the acquirer, and its fair value can be **measured reliably.**

(b)   In the case of a **liability** other than a contingent liability, it is probable that an **outflow** of resources embodying economic benefits will be required to settle the obligation, and its fair value can be **measured reliably**.

(c)   In the case of an **intangible asset**, if it meets the definition in IAS 38 of an intangible asset and its fair value can be measured reliably.

(d)   In the case of a **contingent liability**, its fair value can be **measured reliably**.

The acquiree's identifiable assets and liabilities might include assets and liabilities **not previously recognised** in the acquiree's financial statements. For example:

(a)   A tax benefit arising from the acquiree's tax losses that was not recognised by the acquiree may be recognised by the group if the acquirer has future taxable profits against which the unrecognised tax benefit can be applied.

(b)   Contingent liabilities, which are not recognised in the individual entity accounts in accordance with IAS 37 *Provisions, contingent liabilities and contingent assets*, will be recognised on consolidation at fair value in accordance with IFRS 3 provided the fair value can be reliably measured.

6.3.1 Restructuring and future losses

An acquirer **should not recognise liabilities for future losses** or other costs expected to be incurred as a result of the business combination.

IFRS 3 explains that a plan to restructure a subsidiary following an acquisition is not a present obligation of the acquiree at the acquisition date. Neither does it meet the definition of a contingent liability. Therefore an acquirer **should not recognise a liability for** such **a restructuring plan** as part of allocating the cost of the combination unless the subsidiary was already committed to the plan before the acquisition.

This **prevents creative accounting**. An acquirer cannot set up a provision for restructuring or future losses of a subsidiary and then release this to profit or loss in subsequent periods in order to reduce losses or smooth profits.

6.3.2 Intangible assets

The acquiree may have **intangible assets**, such as development expenditure. These can be recognised separately from goodwill only if they are **identifiable**. An intangible asset is identifiable only if it:

(a)   Is **separable**, ie capable of being separated or divided from the entity and sold, transferred, or exchanged, either individually or together with a related contract, asset or liability, or

(b)   Arises from contractual or other legal rights.

6.3.3 Contingent liabilities

Contingent liabilities of the acquirer are **recognised** if their **fair value can be measured reliably**. This is a departure from the normal rules in IAS 37; contingent liabilities are not normally recognised, but only disclosed.

After their initial recognition, the acquirer should measure contingent liabilities that are recognised separately at the higher of:

(a)   The amount that would be recognised in accordance with IAS 37

(b)   The amount initially recognised.

6.4 Incorporating fair values in the accounts

If there is a difference between the fair value and the carrying value of the net assets acquired, then adjustments must be made to account for this difference. The subsidiary does not normally restate its net assets to fair value at the acquisition date, so this needs to be done on consolidation.

Fair value adjustments affect **three** areas of the consolidated statement of financial position:

(a)   Goodwill

(b)   Group retained earnings (as depreciation charged in the consolidated financial statements must be based on **fair values** rather than the carrying values in the subsidiary's separate financial statements)

(c)   Asset values at the reporting date

The best way to deal with this is to set up an extra working: a fair value table. A proforma working is shown below.

Fair value adjustments

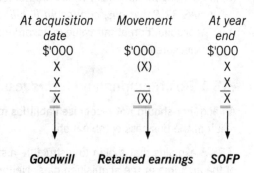

	At acquisition date $'000	Movement $'000	At year end $'000
Plant and equipment	X	(X)	X
Land	X	-	X
	X	(X)	X
	Goodwill	Retained earnings	SOFP

Note that:

(a)   There are always **three** columns, as set out here.

(b)   You need a line for each **class of asset** that is affected by the fair value adjustments. These will differ from question to question.

(c)   The column 'At acquisition date' records the fair value **difference** (usually an increase) for each relevant class of asset at that date. The total uplift can then be taken into the goodwill working.

(d)   The column 'At year end' depends on the nature of the assets, and whether the subsidiary still holds them at the date of the consolidation. The proforma working above assumes:

     (i)   The plant and equipment is still held but additional depreciation must be charged on the uplift (additional depreciation = fair value uplift/remaining useful life).

     (ii)   The land is still held, but as land is not subject to depreciation, the full uplift will still be included.

(e)   The **individual** amounts in the 'At year end' column are added to the relevant items on the consolidated statement of financial position.

(f)   The 'Movement' column contains the differences between the uplift at acquisition and the uplift remaining at the date of the consolidation. The **total** from this column is charged to the retained earnings of the subsidiary as an adjustment in the consolidated retained earnings working.

The following example shows how to incorporate this working with the basic technique you have learned for a consolidated statement of financial position.

Example: fair value adjustments

P Co acquired 100% of the ordinary shares of S Co on 1 September 20X5 when the retained earnings of S Co were $21,000. The statements of financial position of both companies at 31 August 20X6 are given below.

STATEMENTS OF FINANCIAL POSITION AS AT 31 AUGUST 20X6

	P CO $	S CO $
Assets		
Non-current assets		
Property, plant and equipment	63,000	28,000
Investment in S Co at cost	67,000	-
	130,000	
Current assets	82,000	43,000
Total assets	212,000	71,000
Equity and liabilities		
Equity		
Ordinary shares of $1 each	80,000	20,000
Retained earnings	112,000	41,000
	192,000	61,000
Current liabilities	20,000	10,000
Total equity and liabilities	212,000	71,000

At the date of acquisition, the fair values of S Co's assets were equal to their carrying amounts with the exception of the items listed below which exceeded their carrying amounts as follows:

	$
Plant and equipment (3 year remaining useful life)	9,000
Land	14,000
	23,000

S Co has not adjusted the carrying amounts in its own accounts.

Required

Prepare the consolidated statement of financial position of the P group as at 31 August 20X6.

Solution

P GROUP
CONSOLIDATED STATEMENT OF FINANCIAL POSITION AS AT 31 AUGUST 20X6

	$	$
Non-current assets		
Property, plant and equipment (63,000 + 28,000 + (W3) 20,000)	111,000	
Goodwill (W1)	3,000	
		114,000
Current assets (82,000 + 43,000)		125,000
Total assets		239,000

	$	$
Equity and liabilities		
Equity		
Ordinary shares of $1 each	80,000	
Retained earnings (W2)	129,000	
		209,000
Current liabilities (20,000 + 10,000)		30,000
Total equity and liabilities		239,000

1 Goodwill

	$	$
Consideration transferred		67,000
Less net acquisition-date fair value of identifiable assets acquired and liabilities assumed:		
Ordinary share capital	20,000	
Retained earnings at acquisition	21,000	
Fair value adjustment at acquisition (W3)	23,000	
		(64,000)
Goodwill		3,000

2 Retained earnings

	P Co $	S Co $
Per question	112,000	41,000
Fair value movement (W3)	-	(3,000)
Pre-acquisition retained earnings	-	(21,000)
		17,000
Group share of post–acq'n ret'd earnings: S Co	17,000	
Group retained earnings	129,000	

3 Fair value adjustments

	At acquisition date $	Movement $	At year end $
Plant and equipment	9,000	(3,000)*	6,000
Land	14,000	-	14,000
	23,000	(3,000)	20,000
	↓	↓	↓
	Goodwill	**Retained earnings**	**SOFP**

*Extra depreciation $9,000/3 years

Exam skills

In your exam, you may need to calculate the additional depreciation charge so you should make sure you know how to do it: additional depreciation = fair value uplift/remaining useful life.

Question 14.3

Fair value

Learning outcome C1(d)

An asset is recorded in S Co's books at its historical cost of $4,000. On 1 January 20X5 P Co bought 100% of S Co's equity. Its directors attributed a fair value of $3,000 to the asset as at that date. It had been depreciated for two years out of an expected life of four years on the straight line basis. There was no expected residual value. On 30 June 20X5 the asset was sold for $2,600. What is the profit or loss on disposal of this asset to be recorded in S Co's accounts and in P Co's consolidated accounts for the year ended 31 December 20X5?

Section summary

- Fair values are very important in calculating goodwill. **Goodwill** should be calculated **after revaluing** the subsidiary company's assets to **fair value**.

- IFRS 3 sets out **general principles** for arriving at the fair values of a subsidiary's assets and liabilities.

7 Approach to answering exam questions

Introduction

A methodical approach to answering questions on consolidated statements of financial position will help you in the exam. In this section we summarise our recommended approach.

Exam skills

This step by step approach will help you answer exam questions that ask you to prepare a consolidated statement of financial position.

 Read the question and draw out the group structure. Make a note of useful information such as the acquisition date and the pre-acquisition reserves.

 Draw up a proforma for the consolidated statement of financial position. Include a line for goodwill and spaces for any additional items that you might not have noticed at this point. If the question includes an associate (associates are covered in more detail later in this Study Text), include a line for investment in associate.

 Work methodically down the statement of financial position, transferring figures to either the proforma or to workings as necessary.

- Take 100% of all assets/liabilities controlled at the year end aggregated in brackets on the proforma, ready for any adjustments in step 4

- Take the cost of subsidiary/associate and reserves to the workings, setting the workings up as you work down the statement of financial position

- Take share capital and share premium (parent only) to the proforma

Read through the extra information provided in the question again and attempt the adjustments required, showing your workings for all calculations.

Do the double entry for the adjustments onto your proforma answer and onto your group workings (where the group workings are affected by one side of the double entry).

Examples:

- Cancel any intragroup items eg current account balances, loans
- Adjust for unrealised profits
- Make fair value adjustments

Calculate goodwill.

Consideration transferred		X
Less fair value of identifiable net assets acquired:		
Share capital	X	
Share premium	X	
Retained earnings at acquisition	X	
Other reserves at acquisition	X	
Fair value adjustments at acquisition	X	
		(X)
		X
Less: Impairment losses on goodwill to date		(X)
Goodwill		X

If the question contains an associate, calculate the investment in associate. (Note that associates are covered in more detail later in this Study Text.)

Calculate consolidated retained earnings and complete the statement of financial position.

Section summary

Following our step by step approach to preparing a consolidated statement of financial position will help you in the exam.

Chapter Roundup

✓ The basic procedure of consolidation combines the financial statements of a parent and its subsidiaries on a **line by line** basis by adding together like items.

✓ Items which appear as an asset in one company and a liability in another are **cancelled out**.

✓ The asset '**shares in subsidiary companies**' (also called 'investment in subsidiary companies') which appears in the parent company's accounts will be cancelled with the liability '**share capital**' in the subsidiaries' accounts.

✓ If an item appears in the statements of financial position of a parent company and its subsidiary at different amounts, the procedure is to **cancel as far as possible**. The remaining uncancelled amounts will appear in the consolidated statement of financial position.

✓ Dividends paid from a subsidiary to a parent company are **cancelled** on consolidation.

✓ The amount that the parent pays **over and above** the value of identifiable assets and liabilities acquired in the subsidiary is called **goodwill**. Goodwill arising on consolidation is subject to an annual **impairment review**.

✓ **Pre-acquisition retained earnings** of a subsidiary company are **not aggregated** with the parent company's retained earnings on consolidation.

✓ Consideration transferred when a parent acquires a subsidiary could be in the form of cash or shares. Consideration can be **contingent**, **deferred** or in the form of a **share exchange**.

✓ In a consolidated statement of financial position, the only profits recognised should be those **earned by the group** in providing goods or services to outsiders.

✓ Inventory in the consolidated statement of financial position should be valued at **cost to the group**.

✓ Consolidation adjustments are necessary to **remove unrealised profits** in the group.

✓ The consolidated statement of financial position must show **non-current assets** at their **cost to the group** and any depreciation charged must be based on that cost.

✓ Fair values are very important in calculating goodwill. **Goodwill** should be calculated **after revaluing** the subsidiary company's assets to **fair value**.

✓ IFRS 3 sets out **general principles** for arriving at the fair values of a subsidiary's assets and liabilities.

✓ Following our **step by step approach** to preparing a consolidated statement of financial position will help you in the exam.

Quick Quiz

1   Chicken Co owns 100% of Egg Co. Egg Co sells goods to Chicken Co at cost plus 50%. The total invoiced sales to Chicken Co by Egg Co in the year ended 31 December 20X9 were $900,000 and, of these sales, goods which had been invoiced at $60,000 were held in inventory by Chicken Co at 31 December 20X9. What is the reduction in aggregate group gross profit?

2   Major Co, which makes up its accounts to 31 December, has a 100% owned subsidiary Minor Co. Minor Co sells goods to Major Co at a mark-up on cost of 33.33%. At 31 December 20X8, Major had $12,000 of such goods in its inventory and at 31 December 20X9 had $15,000 of such goods in its inventory.

    What is the amount by which the consolidated profit attributable to Major Co's shareholders should be adjusted in respect of the above?

    A $1,000 Debit
    B $800 Credit
    C $750 Credit
    D $750 Debit

3   Goodwill is always positive. True or false?

4   How should contingent consideration on acquisition of a subsidiary be treated in the accounts of the acquirer?

5   North acquired 100% of the ordinary shares in South on 1 July 20X3 at a cost of $300,000. South's reserves at 1 July 20X3 were $36,000, and its issued share capital was $200,000.

At 30 June 20X6, South's reserves were $16,000. What is the amount of goodwill arising on acquisition?

A $64,000
B $84,000
C $123,000
D $138,000

Answers to Quick Quiz

1   $60,000 \times \dfrac{50}{150}$ = $20,000

2   D $(15,000 - 12,000) \times \dfrac{33.3}{133.3}$

3   False. Goodwill can be negative if the purchaser has 'got a bargain'.

4   IFRS 3 requires the acquisition-date **fair value** of contingent consideration to be recognised as part of the consideration for the acquiree in the goodwill calculation.

5   A

	$'000	$'000
Consideration transferred		300
Less fair value of identifiable net assets acquired:		
Ordinary share capital	200	
Reserves at acquisition	36	
		(236)
Goodwill		64

Answers to Questions

14.1 Basic consolidation

P GROUP CONSOLIDATED STATEMENT OF FINANCIAL POSITION AS AT 30 JUNE

	$	$
Assets		
Non-current assets		
Property, plant and equipment (120,000 + 100,000)		220,000
Current assets		
Inventories (50,000 + 60,000)	110,000	
Goods in transit (18,000 – 12,000)	6,000	
Receivables (40,000 + 30,000)	70,000	
Cash (4,000 + 6,000)	10,000	
		196,000
Total assets		416,000
Equity and liabilities		
Equity		
Ordinary shares of $1 each, fully paid (parent)	100,000	
Retained earnings (95,000 + 28,000)	123,000	
		223,000
Non-current liabilities		
10% loan stock	75,000	
12% loan stock (50,000 × 60%)	30,000	
		105,000
Current liabilities		
Payables (47,000 + 16,000)	63,000	
Taxation (15,000 + 10,000)	25,000	
		88,000
Total equity and liabilities		416,000

Note especially how:

(a)   The uncancelled loan stock in S Co becomes a liability of the group

(b)   The goods in transit is the difference between the current accounts ($18,000 – $12,000)

(c)   The investment in S Co's shares is cancelled against S Co's share capital

---

14.2 Unrealised profit

Prepare the proforma statement of financial position and transfer figures from P Co and S Co before calculating workings and making any necessary adjustments.

P GROUP CONSOLIDATED STATEMENT OF FINANCIAL POSITION

	$	$
Assets		
Non-current assets		
Property, plant and equipment (80,000 + 40,000)	120,000	
Goodwill (W1)	4,500	
		124,500
Current assets		
Trade receivables (30,000 + 25,000 – 12,000*)	43,000	
Inventories (10,000 + 5,000 – 2,500**(W2))	12,500	
		55,500
Total assets		180,000

	$	$
Equity and liabilities		
Equity		
Ordinary shares of $1 each	100,000	
Retained earnings (W3)	53,000	
		153,000
Current liabilities		
Trade payables (21,000 + 18,000 – 12,000*)		27,000
Total equity and liabilities		180,000

* To cancel the intra-group receivable and payable

** To remove the unrealised profit on items still in inventories

Workings

1   *Goodwill*

	$	$
Fair value of consideration transferred		46,000
Less net acquisition-date fair value of identifiable assets acquired and liabilities assumed:		
Share capital	30,000	
Retained earnings at acquisition	10,000	
		(40,000)
		6,000
Less impairment losses to date		(1,500)
Goodwill		4,500

2   *Unrealised profit*

	$
Profit on intra-group sales (20% x $50,000)	10,000
Unrealised profit (25% x 10,000)*	2,500

* 25% of the inventories from the intra-group sales remain in inventories at the year end, therefore the unrealised profit is 25% of the overall profit made on the intra-group sales. The rest of the profit from the intra-group sales is now realised as the inventories have been sold outside the group.

3   *Retained earnings*

	P Co $	S Co $
Per question	45,000	22,000
Adjustment (unrealised profit (W2))		(2,500)
Pre-acquisition retained earnings		(10,000)
		9,500
Group share of post-acq'n ret'd earnings: S Co	9,500	
Less group share of impairment losses to date	(1,500)	
Group retained earnings	53,000	

14.3 Fair value

S Co: Carrying amount at disposal (at historical cost) = $4,000 × 1½/4 = $1,500

∴ Profit on disposal = $1,100 (depreciation charge for the year = $500)

P Co: Carrying amount at disposal (at fair value) = $3,000 × 1½/2 = $2,250

∴ Profit on disposal for consolidation = $350 (depreciation for the year = $750).

CONSOLIDATED STATEMENT OF COMPREHENSIVE INCOME

This chapter deals with the consolidated income statement and the consolidated statement of comprehensive income.

Most of the consolidation adjustments will involve the **income statement**, so that is the focus of this chapter.

topic list	learning outcomes	syllabus references	ability required
1 The consolidated income statement	C1(c)	C1(iii)	application
2 The consolidated statement of comprehensive income	C1(c)	C1(iii)	application
3 Approach to answering exam questions	C1(c)	C1(iii)	application

1 The consolidated income statement

Introduction

In the previous chapter you studied how to prepare the consolidated statement of financial position. Now you will learn how to apply those techniques to prepare a consolidated income statement. The aim of the consolidated income statement is to show the results of the group for an accounting period as if it were a **single entity**. Exactly the same philosophy is adopted as for the statement of financial position, ie that of **control**. Accordingly, the consolidated income statement shows the profits resulting from the control exercised by the parent entity.

1.1 Consolidation procedure

It is customary to prepare a working paper (or **consolidation schedule**) on which the individual income statements are set out side by side and totalled to form the basis of the consolidated income statement.

Exam skills

In an examination it is very much quicker not to do this. Use workings to show the calculation of complex figures and show the derivation of others on the income statement itself, as shown in our examples.

Example: consolidated income statement

P Co acquired 100% of the ordinary shares of S Co on that company's incorporation in 20X3. The summarised income statements and movement on retained earnings of the two companies for the year ending 31 December 20X6 are set out below.

	P Co $	S Co $
Sales revenue	75,000	38,000
Cost of sales	(30,000)	(20,000)
Gross profit	45,000	18,000
Administrative expenses	(14,000)	(8,000)
Profit before tax	31,000	10,000
Income tax expense	(10,000)	(2,000)
Profit for the year	21,000	8,000
Note: Movement on retained earnings		
Retained earnings brought forward	87,000	17,000
Profit for the year	21,000	8,000
Retained earnings carried forward	108,000	25,000

Required

Prepare the consolidated income statement and extract from the statement of changes in equity showing retained earnings.

Solution

P GROUP
CONSOLIDATED INCOME STATEMENT FOR THE YEAR ENDED 31 DECEMBER 20X6

	$
Sales revenue (75 + 38)	113,000
Cost of sales (30 + 20)	(50,000)
Gross profit	63,000
Administrative expenses (14 + 8)	(22,000)
Profit before tax	41,000
Income tax expense	(12,000)
Profit for the year	29,000

STATEMENT OF CHANGES IN EQUITY (EXTRACT)

	Retained Earnings $
Balance at 1 January 20X6	104,000
Profit for the year	29,000
Balance at 31 December 20X6	133,000

1.2 Intra-group trading

Like the consolidated statement of financial position, the consolidated income statement should deal with the results of the group as those of a single entity. When one company in a group sells goods to another an identical amount is added to the sales revenue of the first company and to the cost of sales of the second. Yet as far as the group's dealings with outsiders are concerned no sale has taken place.

The consolidated figures for sales revenue and cost of sales should represent **sales to**, and **purchases from, outsiders**. An adjustment is therefore necessary to reduce the sales revenue and cost of sales figures by the value of intra-group sales during the year.

We have also seen in an earlier chapter that any unrealised profits on intra-group trading should be excluded from the figure for group retained earnings. This will occur whenever goods sold at a profit within the group remain in the inventory of the purchasing company at the year end. The best way to deal with this is to **calculate the unrealised profit on unsold inventories at the year end and reduce consolidated gross profit by this amount**. Cost of sales will be the balancing figure.

Example: Intra-group trading

Suppose in our earlier example that S Co had recorded sales of $5,000 at a gross margin of 40% to P Co during 20X6. One half of the goods remained in P Co's inventory at 31 December 20X6. Prepare the revised consolidated income statement.

Solution

The consolidated income statement for the year ended 31 December 20X6 would now be as follows.

	$
Sales revenue (75 + 38 – 5*)	108,000
Cost of sales (30 + 20 – 5* + 1(W))	(46,000)
Gross profit (45 + 18 – 1(W))	62,000
Administrative expenses	(22,000)
Profit before taxation	40,000
Income tax expense	(12,000)
Profit for the year	28,000

*To remove the intra-group sale

Working - unrealised profit

		$
Sale price	100%	5,000
Cost price	60%	(3,000)
Gross profit	40%	2,000
Unrealised profit (2,000 x 1/2)**		1,000

** Half of the inventories from the intra-group sale remain in inventories at the year end, therefore the unrealised profit is half of the overall profit made on the intra-group sale. The rest of the profit from the intra-group sale is now realised as the inventories have been sold outside the group.

An adjustment will be made for the unrealised profit against the inventory figure in the consolidated statement of financial position.

Question 15.1   Intra-group trading I

Learning outcome C1(c)

Pumpkin has held 100% of the equity share capital of Squash for many years. Cost of sales for each entity for the year ended 31 December 20X3 were as follows:

	$
Pumpkin	100,000
Squash	80,000

During the year, Squash sold goods costing $5,000 to Pumpkin for $8,000. At the year end, all these goods remained in inventory.

What figure should be shown as cost of sales in the consolidated income statement of the Pumpkin group for the year ended 31 December 20X3?

Question 15.2   Intra-group trading II

Learning outcome C1(c)

Percy has held 100% of the equity share capital of Mercy for many years. Draft summarised income statements for Percy and Mercy for the year ended 31 December 20X3 are below.

	PERCY	MERCY
	$'000	$'000
Revenue	500	300
Cost of sales	(300)	(200)
Gross profit	200	100
Administrative expenses	(90)	(45)
Profit before taxation	110	55
Income taxes	(10)	(5)
Profit for the year	100	50

During the year, Percy sold goods which cost $20,000 to Mercy at a margin of 20%. At the year end, all of these goods remained in inventory.

Required

Prepare the consolidated income statement for the Percy group as at 31 December 20X3.

1.3 Intra-group dividends

In our example so far we have assumed that S Co retains all of its after-tax profit. It may be, however, that S Co distributes some of its profits as dividends. Group retained earnings are only adjusted for dividends paid to the parent company shareholders. Dividends paid by the subsidiary to the parent are cancelled on consolidation.

Section summary

The table below summarises the main points about the consolidated income statement.

Purpose	To show the results of the group for an accounting period as if it were a single entity.
Sales revenue to profit for year	100% P + 100% S (excluding adjustments for intra-group transactions).
Reason	To show the results of the group which were controlled by the parent company.
Intra-group sales	Strip out intra-group activity from both sales revenue and cost of sales.
Unrealised profit on intra-group sales	Increase cost of sales by unrealised profit.
Depreciation	If the value of S's non-current assets have been subjected to a fair value uplift then any additional depreciation must be charged in the consolidated income statement.
Transfer of non-current assets	Expenses must be increased by any profit on the transfer and reduced by any additional depreciation arising from the increased carrying value of the asset.

2 The consolidated statement of comprehensive income 5/10

Introduction

A consolidated statement of comprehensive income will be easy to produce once you have done the income statement. In this section, we take the last question and add an item of comprehensive income to illustrate this.

Example: consolidated statement of comprehensive income

Using the answer to the previous example (section 1.2), show the consolidated statement of comprehensive income if S Co made a $20,000 revaluation gain on one of its properties during the year.

Solution

CONSOLIDATED STATEMENT OF COMPREHENSIVE INCOME

	$
Sales revenue	108,000
Cost of sales	(46,000)
Gross profit	62,000
Administrative expenses	(22,000)
Profit before taxation	40,000
Income tax expense	(12,000)
Profit for the year	28,000
Other comprehensive income:	
Gain on property revaluation	20,000
Total comprehensive income for the year	48,000

If you were using the two statement format for the statement of comprehensive income you would produce a separate income statement and a separate statement of other comprehensive income. The separate consolidated statement of other comprehensive income would be as follows.

CONSOLIDATED STATEMENT OF OTHER COMPREHENSIVE INCOME

	$
Profit for the year	28,000
Other comprehensive income:	
Gain on property revaluation	20,000
Total comprehensive income for the year	48,000

These amounts would appear in the consolidated statement of changes in equity as follows:

	Retained earnings $	Revaluation surplus $	Total $
Total comprehensive income for the year	28,000	20,000	48,000

Question 15.3

Other comprehensive incom

Learning outcome C1(c)

The following information relates to Osborne Co and its 100% owned subsidiary, Cunney Co, for the year to 30 April 20X7. During the year, Osborne Co made a $30,000 revaluation gain on one of its properties and Cunney Co made a revaluation gain of $10,000 on a piece of land. The additional depreciation charge resulting from the revaluation of Osborne Co's property has already been accounted for in its individual income statement.

INCOME STATEMENTS FOR THE YEAR ENDED 30 APRIL 20X7

	OSBORNE CO	CUNNEY CO
	$'000	$'000
Revenue	1,100	500
Cost of sales	(630)	(300)
Gross profit	470	200
Administrative expenses	(105)	(150)
Profit before taxation	365	50
Income taxes	(65)	(10)
Profit for the year	300	40

Required

Prepare the consolidated statement of comprehensive income for the Osborne group as at 31 April 20X7.

Section summary

The consolidated statement of comprehensive income is produced using the consolidated income statement as a basis.

3 Approach to answering exam questions

Introduction

A methodical approach to answering questions on consolidated statements of comprehensive income will help you in the exam. In this section we summarise our recommended approach.

Exam skills

This step-by-step approach will help you answer exam questions that ask you to prepare a consolidated statement of comprehensive income.

 STEP 1
Read the question and draw out the group structure. Make a note of useful information such as the acquisition date and the pre-acquisition reserves.

 STEP 2
Draw up a proforma for the consolidated statement of comprehensive income (or income statement if there is no other comprehensive income). If the question includes an associate, leave a line space for 'share of profit of associate' before group profit before tax (associates are covered later in this Study Text).

 STEP 3
Work methodically down the income statement, transferring figures to either the proforma or to workings as necessary:

- Put 100% of all income/expenses in brackets on the face of the proforma, ready for any adjustments you need to make

- Exclude dividends received from subsidiaries.

 STEP 4
Read through the extra information provided in the question again and attempt the adjustments required, showing your workings for all calculations. Put the adjustments on to the statement of comprehensive income as necessary.

Finally, if the question contains an associate, calculate share of profit of associate (associates are covered later in this Study Text).

 Section summary

Following our step-by-step approach to preparing a consolidated statement of comprehensive income will help you in the exam.

Chapter Roundup

✓   The table below summarises the main points about the consolidated income statement.

Purpose	To show the results of the group for an accounting period as if it were a single entity.
Sales revenue to profit for year	100% P + 100% S (excluding adjustments for intra-group transactions).
Reason	To show the results of the group which were controlled by the parent company.
Intra-group sales	Strip out intra-group activity from both sales revenue and cost of sales.
Unrealised profit on intra-group sales	Increase cost of sales by unrealised profit.
Depreciation	If the value of S's non-current assets have been subjected to a fair value uplift then any additional depreciation must be charged in the consolidated income statement.
Transfer of non-current assets	Expenses must be increased by any profit on the transfer and reduced by any additional depreciation arising from the increased carrying value of the asset.

✓   The consolidated statement of comprehensive income is produced using the consolidated income statement as a basis.

✓   Following our step-by-step approach to preparing a consolidated statement of comprehensive income will help you in the exam.

Quick Quiz

1   Where does unrealised profit on intra-group trading appear in the income statement?

2   At the beginning of the year a 100% subsidiary transfers a non-current asset to the parent for $500,000. It's carrying value was $400,000 and it has 4 years of useful life left. How is this accounted for at the end of the year in the consolidated income statement?

3   Whales owns 100% of Porpoise. The gross profit for each company for the year ended 31 March 20X7 is calculated as follows:

	Whales $	Porpoise $
Revenue	120,000	70,000
Cost of sales	(80,000)	(50,000)
Gross profit	40,000	20,000

During the year Porpoise made sales to Whales amounting to $30,000. $15,000 of these sales were in inventories at the year end. Profit made on the year end inventories items amounted to $2,000.

Required

Calculate group revenue, cost of sales and gross profit.

4   Barley has owned 100% of the issued share capital of Oats for many years. Barley sells goods to Oats at cost plus 20%. The following information is available for the year.

	Revenue $
Barley	460,000
Oats	120,000

During the year Barley sold goods to Oats for $60,000, of which $18,000 were still held in inventory by Oats at the year end.

At what amount should total revenue appear in the consolidated income statement?

A $520,000
B $530,000
C $538,000
D $562,000

5   Ufton is the sole subsidiary of Walcot. The cost of sales figures for 20X1 for Walcot and Ufton were $11 million and $10 million respectively. During 20X1 Walcot sold goods which had cost $2 million to Ufton for $3 million. Ufton has not yet sold any of these goods.

What is the consolidated cost of sales figure for 20X1?

A $16 million
B $18 million
C $19 million
D $20 million

Answers to Quick Quiz

1   It is added to cost of sales and so deducted from gross profit.

2

	$
Unrealised profit	100,000
Additional depreciation (100 ÷ 4)	(25,000)
Net charge to income statement	75,000

3

	$
Revenue (120 + 70 – 30*)	160,000
Cost of sales (80 + 50 – 30* + 2**)	(102,000)
Gross Profit	58,000

* To remove the intra-group sale

** To remove the unrealised profit

4   A   Revenue = 460,000 + 120,000 – 60,000
            = $520,000

5   C $19m

	$m
Cost of sales (11 + 10 – 3* + 1**)	19

* To remove the intra-group sale

** To remove the unrealised profit

Answers to Questions

15.1 Intra-group trading I

	$
Pumpkin	100,000
Squash	80,000
	180,000
Less intra-group sale	(8,000)
Add unrealised profit	3,000
	175,000

15.1 Intra-group trading II

PERCY GROUP
CONSOLIDATED INCOME STATEMENT AS AT 31 DECEMBER 20X3

	$'000
Revenue (500 + 300 – 25*)	775
Cost of sales (300 + 200 – 25* + 5(W))	(480)
Gross profit (200 + 100 – 5(W))	295
Administrative expenses (90 + 45)	(135)
Profit before taxation	160
Income taxes (10 + 5)	(15)
Profit for the year	145

* To remove the intra-group sale

Working – unrealised profit

		$'000
Sale price	100%	25
Cost price	80%	(20)
Gross profit	20%	5

Unrealised profit = $5,000

15.3 Other comprehensive income

OSBORNE GROUP
CONSOLIDATED STATEMENT OF COMPREHENSIVE INCOME AT 30 APRIL 20X7

	$'000
Revenue (1,100 + 500)	1,600
Cost of sales (630 + 300)	(930)
Gross profit	670
Administrative expenses (105 + 150)	(255)
Profit before taxation	415
Income taxes (65 + 10)	(75)
Profit for the year	340
Other comprehensive income:	
Gain on non-current asset revaluation (30 + 10)	40
Total comprehensive income for the year	380

	Number	Level	Marks	Time
Now try this question from the Exam Question Bank	Q26	Examination	20	36 mins

ASSOCIATES

In this chapter we deal with the treatment of associates in the consolidated financial statements. As the group's share of profit in the associate appears in the income statement section, we have concentrated on the separate income statement.

topic list	learning outcomes	syllabus references	ability required
1 Accounting for associates	C1(c)	C1(iii)	application
2 The equity accounting method	C1(c)	C1(iii)	application
3 More complex situations	C1(c)	C1(iii)	application

1 Accounting for associates

Introduction

Accounting for associates is covered by IAS 28 *Investments in associates*. The investing company does not have control, as it does with a subsidiary, but it does have **significant influence**.

1.1 Definitions

These are the important definitions you need to know.

KEY TERMS

- ASSOCIATE. An entity, including an unincorporated entity such as a partnership, over which an investor has significant influence and which is neither a subsidiary nor an interest in a joint venture.

- SIGNIFICANT INFLUENCE is the power to participate in the financial and operating policy decisions of the investee but is not control or joint control over those policies.

- EQUITY METHOD. A method of accounting whereby the investment is initially recorded at cost and adjusted thereafter for the post-acquisition change in the investor's share of net assets of the investee. The profit or loss of the investor includes the investor's share of the profit or loss of the investee.

We have already looked at how the **status** of an investment in an associate should be determined. Go back to Chapter 13 to revise it.

IAS 28 requires all investments in associates to be accounted for in the consolidated accounts using the equity method, *unless* the investment is classified as 'held for sale' in accordance with IFRS 5 in which case it should be accounted for under IFRS 5.

An investor is exempt from applying the equity method if:

(a)   It is a parent exempt from preparing consolidated financial statements under IAS 27, or

(b)   All of the following apply:

  (i)   The investor is a **wholly-owned subsidiary** or it is a **partially owned subsidiary** of another entity and its other owners, including those not otherwise entitled to vote, have been informed about, and do not object to, the investor not applying the equity method;

  (ii)   The investor's securities are **not publicly traded**

  (iii)   It is **not in the process of issuing securities** in public securities markets; and

  (iv)   The **ultimate or intermediate parent** publishes consolidated financial statements that comply with International Financial Reporting Standards.

The use of the equity method should be **discontinued** from the date that the investor **ceases to have significant influence**. From that date, the investor shall account for the investment in accordance with IAS 39 *Financial instruments: recognition and measurement*.

The following points are also relevant and are similar to a parent-subsidiary consolidation situation.

(a)   Use financial statements drawn up to the **same reporting date.**

(b)   If this is impracticable, adjust the financial statements for **significant transactions/events** in the intervening period. The difference between the reporting date of the associate and that of the investor must be no more than three months.

(c)   Use **uniform accounting policies** for like transactions and events in similar circumstances, adjusting the associate's statements to reflect group policies if necessary.

1.2 Separate financial statements of the investor

If an investor **issues consolidated financial statements** (because it has subsidiaries), an investment in an associate should be *either*:

(a)   Accounted for at **cost**, or
(b)   In accordance with **IAS 39** (at fair value)

in its separate financial statements.

If an investor that does *not* **issue consolidated financial statements** (ie it has no subsidiaries) but has an investment in an associate this should similarly be included in the financial statements of the investor either at cost, or in accordance with IAS 39.

Section summary

IAS 28 requires that, in consolidated accounts, **associates** should be accounted for using **equity accounting principles**.

2   The equity accounting method

Introduction

In this section we look at how to apply the equity method using a simple example. The equity method reflects the parent's significant influence over the associate. If the consolidated statement of financial position contained only an investment at its cost (or fair value) and the statement of comprehensive income included only dividend income, this would not be very informative. The parent has an interest in, and shares responsibility for, the associate's performance.

Exam alert

A Section B exam question could ask you to explain the equity method.

2.1 Consolidated statement of comprehensive income   5/10

The basic principle behind the equity accounting method is that the investing company (X Co) should take account of its **share of the earnings** of the associate, Y Co, whether or not Y Co distributes the earnings as dividends. X Co achieves this by adding to consolidated profit the group's share of Y Co's profit after tax.

Under equity accounting, the associated company's sales revenue, cost of sales and so on are **not amalgamated** with those of the group. Any dividend income received from the associate is removed from consolidated income and instead the **group share** only of the associate's profit after tax is recognised in profit or loss and the **group share** of any other comprehensive income in the associate is recognised as a separate line within other comprehensive income.

Notice the difference between this treatment and the **consolidation** of a subsidiary company's results. If Y Co were a subsidiary X Co would consolidate the whole of its sales revenue, cost of sales etc line by line.

Example: Consolidated statement of comprehensive income

The following statements of comprehensive income relate to the P Co group, consisting of the parent company, an 100% owned subsidiary (S Co) and an associated company (A Co) in which the group has a 30% interest. P Co has owned both of these investments for several years.

STATEMENTS OF COMPREHENSIVE INCOME

	P Co $'000	S Co $'000	A Co $'000
Sales revenue	600	800	300
Cost of sales	(370)	(400)	(120)
Gross profit	230	400	180
Other expenses	(110)	(180)	(80)
	120	220	100
Finance income	30	-	-
	150	220	100
Finance costs	-	(20)	-
Profit before tax	150	200	100
Income tax expense	(55)	(90)	(40)
Profit for the year	95	110	60
Other comprehensive income:			
Gains on property revaluation, net of tax	30	20	10
Total comprehensive income for the year	125	130	70

Required

Prepare the consolidated statement of comprehensive income of the P Group.

Solution

P GROUP CONSOLIDATED STATEMENT OF COMPREHENSIVE INCOME

	$'000
Sales revenue (600 + 800)	1,400
Cost of sales (370 + 400)	(770)
Gross profit	630
Other expenses (110 + 180)	(290)
	340
Finance income	30
	370
Finance costs	(20)
Group profit	350
Group share of associate's profit (30% × 60)	18
	368
Income tax expense	(145)
Profit for the year	223
Other comprehensive income:	
Gains on property revaluation, net of tax (30 + 20)	50
Share of other comprehensive income of associate (30% × 10)	3
Total comprehensive income for the year	276

Note the following

(a) Consolidated sales revenue, group gross profit and expenses **exclude** the sales revenue, gross profit and costs etc of **associates**.

(b) The group share of the associate's **profit after tax** is credited to the group income statement (here, 30% of $60,000 = $18,000). If the associate had been acquired during the year, it would be time apportioned so that only post-acquisition profits are included.

(c) **Taxation** includes only the income tax expense of the **parent company and subsidiaries** in total. (The share of the associate's tax has been dealt with by measuring the share of the associate's profit **net of tax** earlier in the statement.)

(d)   Within other comprehensive income, the amounts relating to the parent and subsidiary are aggregated as usual and the **group share** of the associate's **other comprehensive income** is shown separately.

2.2 Consolidated statement of financial position   5/10, 5/11

In the consolidated statement of financial position, a figure for **investment in associates** is shown as a one line item. At the time of the acquisition this must be stated at cost. This amount will **increase** each year by the amount of the group's share of the associate's profit after tax and will **decrease** by any dividends received from the associate.

Exam skills

In many exam questions, it will be easier to shortcut this and take the original cost plus the group share of the associate's post-acquisition retained earnings.

The investment in the associate must be assessed for any evidence of impairments, in accordance with IAS 39 *Financial Instruments: Recognition and measurement,* and any impairment loss written off against the carrying value of the associate.

A proforma working for the investment in associate figure is as follows.

	$
Cost of associate	X
Share of post-acquisition retained reserves	X/(X)
Less: impairment losses on associate to date	(X)
	X

Example: entries in the consolidated statement of financial position

P Co, a company with subsidiaries, acquires 25,000 of the 100,000 $1 ordinary shares in A Co for $60,000 on 1 January 20X8. In the year to 31 December 20X8, A Co earns profits after tax of $24,000, from which it pays a dividend of $6,000.

How will A Co's results be accounted for in the individual and consolidated accounts of P Co for the year ended 31 December 20X8?

Solution

In the **individual accounts** of P Co, the investment will be recorded on 1 January 20X8 at cost. Unless there is an impairment in the value of the investment, this amount will remain in the individual statement of financial position of P Co permanently. The only entry in P Co's individual income statement will be to record dividends received. For the year ended 31 December 20X8, P Co will:

DEBIT	Cash	$1,500	
CREDIT	Income from shares in associates		$1,500

In the **consolidated accounts** of P Co equity accounting principles will be used to account for the investment in A Co. Consolidated profit after tax will include the group's share of A Co's profit after tax (25% × $24,000 = $6,000). To the extent that this has been distributed as dividend, it is already included in P Co's individual accounts and will automatically be brought into the consolidated results. That part of the group's share of profit in the associate which has not been distributed as dividend (25% × (24,000 – 6,000) = $4,500) will be brought into consolidation by the following adjustment.

DEBIT	Investment in associates	$4,500	
CREDIT	Income from shares in associates		$4,500

The asset 'Investment in associates' is then stated at $64,500, being cost plus the group share of post-acquisition retained earnings.

Example: consolidated statement of financial position

On 1 January 20X6 the net assets of A Co amount to $220,000, financed by 100,000 $1 ordinary shares and revenue reserves of $120,000. P Co, a company with subsidiaries, acquired 30,000 of the shares in A Co for $75,000. During the year ended 31 December 20X6 A Co's profit after tax is $30,000, from which dividends of $12,000 are paid.

Required

Show how P Co's investment in A Co would appear in the consolidated statement of financial position at 31 December 20X6.

Solution

CONSOLIDATED STATEMENT OF FINANCIAL POSITION
AS AT 31 DECEMBER 20X6 (EXTRACT)

	$
Non-current assets	
Investment in associate	
Cost	75,000
Group share of post-acquisition retained earnings (30% × $18,000)	5,400
	80,400

Question 16.1   Associates I

Learning outcome C1(a)

Set out below are the draft accounts of Parent Co and its subsidiaries and of Associate Co. Parent Co acquired 40% of the equity capital of Associate Co three years ago when the latter's reserves stood at $40,000.

SUMMARISED STATEMENTS OF FINANCIAL POSITION

	Parent Co & Subsidiaries	Associate Co
	$'000	$'000
Tangible non-current assets	220	170
Investment in associate at cost	60	–
Loan to Associate Co	20	–
Current assets	100	50
Loan from Parent Co	–	(20)
	400	200
Share capital ($1 shares)	250	100
Retained earnings	150	100
	400	200

SUMMARISED INCOME STATEMENTS

	Parent Co & Subsidiaries	Associate Co
	$'000	$'000
Profit before tax	95	80
Taxation expense	(35)	(30)
Profit for the year	60	50

Required

Prepare the summarised consolidated accounts of Parent Co.

Question 16.2	Associates II

Learning outcome C1(c)

Alfred Co bought a 25% shareholding on 31 December 20X8 in Grimbald Co at a cost of $38,000.

During the year to 31 December 20X9 Grimbald Co made a profit before tax of $82,000 and the taxation charge on the year's profits was $32,000. A dividend of $20,000 was paid on 31 December out of these profits.

Required

Calculate the entries for the associate which would appear in the consolidated accounts of the Alfred group, in accordance with the requirements of IAS 28.

Section summary

Under the **equity method**, the investing company should take account of its share of earnings of the associate by adding to consolidated profit the group's share of the associate's profit after tax.

In the consolidated **statement of financial position**, the investment in associates should be shown as:

– Cost of the investment in the associate; plus

– Group share of post-acquisition retained reserves; less

– Any impairment losses on the investment in associate to date.

3 More complex situations

Introduction

Here we consider how to deal with unrealised profits, losses made by associates and impairment of the investment in an associate.

3.1 Unrealised profits

A group (made up of a parent and its subsidiaries) may trade with its associates. This introduces the possibility of unrealised profits if goods sold within the group are still in inventories at the year end. This is similar to the examples seen earlier involving unrealised profits arising on trading between a parent and a subsidiary. The important thing to remember is that when an associate is involved, **only the group's share is eliminated**.

The precise accounting entries depend on the direction of the transaction. 'Upstream' transactions are sales from an associate to the investor. 'Downstream' transactions are sales of assets from the investor to an associate.

The entries in the consolidated statement of financial position are as follows, where A% is the parent's holding in the associate, and PUP is the provision for unrealised profit.

For upstream transactions (associate sells to parent/subsidiary) where the parent holds the inventories:

DEBIT	Retained earnings of parent/subsidiary	PUP × A%
CREDIT	Group inventories	PUP × A%

OR

For downstream transactions, (parent/subsidiary sells to associate) where the associate holds the inventories:

DEBIT	Retained earnings of parent/subsidiary	PUP x A%
CREDIT	Investment in associate	PUP x A%

In the statement of comprehensive income, the precise treatment of the reduction in profit (a debit entry) also depends on the direction of the transaction:

DEBIT	Cost of sales (increases cost of sales)	PUP x A%	if **parent** made the sales
DEBIT	Share of associate's profit (decreases the profit)	PUP x A%	if **associate** made the sales

Example: downstream transaction

A Co, a parent with subsidiaries, holds 25% of the equity shares in B Co. During the year, A Co makes sales of $1,000,000 to B Co at cost plus a 25% mark-up. At the year end, B Co has all these goods still in inventories. What effect does this transaction have on the consolidated statement of financial position?

Solution

A Co has made an unrealised profit of $200,000 ($1,000,000 × 25/125) on its sales to the associate. The group's share (25%) of this must be eliminated:

DEBIT	Group retained earnings	$50,000
CREDIT	Investment in associate	$50,000

Because the sale was made to the associate, the group's share of the unsold inventory forms part of the investment in the associate at the year-end. If the associate had made the sale to the parent, the adjustment would have been:

DEBIT	Group retained earnings	$50,000
CREDIT	Inventories (consolidated statement of financial position)	$50,000

3.2 Associate's losses

When the equity method is being used and the investor's share of losses of the associate equals or exceeds its interest in the associate, the investor should **discontinue** including its share of further losses. The investment is reported at nil value. The interest in the associate is normally the carrying amount of the investment in the associate, but it also includes any other long-term interests, for example, long-term receivables or loans.

After the investor's interest is reduced to nil, **additional losses** should only be recognised where the investor has incurred obligations or made payments on behalf of the associate (for example, if it has guaranteed amounts owed to third parties by the associate).

3.3 Impairment losses

IAS 39 sets out a list of indications that a financial asset (including an associate) may have become impaired. Any impairment loss is recognised in accordance with IAS 36 *Impairment of assets* for each associate individually.

Section summary

The **group's share** of **unrealised profit** on intra-group transactions with the associate must be **removed** from the consolidated financial statements. The adjustments required depend on which company made the sale.

When the equity method is being used and the investor's share of losses of the associate equals or exceeds its interest in the associate, the investor should **discontinue including its share of further losses**.

Chapter Roundup

✓ IAS 28 requires that, in consolidated accounts, **associates** should be accounted for using **equity accounting principles**.

✓ Under the **equity method**, the investing company should take account of its share of earnings of the associate by adding to consolidated profit the group's share of the associate's profit after tax.

✓ In the consolidated **statement of financial position**, the investment in associates should be shown as:

- Cost of the investment in the associate; plus
- Group share of post acquisition retained reserves; less
- Any impairment losses on the investment in associate to date.

✓ The **group's share** of **unrealised profit** on intra-group transactions with the associate must be **removed** from the consolidated financial statements. The adjustments required depend on which company made the sale.

✓ When the equity method is being used and the investor's share of losses of the associate equals or exceeds its interest in the associate, the investor should **discontinue including its share of further losses**.

Quick Quiz

1 Define an associate.

2 How should associates be accounted for in the separate financial statements of the investor?

3 What is the effect of the equity method on the consolidated income statement and statement of financial position?

Answers to Quick Quiz

1 An entity in which an investor has a significant influence, but which is not a subsidiary or a joint venture of the investor.

2 Either at cost or in accordance with IAS 39.

3 *Income statement.* Investing company includes its share of the earnings of the associate, by adding its share of profit after tax.

Statement of financial position. Investment in associate is initially included in assets at cost. This will be increased (or decreased) each year by the group's share of the post-acquisition retained reserves of the associate. Any impairment of the investment in associate will be deducted from the investment in associate balance.

Answers to Questions

16.1 Associates I

PARENT CO
CONSOLIDATED INCOME STATEMENT

	$'000
Net profit	95
Income from shares in associates (50 × 40%)	20
Profit before tax	115
Taxation	(35)
Profit attributable to the members of Parent Co	80

PARENT CO
CONSOLIDATED STATEMENT OF FINANCIAL POSITION

Assets	$'000
Tangible non-current assets	220
Investment in associate (see note)	84
Loan to Associate Co	20
Current assets	100
Total assets	424
Equity and liabilities	
Share capital	250
Retained earnings (W)	174
Total equity and liabilities	424

Note	
Investment in associate	$'000
Cost of investment	60
Share of post-acquisition retained earnings (W)	24
	84

Working – retained earnings

Retained earnings	Parent & Subsidiaries $'000	Associate $'000
Per question	150	100
Pre-acquisition		(40)
Post-acquisition		60
Group share in associate ($60 × 40%)	24	
Group retained earnings	174	

Note the following points about the treatment of the associate in the consolidated statement of financial position:

(a) An extra column is set out in the retained earnings working to calculate the group share of the associate's post acquisition retained earnings (ie exactly the same calculation as for a subsidiary).

(b) The loan balance asset due from Associate in the books of Parent is **not cancelled out**. There is no cancellation of any balances, whether loans or trading balances, due between the group and the associate. This is because the associate is not fully consolidated so there is no corresponding balance to cancel.

16.2 Associates II

CONSOLIDATED INCOME STATEMENT

	$
Group share of profit of associate (82,000 × 25%)	20,500
Less taxation (32,000 × 25%)	(8,000)
Income from shares in associate	12,500

CONSOLIDATED STATEMENT OF FINANCIAL POSITION

	$
Investment in associate	45,500

Working

	$
Cost of investment	38,000
Share of post-acquisition retained earnings ((82,000 − 32,000 − 20,000) × 25%)	7,500
	45,500

Now try this question from the Exam Question Bank	**Number**	**Level**	**Marks**	**Time**
	Q25	Examination	20	36 mins

PRINCIPLES OF BUSINESS TAXATION

Part D

GENERAL PRINCIPLES OF TAXATION

This chapter forms an introduction to taxation and the general principles you need to know for the exam.

In Section 1, we look at the general principles of taxation, such as the sources of rules and the terminology you need to know.

Section 2 covers how tax is administered and in section 3 we look at the collection of tax and the powers of enforcement of the tax authorities.

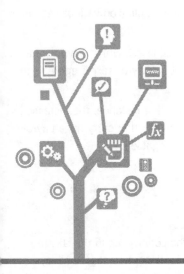

topic list	learning outcomes	syllabus references	ability required
1 General principles of taxation	A1(a),(b),(e), A3(a)	A1(i),(ii),(iii), A3(i)	comprehension
2 Administration of tax	A1(c)	A1(vi),(vii)	comprehension
3 Tax enforcement	A1(c),(d)	A1(viii)	comprehension

1 General principles of taxation

Introduction

In this section we look at the underlying principles of tax and introduce some general tax concepts and terminology. The general principles of tax are not specific to any one country, but should apply to most countries. We have used the UK tax system to illustrate concepts in this chapter.

Exam alert

The Principles of Business Taxation forms 25% of the F1 syllabus and will be examined. Make sure that you work through these chapters and all the examples and questions carefully.

1.1 Characteristics of taxation   5/10

The economist, Adam Smith, wrote about the **canons of taxation.** His original characteristics of a 'good tax' were **equity, certainty, convenience** and **efficiency**. In the US, these characteristics are included among the 10 principles that form the American Institute of Certified Public Accountants' 'Guiding Principles of Good Tax Policy'.

The three **major** principles recognised today are:

(a) **Equity**: the tax burden should be fairly distributed, eg a higher rate tax for wealthier individuals
(b) **Efficiency**: tax should be easy and cheap to collect.
(c) **Economic effects**: the government must consider the effect of taxation policy on various sectors of the economy.

Efficiency is best achieved by the use of 'unpaid tax collectors', such as businesses which have to charge and account for sales tax; and employers who have to collect and account for payroll taxes, eg PAYE in the UK.

Economic effects are sometimes overlooked, with disastrous consequences. For instance, the increase in employers' tax in the UK had a serious effect on many government departments that carry huge payrolls. The government had neglected to take into account that it was, in fact, taxing itself.

1.2 Sources of tax rules

1.2.1 Domestic tax legislation and court rulings

The main source of tax rules arises from the domestic tax legislation of the country, eg in the UK, the annual Finance Act. Although the legislators try to think of all possible situations, business is always changing and so the law may have to be interpreted by the courts. This gives rise to court rulings that have the force of law.

1.2.2 Domestic tax authority practice

Every tax authority develops its own practice on how the law is applied. For example, UK tax law states that employees should be taxed on all 'benefits' supplied by the employer. However, in practice, certain benefits are exempted from the rules because it would be too time consuming to account for them and they yield little in the way of tax.

1.2.3 Supranational bodies

Supranational bodies, such as the European Union (EU), can affect tax rules. The EU has a number of rules on value added or sales tax, which have to be applied by all members of the EU.

1.2.4 International tax treaties

Some businesses trade in many different countries of the world, so called 'multi-national' companies. This means that their profits will be subject to tax in the local countries they trade in, as well as the country where the company has its headquarters. This could mean that the company pays tax on certain profits twice. In order to avoid this 'double tax', countries enter into tax treaties which set out which country gets to tax the profits and to allow relief for local taxes paid, for example withholding taxes. We will look at this in more detail in Chapter 18.

Exam alert

In the exam you will be told what tax rules apply. The tax rules are also released on the CIMA website prior to the exam. Make sure you check the website to see what they are in advance.

www.cimaglobal.com/students/2010-professional-qualification/Operational-level/F1-study-resources/

The tax rules will be given in the following format.

COUNTRY X - TAX REGIME FOR USE THROUGHOUT THE EXAMINATION PAPER

Relevant Tax Rules for Years Ended 31 March 2007 to 2011

Corporate Profits

Unless otherwise specified, only the following rules for taxation of corporate profits will be relevant, other taxes can be ignored:

- Accounting rules on recognition and measurement are followed for tax purposes.

- All expenses other than depreciation, amortisation, entertaining, taxes paid to other public bodies and donations to political parties are tax deductible.

- Tax depreciation is deductible as follows:

  - 50% of additions to Property, Plant and Equipment in the accounting period in which they are recorded

  - 25% per year of the written-down value (ie cost minus previous allowances) in subsequent accounting periods except that in which the asset is disposed of

  - No tax depreciation is allowed on land

- The corporate tax on profits is at a rate of 25%.

- No indexation is allowed on the sale of land.

- Tax losses can be carried forward to offset against future taxable profits from the same business.

Value Added Tax

Country X has a VAT system which allows entities to reclaim input tax paid.

In country X the VAT rates are:

Zero rated   0%
Standard rated   15%

1.3 Classification and characteristics of taxation – the tax base

Although the details of taxes differ between countries, there are certain classes and characteristics of taxation that are common to most tax regimes.

Taxes can be classified according to their **tax base** (what is being taxed). They can be based on any or all of the following items.

- **Income or profits** (personal income tax and company income tax)
- **Assets** (tax on capital gains, wealth and inheritance taxes)
- **Consumption** (or expenditure, eg taxes on alcohol, cigarettes or fuel and sales taxes)

Note that the Organisation for Economic Cooperation and Development (OECD) has a more detailed classification of taxes which can be reviewed at http://www.oecd.org/dataoecd/20/39/35589632.pdf

1.4 Tax terminology

When considering the tax framework, there are a number of terms that you need to be familiar with.

1.4.1 Direct versus Indirect tax

Direct taxation is charged directly on the person, or enterprise, who is intended to pay the tax, and is a tax on income. Examples include personal income taxes, company income tax, tax on capital gains.

Indirect taxation is charged indirectly on the final consumer of the goods or services and is a tax on consumption. An example is sales tax, for example VAT in the UK and TVA in France.

1.4.2 Taxable person

The person liable to pay tax is called a **taxable person**. This includes an individual, an estate of a deceased person, a trust fund, a partnership, a limited company and any other body set up to carry out a trade for profit (eg the bar at a golf club). A taxable person normally only pays tax in the country where he or she is resident. We will look at this in more detail in a later chapter.

1.4.3 Competent jurisdiction   5/10

Jurisdiction relates to the power of a tax authority to charge and collect tax. **Competent jurisdiction** is the authority whose tax laws apply to an entity or person.

1.4.4 Tax rate structure   5/10, 11/10, 5/11

A government will structure its tax rates according to where it wishes the burden of taxation to fall. There is a general agreement that people on higher incomes should pay more tax, but governments have learned that punitive rates at the top lead to higher levels of tax avoidance and evasion.

In the UK, Harold Wilson's Labour government in the 1960s sought to 'soak the rich' with a top rate of 98%. This led to an exodus from the country of film stars and pop singers, who thereafter paid no UK tax at all.

There are three possible tax structures.

- A **proportional** tax rate structure taxes all income at the same rate, so the same proportion of all income is taken in tax.

- A **progressive** tax rate structure takes a higher proportion in tax as income rises.

- A **regressive** structure would take a decreasing proportion as income rises.

Most Western countries use a progressive tax rate structure.

1.4.5 Tax gap

This is the gap between the tax theoretically collectable and the amount actually collected. The tax authorities work unceasingly to minimise this gap.

1.4.6 Hypothecation

The government can choose to ring-fence (ie restrict the use of) certain types of tax revenue for the purposes of certain types of expenditure. This prevents the money being spent on anything else and is known as **hypothecation**.

An example in the UK is the revenue from the 'congestion charge' levied on London motorists which can only be spent on transport in the capital.

1.4.7 Incidence/effective incidence   11/10

The **incidence** of a tax is on the person or organisation that pays it.

It is important to distinguish between **formal** and **effective** incidence.

- The **formal incidence** of a tax is on the person or organisation who has direct contact with the tax authorities. For example, while the formal incidence of a sales tax is on the registered trader who has to pay it to the government.

- The **effective incidence** of a tax is on the person or organisation who actually bears the end cost of the tax. So the effective incidence of a sales tax is on the customer who eventually bears the tax burden.

Section summary

- The three major principles of tax recognised today are **equity, efficiency** and **economic effects**.

- Tax rules arise from a number of sources. There are four main ones:
    - Domestic tax legislation and court rulings
    - Domestic tax authority practice
    - Supranational bodies
    - International tax treaties

- Taxes can be classified according to their **tax base**: **income or profits, assets** or **consumption**.

- Taxation can be one of two forms: **direct** or **indirect.**

- There are three possible tax structures: **proportional, progressive** and **regressive**.

- The **incidence** of a tax is on the person or organisation that pays it. It is important to distinguish between **formal** and **effective** incidence.

2 Administration of tax

Introduction

In this section on administration of tax we cover record keeping, tax returns and deadlines.

2.1 Record keeping and retention   11/10

Tax authorities require businesses to keep records of the tax they pay. It makes no difference if the tax is a cost to the business (eg tax on business profits or gains) or whether the business acts merely as a tax collector (eg employee tax and social security contributions).

Tax records usually need to be kept in more detail than is strictly necessary than for financial reporting purposes. This is so that the business can satisfy the tax authority that is has complied with the law.

For example, businesses will need to keep detailed records of:

- Supporting documents for company income tax and capital gains tax calculations
- Employee pay, income tax and social security contributions
- All sales and purchases subject to VAT or other sales tax, or to excise duties
- Transaction prices for intra-group sales with overseas subsidiaries

Most tax authorities have the power to inspect business records to ensure compliance. If mistakes are made, the tax authority may be able to re-assess earlier years and collect back taxes owed. The UK tax authority, HM Revenue and Customs, has the power to review records from six tax years ago if errors are found. Therefore tax records may need to be kept longer than normal, eg payroll records are usually kept for at least six years in the UK.

Also, tax years may not be the same as accounting years. In the UK, the tax year runs from 6 April in one year to 5 April in the following year. Very few companies have a 5 April accounting year end.

Question 17.1	Retention periods

Learning outcome A1(c)

Blam is incorporated in the UK. Its company year end is 31 December. Until when should it keep the records of employee taxation of the year ended 31 December 20X0?

2.2 Tax returns

Businesses need to submit **tax returns** (ie special tax reports) of the different taxes that they have collected on behalf of the government (eg employee tax, social security contributions, sales tax and so on). They also make returns of their taxable profits and gains, so that they pay the correct income tax and/or capital gains tax.

2.3 Deadlines

There are deadlines for reporting and paying outstanding tax to the tax authorities. Deadlines allow the tax authority to forecast their cash receipts and give them a framework within which interest or penalties for late payment can be imposed. Deadlines also allow companies to forecast their cash outflows as they know when the tax needs to be paid.

There may be different deadlines for the different types of tax.

For instance, in the UK, company income tax for small and medium entities has to be paid within 9 months of the end of the accounting period. The company tax return has to be submitted within 12 months of the end of the period. At this point, any adjustment will be made to the amount originally paid. In contrast, large entities must pay the tax due in four instalments, two during the financial year and two after. Both methods allow the government to collect tax before the company's tax liability is finalised.

In the UK, a business also has to file a return on employee taxes within 6 weeks of the end of the tax year.

Similarly, there are deadlines for the submission of records of VAT (sales tax) and other excise duties. The business may be fined for submitting returns late.

Tax due to, or collected on behalf of the tax authorities must be paid within a time limit. In the UK, employee taxes must be paid to HM Revenue and Customs on a monthly basis by a specified date. Interest is charged for late payment and there may also be penalties charged for persistent late payment.

> ## Section summary
>
> - Tax records usually need to be kept for **different periods** and retained for **longer intervals** than normal accounting records.
> - There are deadlines for reporting and paying outstanding tax to the tax authorities.

3 Tax enforcement

> ## Introduction
>
> This section looks at the enforcement of tax and the powers of tax authorities to deal with non-compliance with tax legislation. We then move on to look at the important distinction between tax avoidance and tax evasion.

3.1 Enforcement

Tax authorities have the power to enforce compliance with the tax rules. These powers generally include the following.

(a) **Power to review and query filed returns.** Tax legislation will usually specify a deadline for the tax authorities to open an enquiry into a filed tax return.

(b) **Power to request special reports or returns.** A special report or return is usually requested when the tax authorities believe that an entity may not be providing full information.

(c) **Power to examine records** (generally extending back some years). This is generally carried out by appointment with the company. In the UK, the tax authorities can go back 20 years in cases where fraud is suspected.

(d) **Powers of entry and search.** When the tax authority believes that fraud has occurred, it can obtain a search warrant to enter a business's premises and seize the records. In the UK, inspections and searches related to VAT are also carried out, sometimes without advance warning if breaches of the VAT rules are suspected.

(e) **Exchange of information with tax authorities in other jurisdictions**. This has become very important as a counter-terrorism measure in recent years. One tax authority may become aware of funds being moved to another country in suspicious circumstances. It will then warn the tax authority in that other jurisdiction. Exchange of information is also useful in dealing with drug smuggling and money laundering. Tax authorities will usually only exchange information where a tax treaty exists with the other country.

3.2 Tax avoidance and tax evasion   5/10, 5/11

KEY TERMS

TAX AVOIDANCE is a way of arranging your affairs to take advantage of the tax rules to pay as little tax as possible. It is perfectly legal and is often referred to as tax planning.

TAX EVASION is a way of paying less tax by **illegal methods,** for example by not declaring income or claiming fictitious expenses.

Tax avoidance and evasion tend to be most common where the following situations apply:

- High tax rates, making it more worthwhile to avoid tax and to spend money on tax advice
- Imprecise wording of the tax laws, leaving loopholes to be exploited
- Insufficient penalties for tax evasion
- Perceived inequity in the tax laws, which makes evasion/avoidance seem more justified

When a tax authority becomes aware that so many businesses are avoiding tax by using a perceived loophole in the law, it may bring in **anti-avoidance legislation** to close the loophole. However this takes time and so modern laws usually include general anti-avoidance clauses in new tax bills to cover any loopholes. In other tax regimes, the tax authority may have to take the case to court to obtain a legal ruling as to whether a scheme is against the spirit of the law.

In countries such as the UK, case law is important in dealing with avoidance and evasion. The revenue authorities regularly bring cases against avoidance schemes and, where the court decides that transactions have been undertaken solely for the purpose of avoiding tax, it will rule that these transactions should be disregarded. This creates a precedent for future cases and in this way loopholes are closed.

However, in the long term, if it wishes to minimise avoidance and evasion, a tax authority has to concentrate on the following:

(a)   reducing opportunity by deducting tax at source whenever possible and keeping the tax system as simple as possible

(b)   increasing the risk of detection by having an efficient system of checking tax returns and good communications with other tax authorities

(c)   maximising penalties for evasion and making sure that this is well publicised

(d)   making sure that the tax system is perceived as equitable and that the tax administration deals fairly and courteously with taxpayers.

Section summary

- Tax authorities have the power to enforce compliance with the tax rules via various means.

- **Tax avoidance** is a way of arranging your affairs to take advantage of the tax rules to pay as little tax as possible. It is perfectly legal.

- **Tax evasion** is a way of paying less tax by **illegal methods**, eg not declaring the income or money laundering.

Chapter Roundup

✓ The three major principles of tax recognised today are **equity, efficiency** and **economic effects**.

✓ Tax rules arise from a number of sources. There are four main ones:

- Domestic tax legislation and court rulings
- Domestic tax authority practice
- Supranational bodies
- International tax treaties

✓ Taxes can be classified according to their **tax base: income or profits, assets** or **consumption**.

✓ Taxation can be one of two forms: **direct** or **indirect**.

✓ There are three possible tax structures: **proportional, progressive** and **regressive**.

✓ The **incidence of a tax** is on the person or organisation that pays it. It is important to distinguish between **formal** and **effective incidence**.

✓ Tax records may need to be kept for **different periods** and retained for **longer intervals** than normal accounting records.

✓ There are deadlines for reporting and paying outstanding tax to the tax authorities.

✓ Tax authorities have the power to enforce compliance with the tax rules via various means.

✓ **Tax avoidance** is a way of arranging your affairs to take advantage of the tax rules to pay as little tax as possible. It is perfectly legal.

✓ **Tax evasion** is a way of paying less tax by **illegal methods**, eg not declaring the income, money laundering.

Quick Quiz

1 Value added tax is an example of which kind of tax?

    A   Indirect tax
    B   Capital gains tax
    C   Direct tax
    D   Income tax

2 Adam Smith's characteristics of a 'good' tax were:...

3 Tax evasion is illegal. True or false?

4 A system of taxation in which a higher proportion is paid in tax as income rises is known as...

5 The tax year should always be the same as the accounting year. True or false?

Answers to Quick Quiz

1   A

2   Equity, certainty, convenience and efficiency

3   True. Tax evasion is illegal, tax avoidance is legal.

4   A **progressive** tax rate structure

5   False

 ## Answers to Questions

17.1 Retention periods

The year ended 31 December 20X0 is part of the year 20X1. Therefore the records need to be kept until at least 5 April 20X7.

TYPES OF TAXATION

In this chapter we look at the different types of taxation – direct taxes, indirect taxes, employee taxes and international taxation.

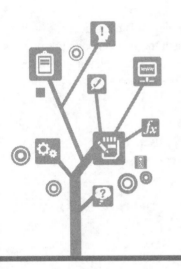

topic list	learning outcomes	syllabus references	ability required
1 Direct tax on company profits and gains	A3(a)	A3(i)	application
2 Interaction of corporate and personal income tax	A3(a)	A3(i)	comprehension
3 International taxation	A2(a),(b)	A2(i), A3(i)	comprehension
4 Indirect taxes	A1(a),(e)	A1(iv)	comprehension
5 Value Added Tax (VAT)	A1(e)	A1(iv)	comprehension
6 Employee taxation	A1(e)	A1(v)	comprehension

1   Direct tax on company profits and gains

Introduction

As we saw in the last chapter, direct taxes are taxes on income and include tax on a company's trading profits and capital gains. In this section, we look in detail at the principles and calculation of these taxes. Note that your syllabus covers the general principles of tax which should be applicable across most countries. In this chapter, we have used the UK tax system to illustrate the principles.

1.1 Schedular systems of company tax

Businesses can have income from many different sources, such as trading profits, capital gains, loan interest, royalties and dividends received. Countries may wish to tax the different income sources according to different rules. This is known as a **schedular system**.

For example, in the UK, the tax system includes the following schedules for company income tax:

(a)   Schedule DI – Trading income
(b)   Schedule DIII – Interest income
(c)   Schedule DV – Income (ie dividends) from overseas subsidiaries.

The rules under each schedule are different. When a company completes a tax return, income must be correctly allocated to each schedule.

1.2 Basis of assessment

The rules for calculating a tax liability are known as the **basis of assessment**. This basis depends on the type of income and the taxable person. In the UK, the bases of assessment for the different types of income are embodied in the schedular system, discussed above. The basis of assessment also governs how the tax liability of a particular person or organisation is computed. The examples below are from the UK tax system.

- An employee is taxed on the income actually earned during the tax year.
- A self-employed person is taxed on the profits of his or her financial year.
- A limited liability company is taxed on the profits of its financial year.

1.3 Company income tax on profits   5/10, 11/10, 5/11

A company pays income tax on the **taxable profits** it generates.

KEY TERM

TAXABLE PROFIT is the accounting profit adjusted according to the tax rules and is the amount on which tax is actually paid.

The financial statements provide the starting point for calculating taxable profits, however some items included in the accounting profit may not be allowed for tax purposes.

The following items are often specifically disallowed:

- Entertaining
- Depreciation
- Formation and acquisition costs
- Donations to political parties

The income tax charge is calculated as taxable profit × tax rate.

Exam alert

Rules for allowed and disallowed items vary according to the tax regime. In the exam you will be told what rules to apply. The tax rules are also released on the CIMA website prior to the exam. Make sure you check the website to see what they are:

www.cimaglobal.com/Students/2010-professional-qualification/Operational-level/F1-study-resources/

1.4 Adjustments to accounting profit

The following statement shows the kind of adjustments to accounting profit needed to arrive at taxable profit.

	$'000	$'000
Accounting profit per financial statements		5,000
Add back items of expense that are not tax allowable:		
Entertaining	50	
Formation and acquisition costs	75	
Donations to political parties	50	
Depreciation	125	
Balancing charge	100	
		400
		5,400
Deduct items of income that are not taxable or tax allowances given:		
Non-taxable income (eg government grants)	70	
Tax depreciation	60	
Balancing allowance	20	
		(150)
Taxable profit		5,250

Here the accounting profit is $5m, but the tax will be paid on the taxable profit of $5.25m. If the tax rate is 30%, the tax due is $1,575,000 (30% × $5,250,000).

The depreciation added back here is the **accounting depreciation** charged in the statement of comprehensive income. This is not normally an allowable expense for tax purposes and so must be added back to taxable profits. Instead, most tax regimes have rules for **'tax depreciation'**. In the UK this allowable tax depreciation is known as **capital allowances**.

Question 18.1	Taxable profit

Learning outcome A3(a)

Talbot is a company resident in country X. The following rules for taxation of corporate profits apply in country X:

(a)   Accounting rules on recognition and measurement are followed for tax purposes.

(b)   All income other than grants received from government bodies is taxable.

(c)   All expenses other than depreciation, amortisation, entertaining, taxes paid to other public bodies and donations to political parties are tax deductible.

(d)   The corporate tax on profits is at a rate of 30%.

Talbot has prepared the following statement of comprehensive income for the year ended 31 December 20X3.

STATEMENT OF COMPREHENSIVE INCOME FOR THE YEAR ENDED 31 DECEMBER 20X3

	$'000	$'000
Revenue		1,150
Cost of sales		(700)
Gross profit		450
Income from government grant		100
		550
Expenses:		
Client entertaining	75	
Telephone costs	10	
Donation to Green Party (political party)	25	
Stationery costs	30	
Travel expenses	35	
Rent and utilities	50	
Depreciation	80	
Amortisation of intangible asset	50	
		(355)
Profit before tax		195

Talbot is entitled to tax depreciation of $100,000 for the year.

Required

Calculate Talbot's taxable profit and tax due for the year ended 31 December 20X3.

1.5 Tax depreciation

Accounting depreciation is not an allowable expense for tax purposes. Instead, tax depreciation is given to compensate entities for the fall in value of their assets. Tax depreciation is calculated in a similar way to accounting depreciation, but following the specific tax rules. Tax depreciation can be used by the government to encourage businesses to invest in particular assets (eg environmentally friendly cars) or to generally boost the economy. This is done by giving **accelerated tax depreciation**, for example a **100% first year allowance**, on these assets in the year they are purchased.

Most countries allow tax depreciation on plant and machinery, including computer equipment and motor vehicles, and on buildings, however, other types of non-current assets may also be included. Many countries do not allow tax depreciation on land.

1.6 Calculating tax depreciation   11/10, 5/11

Exam alert

The rules for calculating tax depreciation vary according to the tax regime. In your exam you will be told what rules apply. The tax rules are also released on the CIMA website prior to the exam. Make sure you check the website to see what they are:

www.cimaglobal.com/Students/2010-professional-qualification/Operational-level/F1-study-resources/

It is likely that these rules will be based on the UK system which is discussed below.

In the UK, similar assets are grouped together and put into a 'pool' of expenditure. A tax depreciation allowance (called the '**writing down allowance**') is given on the **tax written down value** (ie cost less previous allowances) of the pool. The writing down allowance is usually given as a percentage of the written down value.

Over the life of an asset, the tax depreciation should equal the purchase price of the asset less any amount realised on disposal. Therefore, when disposal takes place, there is often a '**balancing charge**' or '**balancing allowance**' to account for any difference.

A balancing charge occurs when the disposal value deducted exceeds the balance remaining in the pool for the asset. The balancing charge equals the excess and is effectively a negative tax depreciation allowance as the entity has been over compensated for the fall in value of the asset.

For instance:

	$
Purchase price of asset	50,000
Tax depreciation allowed	(40,000)
Remaining value for tax purposes	10,000
Amount realised on disposal	(15,000)
Balancing charge	(5,000)

If the asset had realised $7,000 on disposal, the company would have received a balancing allowance of $3,000 – this is effectively an additional tax depreciation allowance to make sure the entity is fully compensated for the fall in value of the asset.

Question 18.2	Tax depreciation

Learning outcome A3(a)

Winton is resident in country Y. In Country Y, tax depreciation is deductible as follows: 50% of additions to plant and machinery in the accounting period in which they are recorded; 25% per year of the written down value in subsequent accounting periods except that in which the asset is disposed of.

Winton makes up accounts 31 December each year. At 31 December 20X7, the tax written down value of plant and machinery is $100,000. During the year to 31 December 20X8, Winton purchases a machine for $20,000 and a van for $10,000. During the year to 31 December 20X9, Winton disposed of the van for $7,000.

Required

Calculate the tax depreciation Winton will claim for the years to 31 December 20X8 and 31 December 20X9.

1.7 Capital gains tax   5/11

When an asset is disposed of for more than its original cost, a '**capital gain**' arises.

KEY POINT

A distinction is made between '**trading profits**' that arise from the trade of the business and '**capital gains**' which result when an asset is disposed of for more than its cost.

Most tax regimes have **separate rules** covering the taxation of capital gains. In the UK, capital gains are included in the total profits chargeable to corporation tax (along with taxable profits from trading activities) and so are taxed at the corporate income tax rate.

Different tax jurisdictions have different rules concerning the taxation of capital gains. In the UK, the largest capital gains are probably made on the sales of residential property, but these are exempt from taxation as long as the property constitutes a 'main residence'. Other items are also excluded, such as cars, boats and caravans. The UK government probably makes most of its capital gains tax revenue from gains made on transfers of shares in companies listed on the Stock Exchange.

The capital gain is usually calculated as the **disposal proceeds less the tax written down value of the asset** being disposed of (ie original cost less tax depreciation allowed). Some countries allow the cost of improvements or the costs incurred to sell the asset to be deducted from the sales proceeds. Some countries also allow the original cost of the asset to be adjusted up to current prices by the use of an index, such as the Retail Price Index, before calculating the capital gain. This prevents the taxpayer from having to pay tax on a gain which is simply the result of inflation.

1.7.1 Indexation allowance

This relief for inflation is known as the **indexation allowance** in the UK and is only available to companies. Companies are entitled to indexation allowance from the date of acquisition until the date of disposal of an asset. It is based on the movement in the Retail Price Index (RPI) between those two dates and is calculated as follows.

Indexation allowance = acquisition cost × indexation factor

where the indexation factor is:

Indexation factor = $\frac{\text{RPI for month of disposal} - \text{RPI for month of acquisition}}{\text{RPI for month of acquisition}}$

Example: Indexation allowance

An asset is acquired by a company in February 20X0 (RPI = 167.5) at a cost of $15,000. The asset is sold for $25,500 in December 20X9 (RPI = 207.2). Gains are taxed at the corporate income tax rate of 25%.

Required

Calculate the capital gain arising and the tax payable. Work to the nearest $1.

Solution

	$	$
Proceeds of sale		25,500
Cost	15,000	
Indexation allowance (15,000 × (207.2 – 167.5)/167.5)	3,555	
Total allowable cost		(18,555)
Capital gain		6,945
Tax payable (6,945 × 25%)		1,736

Indexation allowance **cannot create or increase a capital loss**. If there is a gain before the indexation allowance, the allowance can reduce that gain to zero but no further. If there is a loss before the indexation allowance, there is no indexation allowance.

1.7.2 Capital losses

Capital losses are generally accounted for in the same way as capital gains. Most countries allow capital losses to be offset against current or future capital gains. Some countries allow capital losses to be offset against current or future taxable profits

1.7.3 Rollover relief

An entity may sell an asset and realise a capital gain. However, it may then need to replace the asset. If the entity pays tax on the capital gain, this will reduce the proceeds available for reinvestment. Therefore, some countries allow the tax charge on the disposal of a business asset to be **deferred** until the replacement asset is disposed of. If this is a type of asset that will have to be continuously replaced (such as manufacturing machinery), then this deferral could go on indefinitely. In some tax jurisdictions, this is known as **rollover relief**.

1.8 Treatment of trading losses   11/10

When a company makes a loss instead of a taxable profit, tax relief will be given according to the rules of the tax regime.

In the UK, the position regarding **relief for trading losses** can best be summarised as follows. When an enterprise sustains a trading loss in its financial year, it cannot claim a refund of tax for that year. However, there are a number of other possible ways of that it get tax relief for the loss:

- Carry the loss forward against future **trading profits**
- Offset the loss against other income or **capital gains** of the same period
- Carry the loss back against profits of previous periods
- Offset the loss against the profits of another group company ('group loss relief')

Some countries do not allow **capital gains/losses** to be offset against **trading gains/losses** and vice versa.

Some countries do not allow losses to be carried back and some restrict the number of years for which they can be carried forward. However, when a business ceases trading, there may be provision for carrying back any losses generated in the last year of trading (sometimes known as **terminal losses**) against previous years' taxable profits. In the UK, a business calculates the losses for the last twelve months ending on the day trade ceases. These terminal losses can then be carried back and offset against the final year of assessment and the three previous tax years.

Example: tax losses

Country R has the following tax regulations:

- Taxable profits are subject to income tax at 25%
- Taxable profits are the calculated as the total of trading profits and capital gains for a year
- Trading losses can be carried forwards indefinitely but cannot be carried back to previous years
- Capital gains/losses cannot be offset against trading profits/losses or vice versa.

Entity A started trading in 20X6 and had the following results:

	Trading profits/losses $	Capital gains/losses $
20X6	(50)	100
20X7	(100)	(100)
20X8	350	400

Required

Calculate the amount of tax due for 20X8.

Solution

	Trading profit less trading losses $	Capital gains less capital losses $	Taxable profit $
20X6	(50)	100	100

The trading loss of $50 cannot be offset against the capital gains, but can be carried forward to be offset against future trading losses.

	Trading profit less trading losses	Capital gains less capital losses	Taxable profit
	$	$	$
20X7	(100)	(100)	nil

The trading loss in 20X7 is added to that from 20X6 to give $150 trading losses carried forward. The capital loss of $100 is also carried forward.

	Trading profit less trading losses	Capital gains less capital losses	Taxable profit
	$	$	$
20X8	350 – 150 = 200	400 – 100 = 300	500

The brought forward losses can be offset against trading profits and capital gains for 20X8. The tax due is then calculated as 25% x 500 = $125.

1.9 Group loss relief

Tax rules are also necessary to deal with tax losses in groups. In the UK, losses of one group subsidiary may be set against the profits of another group subsidiary. When assets are transferred between group companies, capital gains tax is deferred until the asset is sold outside the group. In effect, UK group relief rules treat the group as one entity for tax purposes.

This UK treatment is an example of **tax consolidation.** In general, if a group of enterprises are recognised as a **tax group**, it is possible for them to gain relief for trading losses by offsetting the losses of one group member against the profits of another group member. The rules for group relief will vary from country to country, as will the rules for recognition of a tax group (which may differ from the rules under which groups are recognised for financial reporting purposes).

Some countries also have their own regulations for recognising **tax groups for capital gains purposes**. It is not usually possible to offset capital losses and gains between the group members. However, there are usually provisions that allow the transfer of assets between group members without recognising a capital gain or loss. The calculation of the gain and the payment of the tax are usually **deferred** until the asset is sold outside the tax group. Good tax planning is needed to ensure that all asset sales to third parties take place through just one group member. These provisions can then be used to accumulate all the group's capital gains and losses in that member, thereby effectively obtaining offset.

1.10 Recharacterisation rules

An otherwise profitable company may have high interest payments, leading to a low taxable income. This has an adverse effect on government tax revenue. In some countries, such as the US, interest payments above a certain level can be **recharacterised** as dividend payments, which are not an allowable expense. This is likely to be applied where the loans in question are between group companies. This has consequences because **advanced taxes** or **withholding taxes** may be payable.

Advanced taxes may be charged on dividends. This is a proportion of the dividend which is paid to the tax authorities as an advanced payment on account of the final tax liability. If the advanced tax rate is 20%, then the dividend is considered to be 80% and the advanced tax due is 20/80 or 1/4 of the dividend.

Withholding taxes arise when dividends are paid by a company in one tax jurisdiction to a company in a different tax jurisdiction. They are similar to advanced taxes, but can be reduced as a result of a double taxation treaty, which we will cover in the next section.

Section summary

- Entities are subject to **direct taxes** on the **trading profits** and **capital gains** they generate.

- **Company income tax** is paid on the **taxable profit** of an entity. Taxable profit is the accounting profit adjusted according to the tax rules.

- Depreciation is not normally allowable for tax purposes. Instead, entities are allowed to deduct **tax depreciation** which is calculated based on the rules of the tax regime.

- When an asset is disposed of for more than its original cost, a **capital gain** arises that is subject to corporate income tax. An **indexation allowance** may be given to counter the effects of inflation and reduce the gain chargeable to tax.

- **Trading losses** and **capital losses** can usually be **relieved** against profits and gains according to the rules of the tax regime.

2 Interaction of corporate tax and personal income tax   11/10

Introduction

The interaction of the corporate and personal tax systems in a country depends on the system of tax that operates in that country. When a company pays a dividend to its shareholders, it is paid out of the company's taxed profits and therefore has already been subject to tax. If the dividend income received by the individual is then taxed again under personal income tax, the dividend will effectively have been taxed twice. The system of tax which is in operation in a country determines whether this will happen as it specifies the interaction between corporate and personal tax. There are four main systems of tax, which we cover in this short section.

2.1 Classical system

Under the classical system of taxation, company income tax is charged on all of the profits of the entity, whether distributed or not. Dividends are paid out of taxed profits and are then chargeable to personal income tax in the hands of the shareholder. This system is simple to administer but gives rise to **double taxation** of dividends. This system could result in entities being less likely to distribute dividends as it leads to double taxation.

In the UK, where the shareholder is a **company**, the dividend is not liable to UK corporation tax. If this were not the case, the dividend could end up being taxed three times, as it will be included in income by the receiving company and may then be distributed to its own individual shareholders, who will then pay tax on it.

2.2 Imputation system

Under the imputation system, the company income tax that has already been paid is **imputed** to the shareholder as a tax credit. He pays income tax on the dividend but deducts the tax credit. This avoids the problem of double taxation.

The shareholder receives the net dividend. He is taxed on the net dividend and the tax credit is then deducted from his liability.

2.3 Partial imputation system

It is also possible to have a system of **partial imputation**, where the taxpayer receives a tax credit of only part of the underlying company income tax.

2.4 Split rate system

Some tax jurisdictions operate a **split rate system** in which distributed profits are taxable at a lower rate than retained profits. This avoids double taxation of dividends. This can function under the classical, imputation or partial imputation system.

Example: classical versus imputation system

Cadis Co supplies the following information.

	$
Year to 30 June 20X8	
Taxable profits	100,000
Dividend paid for the year (net)	24,500

The corporate income tax rate is 30% and shareholders pay income tax at 40% on dividends received.

Required

Calculate the total tax payable by Cadis Co and its shareholders as at 30 June 20X8 under:

(a) the classical system,
(b) the imputation system; and
(c) a partial imputation system where a tax credit of 25% is allowed.

Solution

(a) **Classical system**

	$
Corporate income tax paid by Cadis Co (100,000 × 30%)	30,000
Tax on dividends paid by shareholders (24,500 × 40%)	9,800
Total tax paid	39,800

(b) **Imputation system**

	$	$
Corporate income tax paid by Cadis Co		30,000
Shareholder:		
Tax at 40% (24,500 × 40%)	9,800	
Less tax credit (24,500 × 30%)	(7,350)	
		2,450
Total tax paid		32,450

(c) **Partial imputation system**

	$	$
Corporate income tax paid by Cadis Co		30,000
Shareholder:		
Tax at 40% (24,500 × 40%)	9,800	
Less tax credit (24,500 × 25%)	(6,125)	
		3,675
Total tax paid		33,675

You can see that the classical system does not encourage the payment of dividends.

Section summary

- There are four main systems of taxing corporate income: **classical, imputation, partial imputation** and **split rate**.
- The classical system is much **simpler** but most countries do not use it.

3 International taxation

Introduction

This section introduces some key concepts in international taxation and looks at double taxation treaties and the OECD model tax convention.

3.1 Corporate residence   5/10, 11/10

Entities usually pay company income tax on their worldwide income in the country they are resident in for tax purposes. Therefore determining an entity's **country of residence** is important. There are different ways to determine the residence of an entity, including its:

(a)   **Place of incorporation (domicile)**
(b)   **Place of effective management** and control
(c)   **Place of permanent establishment**

A permanent establishment means a fixed place of business through which the business of an entity is wholly or partly carried on.

There must be a degree of permanence, for example:

(i)   Place of management
(ii)   Branch
(iii)   Office
(iv)   Factory
(v)   Workshop
(vi)   Mine, oil or gas well, quarry
(vii)   A building site or construction or installation project if it lasts more than 12 months.

A warehouse is not a permanent establishment, it is just a storage area. A permanent establishment is somewhere where trade is carried out or decisions are made.

3.2 Double tax and OECD deemed residence   5/11

Each tax authority will have its own rules on how residence is determined. This can sometimes lead to entities being resident in two countries. For example, suppose a company is incorporated in country X, where residency is determined on the basis of incorporation only. However, the company conducts most of its activities in country Y, where its board of directors meet. In country Y, residency is determined based on the place of management and control. In this situation, the company will be deemed to be resident in both country X and country Y. The company is therefore theoretically subject to tax in both of those countries and may have to pay tax twice on its income. This is known as **double tax**.

The OECD Model Tax Convention addresses the issue of double residence.

In the case where an entity is resident in more than one country, the OECD Model Tax Convention states that the entity will be **deemed** to be **resident only in the country of its effective management**.

A place of effective management is:

- the place where **key management and commercial decisions are made**

- the place where the **board or senior management meet**

An entity can only have one place of effective management, so using the OECD Model Tax Convention rules means that the entity would only be taxed in that country, which solves the problem of double tax.

3.3 Payments remitted from overseas subsidiaries

A group may have overseas subsidiaries which will from time to time pay dividends to the parent company. In this situation, two types of tax become relevant: withholding tax and underlying tax.

3.3.1 Withholding tax   5/10, 11/10

If a company makes payments to an individual or another company or an individual resident in a different country, it may first have to pay **withholding tax (WHT)** to the local tax authority. A withholding tax ensures that the local government gains some income from the dividend payment so that not all of the money earned by the company in that country is remitted overseas.

The rate of withholding tax varies depending on the country. Withholding tax also applies to other types of payment, such as interest payments, royalties, capital gains and rents.

Example: Withholding taxes

P owns 30% of the equity shares in A, an entity resident overseas. P receives a dividend of $40,000 from A, after the deduction of withholding tax at 15%.

Required

Calculate the amount of withholding tax paid by A to the nearest $1.

Solution

P receives $40,000 net of withholding tax at 15%.

Therefore, withholding tax = $40,000 \times 0.15/0.85 = \$7,059$

3.3.2 Underlying tax   5/11

Underlying tax (ULT) is the tax which has already been suffered by the profits from which a dividend is paid. This happens when an entity receives a dividend from a foreign entity when the dividend has been paid out of taxed profits. Under some tax systems, the entity can obtain relief for the tax levied in the foreign country on the amount out of which their dividend was paid.

Underlying tax is calculated as follows.

> Underlying tax = gross dividend $\times$ $\dfrac{\text{tax actually paid by foreign company}}{\text{foreign company's profit after tax}}$
>
> The gross dividend is the dividend paid by the foreign entity before withholding tax.

Example: underlying tax

Continuing the example from above, A had profits after tax for the year of $450,000 and paid corporate income tax of $150,000.

Required

Calculate the amount of ULT that relates to the dividend received by P to the nearest $1.

Solution

Gross dividend = 40,000+ 7,059 = $47,059

$$\text{ULT} = 47,059 \times \frac{150,000}{450,000} = \$15,686$$

3.3.3 Double tax

When a parent company receives a dividend payment from an overseas subsidiary, that dividend will often already have been subject to underlying tax and withholding tax. Because that dividend now forms part of the income of the parent company, it will also be subject to corporate income tax in the country in which the parent is resident. In effect the dividend has been **taxed twice**.

To relieve this burden, **double tax relief** is often available for the overseas tax paid.

3.4 Double tax relief   11/10

There are three main methods for giving double tax relief.

3.4.1 Exemption method

In the Exemption method, the dividend received is exempted from tax in the receiving company's country. So, if income is taxed in Country A, then it will not be taxed in Country B.

3.4.2 Tax Credit method

In the Tax Credit method, the dividend received is subject to tax in the receiving company's country, but the foreign tax already paid is credited against the tax due in the receiving company's country. So the tax paid in Country A is credited against (ie deducted) from the tax due in Country B. No refund of tax is given if the tax already paid in Country A is higher than that due in Country B.

Example: Tax Credit method I

RH, a company resident in Country Y, is a 100% owned subsidiary of APH, a company resident in Country X. At the year end, RH paid a dividend of $54,000, after deduction of a withholding tax of 10%, to APH. RH had reported a profit after tax of $450,000 and paid a corporate income tax bill of $90,000 in Country Y. In Country X:

- Corporate income tax is 40%
- Double tax relief is given by the Tax Credit method.

Required

How much tax is payable by APH in Country X?

Solution

Tax paid in Country Y:

WHT = 54,000 × 10/90 = $6,000

Underlying tax = gross dividend × $\dfrac{\text{tax actually paid by foreign company}}{\text{foreign company's profit after tax}}$

Gross dividend = 54,000 + 6,000 = $60,000

Underlying tax = 60,000 × $\dfrac{90,000}{450,000}$ = $12,000

Tax payable by APH in Country X

	$
Gross dividend (from above)	60,000
Taxed at 40%	24,000
Less: Double tax relief for WHT	(6,000)
Less: Double tax relief for ULT	(12,000)
Tax due in Country X	6,000

Example: Tax Credit method II

SW, a company resident in Country Y, is a 100% owned subsidiary of LR, a company resident in Country X. At the year end, SW paid a dividend of $127,500, after deduction of a withholding tax of 15%, to LR. SW had reported a profit after tax of $200,000 and paid a corporate income tax bill of $50,000 in Country Y. In Country X:

- Corporate income tax is 20%
- Double tax relief is given by the Tax Credit method.

Required

How much tax is payable by LR in Country X?

Solution

Tax paid in Country Y:

WHT = 127,500 × 15/85 = $22,500

Underlying tax = gross dividend × $\dfrac{\text{tax actually paid by foreign company}}{\text{foreign company's profit after tax}}$

Gross dividend = 127,500 + 22,500 = $150,000

Underlying tax = 150,000 × $\dfrac{50,000}{200,000}$ = $37,500

Tax payable by LR in Country X

	$
Gross dividend (from above)	150,000
Taxed at 20%	30,000
Less: Double tax relief for WHT	(22,500)
Less: Double tax relief for ULT (relief restricted to $7,500)	(7,500)
Tax due in Country X	Nil

3.4.3 Deduction method

This is where only the **income after tax** in Country A is taxable in Country B. The example below illustrates the **deduction** method.

Example: Deduction method

RH, a company resident in Country Y, is a 100% owned subsidiary of APH, a company resident in Country X. At the year end, RH paid a dividend of $54,000, after deduction of a withholding tax of 10%, to APH. RH had reported a profit after tax of $450,000 and paid a corporate income tax bill of $90,000 in Country Y.

In Country X:

*   Corporate income tax is 40%

*   Double tax relief is given by the Deduction method.

Required

How much tax is payable by APH in Country X?

Solution

Tax payable by APH in Country X	$
Net dividend received	54,000
Tax payable at 40%	21,600

3.4.4 Double taxation treaties

Often two countries will establish a **double tax treaty** between them to determine which country will tax income and what method of double tax relief will be available to entities that have taxable income in both countries. The starting point for double taxation treaties is often the **OECD's Model Tax Convention**. The Model Tax Convention recommends the use of the Tax Credit method for double tax relief.

You do not need to know the OECD model tax convention in detail. However, it does make good background reading. www.oecd.org

3.5 Other OECD projects

The OECD Forum on Tax Administration encourages discussion between tax administrations. By promoting the sharing of experiences, the forum aims to identify good tax administration practices.

Together the OECD, the International Monetary Fund and the World Bank have created the **International Tax Dialogue** (ITD). The ITD has stated its main objectives as follows.

- Promote effective international dialogue between participating organisations and governments on taxation, giving all countries a real input into the discussion of tax administration and policy issues
- Identify and share good practices in taxation
- Provide a clearer focus for technical assistance on tax matters
- Avoid duplication of effort in respect of existing activities on tax matters.

3.6 Taxable presence

A business trading abroad will have to decide whether it should do so through a **subsidiary** or a **foreign branch**. This decision will not be made principally on the basis of tax considerations, but the following tax issues will be taken into consideration.

Subsidiary

- The parent company is liable to tax on foreign dividends received from the subsidiary.
- Losses made by a non-resident subsidiary are not available for group relief.
- The parent company will not normally be subject to capital gains tax on gains made by a non-resident subsidiary.
- Any capital items transferred to the parent from the non-resident subsidiary may become subject to capital gains tax on transfer.
- Transfer pricing arrangements between parent and foreign subsidiary will be subject to scrutiny from the tax authorities.

Branch

- Money transferred from a branch to the main entity will not be treated as a dividend.
- Losses sustained by a branch are usually immediately available for group relief.
- The main entity will be subject to capital gains tax on any capital gains made by a branch.
- Capital items can usually be transferred to the main entity without triggering capital gains tax.

Section summary

- Where a company pays corporate income tax is determined by which country it is **resident** in.
- The OECD Model Tax Convention defines residence for an entity as being liable to tax in a country by reason of **place of incorporation, place of effective management** or by **place of permanent establishment.**
- If an entity operates in several countries, it could be deemed resident of all those countries, leading to **double taxation**.
- In such circumstances, the OECD Model Tax Convention deems companies to be resident in their **place of effective management**.
- Overseas subsidiary companies often remit dividends to their parent company. These payments will often have been subject to **withholding tax** and **underlying tax**. When the dividend is subsequently taxed as part of the parent company's income, it will have been **taxed twice.**
- **Double tax relief**, is often available in this situation. Relief may be given by **deduction, exemption** or **tax credit**.

4 Indirect taxes

Introduction

This section looks at the different types of indirect taxes. As we saw in Chapter 17, an indirect tax is a tax on expenditure (or 'consumption'), rather than on income.

4.1 Types of indirect taxes   5/10

4.1.1 Unit taxes

Unit taxes are based on the number or weight of items, eg excise duties on cigarettes or tobacco.

4.1.2 Ad valorem taxes

Ad valorem taxes are based on the value of the items, eg a sales tax or value added tax.

4.2 Excise duties

Excise duties are a 'unit' tax – they are levied on the **amount** of the commodity.

Governments apply excise duty to goods that have large sales volumes and are easy to **control**, ie there are a few large producers and products covered by the duty are easily defined.

Excise duty tends to be levied on four major commodities – alcohol, tobacco, oil products and motor vehicles. The tax is collected earlier in the supply chain than sales taxes. By the time the product reaches the final consumer the price will already include excise duty. For instance, each brewery will have an excise officer assigned to it, who will know exactly what quantities are being produced. Because they are collected early in the supply chain from a limited number of products, excise duties yield large amounts of revenue for low collection cost and are therefore popular with governments.

Governments may apply excise duties the basis that increasing the cost of drinking, smoking and motoring is a means of curbing the consumer's enthusiasm for damaging his own health and that of the environment.

Excise duties, unlike sales taxes, are not refundable and so are usually treated as part of the cost of the asset when calculating the amount of sales tax due.

4.3 Wealth and property taxes

Some countries tax individuals and companies on the value of land and buildings or other valuable property or on 'total wealth' – for a company this would be its asset value.

4.3.1 Property taxes

Some countries operate systems under which people are taxed on their property – usually land and buildings, but sometimes including other assets. The UK has a system whereby individuals and businesses are taxed at a local level on the basis of the value of their property.

4.3.2 Wealth taxes

A number of countries levy wealth taxes, either on individuals or on entities or on both. This will involve measurement and valuation of assets each year. The tax is usually a straight percentage, for example 2%, of total net worth (total assets less total liabilities).

Section summary

There are two types of indirect taxes: **unit taxes** and **ad valorem taxes**.

5 Value Added Tax (VAT)

Introduction

In this section we examine VAT and its administration.

5.1 Single-stage versus multi-stage sales taxes   5/10

A sales tax can be single-stage or multi-stage.

Single-stage sales taxes are applied at one stage in the supply chain, either at the manufacturing, wholesale or retail level. Most sales taxes tend to be applied at the retail level (such as the retail sales tax applied in the USA), so the end user will bear the tax burden.

Multi-stage sales taxes are applied at several stages in the supply chain. A multi-stage sales tax is usually **chargeable and deductible** at different points in the supply chain (such as **VAT**), so the business deducts the tax it pays on purchases and pays over the balance to the government. The incidence of tax is therefore on the final consumer of the goods or services. A multi-stage sales tax can also be **cumulative** where no credit is received for tax paid in the previous stage.

5.2 Multi-stage sales tax: VAT   5/10, 11/10, 5/11

VAT is a multi-stage sales tax that is chargeable and deductible at different points in the supply chain. The following example shows how VAT works.

Example: VAT (1)

		Price net of VAT $	VAT @ 17.5% $	Total price $
(a)	Manufacturer buys raw materials	40	7	47
	Manufacturer makes and sells television to wholesaler	200	35	235
	Manufacturer pays VAT		28	
(b)	Wholesaler buys television	200	35	235
	Wholesaler sells television to retailer	320	56	376
	Wholesaler pays VAT		21	
(c)	Retailer buys television	320	56	376
	Retailer sells television	480	84	564
	Retailer pays VAT		28	
(d)	Customer buys television	480	84	564

The total tax of $84 is paid by the customer (the end user). The tax amounts paid by the manufacturer, the wholesaler and the retailer will all have been reclaimed.

	$
Supplier of raw materials	7
Manufacturer	28
Wholesaler	21
Retailer	28
Total VAT paid	84

Exam skills

If you are given a figure including VAT of 20%, multiply this by 20/120 to get the VAT amount.

5.3 VAT business liability

VAT on sales is called **output tax**, while VAT on purchases is called **input tax**. A business owes the tax authority the output tax it collects but deducts from this liability the input tax it pays.

| Output tax | − | Input tax | = | Amount paid to tax authority |

Example: VAT (2)

Carrying on the example from above, how much VAT is paid over to the tax authorities by the Manufacturer, Wholesaler and Retailer?

Solution

		Output VAT	Input VAT	Amount paid to tax authority
		$	$	$
(a)	Manufacturer	35	(7)	28
(b)	Wholesaler buys television	56	(35)	21
(c)	Retailer buys television	84	(56)	28

5.4 Registering for VAT

In most countries, entities are required to register for VAT when their taxable sales (also known as 'taxable supplies') exceed a certain level. Only entities registered for VAT can charge output VAT on their sales and reclaim input VAT on their purchases.

5.5 Rates of VAT

Some activities may be **exempt from VAT**, eg banking services. Traders who carry on exempt activities cannot reclaim VAT on inputs relating to those activities. Other transactions are **outside the scope of VAT**, so VAT is not charged on them. For example , in the UK, toll road charges are outside the scope of VAT.

Transactions which are within the scope of VAT and are not exempt from VAT will be taxable at one of three rates:

(a)   Standard rate. In the UK this is currently 20%.

(b)   Higher or reduced rate. For example in the UK, domestic fuel is taxable at 5%.

(c)   Zero rate (0%). For example, in the UK children's clothing and protective clothing, such as cycle helmets, are taxable at 0%.

Exam alert

In the exam you will be told the rates of VAT to apply. The tax rules are also released on the CIMA website prior to the exam. Make sure you check the website to see what they are:

www.cimaglobal.com/Students/2010-professional-qualification/Operational-level/F1-study-resources/

5.6 Partial exemption

Where an entity has wholly VAT exempt outputs (such as a bank or financial institution), it cannot reclaim any input VAT paid. This is in contrast to traders who have totally zero-rated outputs, such as farmers, who charge output VAT at 0% on their sales and are allowed to obtain a refund of all of their input tax.

However, where a business makes both taxable and exempt supplies, **partial exemption** applies. A number of schemes exist under which the input tax can be apportioned.

The simplest method is that any input tax wholly attributable to exempt outputs is not deductible, any input tax wholly attributable to taxable supplies is deductible in full and any remaining input tax is **apportioned** according to the percentage of exempt outputs.

For instance, if 30% of outputs were exempt, the trader would be able to deduct 70% (100% - 30%) of unallocated input tax.

Example: Partial exemption (1)

A has total sales of $700,000 before VAT. Purchases total $450,000 excluding VAT. The sales tax rate is 15% and 10% of the sales are exempt. How much VAT does A have to pay?

Solution

	$
Output tax (700,000 × 15%) × 90%	94,500
Input tax (450,000 × 15 %) × 90%	(60,750)
Amount payable	33,750

Example: Partial exemption (2)

B has total sales of $700,000 before VAT. Purchases total $450,000 excluding VAT. The VAT rate is 15%, 10% of the sales are exempt and 20% of inputs are directly related to these exempt supplies. How much VAT does B have to pay?

Solution

	$
Output tax (700,000 × 15%) × 90%	94,500
Input tax (450,000 × 15%) × 80% × 90%*	(48,600)
Amount payable	45,900

*The proportion related to exempt supplies (20%) is deducted and the remaining input tax is apportioned between taxable and exempt supplies.

> **Section summary**
>
> - VAT is a **multi-stage sales tax**. It is chargeable and deductible at different points in the supply chain.
>
> - VAT on sales is output tax. VAT on purchases is input tax.
>
> - There are usually three rates of VAT. These are **standard rate, higher or reduced rate** and the **zero rate**.
>
> - Some transactions are **exempt from VAT**. If a business carries out both exempt and taxable activities, then it will be able to recover a proportion of the input tax incurred on purchases.

6 Employee taxation

> **Introduction**
>
> Employees are liable to income tax on their employment income and are responsible for dealing with their own tax liabilities.

6.1 Taxable income

The amount of tax paid depends on the way that earnings are measured. In the UK, an employee is taxed on all income received from the employment in tax year including 'non-cash' items (called **benefits in kind**). Cash income includes basic and overtime pay, bonuses, commission and redundancy pay. Examples of benefits in kind include company cars, private health insurance, free accommodation and cheap loans from the employer.

6.2 Deductible expenses

Tax regimes often allow employees to deduct expenses from their earnings before the tax rate is applied. In the UK an employee can claim that expenses were incurred **wholly, exclusively and necessarily**, in the course of his or her employment. Examples of these expenses include professional subscriptions, business travel, charitable donations through a payroll deduction scheme and contributions to pension plans.

6.3 Employer as a tax collector (PAYE)   11/10, 5/11

Many tax regimes require the employer to deduct employee tax in instalments directly from the employee's pay and pay it over to the tax authorities. In the UK, this system is called 'PAYE' or 'Pay As You Earn'.

If the employee feels that he or she has paid too much tax, it is up to the individual to deal with the tax authority to obtain a refund. The employer merely acts as a tax collector.

While placing a burden on employers, a PAYE system has major advantages for the tax authorities:

- It ensures that employees comply with the tax rules.

- It makes it easier for governments to forecast tax revenues.

- It allows the tax to be collected earlier than would be the case if it were assessed on the employee's earnings at the end of the year, improving cash flows for the government.

- The costs of administering the system are borne by employers, rather than by the government.

- It greatly reduces the risks of default or late payment, helping the government to minimise the tax gap.

It also makes tax payment easier for individuals, who do not have to deal with a large bill once or twice a year.

6.4 Social security contributions

Some taxes are called **social security** contributions because, in theory, they are used to pay for social security items such as pensions. In fact, the money raised is used as part of the general tax revenue. However, it is politically more acceptable to raise social security contributions than to raise taxes. For example, the UK government added a 1% social security levy to pay for hospitals and their needs. In the UK the social security contribution is National Insurance. It is paid by both the employee and the employer.

Section summary

Employee taxation is personal tax; the employer acts as a tax collector.

Chapter Roundup

✓   Entities are subject to **direct taxes** on the **profits** and **capital gains** they generate.

✓   **Company income tax** is paid on the **taxable profit** of an entity. Taxable profit is the accounting profit adjusted according to the tax rules.

✓   Depreciation is not normally allowable for tax purposes. Instead, entities are allowed to deduct **tax depreciation** which is calculated based on the rules of the tax regime.

✓   When an asset is disposed of for more than its original cost, a **capital gain** arises that is subject to corporate tax. An **indexation allowance** may be given to counter the effects of inflation and reduce the gain chargeable to tax.

✓   **Trading losses** and **capital losses** can usually be **relieved** against profits and gains according to the rules of the tax regime.

✓   There are four main systems of taxing corporate income: **classical, imputation, partial imputation** and **split rate**.

✓   The classical system is much **simpler** but most countries do not use it.

✓   Where a company pays corporate income tax is determined by which country it is **resident** in.

✓   The OECD Model Tax Convention defines residence for an entity as being liable to tax in a country by reason of **place of incorporation, place of effective management** or by **place of permanent establishment.**

✓   If an entity operates in several countries, it could be deemed resident of all those countries, leading to **double taxation**.

✓   In such circumstances, the OECD Model Tax Convention deems companies to be resident in their **place of effective management**.

✓   Overseas subsidiary companies often remit dividends to their parent company. These payments will often have been subject to **withholding tax** and **underlying tax**. When the dividend is subsequently taxed as part of the parent company's income, it will have been **taxed twice.**

✓   **Double tax relief**, is often available in this situation. Relief may be given by **deduction, exemption** or **tax credit**.

✓   There are two types of indirect taxes: **unit taxes** and **ad valorem taxes**.

✓   VAT is a **multi-stage sales tax**. It is chargeable and deductible at different points in the supply chain.

✓   VAT on sales is output tax. VAT on purchases is input tax.

✓   There are usually three rates of VAT. These are **standard rate, higher or reduced rate** and the **zero rate**.

✓   Some transactions are **exempt from VAT**. If a business carries out both exempt and taxable activities, then it will be able to recover a proportion of the input tax incurred on purchases.

✓   Employee taxation is personal tax; the employer acts as a tax collector.

Quick Quiz

1   Complete the sentence:

Taxable profit is the .... adjusted according to the tax rules and is the amount on which .... is actually paid.

2   Value added tax (VAT) is an example of which kind of tax?

A   Unit tax
B   Ad valorem tax
C   Direct tax
D   Income tax

3   Peter is a VAT registered trader. In the quarter to 31 March 20X5 Peter sold goods for $40,000 (excluding VAT) and bought stock to sell for $17,900 (including VAT). Calculate Peter's output and input VAT for the quarter and his liability to the tax authorities. The rate of VAT is 17.5%.

4   A withholding tax is:

A tax withheld from the tax authorities   ☐

A tax deducted at source before payment of a dividend   ☐

5   Name three advantages to government of employee income tax deducted at source by employers.

6   Under the OECD Model Tax Convention an entity is considered to be resident in the country of its .... of ....

7   Complete the sentence:

A classical system of company income tax is one where an entity is taxable on all of its .... and .... whether they are .... or not.

Answers to Quick Quiz

1   Accounting profit; tax

2   B

3

	$
Output tax ($40,000 × 17.5%)	7,000
Input tax ($17,900 × 7/47)*	(2,666)
Net VAT payable	4,334

*17.5/117.5 = 7/47

4   A tax deducted at source before payment of a dividend.

5   •   It allows the tax to be collected earlier than would be the case if it were assessed on the employee's earnings at the end of the year.

•   The costs of administering the system are borne by employers, rather than by the government.

•   It greatly reduces the risks of default or late payment, helping government to minimise the tax gap.

6   Place of effective management.

7   Income; gains; distributed.

Answers to Questions

18.1 Taxable profit

		$'000	$'000
Accounting profit			195
Add: disallowable expenditure:	entertaining	75	
	depreciation	80	
	amortisation	50	
	political donation	25	
			230
Less: non-taxable income		100	
tax depreciation		100	
			(200)
Taxable profit			225

The tax rate is 30%, so the tax due is **$67,500** ($225,000 × 30%)

18.2 Tax depreciation

	Plant and machinery pool $'000	Total tax depreciation for the year $'000
Year ended 31 December 20X8		
Opening written down balance	100	
Writing down allowance @25%	(25)	(25)
Additions	30	
First year allowance at 50%	(15)	(15)
Closing written down balance	90	(40)
Year ended 31 December 20X9		
Opening written down balance	90	
Disposal	(7)	
Balancing charge (working)	2	2
	85	
Writing down allowance @25%	(21)	(21)
Closing written down balance	64	(19)

Working

	$
Purchase price of van	10,000
Tax depreciation allowed	(5,000)
Remaining value for tax purposes	5,000
Amount realised on disposal	(7,000)
Balancing charge (added to taxable profit)	(2,000)

Note that the balancing charge increases taxable profit and therefore decreases the amount of tax depreciation allowed in the year.

Now try these questions from the Exam Question Bank

Number	Level	Marks	Time
Q1	Examination	5	9 mins
Q3	Examination	5	9 mins
Q4	Examination	5	9 mins

IAS 12: INCOME TAXES

 This chapter considers the accounting treatment and disclosure requirements contained in IAS 12 *Income taxes* for current and deferred tax in company accounts.

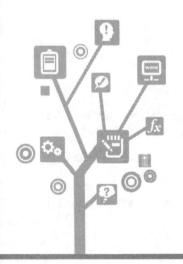

topic list	learning outcomes	syllabus references	ability required
1 Current tax	A4(a)	A4(i)	application
2 Deferred tax	A4(a)	A4(i)	application
3 Taxable temporary differences	A4(a)	A4(i)	application
4 Deductible temporary differences	A4(a)	A4(i)	application
5 Disclosure of taxation	A4(a)	A4(i)	application

1   Current tax

Introduction

IAS 12 uses the term *income taxes* to refer to taxes on profits and gains of an entity. IAS 12 considers both current and deferred tax. In this section we will look at current tax.

1.1 Current tax versus deferred tax

Before we go any further, let us be clear about the difference between current and deferred tax.

(a)   **Current tax** is the amount *actually payable* to the tax authorities in relation to the trading activities of the enterprise during the period.

(b)   **Deferred tax** is an *accounting measure*, used to match the tax effects of transactions with their accounting impact and thereby produce less distorted results.

You should understand this distinction a little better after working through section 2 of this chapter.

Exam alert

In your exam, current and deferred tax are highly examinable as section A and section B questions. They are also likely to feature as part of a longer question on the preparation of financial statements.

1.2 IAS 12 definitions

These are some of the important definitions given in IAS 12 relevant to current tax.

KEY TERMS

ACCOUNTING PROFIT. Net profit or loss for a period before deducting tax expense.

TAXABLE PROFIT (TAX LOSS). The profit (loss) for a period, determined in accordance with the rules established by the taxation authorities, upon which income taxes are payable (recoverable).

TAX EXPENSE (TAX INCOME). The aggregate amount included in the determination of net profit or loss for the period in respect of current tax and deferred tax.

CURRENT TAX. The amount of income taxes payable (recoverable) in respect of the taxable profit (tax loss) for a period.   *(IAS 12)*

1.3 Accounting entries   5/10, 11/10

You may have assumed until now that accounting for income tax was a very simple matter for companies. You would calculate the amount of tax due to be paid on the company's taxable profits and you would:

DEBIT   Tax charge (statement of comprehensive income)
CREDIT   Tax liability (statement of financial position)

with this amount.

However, it may take some time to finalise the company's accounts and therefore its tax liability.

Example: The company's tax charge for 20X5 is estimated at $55,000. The following entry is made in the financial statements:

DEBIT   Statement of comprehensive income (tax expense) $55,000
CREDIT   Statement of financial position (tax payable) $55,000

When the final tax liability is agreed with the tax authority, the amount payable is $58,000, and this amount is paid and posted as:

DEBIT	Statement of financial position (tax payable)	$58,000
CREDIT	Cash	$58,000

The account on the statement of financial position now has a DR balance of $3,000. This represents an **underprovision** of tax for 20X5. This tax has been paid but not charged to the statement of comprehensive income.

In the accounts for 20X6, this underprovision will be accounted for. If the estimated liability for 20X6 is $60,000, the following entries will be made:

DEBIT	Statement of comprehensive income	$60,000	*Being current tax*
		$3,000	*Being prior year underprovision*
CREDIT	Statement of financial position	$63,000	

The statement of financial position will now have a balance of $60,000, being the amount payable for the current year.

Complexities also arise when we consider the future tax consequences of what is going on in the accounts now. This is an aspect of tax called **deferred tax**, which we will look at in the next section.

1.3.1 Recognition of current tax liabilities and assets

IAS 12 requires any **unpaid tax** in respect of the current or prior periods to be recognised as a **liability**.

Conversely, any **excess tax** paid in respect of current or prior periods over what is due should be recognised as an asset.

Question 19.1
Tax charge and tax payable

Learning outcome A4(a)

In 20X8 Darton Co had taxable profits of $120,000. In the previous year (20X7) income tax on 20X7 profits had been estimated as $30,000. Tax is payable at 30%.

Required

Calculate tax payable and the charge for 20X8 if the tax due on 20X7 profits was subsequently agreed with the tax authorities as:

(a) $35,000; or
(b) $25,000.

Any under or over payments are not settled until the following year's tax payment is due.

Taking this a stage further, IAS 12 also requires recognition as an asset of the benefit relating to any tax loss that can be **carried back** to recover current tax of a previous period. This is acceptable because it is probable that the benefit will flow to the entity *and* it can be reliably measured.

Example: tax losses carried back

In 20X7 Eramu Co paid $50,000 in tax on its profits. In 20X8 the company made tax losses of $24,000. The local tax authority rules allow losses to be carried back to offset against current tax of prior years.

Required

Show the tax charge and tax liability for 20X8.

Solution

Tax repayment due on tax losses = 30% × $24,000 = $7,200.

The double entry will be:

| DEBIT | Tax receivable (statement of financial position) | $7,200 |
| CREDIT | Tax repayment (statement of comprehensive income) | $7,200 |

The tax receivable will be shown as an asset until the repayment is received from the tax authorities.

1.3.2 Presentation of current tax assets and liabilities

In the statement of financial position, current **tax assets and liabilities** should be shown separately from other assets and liabilities.

Current tax assets and liabilities can be **offset**, but this should happen only when certain conditions apply:

(a) The entity has a **legally enforceable right** to set off the recognised amounts.

(b) The entity intends to settle the amounts on a **net basis**, or to realise the asset and settle the liability at the same time.

The **tax expense (income)** related to the profit or loss should be shown in the statement of comprehensive income. Remember that the tax expense will include the tax charge for the year, any under or overprovision of income tax from the previous year and any increase or decrease in the deferred tax provision.

The **disclosure requirements** of IAS 12 are extensive and we will look at these later in the chapter.

Section summary

- Taxation consists of two components: current and deferred tax.

- Current tax is the amount actually payable to the tax authorities in relation to the trading activities of the entity during the period.

2 Deferred tax   5/10, 11/10, 5/11

Introduction

Deferred tax is an accounting measure used to match the tax effects of transactions with their accounting impact. It does *not* represent tax payable to the tax authorities. Deferred tax is quite complex so read this section carefully working through all the examples.

Exam alert

Students invariably find deferred tax very confusing. You are unlikely to be asked any very complicated questions on deferred tax in this paper, so concentrate on understanding and being able to explain the purpose of deferred tax and carry out basic calculations.

2.1 What is deferred tax?

Deferred tax is an **accounting adjustment**. It is not a tax which is paid to the tax authorities. Deferred tax arises because the accounting treatment of a transaction is different to the tax treatment of the transaction. Some of these differences are **permanent** and some of these differences are **temporary**. Permanent differences, for example, are expenses that are included in the income statement (eg entertaining, donations to political parties) but which will never be deductible for tax purposes. Temporary differences arise because of timing differences between the tax treatment and the accounting treatment, for example, items that are accounted for on an accruals basis for the financial statements, but are treated on a cash basis when calculating the tax due.

Deferred tax is the tax attributable to temporary differences.

2.2 Definitions

Here are the definitions relating to deferred tax given in IAS 12.

KEY TERMS

DEFERRED TAX LIABILITIES are the amounts of income taxes payable in future periods in respect of taxable temporary differences.

DEFERRED TAX ASSETS are the amounts of income taxes recoverable in future periods in respect of:

- Deductible temporary differences
- The carry forward of unused tax losses
- The carry forward of unused tax credits

TEMPORARY DIFFERENCES are differences between the carrying amount of an asset or liability in the statement of financial position and its tax base. Temporary differences may be either:

- TAXABLE TEMPORARY DIFFERENCES, which are temporary differences that will result in taxable amounts in determining taxable profit (tax loss) of future periods when the carrying amount of the asset or liability is recovered or settled

- DEDUCTIBLE TEMPORARY DIFFERENCES, which are temporary differences that will result in amounts that are deductible in determining taxable profit (tax loss) of future periods when the carrying amount of the asset or liability is recovered or settled

The TAX BASE of an asset or liability is the amount attributed to that asset or liability for tax purposes.

(IAS 12)

So to summarise: deferred tax is the tax attributable to **temporary differences**. Temporary differences are the differences between the **carrying amount** of an asset or liability in the financial statements and the **tax base** of an asset or liability. There are two types of temporary differences: **taxable temporary differences** which lead to **deferred tax liabilities**, and **deductible temporary differences** which lead to **deferred tax assets**.

The procedure to follow in calculating deferred tax is as follows.

 Identify situations where the tax treatment is **different** from the accounting treatment.

 Work out whether the differences caused by the tax treatment and the accounting treatment result in a **temporary or permanent difference**. If the difference is permanent, there will be no deferred tax.

 If the difference is **temporary**: work out the tax base of the asset or liability (ie the carrying value according to the tax authorities) and compare it to the carrying value in the financial statements. This is the temporary difference.

Calculate the deferred tax liability or asset: **temporary difference × tax rate**.

Now we need to look at some of the definitions in IAS 12 in more detail.

2.3 Tax base

2.3.1 Assets

The tax base of an asset is its value for tax purposes.

This is the amount that will be deductible for tax purposes against any taxable economic benefits that will flow to the entity when it recovers the carrying value of the asset. Where those economic benefits are not taxable, the tax base of the asset is the same as its carrying amount.

Question 19.2	Tax base (1)

Learning outcome A4(a)

State the tax base of each of the following assets.

(a)   A machine cost $10,000. For tax purposes, depreciation of $3,000 has already been deducted in the current and prior periods and the remaining cost will be deductible in future periods, either as depreciation or through a deduction on disposal. Revenue generated by using the machine is taxable, any gain on disposal of the machine will be taxable and any loss on disposal will be deductible for tax purposes.

(b)   Interest receivable has a carrying amount of $1,000. The related interest revenue will be taxed on a cash basis (ie when it is received).

(c)   Trade receivables have a carrying amount of $10,000. The related revenue has already been included in taxable profit (tax loss).

(d)   A loan receivable has a carrying amount of $1m. The repayment of the loan will have no tax consequences.

2.3.2 Liabilities

In the case of a liability, the tax base will be its carrying amount, less any amount that will be deducted for tax purposes in relation to the liability in future periods. For revenue received in advance, the tax base of the resulting liability is its carrying amount, less any amount of the revenue that will *not* be taxable in future periods.

Question 19.3	Tax base (2)

Learning outcome A4(a)

State the tax base of each of the following liabilities.

(a)   Current liabilities include accrued expenses with a carrying amount of $1,000. The related expense will be deducted for tax purposes on a cash basis.

(b)   Current liabilities include interest revenue received in advance, with a carrying amount of $10,000. The related interest revenue was taxed on a cash basis.

(c)   Current liabilities include accrued expenses with a carrying amount of $2,000. The related expense has already been deducted for tax purposes.

(d)   Current liabilities include accrued fines and penalties with a carrying amount of $100. Fines and penalties are not deductible for tax purposes.

(e)   A loan payable has a carrying amount of $1m. The repayment of the loan will have no tax consequences.

IAS 12 gives the following examples of circumstances in which the carrying amount of an asset or liability will be **equal to its tax base**.

*   **Accrued expenses** which have already been deducted in determining an enterprise's current tax liability for the current or earlier periods.

*   A **loan payable** is measured at the amount originally received and this amount is the same as the amount repayable on final maturity of the loan.

*   **Accrued expenses** which will never be deductible for tax purposes.

*   **Accrued income** will never be taxable.

2.4 Temporary differences

You may have found the definition of temporary differences somewhat confusing. Remember that accounting profits form the basis for computing **taxable profits**, on which the tax liability for the year is calculated, however, accounting profits and taxable profits are different. There are two reasons for the differences.

(a)   **Permanent differences**. These occur when certain items of revenue or expense are excluded from the computation of taxable profits (for example, entertainment expenses may not be allowable for tax purposes).

(b)   **Temporary differences**. These occur when items of revenue or expense are included in both accounting profits and taxable profits, but not for the same accounting period. For example, an expense which is allowable as a deduction in arriving at taxable profits for 20X7 might not be included in the financial statements until 20X8 or later. In the long run, the total taxable profits and total accounting profits will be the same (except for permanent differences) so that timing differences originate in one period and are capable of reversal in one or more subsequent periods. **Deferred tax** is the tax attributable to **temporary differences.**

The distinction made in the definition between **taxable temporary differences** and **deductible temporary differences** can be made clearer by looking at the explanations and examples given in IAS 12 and its appendices.

Exam skills

You should understand the difference between **permanent** and **temporary differences**.

Section summary

*   Deferred tax is an **accounting device**. It does *not* represent tax payable to the tax authorities.
*   The **tax base** of an asset or liability is the value of that asset or liability for tax purposes.
*   Deferred tax is the tax attributable to **temporary differences**.

3 Taxable temporary differences

Introduction

In this section we will see how deferred tax assets and liabilities arise from taxable and deductible temporary differences.

3.1 Taxable temporary differences

KEY POINT

The rule to remember is that:

'A taxable temporary difference gives rise to a deferred tax liability.'

3.2 Examples

The following are examples of circumstances that give rise to taxable temporary differences.

(a) **Interest revenue** received in arrears and included in accounting profit on the basis of time apportionment. It is included in taxable profit, however, on a cash basis.

(b) **Depreciation** of an asset is accelerated for tax purposes. When new assets are purchased, allowances may be available against taxable profits which exceed the amount of depreciation chargeable on the assets in the financial accounts for the year of purchase.

(c) **Development costs** which have been capitalised will be amortised in the statement of comprehensive income, but they were deducted in full from taxable profit in the period in which they were incurred.

Try to **understand the reasoning** behind the recognition of deferred tax liabilities on taxable temporary differences.

(a) When an **asset is recognised**, it is expected that its carrying amount will be recovered in the form of economic benefits that flow to the entity in future periods.

(b) If the carrying amount of the asset is **greater than** its tax base, then taxable economic benefits will also be greater than the amount that will be allowed as a deduction for tax purposes.

(c) The difference is therefore a **taxable temporary difference** and the obligation to pay the resulting income taxes in future periods is a **deferred tax liability**.

(d) As the entity recovers the carrying amount of the asset, the taxable temporary difference will **reverse** and the entity will have taxable profit.

(e) It is then probable that economic benefits will flow from the entity in the form of **tax payments**, and so the recognition of all deferred tax liabilities (except those excluded above) is required by IAS 12.

Example: taxable temporary differences

A company purchased an asset costing $1,500. At the end of 20X8 the carrying amount is $1,000. The cumulative depreciation for tax purposes is $900 and the current tax rate is 25%.

Required

Calculate the deferred tax liability for the asset.

LEARNING MEDIA

Solution

Firstly, what is the tax base of the asset? It is $1,500 – $900 = $600.

In order to recover the carrying value of $1,000, the entity must earn taxable income of $1,000, but it will only be able to deduct $600 as a taxable expense in the future as this is the tax base of the asset. The entity must therefore pay income tax of $400 × 25% = $100 when the carrying value of the asset is recovered.

The entity must therefore recognise a deferred tax liability of $400 × 25% = $100, recognising the difference between the carrying amount of $1,000 and the tax base of $600 as a taxable temporary difference.

3.3 Accounting entries

The double entry to account for the creation or increase in a deferred tax provision is as follows:

DEBIT   Statement of comprehensive income (tax expense)
CREDIT   Statement of financial position (deferred tax provision)

To account for the decrease in a deferred tax provision:

DEBIT   Statement of financial position (deferred tax provision)
CREDIT   Statement of comprehensive income (tax expense)

3.4 Timing differences   5/10

Some temporary differences are often called **timing differences**, when income or expense is included in accounting profit in one period, but is included in taxable profit in a different period. The main types of taxable temporary differences which are timing differences and which result in deferred tax liabilities are included in the examples given below.

- **Interest received** which is accounted for on an accruals basis, but which for tax purposes is included on a cash basis.

- **Accelerated depreciation** for tax purposes.

- Capitalised and amortised **development costs**.

Question 19.4   Current and deferred tax

Learning outcome A4(a)

Jonquil Co buys equipment for $50,000 at the beginning of 20X1 and depreciates it on a straight line basis over its expected useful life of five years. For tax purposes, the equipment is depreciated at 25% per annum on a straight line basis. Tax losses may be carried back against taxable profit of the previous five years. In year 20X0, the entity's taxable profit was $25,000. The tax rate is 40%.

Required

Assuming nil profits/losses after depreciation in years 20X1 to 20X5 show the current and deferred tax impact in years 20X1 to 20X5 of the acquisition of the equipment.

Exam alert

Questions on deferred tax in your exam will probably not be complex and are likely to just be on depreciation/tax depreciation. So make sure you understand the question above.

Section summary

- With one or two exceptions, all taxable temporary differences give rise to a **deferred tax liability**.

- Many taxable temporary differences are **timing differences**.

- Timing differences arise when income or an expense is included in accounting profit in one period, but in taxable profit in a **different period**.

4 Deductible temporary differences

Introduction

In this section we look at what deductible temporary differences are, and how they give rise to a deferred tax asset.

4.1 Definition

KEY POINT

The rule to remember is that:

'A deductible temporary difference gives rise to a deferred tax asset'.

However, the deferred tax asset must also satisfy the **recognition criteria** given in IAS 12. This is that a deferred tax asset should be recognised for all deductible temporary differences to the extent that it is **probable that taxable profit will be available** against which it can be utilised. This is an application of prudence.

4.2 Deductible temporary differences

Let us consider some examples of deductible temporary differences:

(a) **Retirement benefit costs** (pension costs) are deducted from accounting profit as service is provided by the employee. They are not deducted in determining taxable profit until the entity pays either retirement benefits or contributions to a fund. (This may also apply to similar expenses.)

(b) **Accumulated depreciation** of an asset in the financial statements is greater than the accumulated depreciation allowed for tax purposes up to the balance sheet date.

(c) **Research costs** (or organisation/other start-up costs) are recognised as an expense for accounting purposes but are not deductible against taxable profits until a later period.

(d) Income is **deferred** in the statement of financial position, but has already been included in taxable profit in current/prior periods.

Example: Deductible temporary differences

Pargatha Co recognises a liability of $10,000 for accrued product warranty costs on 31 December 20X7. These product warranty costs will not be deductible for tax purposes until the entity pays claims. The tax rate is 25%.

Required

State the deferred tax implications of this situation.

Solution

What is the tax base of the liability? It is nil (carrying amount of $10,000 less the amount that will be deductible for tax purposes in respect of the liability in future periods).

When the liability is settled for its carrying amount, the entity's future taxable profit will be reduced by $10,000 and so its future tax payments by $10,000 × 25% = $2,500.

The difference of $10,000 between the carrying amount ($10,000) and the tax base (nil) is a deductible temporary difference. The entity should therefore recognise a deferred tax asset of $10,000 × 25% = $2,500 **provided that** it is probable that the entity will earn sufficient taxable profits in future periods to benefit from a reduction in tax payments.

4.3 Tax losses

An entity may have tax losses that it can carry forward to deduct against **future** taxable profits. IAS 12 requires that these tax credits be recognised as deferred tax assets where it is probable that the entity will generate future taxable profits against which they can offset the losses.

Section summary

- Deductible temporary differences give rise to a **deferred tax asset**.
- **Prudence** dictates that deferred tax assets can only be recognised when **sufficient future taxable profits** exist against which they can be utilised.

5 **Disclosure of taxation**   5/10

Introduction

IAS 12 contains rules for and disclosure of taxation items. In this section we look at the key disclosure requirements.

As you would expect, the major components of tax expense or income should be disclosed separately.

These will generally include the following.

(a) The major components of tax expense, eg:

	$
Current tax expense	X
Under/overprovisions relating to prior periods	X/(X)
Increases/decreases in the deferred tax balance	X/(X)
	X

(b) Tax expense relating to discontinued operations

(c) An explanation of the difference between accounting and taxable profits

(d) Details of temporary differences and the deferred tax assets/liabilities recognised in relation to them.

Example of tax presentation

Alpha has a balance brought forward on current tax of $5,000,000. Tax paid during the period was $4,900,000 and the provision for the period is $3,000,000.

Alpha also has a balance brought forward on deferred tax of $2,600,000. The charge to the statement of comprehensive income for the period is $400,000.

Draw up the current and deferred tax accounts for the accounting period and show the disclosure in the statement of comprehensive income and statement of financial position.

Solution

CURRENT TAX

	$		$
Bank account	4,900,000	Bal b/f	5,000,000
Bal c/f	3,000,000	Statement of comprehensive income	2,900,000
	7,900,000		7,900,000
		Bal c/f	3,000,000

DEFERRED TAX

	$		$
Bal c/f	3,000,000	Bal b/f	2,600,000
		Statement of comprehensive income	400,000
	3,000,000		3,000,000
		Bal c/f	3,000,000

STATEMENT OF COMPREHENSIVE INCOME (EXTRACT)

Tax (Note 1)	3,300,000

STATEMENT OF FINANCIAL POSITION (EXTRACT)

Current liabilities	
Tax payable	3,000,000
Non current liabilities	
Deferred tax (Note 2)	3,000,000

Notes to the accounts

1   *Tax expense*

	$
Bal b/f	(5,000,000)
Tax paid	4,900,000
Tax for current period	3,000,000
Increase in deferred tax	400,000
Statement of comprehensive income	3,300,000

2   *Deferred tax*

	$
Bal b/f	2,600,000
Increase in period	400,000
	3,000,000

Section summary

Deferred tax assets and liabilities must be presented separately from other assets and liabilities in the statement of financial position.

Chapter Roundup

✓   Taxation consists of **two components**: current tax and deferred tax.

✓   Current tax is the amount actually payable to the tax authorities in relation to the trading activities of the enterprise during the period.

✓   Deferred tax is an **accounting device**. It does *not* represent tax payable to the tax authorities.

✓   The tax base of an asset or liability is the value of that asset or liability for tax purposes.

✓   Deferred tax is the attributable to **temporary differences**.

✓   With one or two exceptions, all taxable temporary differences give rise to a **deferred tax liability**.

✓   Many taxable temporary differences are **timing differences**.

✓   Timing differences arise when income or an expense is included in accounting profit in one period, but in taxable profit in a **different period**.

✓   Deductible temporary differences give rise to a **deferred tax asset**.

✓   **Prudence** dictates that deferred tax assets can only be recognised when sufficient future taxable profits exist against which they can be utilised.

✓   Deferred tax assets and liabilities must be presented separately from other assets and liabilities in the statement of financial position.

Quick Quiz

1   The tax expense related to the profit from ordinary activities should be shown in the statement of comprehensive income.

    True ☐

    False ☐

2   Deferred tax liabilities are the amounts of income taxes payable in future periods in respect of
    ....

3   Give three examples of taxable temporary differences.

4   Current tax is the amount of income tax payable in respect of the .... for a period.

5   Deductible temporary differences give rise to a:

    A   Deferred tax asset
    B   Deferred tax liability

Answers to Quick Quiz

1   True

2   Taxable temporary differences

3   Examples are:

- Interest revenue
- Depreciation
- Development costs
- Prepayments
- Sale of goods revenue

4   Taxable profit

5   A

Answers to Questions

19.1 Tax charge and tax payable

(a)

	$
Tax due on 20X8 profits ($120,000 × 30%)	36,000
Underpayment for 20X7	5,000
Tax charge and liability	41,000

(b)

	$
Tax due on 20X8 profits (as above)	36,000
Overpayment for 20X7	(5,000)
Tax charge and liability	31,000

Alternatively, the rebate due could be shown separately as income in the statement of comprehensive income and as an asset in the statement of financial position. An offset approach like this is, however, most likely.

19.2 Tax base (1)

(a)   The tax base of the machine is $7,000.
(b)   The tax base of the interest receivable is nil.
(c)   The tax base of the trade receivables is $10,000.
(d)   The tax base of the loan is $1m.

19.3 Tax base (2)

(a)   The tax base of the accrued expenses is nil.
(b)   The tax base of the interest received in advance is nil.
(c)   The tax base of the accrued expenses is $2,000.
(d)   The tax base of the accrued fines and penalties is $100.
(e)   The tax base of the loan is $1m.

19.4 Current and deferred tax

Jonquil Co will recover the carrying amount of the equipment by using it to manufacture goods for resale. Therefore, the entity's current tax computation is as follows.

	Year				
	20X1	20X2	20X3	20X4	20X5
Accounting profit	0	0	0	0	0
Add back depreciation	10,000	10,000	10,000	10,000	10,000
Taxable income	10,000	10,000	10,000	10,000	10,000
Depreciation for tax purposes	(12,500)	(12,500)	(12,500)	(12,500)	0
(Tax loss)/Taxable profit	(2,500)	(2,500)	(2,500)	(2,500)	10,000
Current tax (income)/expense at 40%	(1,000)	(1,000)	(1,000)	(1,000)	4,000

The temporary differences associated with the equipment and the resulting deferred tax asset and liability and deferred tax expense and income are as follows.

	Year				
	20X1	20X2	20X3	20X4	20X5
Carrying amount	40,000	30,000	20,000	10,000	0
Tax base	37,500	25,000	12,500	0	0
Taxable temporary difference	2,500	5,000	7,500	10,000	0
Opening deferred tax liability	0	1,000	2,000	3,000	4,000
Deferred tax expense/(income): bal fig	1,000	1,000	1,000	1,000	(4,000)
Closing deferred tax liability @ 40%	1,000	2,000	3,000	4,000	0

The entity recognises the **deferred tax liability** in years 20X1 to 20X4 because the reversal of the taxable temporary difference will create taxable income in subsequent years. The entity's income statement is as follows.

	Year				
	$	$	$	$	$
Income	10,000	10,000	10,000	10,000	10,000
Depreciation	10,000	10,000	10,000	10,000	10,000
Profit before tax	0	0	0	0	0
Current tax expense (income)	(1,000)	(1,000)	(1,000)	(1,000)	4,000
Deferred tax expense (income)	1,000	1,000	1,000	1,000	(4,000)
Total tax expense (income)	0	0	0	0	0
Net profit for the period	0	0	0	0	0

Now try these questions from the Exam Question Bank	Number	Level	Marks	Time
	Q2	Examination	5	9 mins
	Q5	Examination	5	9 mins
	Q24	Examination	5	9 mins

BPP LEARNING MEDIA

APPENDIX

MATHS TABLES AND FORMULAE

Present value table

Present value of $1, that is $(1 + r)^{-n}$ where r = interest rate; n = number of periods until payment or receipt.

Periods (n)	Interest rates (r)									
	1%	2%	3%	4%	5%	6%	7%	8%	9%	10%
1	0.990	0.980	0.971	0.962	0.952	0.943	0.935	0.926	0.917	0.909
2	0.980	0.961	0.943	0.925	0.907	0.890	0.873	0.857	0.842	0.826
3	0.971	0.942	0.915	0.889	0.864	0.840	0.816	0.794	0.772	0.751
4	0.961	0.924	0.888	0.855	0.823	0.792	0.763	0.735	0.708	0.683
5	0.951	0.906	0.863	0.822	0.784	0.747	0.713	0.681	0.650	0.621
6	0.942	0.888	0.837	0.790	0.746	0.705	0.666	0.630	0.596	0.564
7	0.933	0.871	0.813	0.760	0.711	0.665	0.623	0.583	0.547	0.513
8	0.923	0.853	0.789	0.731	0.677	0.627	0.582	0.540	0.502	0.467
9	0.914	0.837	0.766	0.703	0.645	0.592	0.544	0.500	0.460	0.424
10	0.905	0.820	0.744	0.676	0.614	0.558	0.508	0.463	0.422	0.386
11	0.896	0.804	0.722	0.650	0.585	0.527	0.475	0.429	0.388	0.350
12	0.887	0.788	0.701	0.625	0.557	0.497	0.444	0.397	0.356	0.319
13	0.879	0.773	0.681	0.601	0.530	0.469	0.415	0.368	0.326	0.290
14	0.870	0.758	0.661	0.577	0.505	0.442	0.388	0.340	0.299	0.263
15	0.861	0.743	0.642	0.555	0.481	0.417	0.362	0.315	0.275	0.239
16	0.853	0.728	0.623	0.534	0.458	0.394	0.339	0.292	0.252	0.218
17	0.844	0.714	0.605	0.513	0.436	0.371	0.317	0.270	0.231	0.198
18	0.836	0.700	0.587	0.494	0.416	0.350	0.296	0.250	0.212	0.180
19	0.828	0.686	0.570	0.475	0.396	0.331	0.277	0.232	0.194	0.164
20	0.820	0.673	0.554	0.456	0.377	0.312	0.258	0.215	0.178	0.149

Periods (n)	Interest rates (r)									
	11%	12%	13%	14%	15%	16%	17%	18%	19%	20%
1	0.901	0.893	0.885	0.877	0.870	0.862	0.855	0.847	0.840	0.833
2	0.812	0.797	0.783	0.769	0.756	0.743	0.731	0.718	0.706	0.694
3	0.731	0.712	0.693	0.675	0.658	0.641	0.624	0.609	0.593	0.579
4	0.659	0.636	0.613	0.592	0.572	0.552	0.534	0.516	0.499	0.482
5	0.593	0.567	0.543	0.519	0.497	0.476	0.456	0.437	0.419	0.402
6	0.535	0.507	0.480	0.456	0.432	0.410	0.390	0.370	0.352	0.335
7	0.482	0.452	0.425	0.400	0.376	0.354	0.333	0.314	0.296	0.279
8	0.434	0.404	0.376	0.351	0.327	0.305	0.285	0.266	0.249	0.233
9	0.391	0.361	0.333	0.308	0.284	0.263	0.243	0.225	0.209	0.194
10	0.352	0.322	0.295	0.270	0.247	0.227	0.208	0.191	0.176	0.162
11	0.317	0.287	0.261	0.237	0.215	0.195	0.178	0.162	0.148	0.135
12	0.286	0.257	0.231	0.208	0.187	0.168	0.152	0.137	0.124	0.112
13	0.258	0.229	0.204	0.182	0.163	0.145	0.130	0.116	0.104	0.093
14	0.232	0.205	0.181	0.160	0.141	0.125	0.111	0.099	0.088	0.078
15	0.209	0.183	0.160	0.140	0.123	0.108	0.095	0.084	0.079	0.065
16	0.188	0.163	0.141	0.123	0.107	0.093	0.081	0.071	0.062	0.054
17	0.170	0.146	0.125	0.108	0.093	0.080	0.069	0.060	0.052	0.045
18	0.153	0.130	0.111	0.095	0.081	0.069	0.059	0.051	0.044	0.038
19	0.138	0.116	0.098	0.083	0.070	0.060	0.051	0.043	0.037	0.031
20	0.124	0.104	0.087	0.073	0.061	0.051	0.043	0.037	0.031	0.026

Cumulative present value of $1 per annum, Receivable or Payable at the end of each year for n years $\dfrac{1-(1+r)^{-n}}{r}$

Periods (n)	Interest rates (r)									
	1%	2%	3%	4%	5%	6%	7%	8%	9%	10%
1	0.990	0.980	0.971	0.962	0.952	0.943	0.935	0.926	0.917	0.909
2	1.970	1.942	1.913	1.886	1.859	1.833	1.808	1.783	1.759	1.736
3	2.941	2.884	2.829	2.775	2.723	2.673	2.624	2.577	2.531	2.487
4	3.902	3.808	3.717	3.630	3.546	3.465	3.387	3.312	3.240	3.170
5	4.853	4.713	4.580	4.452	4.329	4.212	4.100	3.993	3.890	3.791
6	5.795	5.601	5.417	5.242	5.076	4.917	4.767	4.623	4.486	4.355
7	6.728	6.472	6.230	6.002	5.786	5.582	5.389	5.206	5.033	4.868
8	7.652	7.325	7.020	6.733	6.463	6.210	5.971	5.747	5.535	5.335
9	8.566	8.162	7.786	7.435	7.108	6.802	6.515	6.247	5.995	5.759
10	9.471	8.983	8.530	8.111	7.722	7.360	7.024	6.710	6.418	6.145
11	10.368	9.787	9.253	8.760	8.306	7.887	7.499	7.139	6.805	6.495
12	11.255	10.575	9.954	9.385	8.863	8.384	7.943	7.536	7.161	6.814
13	12.134	11.348	10.635	9.986	9.394	8.853	8.358	7.904	7.487	7.103
14	13.004	12.106	11.296	10.563	9.899	9.295	8.745	8.244	7.786	7.367
15	13.865	12.849	11.938	11.118	10.380	9.712	9.108	8.559	8.061	7.606
16	14.718	13.578	12.561	11.652	10.838	10.106	9.447	8.851	8.313	7.824
17	15.562	14.292	13.166	12.166	11.274	10.477	9.763	9.122	8.544	8.022
18	16.398	14.992	13.754	12.659	11.690	10.828	10.059	9.372	8.756	8.201
19	17.226	15.679	14.324	13.134	12.085	11.158	10.336	9.604	8.950	8.365
20	18.046	16.351	14.878	13.590	12.462	11.470	10.594	9.818	9.129	8.514

Periods (n)	Interest rates (r)									
	11%	12%	13%	14%	15%	16%	17%	18%	19%	20%
1	0.901	0.893	0.885	0.877	0.870	0.862	0.855	0.847	0.840	0.833
2	1.713	1.690	1.668	1.647	1.626	1.605	1.585	1.566	1.547	1.528
3	2.444	2.402	2.361	2.322	2.283	2.246	2.210	2.174	2.140	2.106
4	3.102	3.037	2.974	2.914	2.855	2.798	2.743	2.690	2.639	2.589
5	3.696	3.605	3.517	3.433	3.352	3.274	3.199	3.127	3.058	2.991
6	4.231	4.111	3.998	3.889	3.784	3.685	3.589	3.498	3.410	3.326
7	4.712	4.564	4.423	4.288	4.160	4.039	3.922	3.812	3.706	3.605
8	5.146	4.968	4.799	4.639	4.487	4.344	4.207	4.078	3.954	3.837
9	5.537	5.328	5.132	4.946	4.772	4.607	4.451	4.303	4.163	4.031
10	5.889	5.650	5.426	5.216	5.019	4.833	4.659	4.494	4.339	4.192
11	6.207	5.938	5.687	5.453	5.234	5.029	4.836	4.656	4.486	4.327
12	6.492	6.194	5.918	5.660	5.421	5.197	4.988	7.793	4.611	4.439
13	6.750	6.424	6.122	5.842	5.583	5.342	5.118	4.910	4.715	4.533
14	6.982	6.628	6.302	6.002	5.724	5.468	5.229	5.008	4.802	4.611
15	7.191	6.811	6.462	6.142	5.847	5.575	5.324	5.092	4.876	4.675
16	7.379	6.974	6.604	6.265	5.954	5.668	5.405	5.162	4.938	4.730
17	7.549	7.120	6.729	6.373	6.047	5.749	5.475	5.222	4.990	4.775
18	7.702	7.250	6.840	6.467	6.128	5.818	5.534	5.273	5.033	4.812
19	7.839	7.366	6.938	6.550	6.198	5.877	5.584	5.316	5.070	4.843
20	7.963	7.469	7.025	6.623	6.259	5.929	5.628	5.353	5.101	4.870

Formulae

Annuity

Present value of an annuity of $1 per annum, receivable or payable for n years, commencing in one year, discounted at r% per annum:

$$PV = \frac{1}{r}\left[1 - \frac{1}{[1 + r]^n}\right]$$

Perpetuity

Present value of $1 per annum, payable or receivable in perpetuity, commencing in one year, discounted at r% per annum:

$$PV = \frac{1}{r}$$

OBJECTIVE TEST QUESTION AND ANSWER BANK

390

1   A company makes an accounting profit of $300,000 during the year. This includes non-taxable income of $50,000 and book depreciation of $30,000. In addition, expenses of $25,000 are disallowable for tax purposes. If the tax allowable depreciation totals $24,000, what is the taxable profit?

    A $279,000
    B $281,000
    C $319,000
    D $321,000

2   A company has sales of $200,000, excluding sales tax, in a period. Its purchases, excluding sales tax, total $150,000. It has no zero-rated sales but 20% of its purchases are zero-rated. Sales tax is 17.5%. What is the sales tax payable for the period?

    A $7,447
    B $8,750
    C $14,000
    D $29,750

3   Define the accruals basis of accounting in no more than 35 words.

4   When carrying out an audit an external auditor must satisfy himself of a number of matters. Which one of the following is not one of those matters?

    A   The accounts have been prepared by a qualified accountant
    B   Adequate accounting records have been kept
    C   The accounts have been prepared in accordance with the legislation
    D   The accounts are in agreement with accounting records

5   According to the IASB *Framework* the qualitative characteristics of financial statements are

    A   Understandability, consistency, reliability and going concern
    B   Understandability, prudence, reliability and relevance
    C   Understandability, relevance, reliability and comparability
    D   Prudence, consistency, relevance and accruals

6   T purchases production machinery costing $200,000 and having an estimated useful life of 20 years with a residual value of $4,000. After being in use for 6 years the remaining useful life of the machinery is revised and estimated to be 25 years, with an unchanged residual value. The annual depreciation charge after these events is $......................

7   Fill in the two series of missing words.

    An asset is a resource controlled by an entity as a result of .... and from which .... are expected to flow to the entity.

8   IAS 37 *Provisions, contingent liabilities and contingent assets* requires that material contingencies, other than those where the probability of the outcome is remote, existing at the end of the reporting period should be treated as follows.

    A   Contingent assets and contingent liabilities must always be either accrued or disclosed in the financial statements

    B   Contingent liabilities must always be accrued and contingent assets must always be disclosed in the financial statements

    C   Contingent liabilities must always be either accrued or disclosed and contingent assets must always be disclosed in the financial statements

    D   Neither contingent assets nor contingent liabilities can be accrued in the financial statements

9   A company purchases a new machine and the costs involved in this are given below.

	$
Purchase price	680,000
Delivery costs	30,000
Installation costs	80,000
Cleaning costs after first production run	4,000

At what figure would the machine initially be included in the statement of financial position?
$........................

10   Which of the following is a source of tax rules?

A   International accounting standards
B   Local company legislation
C   Local tax legislation
D   Domestic accounting practice

11   H has prepared its financial statements for the year ending 30 June 20X8. On 15 July a major fraud was uncovered by the auditors which had taken place during the year to 30 June. On 31 July the company made a large loan stock issue which has significantly increased the company's gearing level.

In accordance with IAS 10 *Events after the reporting period*, how should the two events be treated in the financial statements?

	Fraud	Loan stock issue
A	Accrued in accounts	Disclosed in notes
B	Accrued in accounts	Accrued in accounts
C	Disclosed in notes	Disclosed in notes
D	Disclosed in notes	Accrued in accounts

12   F. Co. estimates its tax due for the year ended 30 June 20X8 to be $520,000. Tax for the year ended 30 June 20X7 was estimated at $475,000 and eventually settled at $503,000. A taxable temporary difference of $76,000 has arisen during the year due to accelerated tax allowances. The tax rate is 30%.

What is the tax charge in the statement of comprehensive income for the year ended 30 June 20X8?

A $520,000
B $542,800
C $548,000
D $570,800

13   According to IAS 36 *Impairment of assets* what is the recoverable amount of a non-current asset?

A   Net selling price
B   Value in use
C   The higher of net selling price and value in use
D   The lower of net selling price and value in use

14   Which of the following types of research and development expenditure must be written off in the year it is incurred?

A   Market research costs confirming the ultimate commercial viability of a product
B   Legal costs in connection with registration of a patent
C   Costs of searching for possible alternative products
D   Costs of research work which are to be reimbursed by a customer

15 If an auditor believes an item in the financial statements is materially misstated and he considers that the effect on the financial statements is *material,* but not *pervasive*, what type of audit opinion would be issued?

    A   Unmodified opinion
    B   Qualified opinion
    C   Disclaimer of opinion
    D   Adverse opinion

16 Which of the following statements are true with regards to an ethical code.

    1   A code based on a set of principles rather than rules is more flexible in a rapidly changing environment

    2   The CIMA *Code of ethics for professional accountants* is principles based

    3   A code based on a set of rules requires accountants to evaluate and address threats to independence

    A   2 only
    B   1 and 2 only
    C   2 and 3 only
    D   1, 2 and 3

17 A provision for the cost of removing pollution arising from a company's operations should be recognised if?

    A   The accounts would reveal an understated net profit figure without the provision

    B   The directors recognise that there is a legal or constructive obligation to remove the pollution by spending money in the future

    C   Other companies in the same industry have recognised similar provisions

    D   The company auditors instruct the directors to set up a provision.

18 According to IAS 36 *Impairment of assets*, how often should assets be tested for impairment?

    A   Every year
    B   Every 3 years
    C   Every time non-current assets are revalued
    D   When there is an indication that impairment may have occurred

19 G has revalued one of its buildings to $1,200,000 at 31 December 20X8. The building was purchased 8 years ago at a cost of $840,000 and is being depreciated over a period of 40 years.

The depreciation charge for the year ending 31 December 20X9 will be $........................

20 Given below are details of one of S's construction contracts.

	$
Costs incurred to date	240,000
Estimated costs to completion	280,000
Progress payments invoiced	280,000
Total contract price	680,000

The contract is estimated to be 45% complete.

What figure would appear on the statement of financial position for the gross amount due from customers? $ ....

21 According to IAS 24 Related party disclosures, which of the following would not be a related party of Chen Co?

    A   An associated undertaking of Chen Co

    B   The managing director of Chen Co's parent company

    C   A company in which Chen Co holds a 10% investment

    D   Chen Co's pension fund for its employees

22 State the definition of a non-adjusting event in no more than twenty-five words.

23 Define a provision in no more than ten words.

24 Which of the following does not accurately describe '*true and fair view*'?

    A   It is a dynamic concept that evolves in response to changes in accounting and business practice

    B   Even reasonable business people and accountants may not share a consensus as to the degree of accuracy and completeness required

    C   Courts are likely to examine the meanings of the word 'true' and the word 'fair' in interpreting the meaning of 'true and fair'

    D   Courts are likely to look to the ordinary practices of professional accountants

25 A company is resident in Country Z. It has a branch in Country Y. The branch has taxable profits of $100,000, on which tax of $5,000 is paid. The tax rate in Country Z is 20% and there is a double taxation treaty between Countries Y and Z that allows tax relief on the full deduction basis. If the company has total taxable profits including those of the branch of $200,000, how much tax will it pay in Country Z?

    A $20,000

    B $25,000

    C $35,000

    D $40,000

26 Where is employee tax recorded in a set of financial statements?

    A   Charged to employee costs in the statement of comprehensive income

    B   Not included in the financial statements at all

    C   Included as a payable in the statement of financial position

    D   Included as a receivable in the statement of financial position

27 A company has sales of $800,000, excluding sales tax, in a period. Its purchases, including sales tax, total $550,000. The rate of sales tax is 10%. If 25% of all sales are zero rated, what is the sales tax payable for the period?

    A $10,000

    B $20,000

    C $22,500

    D $30,000

28 A professional accountant in business has an immediate manager who is a very forceful, domineering individual. The manager has stated work in progress has increased by 200% during the current reporting period and instructed the professional accountant to report this level in the financial statements. Evidence is available which indicates that the work in progress has not increased by anywhere near the rate advised by the manager. What kind of threat to compliance with the fundamental principles for accountants in business is this?

29   A company has an accounting profit of $200,000 for the year. This includes depreciation of $25,000 and disallowable expenses of $10,000. If the tax allowable depreciation totals $30,000 and the tax rate is 30%, what is the tax payable?

    A $55,500
    B $58,500
    C $60,000
    D $61,500

30   Which of the following must be presented in the income statement according to IAS 1 (revised) *Presentation of Financial Statements*?

    1   Tax expense
    2   Revenue
    3   Finance costs
    4   Depreciation expense

    A   1, 2, 3 and 4
    B   1, 2 and 3 only
    C   1, 3 and 4 only
    D   2 and 4 only

31   When considering IFRS 5 *Non-current Assets Held for Sale and Discontinued Operations*, which of the following statements is true?

    1   A discontinued operation must have been disposed of by the end of the reporting period.

    2   A discontinued operation must be a separate major line of business or geographical area of operation.

    3   A discontinued operation must be clearly distinguished operationally and for financial reporting purposes.

    A   1, 2 and 3
    B   1 and 2 only
    C   2 and 3 only
    D   1 and 3 only

32   Classify the following situations as finance or operating leases.

Situation	Lease type
A company leases machine tools. Legal title is transferred after three years.	
A company leases a photocopier. The present value of minimum lease payments is $2,000 but the fair value of the asset is $10,000.	
A company leases a car for a sales representative for a five-year period, after which the car will have come to the end of its useful economic life.	
A company acquires some equipment made bespoke to its specifications. To sell the equipment to a third party would require substantial modification.	

33 Information from the statement of cash flows and related notes of Gresham Co for the year ended 31 December 20X9 can be found in the table below.

	$
Depreciation	30,000
Profit on sale of non-current assets	5,000
Proceeds from sale of non-current assets	20,000
Purchase of non-current assets	25,000

If the carrying amount of property, plant and equipment was $110,000 on 31 December 20X8, what was it on 31 December 20X9?

A $85,000
B $90,000
C $70,000
D $80,000

34 A company has $500,000 4% redeemable preference shares in issue. According to IAS 32 *Financial Instruments: Presentation*, where will the dividend charge for the year be shown in the income statement?

A Dividends received
B Interest received
C Dividends paid
D Finance costs

35 Define a subsidiary in no more than 15 words.

36 Vaynor Co acquired 100% of the ordinary shares in Weeton Co and Yarlet Co some years ago. Extracts from the statements of financial position of the three companies as on 30 September 20X7 were as follows.

	Vaynor Co $'000	Weeton Co $'000	Yarlet Co $'000
Retained earnings	90	40	70

At acquisition Weeton Co had retained losses of $10,000 and Yarlet Co had retained earnings of $30,000.

The consolidated retained earnings of Vaynor Co on 30 September 20X7 were:

A $160,000
B $180,000
C 200,000
D $220,000

37 Milton Co owns all the share capital of Keynes Co. The following information is extracted from the individual company statements of financial position as on 31 December 20X1.

	Milton Co $	Keynes Co $
Current assets	500,000	200,000
Current liabilities	220,000	90,000

Included in Milton Co's purchase ledger is a balance in respect of Keynes Co of $20,000. The balance on Milton Co's account in the sales ledger of Keynes Co is $22,000. The difference between those figures is accounted for by cash in transit.

If there are no other intra-group balances, what is the amount of current assets less current liabilities in the consolidated statement of financial position of Milton Co and its subsidiary?

A $368,000
B $370,000
C $388,000
D $390,000

38   Oxford Co owns 100% of the issued share capital of Cambridge Co, and sells goods to its subsidiary at a profit margin of 20%. At the year end their statements of financial position showed inventories of:

Oxford Co $290,000
Cambridge Co $160,000

The inventory of Cambridge Co included $40,000 of goods supplied by Oxford Co and there was inventory in transit from Oxford to Cambridge amounting to a further $20,000. At what amount should inventory be carried in the consolidated statement of financial position?

A $438,000
B $442,000
C $458,000
D $462,000

Using the following information answer questions 39 and 40

Patience Co has a wholly owned subsidiary, Bunthorne Co. During 20X1 Bunthorne Co sold goods to Patience Co for $40,000 which was cost plus 25%. At 31 December 20X1 $20,000 of these goods remained unsold.

39   In the consolidated income statement for the year ended 31 December 20X1 the revenue will be reduced by

A $20,000
B $30,000
C $32,000
D $40,000

40   In the consolidated income statement for the year ended 31 December 20X1 the profit will be reduced by

A $4,000
B $6,000
C $8,000
D $10,000

41   The following figures related to Sanderstead Co and its 100% subsidiary Croydon Co for the year ended 31 December 20X9.

	Sanderstead Co $	Croydon Co $
Revenue	600,000	300,000
Cost of sales	(400,000)	(200,000)
Gross profit	200,000	100,000

During the year Sanderstead Co sold goods to Croydon Co for $20,000, making a profit of $5,000.

These goods were all sold by Croydon Co before the year end.

What are the amounts for total revenue and gross profit in the consolidated income statement of Sanderstead Co for the year ended 31 December 20X9?

	Revenue	Gross profit
A	$900,000	$300,000
B	$900,000	$295,000
C	$880,000	$300,000
D	$880,000	$295,000

42 Extracts from the income statements of Pik Co and its subsidiaries and Wik Co, its associate, for the year ended 31 March 20X6 are as follows.

	Pik Co (inc subsidiaries) $'000	Wik Co $'000
Gross profit	2,900	1,600
Administrative expenses	(750)	(170)
Distribution costs	(140)	(190)
Dividends from Wik Co	20	–
Profit before tax	2,030	1,240
Income tax expense	(810)	(440)
Profit for the year	1,220	800

Pik Co acquired 25% of the ordinary shares in Wik Co on 1 April 20X3 when the retained earnings of Wik Co were $80,000.

At what amount should the profit before tax be shown in the consolidated income statement of Pik Co for the year ended 31 March 20X6?

A $2,010,000
B $2,210,000
C $2,340,000
D $3,270,000

43 Austen Co has owned 100% of Kipling Co and 30% of Dickens Co, an associate, for many years. At 31 December 20X5 the trade receivables and trade payables shown in the individual company statements of financial position were as follows.

	Austen Co $'000	Kipling Co $'000	Dickens Co $'000
Trade receivables	50	30	40
Trade payables	30	15	20
Trade payables included amounts owing to			
Austen Co	–	–	–
Kipling Co	2	–	4
Dickens Co	7	–	–
Other suppliers	21	15	16
	30	15	20

The inter-company accounts agreed after taking into account the following.

(1) An invoice for $3,000 posted by Kipling Co on 31 December 20X5 was not received by Austen Co until 2 January 20X6.

(2) A cheque for $6,000 posted by Austen Co on 30 December 20X5 was not received by Dickens Co until 4 January 20X6.

What amount should be shown as trade receivables in the consolidated statement of financial position of Austen Co?

A $75,000
B $79,000
C $87,000
D $115,000

1   B

		$	$
Accounting profit			300,000
Add:	depreciation	30,000	
	disallowed expenses	25,000	
			55,000
			355,000
Less:	non-taxable income	50,000	
	tax allowable depreciation	24,000	
			74,000
Taxable profit			281,000

2   C

	$
Output tax (200,000 × 17.5%)	35,000
Input tax ((150,000 × 80%) × 17.5%)	21,000
Payable	14,000

3   The accruals basis of accounting requires that the effects of transactions and other events are recognised when they occur, and they are recorded in the accounting records and reported in the financial statements of the periods to which they relate.

4   A   In order to state that the financial statements show a true and fair view the auditor must satisfy himself that the other three matters are valid.

5   C

6 $5,488

	$
Cost	200,000
Depreciation $6 \times \left(\dfrac{200,000 - 4,000}{20} \right)$	58,800
NBV end year 6	141,200
Depreciation year 7 $\dfrac{141,200 - 4,000}{25}$	$5,488

7   An asset is a resource controlled by an entity as a result of **past transactions or events** and from which **future economic benefits** are expected to flow to the entity.

8   D   Probable liabilities should be accrued

Possible liabilities should be disclosed

Contingent assets are only disclosed if they are probable

9 $790,000. The cost to appear initially in the statement of financial position is the cost of getting the machine ready for production. This will include the delivery and installation costs but not the cleaning costs after the first production run.

10   C   Local tax legislation forms the basis of local taxation and so is a source of tax rules. The other options are all sources of accounting rules.

11   A   The fraud is an adjusting event as it took place during the year to 30 June although it was not discovered until after the year end. The loan stock issue is a non-adjusting event but due to its materiality should be disclosed in the notes.

12   D

	$'000
Estimated charge 20X8	520,000
Underprovision 20X7	28,000
Transfer to deferred tax (76,000 × 30%)	22,800
	570,800

13   C   The higher of net selling price and value in use.

14 C Items A and B are costs incurred in the *development* of a product. Note that while market research costs are not normally development costs, they *may be* treated as such when confirming ultimate commercial viability.

C is research and therefore must be written off.

D is work in progress (inventory) which you are being paid to do.

15 B Qualified opinion. See ISA 705 Modifications to the opinion in the independent auditor's report.

16 B A rules based system tends to remove the need to evaluate, as accountants can just check whether certain rules are being met or not, rather than applying the principles to given situations.

17 B It is the existence of an obligation which creates the need for a provision.

18 D

19 Depreciation charge $= \dfrac{\$1,200,000}{32 \text{ years}} = \$37,500$

20 $32,000

	$
Costs to date	240,000
Attributable profit (45% × (680 – 240 – 280))	72,000
Progress billings	(280,000)
Gross amount due from customers	32,000

21 C IAS 24 states that two or more parties are related if:

- One party has control of the other
- The parties are subject to common control
- One party has significant influence over the financial and operating policies of the other party
- One party has joint control over the other

A 10% investment in another company does not fall into any of these categories.

22 Non-adjusting events **arise after the end of the reporting period** and concern **conditions** which did **not exist** at that time.

23 A provision is a liability of uncertain timing or amount.

Note. Although the amount is uncertain, it should be susceptible to **measurement** with **sufficient reliability**. Where no reliable estimate can be made, a liability exists which cannot be recognised. Such a liability should be disclosed as a contingent liability.

24 C Courts are **not likely** to examine the individual meanings of the word 'true' and the word 'fair' in interpreting the meaning of 'true and fair'. The courts are likely to use an approach that applies the **concepts implied** by the **expression** *'true and fair'*.

25 C Total tax due is $40,000 ($200,000 x 20%) less double taxation relief for $5,000, leaves $35,000 to pay.

26 C The company acts as a tax collector on behalf of the tax authority. Therefore any tax deducted is put in a payable account until the money is actually paid to the tax authority. The balance on the payable account represents the amount collected but not yet paid over.

27 A

	$
Output tax (800,000 x 75% x 10%)	60,000
Input tax (550,000/110 x 10)	50,000
Payable	10,000

The important point to remember is that zero rated sales are still taxable supplies; they just pay tax at 0%. Therefore input tax does not need to be restricted.

28 Intimidation. The professional accountant is being intimidated by a dominant personality.

29 D

	$	$
Accounting profit		200,000
Add: depreciation	25,000	
disallowed expenses	10,000	
		35,000
		235,000
Less: tax allowable depreciation		30,000
Taxable profit		205,000

Tax payable = $205,000 x 30% = $61,500.

30 B All these items should be shown in the income statement except depreciation which may be disclosed in a note as per IAS 1 (revised)

31 C In order to be classified as discontinued, a component must either have been disposed of or be held for sale (provided that it is highly probable that it will be sold within 12 months of classification.

32

Situation	Lease type
A company leases machine tools. Legal title is transferred after three years.	Finance lease, because title is transferred and the company enjoys the risks and rewards of ownership before-hand.
A company leases a photocopier. The present value of minimum lease payments is $2,000 but the fair value of the asset is $10,000.	Operating lease, as the fair value of the asset is a lot more than the minimum lease payments.
A company leases a car for a sales representative for a five-year period, after which the car will have come to the end of its useful economic life.	Finance lease
A company acquires some equipment made bespoke to its specifications. To sell the equipment to a third party would require substantial modification.	Finance lease

33 B $90,000

NON-CURRENT ASSETS (CARRYING VALUE)

	$		$
Balance b/d	110,000	Depreciation	30,000
Additions	25,000	Disposals (Carrying value)	15,000
		Balance c/d	90,000
	135,000		135,000

34 D Payment of dividends on redeemable preference shares is treated as if it were payment of the finance charge on a redeemable loan.

35 A subsidiary is an entity that is controlled by another entity (known as the parent).

36 B

		$'000
Vaynor Co		90
Weeton Co (40+10)		50
Yarlet Co (70-30)		40
		180

37 D

	Milton Co $'000	Keynes Co $'000	Adjustment $'000	Consolidated $'000
Current assets	500	200	-22+2	680
Current liabilities	(220)	(90)	20	(290)
	280	110		390

38 C

	$'000
Oxford Co	290
Cambridge Co	160
In transit to Cambridge Co	20
Less: PURP ((40+20)x20%)	(12)
	458

39 D Reduce revenue by intra-group sales of $40,000.

40 A Reduce consolidated profit by provision for unrealised profit.

$$20,000 \times \frac{25}{125} = \$4,000$$

41 C

	Sanderstead Co $	Croydon Co $	Adj $	Consol $
Revenue	600,000	300,000	(20,000)	880,000
Cost of sales	(400,000)	(200,000)	20,000	(580,000)
Gross profit				300,000

42 B

	$'000
Pik Co (incl subsidiaries)	
Gross profit	2,900
Less Administrative expenses	(750)
Distribution costs	(140)
Share of profit of associates (25% × 800)	200
	2,210

43 A

	$'000	$'000
Austen Co		50
Kipling Co	30	
Less Intra group (2 + 3)	(5)	
		25
		75

EXAM QUESTION AND ANSWER BANK

What the examiner means

The very important table below has been prepared by CIMA to help you interpret exam questions.

Learning objectives	Verbs used	Definition
1 Knowledge What are you expected to know	• List • State • Define	• Make a list of • Express, fully or clearly, the details of/facts of • Give the exact meaning of
2 Comprehension What you are expected to understand	• Describe • Distinguish • Explain • Identify • Illustrate	• Communicate the key features of • Highlight the differences between • Make clear or intelligible/state the meaning of • Recognise, establish or select after consideration • Use an example to describe or explain something
3 Application How you are expected to apply your knowledge	• Apply • Calculate/ compute • Demonstrate • Prepare • Reconcile • Solve • Tabulate	• Put to practical use • Ascertain or reckon mathematically • Prove with certainty or to exhibit by practical means • Make or get ready for use • Make or prove consistent/compatible • Find an answer to • Arrange in a table
4 Analysis How you are expected to analyse the detail of what you have learned	• Analyse • Categorise • Compare and contrast • Construct • Discuss • Interpret • Prioritise • Produce	• Examine in detail the structure of • Place into a defined class or division • Show the similarities and/or differences between • Build up or compile • Examine in detail by argument • Translate into intelligible or familiar terms • Place in order of priority or sequence for action • Create or bring into existence
5 Evaluation How you are expected to use your learning to evaluate, make decisions or recommendations	• Advise • Evaluate • Recommend	• Counsel, inform or notify • Appraise or assess the value of • Propose a course of action

Guidance in our Practice and Revision Kit focuses on how the verbs are used in questions.

1 Convex　　　　　　　　　　　　　　　　　　　　9 mins

Learning outcome A2(b)

Convex is a limited liability company incorporated in Switzerland. However its board are all English and board meetings are held regularly in London. Head office is in Switzerland but the main accountancy offices are in London and the chairman and the chief executive are based in London.

Required

(a)　Where is the place of management of Convex?　　　　　　　　　　　　　　**(2 marks)**

(b)　Would your answer to part (a) change if the following were the case?

　　(i)　The Board are all Swiss nationals?

　　(ii)　Board meetings are held in Switzerland with the main accounts offices in London and the chairman and chief Executive based in Switzerland?　　　　　**(3 marks)**

　　　　　　　　　　　　　　　　　　　　　　　　　　　　　　　(Total = 5 marks)

2 AB　　　　　　　　　　　　　　　　　　　　　　9 mins

Learning outcomes A4(a), C1(a)

AB has an allotted capital of $350,000 in fully paid 50c ordinary shares. At 31 December 20X6 the following balances were included in the company's statement of financial position.

	$
Estimated income tax liability on 20X6 profits	5,000
Deferred taxation account	29,400
Retained earnings b/f (credit)	43,000

The following information relates to the year ended 31 December 20X7.

(a)　Income tax liability for 20X6 was agreed at $3,800 (December), paid January 20X8.

(b)　Net profit for 20X7 (before tax) was calculated at $100,000.

(c)　Income tax based on the 20X7 profits was estimated at $36,000.

(d)　A transfer to the deferred taxation account of $7,000 for 20X7 is to be made in respect of capital allowances in excess of depreciation charges (the entire balance on the deferred tax account being of a similar nature).

Required

Complete the statement of comprehensive income for 20X7 starting with profit before tax and show how the final balances would be included in the statement of financial position at 31 December 20X7. Show the details given in the notes to the accounts.

Assume income tax at 25%.　　　　　　　　　　　　　　　　　　　　**(5 marks)**

3 Tax and dividends

9 mins

Learning outcome A3(a)

(a)   Company A has an accounting profit of $750,000. This total is after charging book depreciation of $300,000, formation expenses of $15,000 and entertaining expenses of $75,000. The figure also includes government grants received of $25,000.

The tax rate is 25%. Under A's tax regime, government grants are tax-free and formation and entertaining expenses are disallowable. If the tax allowable depreciation is $350,000, calculate the tax due for the current period.   **(2 marks)**

(b)   Company A has paid a dividend during the accounting period of $1,500,000. It operates in a country where a full imputation system applies. Corporate income tax is 25% and personal income tax is 30%.

How much tax will be paid by its shareholders?   **(3 marks)**

(Total = 5 marks)

4 VAT

9 mins

Learning outcome A1(e)

A company has sales of $570,000 including VAT. Its purchases for the same period were $300,000 excluding VAT. The sales tax rate is 17.5%. Calculate the tax payable to the tax authorities if 20% of sales are zero-rated but only 15% of its purchases are zero-rated.   **(5 marks)**

5 Company tax

9 mins

Learning outcome A4(a)

J is a retail entity. Its tax rate is 25%. It has current tax payable brought forward from the year ended 30 June 20X4 of $765,000 and deferred tax payable of $200,000.

On 30 June 20X5, the estimated tax charge for the year ended 30 June 20X5 was $976,000. The actual tax charge for the year ended 30 June 20X4 was agreed with the tax authority and settled with a payment of $794,000. The deferred tax payable needs to be increased to $300,000 as at 30 June 20X5.

Required

Prepare the notes in respect of current and deferred tax as they would appear in the statement of comprehensive income and statement of financial position of J for the year ended 30 April 20X5.

(5 marks)

6 Regulatory influences

9 mins

Learning outcome B1(a)

State three different regulatory influences on the preparation of the published accounts of quoted companies and briefly explain the role of each one. Comment briefly on the effectiveness of this regulatory system.

(5 marks)

7 Accounting standards   9 mins

Learning outcome B1(a)

There are those who suggest that any standard setting body is redundant because accounting standards are unnecessary. Other people feel that such standards should be produced, but by the government, so that they are legislated.

Required

Discuss the statement that accounting standards are unnecessary for the purpose of regulating financial statements.   **(5 marks)**

8 IASB   9 mins

Learning outcome B1(c)

Consider to what extent the IASB has succeeded in its aims and what problems it still faces.

(5 marks)

9 External auditors   9 mins

Learning outcome B1(g)

Describe the external auditors' responsibilities with respect to the financial statements.

(5 marks)

10 Audit report   9 mins

Learning outcome B1(g)

Explain what is meant by a 'modified' audit report and describe the differences between a 'modified' and an 'unmodified' report.

(5 marks)

11 New project   9 mins

Learning outcome B2(c)

A professional accountant in business has recently been put in charge of a new project by the finance director. However, the accountant does not have the required level of expertise for this project. The accountant is uncomfortable carrying out the work and is uncertain about what to say to the finance director.

Required

Identify the ethical issues in this situation and describe the action the accountant should take.

(5 marks)

12 C

Learning outcome C2(a)

C is a civil engineering company. It started work on two construction projects during the year ended 31 December 20X0. The following figures relate to those projects at the end of the reporting period.

	Maryhill bypass $'000	Rottenrow Centre $'000
Contract price	9,000	8,000
Costs incurred to date	1,400	2,900
Estimated costs to completion	5,600	5,200
Value of work certified to date	2,800	3,000
Cash received from customer	2,600	3,400

C recognises revenues and profits on construction contracts on the basis of work certified to date.

Required

Calculate the figures which would appear in C's financial statements in respect of these two projects.

(5 marks each)

(Total = 10 marks)

13 IFRS 5

Learning outcome C2(a)

At 30 November a manufacturing company decided to sell one of its processing plants and steps were taken to locate a buyer. After consultation with a property agent, who advised that prices in the area were expected to rise sharply over the next twelve months, senior management decided to raise the price of the building in anticipation of this. The buyers who were interested have now withdrawn due to the price rise but the directors are confident that in the new year, when property prices rise, they will obtain the price required. In the meantime, the processing plant is continuing to operate and handle customers orders.

At 31 December, will this plant be classified as 'held for sale' under IFRS 5? Explain your answer.

(5 marks)

14 Leases

Learning outcome C2(a)

The following definitions have been taken from the International Accounting Standards Board's *Framework for the Preparation and Presentation of Financial Statements*.

- 'An asset is a resource controlled by the entity as a result of past events and from which future economic benefits are expected to flow to the entity.'

- 'A liability is a present obligation of the entity arising from past events, the settlement of which is expected to result in an outflow from the entity of resources embodying economic benefits.'

IAS 17 *Leases* requires lessees to capitalise finance leases in their financial statements.

Required

Explain how IAS 17's treatment of finance leases applies the definitions of assets and liabilities.

(5 marks)

15 T

54 mins

Learning outcome C1(a)

T is a quoted company which owns a large number of hotels throughout the UK. The company's latest trial balance at 31 December 20X1 is as follows.

	$'000	$'000
Administrative expenses	3,000	
Bank	300	
Payables		1,700
Distribution costs	4,000	
Food purchases	2,100	
Heating and lighting (to be included in cost of sales)	3,000	
Hotel buildings: cost	490,000	
depreciation to date		46,200
Hotel fixtures and fittings: cost	18,000	
depreciation to date		9,400
Loan interest	4,950	
Interim dividend paid	1,000	
Loans, repayable 20X9		110,000
Retained earnings		86,000
Sales of accommodation and food		68,500
Share capital: $1 shares, fully paid		220,000
Inventory as at 31 December 20X0	400	
Taxation	50	
Wages: administrative staff	6,000	
housekeeping and restaurant staff	9,000	
	541,800	541,800

Additional information

(a) During the year the company spent a total of $12m on a new hotel and purchased new fixtures for $7m. These acquisitions have been included in the relevant trial balance totals.

(b) Hotels are to be depreciated by 2 per cent of cost, and fixtures and fittings by 25 per cent of the reducing balance, with a full year's depreciation to be charged in the year of acquisition. Depreciation is charged to cost of sales.

(c) Closing inventories of foodstuffs and other consumables were valued at $470,000 on 31 December 20X1.

(d) The balance on the taxation account is an underprovision remaining after the payment of the estimated income tax liability for the year ended 31 December 20X0. The directors have estimated the income tax liability for the year ended 31 December 20X1 at $10.2m.

(e) T took out a contract on 1 July 20X1 to lease a fleet of refrigerated vans. The lease agreement provided for 6 6-monthly payments in arrears of $60,000. The cash price of the vans would have been $300,000. The payment made in 20X1 has been charged to administrative expenses. T has now been advised that this is a finance lease and that the applicable interest rate is 10%. The vehicles should be depreciated by 20% per annum reducing balance.

(f) During 20X1 T issued 50m new shares at $1.20. The proceeds have all been credited to share capital.

Required

Prepare T's statement of comprehensive income for the year ended 31 December 20X1 and its statement of financial position at that date.

Notes to the accounts are not required.

(30 marks)

16 CEC
9 mins

Learning outcome C2(a)

After its end of year physical inventory count and valuation, the accounts staff of CEC have reached a valuation of $153,699 at cost for total inventories held at the year end.

However, on checking the figures, the chief bookkeeper has come across the following additional facts.

(a)   The count includes damaged goods which originally cost $2,885. These could be repaired at a cost of $921 and sold for $3,600.

(b)   The count excludes 300 units of item 730052 which were sold to a customer SC on a sale or return basis, at a price of $8 each. The original cost of the units was $5 each. SC has not yet indicated to CEC whether these goods have been accepted, or whether they will eventually be returned.

(c)   The count includes 648 units of item 702422. These cost $7.30 each originally but because of dumping on the market by overseas suppliers, a price war has flared up and the unit cost price of the item has fallen to $6.50. The price reduction is expected to be temporary, lasting less than a year or so, although some observers of the market predict that the change might be permanent. CEC has already decided that if the price reduction lasts longer than six months, it will reduce its resale price of the item from $10.90 to about $10.

Required

Calculate the closing inventory figure for inclusion in the annual accounts of CEC, making whatever adjustments you consider necessary in view of items (a) to (c). Explain your treatment of each item.

(5 marks)

17 Plant and equipment
9 mins

Learning outcome C2(a)

A business's plant and equipment account and depreciation account at 31 December 20X8 show the following:

Year of purchase	Cost $	Accumulated depreciation $
20X5	100,000	80,000
20X6	70,000	42,000
20X7	50,000	20,000
20X8	30,000	6,000
	250,000	148,000

Depreciation is calculated at 20% on a straight line basis with a full year's charge in the year of acquisition and none in the year of disposal.

During 20X9 the following transactions took place:

(a)   Purchases of plant and equipment amounted to $150,000
(b)   Plant that had been bought in 20X5 for $40,000 was sold for $5,000
(c)   Plant that had been bought in 20X7 for $10,000 was damaged and had to be scrapped.

Required

Prepare the following ledger accounts as at 31 December 20X9:

Plant and equipment   – cost
                      – accumulated depreciation
                      – disposals

(5 marks)

18 IT   9 mins

Learning outcome C2(a)

The accounts of IT at 1 January 20X6 include capitalised development costs of $26,500. During the year ended 31 December 20X6 IT purchased a new business. The consideration paid to the proprietor included $4,800 in respect of goodwill. The company also spent $7,900 in research and $3,500 on development activities.

The directors of IT intend to write off $1,200 in respect of impairment of goodwill. They believe that $22,600 of development costs should be carried forward at 31 December 20X6, in accordance with IAS 38.

Show the ledger accounts for goodwill and research and development in the books of IT.

(5 marks)

19 F   9 mins

Learning outcome C2(a)

F, an engineering company, makes up its financial statements to 31 March in each year. The financial statements for the year ended 31 March 20X1 showed revenue of $3m and trading profit of $400,000.

Before approval of the financial statements by the board of directors on 30 June 20X1 the following events took place.

(a)   The financial statements of P for the year ended 28 February 20X1 were received which indicated a permanent decline in that company's financial position. F had bought shares in P some years ago and this purchase was included in unquoted investments at its cost of $100,000. The financial statements received indicated that this investment was now worth only $50,000.

(b)   There was a fire at the company's warehouse on 30 April 20X1 when inventory to the value of $500,000 was destroyed. It transpired that the inventory in the warehouse was under-insured by some 50%.

(c)   It was announced on 1 June 20X1 that the company's design for tank cleaning equipment had been approved by the major oil companies and this could result in an increase in the annual revenue of some $1m with a relative effect on profits.

Required

You are required to explain how, if at all, items (a) to (c) above should be reflected in the accounts of F for the year ended 31 March 20X1.

(5 marks)

20 B

54 mins

Learning outcome C1(a)

The draft financial statements for B, a limited liability company, are set out below.

STATEMENT OF COMPREHENSIVE INCOME FOR THE YEAR ENDED 30 SEPTEMBER 20X1

	$'000
Revenue	600
Cost of sales	(410)
Gross profit	190
Profit on sale of non-current asset	10
	200
Depreciation	(30)
Other expenses	(70)
Interest expense	(15)
Profit for the year	85

STATEMENT OF FINANCIAL POSITION AS AT 30 SEPTEMBER

	20X1		20X0	
	$'000	$'000	$'000	$'000
Non-current assets (see note)		450		520
Current assets				
Inventory	65		50	
Receivables	80		30	
Bank and cash	30		15	
		175		95
Total assets		625		615
Equity and liabilities				
Share capital		400		400
Retained earnings		145		95
Non-current liability				
Loan		20		100
Current liabilities				
Payables		60		20
		625		615

Notes

The company purchased non-current assets for $40,000 during the year ended 30 September 20X1.

Dividends of $35,000 were paid during the year.

Ignore taxation.

Required

(a)   Prepare a statement of cash flows for B for the year ended 30 September 20X1.   **(15 marks)**

(b)   In the year to 30 September 20X2 B had the following results:

	$'000
Revenue	640
Cost of sales	(400)
Gross profit	240
Depreciation	(30)
Other expenses	(35)
Interest expense	(15)
Profit for the year	160

Notes

1   Interest was paid up to date and the remaining loan paid off
2   There were no purchases or sales of non-current assets
3    $615,000 was received from customers and $390,000 paid to suppliers.
4   Cost of sales was:

	$'000
Opening inventory	65
Purchases	410
Closing inventory	(75)
	400

Required

Prepare the statement of financial position as at 30 September 20X2   **(15 marks)**

(Total = 30 marks)

21 Cat   **54 mins**

Learning outcome C1(a)

Set out below are the statements of financial position of Cat Co as at 30 June 20X1 and 20X2.

CAT CO
STATEMENT OF FINANCIAL POSITION AS AT 30 JUNE

	20X1		*20X2*	
	$	$	$	$
Assets				
Non-current assets				
Cost	85,000		119,000	
Depreciation	26,000		37,000	
		59,000		82,000
Current assets				
Inventories	34,000		40,000	
Receivables (trade)	26,000		24,000	
Cash at bank	10,000		13,500	
		70,000		77,500
Total assets		129,000		159,500
Equity and liabilities				
Equity				
Ordinary $1 shares	26,000		28,000	
Share premium	12,000		13,000	
Retained earnings	44,000		70,500	
		82,000		111,500
Non-current liabilities				
10% loan stock		20,000		10,000
Current liabilities				
Payables (trade)	15,000		23,000	
Taxation	12,000		15,000	
		27,000		38,000
Total equity and liabilities		129,000		159,500

Notes

1   No non-current assets were disposed of during the year.
2   Of the 10% loan stock, $10,000 was redeemed at par on 31 December 20X1.
3   Dividends of $13,000 were paid during the year.

Required

(a)   Prepare a statement of cash flows for the year to 30 June 20X2, using the format specified in IAS 7.   **(18 marks)**

(b)   The 20X2 statement of financial position was drafted without taking account of the following adjustments:

(i)   Capital allowances were received during 20X2 which exceeded depreciation by $15,000. The tax rate is 30%.

(ii)   Inventory valued at $9,000 has been damaged. It can be sold for $6,000 following $2,000 remedial work.

(iii)   A provision of $8,000 was made for possible costs following a legal case. This was incorrectly included in trade payables. The case has now been decided and only $3,000 is payable.

Required

Redraft the 20X2 statement of financial position to take account of these adjustments.

Note. This does **not** affect your answer to (a)   **(12 marks)**

(Total = 30 marks)

22 ABA   9 mins

Learning outcome C2(a)

The directors of ABA, a limited liability company, are reviewing the draft accounts for the year ended 30 June 20X9. The net profit before tax currently stands at $923,000. The auditors have drawn their attention to the following matters:

(a)   An announcement was made on 4 July that one of their customers, IMX, had gone into liquidation. The liquidator is estimating that suppliers will receive 30c in the $. The receivable in ABA's accounts regarding IMX is $325,000 at 30 June.

(b)   A line of inventory valued at cost of $150,000 has become obsolete. It can only be disposed of for $200,000 via an agent who will require 20% of selling price as commission for selling it. Other disposal costs will amount to $25,000.

(c)   An outstanding claim for damages by an ex-employee who was injured in the warehouse is likely to amount to $50,000. No provision has been made for this as it was expected to be covered by insurance. However the insurance company are now claiming that certain safety procedures were not in place, rendering the cover invalid.

Required

Explain how each of these issues should be dealt with and show the effect on the net profit before tax.

(5 marks)

23 L   **9 mins**

Learning outcome C2(b)

L, a limited liability company, has the following capital structure:

	$'000
Share capital	
50c ordinary shares (fully paid)	15,000
Share premium	3,000
Retained earnings	27,000
	45,000

The following share issues are made:

(a)   A 3 for 2 bonus issue, and then

(b)   A 1 for 2 rights issue at 80c.

Show the capital structure following these issues, assuming all rights are taken up.   **(5 marks)**

24 International tax   **9 mins**

Learning outcome A2(a)

J has an overseas branch L, which made a profit adjusted for tax purposes of $8 million for the year ended 30 June 20X6. This figure is included in the financial statements to 30 June 20X6. Taxable profits of the overseas branch have suffered local tax at a rate of 15%. J calculates that its tax liability for the year to 30 June 20X6 will be $1.5m. Overseas tax has not been taken into account in computing this tax liability. The liability for the year ended 30 June 20X5 has been agreed at $970,000. The deferred tax payable needs to be reduced to $290,000 at 30 June 20X6. J has the following balances brought forward: Current tax: $976,000; Deferred tax: $300,000.

Required

Prepare the notes in respect of current and deferred tax as they would appear in the financial statements of J for the year ended 30 April 20X6.

(5 marks)

25 A Co, B Co and C Co   **36 mins**

Learning outcome C1(c)

The income statements and statements of financial position for the year 20X2 for A Co, B Co and C Co are given below.

INCOME STATEMENTS FOR THE YEAR ENDED 31 DECEMBER 20X2

	A Co	B Co	C Co
	$'000	$'000	$'000
Revenue	10,000	7,000	9,000
Cost of sales	(6,000)	(2,000)	(4,500)
Gross profit	4,000	5,000	4,500
Expenses	(2,200)	(1,200)	(1,900)
Profit before taxation	1,800	3,800	2,600
Taxation	(800)	(800)	(600)
Profit for the year	1,000	3,000	2,000

STATEMENTS OF FINANCIAL POSITION AT 31 DECEMBER 20X2

	A Co $'000	B Co $'000	C Co $'000
Assets			
Non-current assets			
Property, plant and equipment	25,300	9,000	10,000
Investment in B Co at cost	4,000	–	–
Investment in C Co at cost	1,000	–	–
	30,300	9,000	10,000
Current assets	21,500	7,000	4,000
Total assets	51,800	16,000	14,000
Equity and liabilities			
Equity			
Ordinary share capital	10,000	4,000	3,000
Share premium account	4,000	–	–
Retained earnings	2,800	7,000	4,000
Total equity	16,800	11,000	7,000
Non-current liabilities	10,000	2,000	3,000
Current liabilities	25,000	3,000	4,000
Total equity and liabilities	51,800	16,000	14,000

Additional information

(a) A Co has owned 100% of B Co since incorporation.

(b) A Co purchased 25% of the shares in C Co for $1 million on 1 January 20X2. Pre-acquisition retained earnings were $2 million.

(c) During the year, A Co sold goods to C Co for $1.5 million at cost plus a 20% mark-up. These goods were still in the inventories of C Co at year-end.

Required

Prepare, for A Co, the consolidated income statement for the year ended 31 December 20X2 and the consolidated statement of financial position at that date.

(20 marks)

26 Fallowfield and Rusholme   36 mins

Learning outcome C1(c)

Fallowfield acquired a 100% holding in Rusholme three years ago when Rusholme's retained earnings balance stood at $16,000. Both businesses have been very successful since the acquisition and their respective income statements for the year ended 30 June 20X8 are as follows:

	Fallowfield $	Rusholme $
Revenue	403,400	193,000
Cost of sales	(207,400)	(92,600)
Gross profit	196,000	100,400
Other income	6,000	–
Distribution costs	(16,000)	(14,600)
Administrative expenses	(24,250)	(17,800)
Dividends from Rusholme	25,000	–
Profit before tax	186,750	68,000
Income tax expense	(61,750)	(22,000)
Profit for the year	125,000	46,000

STATEMENT OF CHANGES IN EQUITY (EXTRACTS)

	Fallowfield Retained earnings $	Rusholme Retained earnings $
Balance at 1 July 20X7	163,000	61,000
Dividends	(40,000)	(25,000)
Total comprehensive income for the year	125,000	46,000
Balance at 30 June 20X8	248,000	82,000

(a)   During the year Rusholme sold some goods to Fallowfield for $40,000, including 25% mark up. Half of these items were still in inventories at the year-end.

(b)   Fallowfield sold plant costing $22,000 to Rushholme during the year. The profit on the sale has been shown as other income. Depreciation on plant is charged at 25%.

Required

Produce the consolidated income statement of Fallowfield Co and its subsidiary for the year ended 30 June 20X8, and an extract from the statement of changes in equity, showing retained earnings. Goodwill is to be ignored. **(20 marks)**

1 Convex

(a) Although the head office is in Switzerland, board meetings are held in London and the chairman and chief executive are based in London. **Therefore the place of management is London.**

(b) (i) The nationality of the Board Members is irrelevant to the place of management. Therefore the place of management is London.

(ii) As board meetings are held in Switzerland and the chairman and chief executive are based in Switzerland, **the place of management is Switzerland**. Although the accounting offices are in London, this does not affect the place where management decisions are made.

2 AB

> **Top tips.** This question is easier than it looks and similar to what you may see in the exam. Make sure you understand the answer.

STATEMENT OF COMPREHENSIVE INCOME FOR THE YEAR ENDED 31 DECEMBER 20X7 (EXTRACT)

	Note	$
Profit before tax		100,000
Income tax expense	3	(41,800)
Profit for the year		58,200

STATEMENT OF FINANCIAL POSITION AT 31 DECEMBER 20X7 (EXTRACT)

	$	Note
Equity and liabilities		
Issued capital of 700,000 50c ordinary shares fully paid	350,000	
Retained earnings	101,200	4
Non-current liabilities		
Deferred tax	36,400	2
Current liabilities		
Current tax	39,800	1

Notes to the statement of financial position and statement of financial position

1 *Current tax comprises*

	$
Income tax (3,800 + 36,000)	39,800

2 *Deferred tax*

	$
Balance at 1.1.20X7	29,400
Deferred tax expense	7,000
Balance at 31.12.20X7	36,400

3 *Tax on profit for the year*

	$
Income tax (at 25% on taxable profits of 20X7)	36,000
less overprovision on profits of 20X6	(1,200)
Transfer to deferred tax	7,000
	41,800

4 *Retained earnings*

	$
Profit for the year	58,200
Retained brought forward	43,000
Retained carried forward	101,200

3 Tax and dividends

> **Top tips.** Remember that the dividend is a **net** amount.

(a)

	$'000	$'000
Accounting profit		750
Add: disallowable expenditure: entertaining	75	
formation expenses	15	
book depreciation	300	
		390
		1,140
Less: non-taxable income	25	
tax allowable depreciation	350	
		(375)
Taxable profit		765

The tax rate is 25%, so the tax due is $191,250 (25% × $765,000).

(b)

	$'000
Net dividend received	1,500
Tax at 30%	450
Less tax credit (1,500 × 25%)	(375)
Payable by shareholders	75

4 VAT

	$
Output tax (see note)	70,000
Input tax (300,000 x 85%) x 17.5%	44,625
Tax payable	25,375

Note

Assume sales excluding VAT are Y.

Then zero-rated sales are 20% x Y and standard rated gross sales are Y x 80% x 1.175%.

So:

(20% x Y) + (Y x 80% x 1.175%) = 570,000

0.2Y + 0.94Y = 570,000

1.14Y = 570,000

Y = 500,000

Check: Net sales are $500,000, so VAT due is $500,000 x 80% x 17.5% ($70,000). This gives sales including VAT of $570,000.

5 Company tax

> **Top tips.** Writing out T accounts will probably help here.

Tax on profit on ordinary activities – note to statement of comprehensive income

	$'000
Current tax	
Tax on profit for the year	976
Underprovision for previous period ($794,000 – $765,000)	29
Deferred tax	
Increase in provision ($300,000 - $200,000)	100
Total tax charge	1,105

Statement of financial position

	$'000
Non-current liabilities	
Deferred tax	300
Current liabilities	
Current tax	976

6 Regulatory influences

> **Top tips.** Do not omit the requirement to **explain**. It is best to use **headings** to divide your answer.

Stock Exchange

A quoted company is a company whose shares are bought and sold on a stock exchange. This involves the signing of an agreement which requires compliance with the rules of that stock exchange. This would normally contain amongst other things the stock exchange's detailed rules on the information to be disclosed in listed companies' accounts. This, then, is one regulatory influence on a listed company's accounts. The stock exchange may enforce compliance by monitoring accounts and reserving the right to withdraw a company's shares from the stock exchange: ie the company's shares would no longer be traded through the stock exchange. In many countries there is, however, no statutory requirement to obey these rules.

Local legislation

In most countries, companies have to comply with the local companies legislation, which lays down detailed requirements on the preparation of accounts. Company law is often quite detailed, partly because of external influences such as EU Directives. Another reason to increase statutory regulation is that listed companies are under great pressure to show profit growth and an obvious way to achieve this is to manipulate accounting policies. If this involves breaking the law, as opposed to ignoring professional guidance, company directors may think twice before bending the rules - or, at least, this is often a government's hope.

Standard-setters

Professional guidance is given by the national and international standard-setters. Prescriptive guidance is given in accounting standards which must be applied in all accounts intended to show a 'true and fair view' or 'present fairly in all material respects'. IFRSs and national standards are issued after extensive consultation and are revised as required to reflect economic or legal changes. In some countries, legislation requires details of non-compliance to be disclosed in the accounts. 'Defective' accounts can be revised under court order if necessary and directors signing such accounts can be prosecuted and fined (or even imprisoned).

The potential for the IASB's influence in this area is substantial.

7 Accounting standards

The users of financial information – shareholders, suppliers, management, employees, business contacts, financial specialists, government and the general public - are entitled to this information about a business entity to a greater or lesser degree. However, the needs and expectations of these groups will vary.

The preparers of the financial information often find themselves in the position of having to reconcile the interests of different groups in the best way for the business entity. For example whilst shareholders are looking for increased profits to support higher dividends, employees will expect higher wage increases; and yet higher profits without corresponding higher tax allowances (increased capital allowances for example) will result in a larger tax bill.

Without accounting standards to prescribe how certain transactions should be treated, preparers **would be tempted to produce financial information which meets the expectations of the favoured user group**. For example creative accounting methods, such as off balance sheet finance, could be used to enhance a company's statement of financial position to make it more attractive to investors/lenders.

The aim of accounting standards is that they should regulate financial information in order that it shows the following characteristics, amongst others.

(a)   Objectivity
(b)   Comparability
(c)   Completeness
(d)   Consistency

8 IASB

The main aims of the IASB are:

(a)   to develop a single set of high quality, understandable, enforceable and globally accepted international financial reporting standards

(b)   to promote the use and rigorous application of those standards

(c)   to take account of the financial reporting needs of emerging economies and small and medium-sized entities

(d)   to bring about convergence of national accounting standards and IFRSs to high quality solutions.

The tendency of the IASB has been to concentrate on the development of standards, leaving the others, which are slightly more vague aims to follow behind.

One of IASB's targets has been to produce a set of 'core standards' which the worldwide body representing stock exchanges, IOSCO, can accept for all cross-border listings. In theory, this would mean that, say, a German company that prepares its accounts using IFRSs would be accepted for a listing on the Tokyo Stock Exchange.

IOSCO has given the core standards qualified endorsement and with the new standards and improvements to existing standards issued in 2003 and 2004, the IASB claims to have now established a 'stable platform' of standards.

However, individual stock exchanges may still make life difficult for foreign companies by insisting on substantial additional disclosures. The IASB is facing an uphill struggle, but there have been substantial successes, notably the EU decision that the consolidated accounts of listed companies must comply with IFRS from 2005.

In recent years the IASB has also been pursuing the convergence of IFRSs and standards produced in the US by the FASB. There is now a timetable for convergence between IFRS and US GAAP. When this is achieved it will greatly increase the influence of the IASB.

9 External auditors

The external auditors' responsibilities with respect to the financial statements are concerned with deciding whether the accounts show a **true and fair view** of the affairs of the company for the year. The auditors must express an **opinion** on the financial statements to this effect.

The auditors conduct an audit which examines the figures in the financial statements and agrees them back to the underlying accounting information. They are required to satisfy themselves that the directors have prepared the accounts correctly and that there is no materially misleading information within them. To this end the auditors have a statutory right to all information and explanations deemed necessary to perform the audit.

The external auditors report to the members of the company and their responsibility is limited to the expression of this opinion.

They are not responsible for the accounting systems, or for the detection of all fraud and error. While auditors will report on whether or not the accounting system is satisfactory, and will design their tests in order to have **a good chance of detecting any material fraud or error**, these issues are the responsibility of the directors.

10 Audit report

If the auditor's work leads them to conclude that the financial statements are free from material error or misstatement and that they give a true and fair view of the financial affairs of the company then they will issue an **unmodified opinion**. This opinion covers the statement of comprehensive income, the statement of financial position, the statement of changes in equity, the statement of cash flows and the notes to the accounts. They also review the directors report to ensure that this does not contain information which is materially misleading or which conflicts with elements of the financial statements. The auditor's report is the statement of their opinion on these elements of the financial statements. They state explicitly that the statement of financial position reflects the state of the company's affairs at the year end and that the statement of comprehensive income gives the company's profit or loss for the year. The report also covers a number of other elements, such as the fact that adequate accounting records were kept, by exception.

A modified report contains a modified opinion because the auditors are concerned that the financial statements do not or may not give a true and fair view. This may occur due to the auditor concluding that the financial statements are as a whole are not free from material misstatements or because the auditor cannot obtain sufficient appropriate audit evidence to conclude that the financial statements as a whole are free from material misstatement.

The extent of the modification is determined by whether the misstatement or inability to obtain sufficient appropriate audit evidence is merely **material** or is **pervasive**.

When the auditors issue a modified report it must contain a full explanation of the reasons for the modification and, where possible, a quantification of the effects on the financial statements. This means that a modified report will contain at least one more paragraph than an unmodified report.

The modified report should leave the reader in no doubt as to its meaning and the implications it has on an understanding of the financial statements.

11 New project

Ethical issues

The accountant has been asked to manage a project for which he or she does not have sufficient expertise. This is a threat to the fundamental principle of **professional competence and due care**. The CIMA *code of ethics for professional accountants* specifically requires accountants to only undertake tasks for which they have sufficient experience.

The finance director may be unaware that the accountant does not possess the requisite knowledge for the project in question. It may be tempting for the accountant to ignore the issue, especially if he or she is concerned that their reputation is discredited or they are hoping for a promotion within the business. This is a threat to the fundamental principle of **professional behaviour**. Under the CIMA Code, accountants in business should not intentionally mislead employers as to their level of expertise.

Action to take

Initially, the accountant should inform the finance director of his or her concerns and discuss an appropriate course of action. The problem may be alleviated by the accountant attending further training or if there are only specific areas where he or she lacks expertise, consulting with others on these areas. If none of these safeguards are appropriate then the management of the project should be reassigned to a member of staff with the correct experience.

If the finance director insists the accountant manages the project after being made aware of his or her lack of expertise, the accountant should raise the matter with the next level of management, if this exists.

The accountant should only contact external parties if a satisfactory response cannot be obtained internally. It may be appropriate to contact CIMA or an independent professional advisor. As confidentiality rules apply, legal advice should be sought before contacting an external party.

The accountant should only refuse to manage the new project as a last resort.

12 C

> **Top tips.** Begin by working out the profit/loss on each contract. The loss is recognised in full. Cost of sales is a balancing figure.

Profit/loss on contract

Maryhill bypass

	$'000
Final contract price	9,000
Less: costs to date	(1,400)
estimated future costs	(5,600)
Estimated final profit	2,000

Recognised profit for the period $= 2,000 \times \dfrac{2,800}{9,000} = 622$

Rottenrow Centre

	$'000
Final contract price	8,000
Less: costs to date	(2,900)
estimated future costs	(5,200)
Estimated final loss	(100)

	Maryhill bypass $'000	Rottenrow Centre $'000
Statement of comprehensive income		
Revenue	2,800	3,000
Cost of sales (balancing figure)	(2,178)	(3,100)
Profit/(loss)	622	(100)
Statement of financial position		
Costs to date	1,400	2,900
Recognised profits less recognised losses	622	(100)
	2,022	2,800
Less: progress billings to date	(2,600)	(3,400)
Gross amount due to customers (liability)	(578)	(600)

13 IFRS 5

> **Top tips.** Read this question carefully. The definition of 'held for sale' is quite specific.

The plant will not be classified as 'held for sale'.

For this to be the case, the asset must be available for immediate sale and its sale must be **highly probable**. For the sale to be highly probable, the asset must be actively marketed for sale at a price that is reasonable in relation to its current fair value.

This property is being marketed at a price which is **above** its current fair value. It is improbable that it will be sold at that price until property prices rise. This delay has been imposed by the seller, so it cannot be said that his intention is to sell the plant immediately. Therefore it cannot be classified as 'held for sale'.

14 Leases

> **Top tips.** The principle of 'substance over form' is important here. Consider what the position would be if lessees were not required to capitalise finance leases.

IAS 17 is an example of substance triumphing over form. In legal terms **the lessor may be the owner of the asset, but the lessee enjoys all the risks and rewards which ownership of the asset would convey**. This is the key element to IAS 17. The lessee is deemed to have an asset as they must maintain and run the asset through its useful life.

The lessee enjoys the future economic benefits of the asset as a result of entering into the lease. There is a corresponding liability which is the obligation to pay the instalments on the lease until it expires. Assets and liabilities cannot be netted off. If finance leases were treated in a similar manner to the existing treatment of operating leases then no asset would be recognised and lease payments would be recognised in profit or loss as they were incurred. This is off balance sheet finance. The company has assets in use and liabilities to lessors which are not recorded in the financial statements. This would be misleading to the users of the accounts and make it appear as though the assets which were recorded were more efficient in producing returns than was actually the case.

15 T

> **Top tips.** This is similar to Section C questions in the exam. Make all your workings very clear, so you can see what you are doing.

T: STATEMENT OF COMPREHENSIVE INCOME
FOR THE YEAR ENDED 31 DECEMBER 20X1

	$'000
Revenue	68,500
Cost of sales (W2)	(26,010)
Gross profit	42,490
Distribution costs	(4,000)
Administrative expenses (W3)	(8,940)
	29,550
Financial costs (W9)	(4,965)
Profit before tax	24,585
Taxation (10,200 + 50) (W5)	(10,250)
Profit for the year	14,335

STATEMENT OF FINANCIAL POSITION AT 31 DECEMBER 20X1

	$'000	$'000
Non-current assets		
Property, plant and equipment		440,720
Current assets		
Inventory	470	
Cash at bank	300	
		770
Total assets		441,490
Equity and liabilities		
Equity		
Share capital (W8)		210,000
Share premium		10,000
Retained earnings (W6)		99,335
Non-current liabilities		
Loans		110,000
Amount due under finance lease		158
Current liabilities		
Trade payables	1,700	
Taxation	10,200	
Amount due under finance lease	97	
		11,997
Total equity and liabilities		441,490

Workings

1   *Depreciation*

	$'000
Hotels 490,000 @ 2%	9,800
Fixtures and fittings (18,000 – 9,400) @ 25%	2,150
Vans (300,000 × 20% × 6/12)	30
	11,980

2   *Cost of sales*

	$'000
Food purchases	2,100
Heating and lighting	3,000
Housekeeping and restaurant staff	9,000
Opening inventory	400
Closing inventory	(470)
Depreciation	11,980
	26,010

3   *Administrative expenses*

	$'000
Administration	3,000
Staff wages	6,000
Lease payment	(60)
	8,940

4   *Property, plant and equipment*

	Hotels $'000	Fixtures and fittings $'000	Vehicles $'000	Total $'000
Cost or valuation				
As at 1 January 20X1	478,000	11,000	–	489,000
Additions	12,000	7,000	300	19,300
As at 31 December 20X1	490,000	18,000	300	508,300
Depreciation				
As at 1 January 20X1	46,200	9,400	–	55,600
Charge for the year	9,800	2,150	30	11,980
As at 31 December 20X1	56,000	11,550	30	67,580
Net book value as at 31 December 20X1	434,000	6,450	270	440,720
Net book value as at 1 January 20X1	431,800	1,600	–	433,400

5   *Taxation*

	$'000
Taxation charge for the year	10,200
Underprovision from the previous year	50
	10,250

6   *Retained earnings*

	$'000
Profit for the year	14,335
Dividend paid	(1,000)
Retained for the period	13,335
Retained earnings b/f	86,000
Retained earnings c/f	99,335

7   *Finance lease*

	$'000
Cash price	300
Interest 10% × 6/12	15
Instalment 31/12/X1	(60)
Balance 31/12/X1	255
Interest 10% × 6/12	13
Instalment 30/6/X2	(60)
	208
Interest 10% × 6/12	10
Instalment 31/12/X2	(60)
Balance 31/12/X2	158
Balance 31/12/X1	255
Due within 1 year	
(120 – 13 – 10)	97
Due after 1 year	158
	255

8   *Share capital*

	$'000
Balance per trial balance	220,000
Transfer to share premium ($50m x 0.20)	(10,000)
	210,000

9   *Finance costs*

	$'000
Loan interest	4,950
Finance lease interest (W7)	15
	4,965

16 CEC

> **Top tips.** This is a fairly easy question. Remember to **explain** each item.

		Adjustment	
Item	Explanation	Add to inventory value $	Subtract from inventory value $
(a)	Cost $2,885. Net realisable value $(3,600 – 921) = $2,679. The inventory should be valued at the lower of cost and NRV. Since NRV is lower, the original valuation of inventories (at cost) will be reduced by $(2,885 – 2,679)		206
(b)	Inventory issued on sale or return and not yet accepted by the customer should be included in the valuation and valued at the lower of cost and NRV, here at $5 each (cost)	1,500	
(c)	The cost ($7.30) is below the current and foreseeable selling price ($10 or more) which is assumed to be the NRV of the item. Since the current valuation is at the lower of cost and NRV, no change in valuation is necessary		
		1,500	206

	$	$
Original valuation of inventories, at cost		153,699
Adjustments and corrections:		
To increase valuation	1,500	
To decrease valuation	(206)	
		1294
Valuation of inventories for the annual accounts		154,993

17 Plant and equipment

> **Top tips.** Do not forget the annual depreciation charge.

PLANT AND EQUIPMENT – COST

	DR $		CR $
Balance b/f	250,000	Plant 20X5 disposal	40,000
Purchases	150,000	Plant 20X7 disposal	10,000
		Balance c/d	350,000
	400,000		400,000
Balance b/d	350,000		

PLANT AND EQUIPMENT – ACCUMULATED DEPRECIATION

	DR $		CR $
Plant 20X5 disp	32,000	B/f	148,000
Plant 20X7 disp	4,000	Current year chg – 350,000 x 20%	70,000
Balance c/d	182,000		
	218,000		218,000
		Balance b/d	182,000

PLANT AND EQUIPMENT – DISPOSALS

	DR $		CR $
Plant 20X5	40,000	Plant 20X5 depn	32,000
Plant 20X7	10,000	Plant 20X7 depn	4,000
		Plant 20X5 proceeds	5,000
		Losses on disposals	9,000
	50,000		50,000

18 IT

> **Top tips.** The important point is to distinguish between the amounts actually spent during the year and the amounts taken to profit or loss.

PURCHASED GOODWILL

	$		$
Cash	4,800	Income statement: impairment loss	1,200
		Balance c/d	3,600
	4,800		4,800
Balance b/d	3,600		

RESEARCH AND DEVELOPMENT EXPENDITURE

	$		$
Balance b/f	26,500	∴ Income statement (7,900 +	
Cash: research	7,900	(26,500 + 3,500 − 22,600))	15,300
development	3,500	Development costs c/d	22,600
	37,900		37,900
Balance b/d	22,600		

19 F

> **Top tips.** Remember that some events after the end of the reporting period, while not adjusting events, may still require disclosure.

The treatment of the events arising in the case of F would be as follows.

(a)   The fall in value of the investment in P has arisen over the previous year and that company's financial accounts for the year to 28 February 20X1 provide additional evidence of conditions that existed at the end of the reporting period. The loss of $50,000 is material in terms of the trading profit figure and it should therefore be reflected in the financial statements of F. Due to the size and nature of the loss, it should be disclosed separately either in profit or loss or in the notes, according to IAS 1.

(b)   The destruction of inventory by fire on 30 April (one month after the end of the reporting period) must be considered as a new condition which did not exist at the end of the reporting period. Since the loss is material, being $250,000, it should be disclosed separately, by way of a note describing the nature of the event and giving an estimate of its financial effect.

(c)   The approval on 1 June of the company's design for tank cleaning equipment creates a new condition which did not exist at the end of the reporting period. This is, therefore, an event which does not require adjustment under IAS 10.

20 B

> **Top tips.** This is very likely to be examined. Make sure you know the format. Do not neglect part (b).

(a)   STATEMENT OF CASH FLOWS FOR THE YEAR ENDED 30 SEPTEMBER 20X1

	$'000	$'000
Profit before tax (85 + 15)		100
Adjustment for non-cash-flow items		
Profit on sale of non-current asset		(10)
Depreciation		30
Adjustment for working capital		120
Inventory		(15)
Receivables		(50)
Payables		40
Cash generated from operations		95
Interest paid		(15)
Net cash from operating activities		80
Cash flows from investing activities		
Sale of non-current asset (W2)	90	
Purchase of non-current assets	(40)	
Net cash from investing activities		50
Cash flows from financing activities		
Dividends paid	(35)	
Loan repaid	(80)	
Net cash used in financing activities		(115)
Net increase in cash and cash equivalents		15
Cash and cash equivalents at beginning of period		15
Cash and cash equivalents at end of period		30

Working

Sale of non-current assets

	$'000
Net book value (520 + 40 – 30 – 450)	80
Profit from sale	10
Proceeds on sale	90

(b)   STATEMENT OF FINANCIAL POSITION AS AT 30 SEPTEMBER 20X2

	$'000	$'000
Non-current assets (450 – 30)		420
Current assets		
Inventory	75	
Receivables (80 + 640 – 615)	105	
Bank and cash (W)	220	400
Total assets		820
Equity and liabilities		
Share capital		400
Retained earnings (145 + 160)		305
Current liabilities (60 + 410 + 35 – 390)		115
		820

Working

Bank and cash

	$'000
Balance at 30 September 20X1	30
Received from customers	615
Paid to suppliers	(390)
Interest paid	(15)
Loan paid off	(20)
	220

21 Cat

> **Top tips.** This question is easier than it looks. Work through it methodically.

(a)   CAT CO
        STATEMENT OF CASH FLOWS FOR THE YEAR ENDED 30 JUNE 20X2

	$	$
Cash flows from operating activities		
Profit before tax (W1)	54,500	
Interest expense	1,500	
Depreciation (37,000 – 26,000)	11,000	
Increase in inventories	(6,000)	
Decrease in receivables	2,000	
Increase in payables	8,000	
Interest paid	(1,500)	
Dividends paid	(13,000)	
Income tax paid (W2)	(12,000)	
Net cash from operating activities		44,500
Cash flows from investing activities		
Payments to acquire non-current assets (W3)		(34,000)
Net cash used in investing activities		10,500
Cash flows from financing activities		
Issue of ordinary share capital	3,000	
Redemption of loan stock	(10,000)	
Net cash used in financing activities		(7,000)
Net increase in cash and cash equivalents		3,500
Cash and cash equivalents at beginning of year		10,000
Cash and cash equivalents at end of year		13,500

Workings

1   *Profit before tax*

RETAINED EARNINGS

	$		$
Taxation	15,000	Balance b/f 1.7.X1	44,000
Dividends	13,000	Profit before tax (bal fig)	54,500
Balance c/f 30.6.X2	70,500		
	98,500		98,500

Profit for the year is after charging loan interest of 10% × 10,000 for 12 months and 10% × 10,000 for 6 months.

2   *Tax paid*

TAXATION

	$		$
Tax paid*	12,000	Balance b/f 1.7.X1	12,000
Balance c/f 30.6.X2	15,000	Tax charge	15,000
	27,000		27,000

*Note. The tax paid will be last year's year-end provision

3   *Non-current assets*

NON-CURRENT ASSETS

	$		$
Balance b/f 1.7.X1	85,000		
Purchases (bal fig)	34,000	Balance c/f 30.6.X2	119,000
	119,000		119,000

(b)   STATEMENT OF FINANCIAL POSITION AS AT 30 JUNE 20X2

	$	$
Assets		
Non-current assets		
Cost	119,000	
Depreciation	(37,000)	
		82,000
Current assets		
Inventories (40,000 – 3,000 – 2,000)	35,000	
Receivables	24,000	
Cash	13,500	
		72,500
Total assets		154,500
Equity and liabilities		
Equity		
Ordinary $1 shares	28,000	
Share premium	13,000	
Retained earnings (W)	66,000	
		107,000
Non-current liabilities		
10% loan stock	10,000	
Deferred tax	4,500	
		14,500
Current liabilities		
Provision for legal costs	3,000	
Trade payables (23,000 – 8,000)	15,000	
Taxation	15,000	
		33,000
Total equity and liabilities		154,500

Working: Retained earnings

	$'000
As per draft statement of financial position	70,500
Transfer to deferred tax (15,000 x 30%)	(4,500)
Inventory adjustment	(5,000)
Reduction in provision	5,000
	66,000

22 ABA

Top tips. Do not forget to show effect of these adjustments on the net profit before tax.

(a) The value of the IMX receivable will have to be written down. If, as appears likely, something can be recovered, then the debt will not need to be written off entirely. It can be written down to 30c in the $. The write-down needed will be $227,500.

(b) NRV of this inventory is now:

	$
Sales proceeds	200,000
Less agents commission 20%	(40,000)
Less disposal costs	(25,000)
	135,000

As this is less than cost, the inventory should be written down by $15,000.

(c) It currently looks probable that this liability will not be met by the insurance company, so it should be provided for in full in accordance with IAS 37.

Effect on net profit before tax

	$
Draft net profit	923,000
IMX write-down	(227,500)
Inventory write-down	(15,000)
Provision for damages	(50,000)
Adjusted net profit	630,500

23 L

(a) '3 for 2' bonus issue

This involves the issue of 45m new 50c shares, financed from the share premium account and the retained earnings. The capital structure following this issue will be:

	$'000
Share capital (15,000 + 22,500)	37,500
Share premium	–
Retained earnings (27,000 – 19,500)	7,500
	45,000

(b)   '1 for 2' rights issue at 80c

37.5m shares are now issued at 80c.

	$'000
Share capital (37,500 + 18,750)	56,250
Share premium (37.5m × 30c)	11,250
Retained earnings	7,500
	75,000

24 International tax

Tax on profit on ordinary activities – note to statement of comprehensive income

	$'000
Current tax	
Tax on profit for the year	1,500
Overseas tax paid (note)	(1,200)
Overprovision for previous period ($976,000 - $970,000)	(6)
Deferred tax	
Decrease in provision ($300,000 - $290,000)	(10)
Total tax charge	284

Note: Tax paid by overseas branch = $8m x 15% = $1.2m.

STATEMENT OF FINANCIAL POSITION

	$m
Non-current liabilities	
Deferred tax	290
Current liabilities	
Current tax	300

25 A Co, B Co and C Co

A CO
CONSOLIDATED INCOME STATEMENT FOR THE YEAR ENDED 31 DECEMBER 20X2

	$'000
Revenue (10,000 + 7,000)	17,000
Cost of sales (6,000 + 2,000 + 63 (W1))	(8,063)
Gross profit	8,937
Expenses (2,200 + 1,200)	(3,400)
Share of profit of associate (2,000 × 25%)	500
Profit before taxation	6,037
Taxation (800 + 800)	(1,600)
Profit for the year	(4,437)

A CO
CONSOLIDATED STATEMENT OF FINANCIAL POSITION AT 31 DECEMBER 20X2

	$
Assets	
Non-current assets	
Property, plant and equipment (25,300 + 9,000)	34,300
Investment in associate (W2)	1,437
Current assets (21,500 + 7,000)	28,500
Total assets	64,237
Equity and liabilities	
Ordinary share capital	10,000
Share premium account	4,000
Retained earnings (2,800 + 7,000 + 500 – 63 (W2))	10,237
Total equity	24,237
Non-current liabilities (10,000 + 2,000)	12,000
Current liabilities (25,000 + 3,000)	28,000
Total equity and liabilities	64,237

Points to note

1   A Co has owned the shares in B Co since incorporation and the shares were acquired at nominal value (4,000 shares for $4 million). There is therefore no difference between the value of the consideration transferred by A Co and the value of the assets it acquired.

Workings

1   *Unrealised profit*

$$1,500 \times \frac{20}{120} \times 25\% = 63$$

2   *Investment in associate*

	$'000
Cost of investment	1,000
Share of post-acquisition retained earnings ((4,000 – 2,000) × 25%)	500
Unrealised profit (W1)	(63)
	1,437

26 Fallowfield and Rusholme

CONSOLIDATED INCOME STATEMENT FOR THE YEAR ENDED 30 JUNE 20X8

	$
Revenue (403,400 + 193,000 – 40,000)	556,400
Cost of sales (207,400 + 92,600 – 40,000 + 4,000)	(264,000)
Gross profit	292,400
Distribution costs (16,000 + 14,600)	(30,600)
Administrative expenses (24,250 + 17,800 – (6,000 × 25%))	(40,550)
Profit before tax	221,250
Income tax expense (61,750 + 22,000)	(83,750)
Profit for the year	137,500

STATEMENT OF CHANGES IN EQUITY (EXTRACT)

	Retained earnings $
Balance at 1 July 20X7 (W1)	208,000
Dividends	(40,000)
Total comprehensive income for the year	137,500
Balance at 30 June 20X8 (W2)	305,500

Workings

1   *Retained earnings brought forward*

	Fallowfield $	*Rusholme* $
Per question	163,000	61,000
Pre-acquisition retained earnings	–	(16,000)
Share of Rusholme	163,000	45,000
	45,000	
	208,000	

2   *Retained earnings carried forward*

	Fallowfield $	*Rusholme* $
Per question	248,000	82,000
PUP	–	(4,000)
Pre-acquisition retained earnings		(16,000)
Disposal of plant		
Profit	(6,000)	
Depreciation (6,000 x 25%)	1,500	
	243,500	62,000
Share of Rusholme post-acquisition earnings	62,000	
	305,500	

INDEX

Note: **Key Terms** and their references are given in **bold**.

Review Form – Paper F1 Financial Operations (6/11)

Please help us to ensure that the CIMA learning materials we produce remain as accurate and user-friendly as possible. We cannot promise to answer every submission we receive, but we do promise that it will be read and taken into account when we up-date this Study Text.

Name: _____   Address: _____

_____

_____

How have you used this Study Text?
(Tick one box only)

☐ Home study (book only)

☐ On a course: college _____

☐ With 'correspondence' package

☐ Other _____

Why did you decide to purchase this Study Text? *(Tick one box only)*

☐ Have used BPP Texts in the past

☐ Recommendation by friend/colleague

☐ Recommendation by a lecturer at college

☐ Saw information on BPP website

☐ Saw advertising

☐ Other _____

During the past six months do you recall seeing/receiving any of the following?
(Tick as many boxes as are relevant)

☐ Our advertisement in *Financial Management*

☐ Our advertisement in *Pass*

☐ Our advertisement in *PQ*

☐ Our brochure with a letter through the post

☐ Our website www.bpp.com

Which (if any) aspects of our advertising do you find useful?
(Tick as many boxes as are relevant)

☐ Prices and publication dates of new editions

☐ Information on Text content

☐ Facility to order books off-the-page

☐ None of the above

Which BPP products have you used?

Text	☑	*Success CD*	☐
Kit	☐	*i-Pass*	☐
Passcard	☐	*Interactive Passcard*	☐

Your ratings, comments and suggestions would be appreciated on the following areas.

	Very useful	Useful	Not useful
Introductory section	☐	☐	☐
Chapter introductions	☐	☐	☐
Key terms	☐	☐	☐
Quality of explanations	☐	☐	☐
Case studies and other examples	☐	☐	☐
Exam skills and alerts	☐	☐	☐
Questions and answers in each chapter	☐	☐	☐
Fast forwards and chapter roundups	☐	☐	☐
Quick quizzes	☐	☐	☐
Question Bank	☐	☐	☐
Answer Bank	☐	☐	☐
OT Bank	☐	☐	☐
Index	☐	☐	☐

Overall opinion of this Study Text   Excellent ☐   Good ☐   Adequate ☐   Poor ☐

Do you intend to continue using BPP products?   Yes ☐   No ☐

On the reverse of this page is space for you to write your comments about our Study Text. We welcome your feedback.

The BPP Learning Media author of this edition can be e-mailed at: rebeccahart@bpp.com

Please return this form to: Adrian Sims, CIMA Publishing Director, BPP Learning Media Ltd, FREEPOST, London, W12 8BR

TELL US WHAT YOU THINK

Please note any further comments and suggestions/errors below. For example, was the text accurate, readable, concise, user-friendly and comprehensive?